CW01184255

A History of the European Restorations

A History of the European Restorations

Volume One
Governments, States and Monarchy

Edited by

Michael Broers and Ambrogio A. Caiani

Sub-editors:

Stephen Bann, Gaynor Johnson and Munro Price

BLOOMSBURY ACADEMIC
LONDON • NEW YORK • OXFORD • NEW DELHI • SYDNEY

BLOOMSBURY ACADEMIC
Bloomsbury Publishing Plc
50 Bedford Square, London, WC1B 3DP, UK
1385 Broadway, New York, NY 10018, USA

BLOOMSBURY, BLOOMSBURY ACADEMIC and the Diana logo are trademarks of
Bloomsbury Publishing Plc

First published in Great Britain 2020
Reprinted 2020

Copyright © Michael Broers and Ambrogio A. Caiani, 2020

Michael Broers and Ambrogio A. Caiani have asserted their right under the Copyright,
Designs and Patents Act, 1988, to be identified as Editors of this work.

For legal purposes the Acknowledgements on p. vii constitute an extension
of this copyright page.

Cover design: Terry Woodley
Cover image: *'Brother, the Lord is with us'. The Emperor of Russia, King of Prussia
and the Emperor of Austria*, London 1815. Courtesy of Stephen Bann

All rights reserved. No part of this publication may be reproduced or transmitted
in any form or by any means, electronic or mechanical, including photocopying,
recording, or any information storage or retrieval system, without prior permission
in writing from the publishers.

Bloomsbury Publishing Plc does not have any control over, or responsibility for, any
third-party websites referred to or in this book. All internet addresses given in this
book were correct at the time of going to press. The author and publisher regret
any inconvenience caused if addresses have changed or sites have ceased to
exist, but can accept no responsibility for any such changes.

A catalogue record for this book is available from the British Library.

ISBN:	HB:	978-1-7883-1803-7
	ePDF:	978-1-7867-3658-1
	eBook:	978-1-7867-2652-0

Series: International Library of Historical Studies

Typeset by RefineCatch Limited, Bungay, Suffolk
Printed and bound in Great Britain

To find out more about our authors and books visit www.bloomsbury.com
and sign up for our newsletters.

Contents

Acknowledgements vii
Note on Translations ix
List of Contributors x
List of Plates xvi
Introduction   *Ambrogio A. Caiani* 1

Part 1   New Order, New Diplomacy?

1   Neutrality, Restoration and Restraint: The Congress System at Work after 1815   *Maartje Abbenhuis* 17
2   Russia, the General Alliance and the Russo-Ottoman War Scare of 1821–2   *Elise Kimerling Wirtschafter* 29
3   An Imperial Affair: The Allied Council of Ambassadors and the Occupation of France, 1815–18   *Beatrice de Graaf* 39
4   Restoring International Order: Managing Multi-Polarity 1814–30 and the Foundation of the Concert of Europe   *Richard Langhorne* 53
5   The Art of Diplomacy: Jean-Baptiste Isabey at the Congress of Vienna   *Daniel Harkett* 67
6   Cosmopolitan Conspirators: The Conspiracy against the Holy Alliance during the French Intervention in Spain   *Jean-Noël Tardy* 79

Part 2   Charters and Constitutional Monarchy

7   Louis XVIII and the Charter of 4 June 1814: Time, Memory and Oblivion   *Emmanuel de Waresquiel* 91
8   Constitutional Monarchism in Post-Napoleonic Europe   *Markus J. Prutsch* 109
9   The Practical Politics of Restoration Constitutionalism: The Cases of Scandinavia and South Germany   *Morten Nordhagen Ottosen* 121
10   Royal Opposition against the *Ancien Régime*: The Case of Württemberg   *Georg Eckert* 133

Part 3 Composite Monarchy Restored

11 The Austrian Empire as a Composite Monarchy after 1815
   Karin Schneider 147
12 A Monarchical Regime based on Republican Antecedents: The
   Constitution of the United Kingdom of the Netherlands   *Ido de Haan* 159
13 Ruling over the Ruling Class: Doctrine and Practice of Government
   in the Kingdom of Sardinia   *Enrico Genta Ternavasio* 171

Part 4 Dynasty Re-Invented

14 Heroic Heirs: Monarchical Succession and the Role of the Military
   in Restoration Spain and France   *Heidi Mehrkens and Richard
   Meyer Forsting* 183
15 Southern Influences on Nordic Political Culture: Bernadotte as
   King of Norway and Sweden   *Bård Frydenlund* 201
16 Madame Adélaïde, Female Political Power and the July Monarchy
   Munro Price 213

Part 5 New States, New Borders

17 '... to be Norwegians, not Swedish': Identity Adaptations in the
   Norwegian Officers Corps, 1814–45   *Roald Berg* 225
18 The Construction of the Boundaries in Restoration Italy: A
   Comparative Perspective   *Marco Meriggi* 235
19 When Size Mattered: The Threshold Principle and the Existential
   Fear of Being too Small   *Rasmus Glenthøj* 245

Part 6 Re-Imagining Restoration

20 Was Moderate Representative Government Possible in Spain
   (1814–32)?   *Gonzalo Butrón Prida* 259
21 The Poles and their next 'Saviour': Alexander I and the Kingdom of
   Poland   *Jarosłtaw Czubaty* 269
22 Peace through Legislation: Law Codes and Social Control in Restoration
   Italy   *Marco Bellabarba* 277

Conclusion

23 Metternich-Kissinger: Interpreting the Restoration
   Luigi Mascilli Migliorini 289

Index 297

Acknowledgements

The editors of these two volumes did not expect that an enjoyable lunch in London in January 2014 would lead to this edited collection comprising forty-seven chapters in total. Our aim was simple; we noted that recent bicentennial commemorations for the Napoleonic Empire had led to some fantastic new research, and we wondered if the same could be achieved for the European Restorations. We were deeply heartened by the enthusiastic response that we received from almost fifty scholars working in over a dozen European countries and the US. It will come as little surprise that in these four years we have accumulated a very substantial number of debts. First and foremost, we wish to thank the Kent Institute for Advanced Studies in the Humanities, the School of History at Kent and the British International History Group for their financial support. They funded a conference that took place, in August 2016, at the University of Kent in Paris, entitled: 'The Price of Peace: Modernising the *Ancien Régime*? 1815–1848.' These two volumes are an expanded version and loosely based on the proceedings of this conference.

We are delighted to acknowledge Frank Mikus, Kent's Paris Administrator, for his assistance in facilitating our conference. Bettina Frederking was also vital in spreading the word in Paris and helping with the general organization. Our biggest debt is towards Prof. Gaynor Johnson, who from the beginning encouraged this project with infectious enthusiasm and also provided generous financial support from her own research allowance. Without her these volumes would never have seen the light of day. We are also grateful to Dr Juliette Pattinson, Head of the School of History, Kent, for her support throughout the good and the bad moments.

We are deeply grateful to all our contributors, who have shown incredible patience, resilience and enthusiasm throughout the entire process. They have been our greatest champions and we are truly in their debt. A special word of thanks should go to Drs Rasmus Glenthøj and Morten Ottosen, who generously invited the editors to a wonderful summer conference at the Danish-Norwegian institute in Copenhagen in July 2015. This provided a magnificent forum in which we tested our ideas and drew much inspiration from the highly original work being undertaken in Scandinavia. Very sadly Dr Tom Munch-Petersen of UCL passed away in January 2016 and was scheduled to contribute a paper on 'Scandinavia and Congress Diplomacy'. Tom was a wonderful man and very generous with his time when it came to helping younger scholars. We regret his passing both as a scholar and a friend, our thoughts are with his widow. He will be deeply missed.

Profs Munro Price and Gaynor Johnson very kindly helped when it came to editing some of the chapters from volume one. We owe a huge debt of gratitude to Prof. Stephen Bann, who not only gave the keynote opening address at our conference but also assembled a superlative history of art section in volume two. His encouragement, inspiration and original mind have been invaluable in getting political historians to think more imaginatively about their own *oeuvre*. We also have a debt of gratitude to him for helping us select and obtain the cover images for both volumes. Finally, we wish to thank Joanna Godfrey for encouraging us to expand these essays beyond the original scope of the conference and to her team at Bloomsbury for their genuine excitement for our work and for accepting this massive undertaking. We hope that what follows will be worthy of the generosity and support we have received in the past four years.

Ambrogio A. Caiani and Michael Broers

Note on Translations

Unless otherwise stated all translations in these volumes are the contributors' own. We have tended in general to opt in favour of a simple translation into modern English rather a literal rendition of the original, and somewhat antiquated, nineteenth-century language used by contemporaries. What this may lose in authenticity we hope it will gain in comprehensibility.

A number of key chapters were translated by some of our contributors. We wish to acknowledge them below.

Volume I

Ch. 6 Cosmopolitan Conspirators: The Conspiracy against the Holy Alliance during the French Intervention in Spain. Jean-Noël Tardy. Translated from the original French by Richard Nowell.

Ch. 7 Louis XVIII and the Charter of 4 June 1814: Time, Memory and Oblivion. Emmanuel de Waresquiel. Translated from the original French by Prof. Munro Price.

Ch. 23 Metternich-Kissinger: Interpreting the Restoration. Luigi Mascilli Migliorini. Translated from the original Italian by Dr Ambrogio A. Caiani.

Volume II

Ch. 5 Was a State–Church Alliance Really Possible? The Case of the Spanish Episcopate and the Crown (1814–33). Andoni Artola. Translated from the original Spanish into English by Guillermo Sven-Reher.

Ch. 8 Politicization and Conspiracies against the Bourbons, 1816–23: A Double Repression of Popular Involvement? Jean-Noël Tardy. Translated from the original French by Richard Nowell.

Ch. 15 Ideological Change and National Frontiers, From the Fall of Napoleon's Empire to the Savoyard Restoration in Subalpine Italy 1814–21. Michael Broers. Translated from the original Italian by Dr Ambrogio A. Caiani.

Contributors

Maartje Abbenhuis is Associate Professor in History at the University of Auckland. She works on the history of war, peace, neutrality and internationalism, with a particular focus on the 1815-1919 period. She has published two monographs: *The Art of Staying Neutral: The Netherlands in the First World War 1914-1918* (Amsterdam University Press, 2006) and *An Age of Neutrals: Great Power Politics 1815-1914* (Cambridge University Press, 2014). Her third book, *The Hague Conferences in International Politics 1898-1915*, was published by Bloomsbury in 2018.

Marco Bellabarba is Professor of Early Modern History at the University of Trento (Italy). His main research fields are the history of justice in the early modern age (*La giustizia ai confini. Il principato vescovile di Trento nella prima età moderna*, Bologna 1986; *Storia della giustizia nell'Italia moderna*, Roma-Bari 2008), the feudal principalities in the east (Trent, Bressanone/Brixen, Aquileia, Tyrol and Gorizia, in *The Italian Renaissance State*, Cambridge 2012) and the history of the Habsburg Empire in the nineteenth century (with B. Mazohl, M. Verga and R. Stauber, eds, *Gli imperi dopo l'Impero nell'Europa del XIX secolo*, Bologna 2008; *L'impero asburgico*, Bologna 2014).

Roald Berg is Professor of Modern History at the University of Stavanger and a specialist in Defence and Foreign Policy History. He has been a visiting fellow at University of Cambridge (Wolfson & SPRI), and a research fellow at the Norwegian Institute of Defence Studies, Oslo. His recent publications include *Norsk utanrikspolitikk etter 1814* [Norway's foreign politics after 1814] (2016), 'Mod som en konge'. *Bøndene, makten og politikken 1800-1850* [farmers and political power in Norway, 1800-1850] (co-editor) (2015), and 'Norwegian attitudes towards Britain, 1814-1914', in *Britain and Norway. Special relationships*, ed. Helge Ø. Pharo & Patrick Salmon (2012).

Michael Broers is Professor of Western European History at the University of Oxford and Fellow of Lady Margaret Hall. His book, *The Napoleonic Empire in Italy, 1796-1814: Cultural Imperialism in a European Context?* (2005) won the Prix Napoléon of the foundation Napoléon. He has been a visiting member of the Institute for Advanced Study, Princeton. His most recent books are *Napoleon's Other War: Bandits, Rebels and Their Pursuers in the Age of revolutions* (2010) and *Napoleon: Solider of Destiny 1769-1805* (2014). The second volume of his life of Napoleon, *The Spirit of the Age, 1805-1810*, was published by Faber & Faber in March 2018.

Gonzalo Butrón Prida is Professor of Modern History at the University of Cádiz (Spain) and was Academic Visitor at the University of Oxford in 2015 (Faculty of History) and 2017 (Latin American Centre). He holds a PhD in Modern History from the University of Cádiz (1995), and has conducted extensive research on Spain's transition to Liberalism and its transnational implications. Currently, he is working in a cross-national research project on Revolution and Counterrevolution coordinated by the University of Zaragoza (Spain). He has published several works on the Peninsular War (2014), the European impact of the 1812 Spanish Constitution (2006) and the French occupation of Spain in 1823–8 (1996), as well as articles in journals such as *Ayer* (2001), *Spagna Contemporanea* (2004), *Mélanges de la Casa de Velázquez* (2008), *Historia Constitucional* (2012) and *Historia Contemporánea* (2016).

Ambrogio A. Caiani is Senior Lecturer in Modern European History at the University of Kent. His main research interests have focused on Revolutionary France and Napoleonic Italy. His doctorate examined the declining fortunes of Louis XVI's court during the early French Revolution and was published by Cambridge University Press in 2012. He is currently working on a second book project with the provisional title 'Napoleon and the Pope'. He is also very interested in how the *ancien régime* was re-invented and conceptualized during the nineteenth century.

Jarosław Czubaty is Professor of History at the University of Warsaw, Poland. His published work includes *The Duchy of Warsaw, 1807–1815: A Napoleonic Outpost in Central Europe* (2016); 'The Attitudes of the Polish Political Elite towards the State in the Period of the Duchy of Warsaw, 1807–1815', in *Collaboration and Resistance in Napoleonic Europe: State Formation in an Age of Upheaval, c. 1800–1815*, ed. M. Rowe (2003); 'Glory, Honor and Patriotism: The Notion of a Military Career in the Duchy of Warsaw, 1806–1815', in *Soldiers, Citizens and Civilians: Experiences and Perceptions of the French Wars 1790–1820*, ed. Alan Forrest, Karen Hagemann and Jane Rendall (2008); 'The Army of the Duchy of Warsaw', in *Armies of the Napoleonic Wars*, ed. G. Fremont-Barnes (2011).

Georg Eckert is Privatdozent of Modern History at the Bergische Universität Wuppertal. His research centres on the transformation of Europe especially in the eighteenth and nineteenth centuries. He is particularly interested in the analysis of social, political and intellectual change – before, during and after Napoleon. His most recent book is *Zeitgeist auf Ordnungssuche: Die Begründung des Königreiches Württemberg 1797–1819* (2016).

Richard Meyer Forsting is a member of the AHRC-funded Heirs to the Throne project, directed by Professor Frank Müller. His research interest lies in nineteenth-century Spanish constitutional and monarchical history. His work so far has focused on monarchs-in-waiting, their interaction with the armed forces and their public portrayal during their youth. His most recent publication is a study entitled *Raising Heirs to the Throne in Nineteenth-Century Spain* (Palgrave Macmillan, 2018).

Bård Frydenlund is Director/CEO at Eidsvoll 1814 – Centre of Constitutional History and National Monument of Norway (Historic House Eidsvoll Estate). He has formerly served as Director at the Norwegian Iron Works Museum and as Research

Fellow at the Department of Archaeology, Conservation and History, University of Oslo, Norway. His published works include *Spillet om Norge: Det politiske året 1814* (2014); 'Defying the Continental System in the Periphery: Political Strategies and Protests by Norwegian Magnates', in *Revisiting Napoelon's Continental System: Local, Regional and European Experiences* (2014); 'Political Practices among Merchants in Denmark and Norway in the Period of Absolutism', in *Scandinavia in the Age of Revolutions: Nordic Political Culture 1740–1820* (2011); and *Stormannen Peder Anker: En biografi* (2009).

Enrico Genta Ternavasio is Professor of History of Italian and European Law (in the field History of Medieval and Modern Law) in the Faculty of Law, University of Turin, where he has convened courses in *dirittio comune* for years as well as teaching at the Alexandria campus of the University of Turin. Among his recent publications are *Dalla Restaurazione al Risorgimento. Diritto, Diplomazia, Personaggi* (2012); 'Codici della (piccola?) borghesia. Note su proprietà, successioni e maggioraschi dal Codice Napoleone al Codice Albertino', in *Etudes d'Histoire du droit privé en souvenir de Maryse Carlin* (2008); 'Nobiltà, studi e carriere nel Piemonte sabaudo: Filippo e Amedeo Avogadro', in *Avogadro e la cultura scientifica del primo Ottocento*, edited by M. Ciardi (2007); *Storia del diritto contemporaneo* with G. S. Pene Vidari (2005); *Principi e regole internazionali tra forza e costume* (2004); *Una rivoluzione liberale mancata* (2000); 'Genealogia, araldica, nobiltà nella storia del diritto tra realtà e finzione', in *Rivista di storia del diritto italiano LXXII* (1999); *Intendenti e comunità nel Piemonte settecentesco*, in *Comunità e poteri centrali negli antichi Stati italiani* (1996).

Rasmus Glenthøj is a Carlsberg Foundation Distinguished Associate Professor at the University of Southern Denmark. He is a Knight of the Royal Norwegian Order for Merit, the recipient of the Elite Travel-Scholarship (the Danish Ministry for Science, 2009), and the winner of the H.O. Lange Prize for Outstanding Research Dissemination (2014) and the Nordic History Book Prize (2017, together with Morten Nordhagen Ottosen). Glenthøj has published widely on Scandinavian nineteenth-century history in a comparative perspective, including *Experiences of War and Nationality in Denmark and Norway, 1807–1815* (2014, co-written with Morten Nordhagen Ottosen) and *1864 – Sønner af de slagne* (2014).

Beatrice de Graaf is Professor History for the International Relations at Utrecht University, and head of this department. In 2016, she is visiting fellow at St Catharine's College/History Faculty of Cambridge University where she is writing a monograph, *The Balancers: How Europe Waged Peace after 1815*. She is also the PI for an ERC Consolidator Grant Project and runs the research group 'SECURE: The making of a security culture in Europe and beyond, 1815–1914', www.uu.nl/securing-europe.

Ido de Haan is Professor of Political History at University of Utrecht. His special focus is on the impact of regime changes, revolutions and widespread violence, especially the Holocaust. He is concerned with the history of political thought, the development of citizenship, state and civil society in Western Europe and Dutch political history in the nineteenth and twentieth centuries. His publications include *Een nieuwe staat: het begin van het Koninkrijk der Nederlanden* [*A New State: The Beginnings of the Kingdom of the Netherlands*] edited with Paul den Hoed, Henk te Velde and Eveline Koolhaas-Grosfeld (2013); with Beatrice de Graaf and Brian Vick he has edited *Securing Europe After Napoleon: 1815 and the New European Security Culture* (Cambridge University Press, 2018).

Daniel Harkett is Associate Professor of Art at Colby College. His research focuses on early nineteenth-century French art, especially its intersection with cultures of display. He has published essays on topics including Jacques-Louis David's exhibition practice, Louis Daguerre's Diorama, Juliette Récamier's salon and Delphine Gay's self-fashioning. He is the co-editor, with Katie Hornstein, of *Horace Vernet and the Thresholds of Nineteenth-Century Visual Culture* (2017).

Richard Langhorne studied at Cambridge and lectured in History at the University of Kent, where he was also Master of Rutherford College. He was then Fellow of St John's College and Director of the Centre of International Studies, University of Cambridge. In 1993–6 he worked for the British Government as Director and Chief Executive of Wilton Park Executive Agency, Foreign and Commonwealth Office. Since then he has been Full Professor of Political Sciences and Director of the Graduate Division of Global Affairs, Rutgers University, USA. He was President of the British International History Association, 1988–93, and he has been a visiting professor at universities in Ecuador, China, the USA and Russia. His books include *The Practice of Diplomacy: Its Evolution, Theory and Administration* (1994, with K. A. Hamilton); *The Coming of Globalization: Its Evolution and Contemporary Consequences* (2001); *Diplomacy* (2004, with Christer Jonsson); *The Essentials of Global Politics* (2006).

Luigi Mascilli Migliorini is Professore Ordinario of Storia del Mediterraneo moderno e contemporaneo e di Storia moderna at the Università degli Studi di Napoli 'L'Orientale. He is an expert on eighteenth- and nineteenth-century history and has published widely on the Napoleonic and Restoration period. In 2015 the French Republic honoured him with the decoration *commandeur de l'ordre des palmes académiques*. His most recent books include: *Napoleone. L'uomo che esportò la Rivoluzione in tutta Europa* (2001, now in its third edition); *Il mito dell'eroe: Italia e Francia nell'età della Restaurazione* (2003); *Metternich. L'artefice dell'Europa nata dal Congresso di Vienna* (2014); and most recently, *500 giorni. Napoleone dall'Elba a Sant'Elena* (2016).

Marco Meriggi is Professor in History of Political Institutions at the Federico II University in Naples. His key research interests include the relationship between society and political power in Europe (eighteenth to twentieth centuries), as well as the fields of comparative, transnational and world history. His recent works include: *Racconti di confine. Nel Mezzogiorno del Settecento* (2016); *Gli Stati italiani prima dell'unità. Una storia istituzionale* (2011); *World History. Le nuove rotte della storia* (2011, jointly written with Laura Di Fiore); *L'Europa dall'Otto al Novecento* (2006).

Heidi Mehrkens is particularly interested in political cultural history, military and media history as well as the history of the monarchy in nineteenth-century Europe. From 2012 to 2016 she worked with the AHRC-funded research project 'Heirs to the Throne in the Constitutional Monarchies of Nineteenth-Century Europe (1815–1914)' at the University of St Andrews. Her current research focuses on royal succession in the constitutional political systems of nineteenth-century Prussia, France and Great Britain; she is also co-editor of the book series 'Studies in Modern Monarchy' (Palgrave Macmillan).

Morten Nordhagen Ottosen holds a PhD in History from the University of Oslo and has previously worked at the University of Southern Denmark. His publications include *Experiences of War and Nationality in Denmark and Norway, 1807–1815* (2014, co-authored with Rasmus Glenthøj) and the forthcoming *Scandinavia between Napoleon and Bismarck: Scandinavianism as a Pan-National Movement* (also co-authored with Glenthøj). He has also published articles and book chapters on nationalism, constitutionalism, popular war experiences and religious reform in Scandinavia and Continental Europe during and after the Napoleonic Wars.

Munro Price is Professor of Modern History at the University of Bradford and has a particular focus on the French Revolution. He has written a number of works including *Napoleon: The End of Glory* (2014); *The Fall of the French Monarchy: Louis XVI, Marie Antoinette and the Baron de Breteuil*, which won the 2002 Franco-British Society Literary Prize, and *The Perilous Crown: France Between Revolutions*. He is a regular reviewer for national newspapers and magazines and has appeared on television and radio in the UK and France.

Markus J. Prutsch is Senior Researcher and Research Administrator at the European Parliament. He has a background in history and political science and received his PhD from the European University Institute in Florence, Italy, in 2009. He has been awarded the Bruno-Kreisky-Prize for Political Literature and was a researcher at the University of Helsinki, Finland, until 2012. He teaches at Heidelberg University and is a fellow of the Heidelberg Academy of Sciences and Humanities. His recent publications include *Making Sense of Constitutional Monarchism in Post-Napoleonic France and Germany* (2013) and *Constitutionalism, Legitimacy, and Power: Nineteenth-Century Experiences* (2014).

Karin Schneider is Research Associate at the Institute for Modern and Contemporary Historical Research at the Austrian Academy for Sciences with a focus on Austrian History in the first decades of the nineteenth century. She is the head of the project 'The Congresses of Troppau and Laibach 1820/21' (funded by the Austrian Science Fund FWF) and has published several works about the Congress of Vienna, among them *Europa in Wien. Who is who beim Wiener Kongress* (together with Eva Maria Werner).

Jean-Noël Tardy graduated with a PhD from the University of Paris Panthéon-Sorbonne in 2011. His doctorate dealt with the meaning and the uses of conspiracy in

French politics during the nineteenth century and was published by Les Belles Lettres in 2015. His current research focuses on political vengeance in Post-Revolutionary Europe. His recent publications include 'Les Funérailles de l'utopie: les funérailles de Pierre Leroux et la Commune de Paris' (*Revue historique*, 2017).

Emmanuel de Waresquiel is Docteur en Histoire and Professeur at École Pratique des Hautes Études. He is the recipient of numerous honours and prizes, most notably Chevalier des Arts et des Lettres (2005) and Chevalier de la Légion d'honneur (2011). He is the author of many important works on the Revolution, Empire and Restoration. He has written biographies of Talleyrand (2015), Fouché (2014) and the Duke of Richelieu (1990) Other notable works include: (with Benoît Yvert) *Histoire de la Restauration, 1814–1830: Naissance de la France moderne* (1996); also, *Un groupe d'hommes considérables: Les pairs de France et la Chambre des pairs héréditaire de la Restauration 1814–1831* (2006); *Cent-Jours: la tentation de l'impossible, mars–juillet, 1815* (2014); *L'histoire a rebrousse-poil: les elites, la Restauration, la Revolution* (2014); and most recently, *Juger la reine: 14, 15, 16 octobre 1793* (2016), which has profoundly changed our perception of Marie Antoinette and her trial.

Elise Kimerling Wirtschafter is Professor of History at California State Polytechnic University in Pomona. She received her PhD from Columbia University and has written six books on Russian social and cultural history. Her current research project, 'Russia in concert: tsarist diplomacy and European politics, 1815–23', is devoted to diplomatic thought, particularly understandings of European order, in the decade following the Congress of Vienna. Her previous books include: *From Serf to Russian Soldier* (1990); *Structures of Society: Imperial Russia's 'People of Various Ranks'* (1994); *Social Identity in Imperial Russia* (1997); *The Play of Ideas in Russian Enlightenment Theatre* (2003); and *Religion and Enlightenment in Catherinian Russia* (2013). Professor Wirtschafter has been a fellow of the John Simon Guggenheim Memorial Foundation and has held visiting professorships at the École des Hautes Études en Sciences Sociales, the National Research University Higher School of Economics in Moscow and the University of Tübingen.

Plates

1 Jean-Baptiste Isabey, *Costume of an Inspector General of Artillery*.

2 Jean-Baptiste Isabey, *Isabey and His First Wife, His Brother Louis and His Wife, Their Four Children*.

3 Jean-Baptiste Isabey, *Frederick William III of Prussia*, 1815.

4 Gerard ter Borch, *The Swearing of the Oath of Ratification of the Treaty of Münster*, 1648.

5 Jean-Baptiste Isabey, *The Congress of Vienna*, 1815.

6 Detail of Jean-Baptiste Isabey, *The Congress of Vienna*, 1815.

7 Louis-Léopold Boilly, *Gathering of Artists in the Studio of Isabey*, Salon of 1798.

8 Jean-Baptiste Isabey, *The Congress of Vienna*, 1815.

9 Jean-Baptiste Isabey, *Costume Study for Count Rasoumoffsky*.

10 Detail of Jean-Baptiste Isabey, *The Congress of Vienna*, 1815.

11 Jacques-Louis David, drawing for *Oath of the Tennis Court*, 1791.

12 Jacques-Louis David, painted sketch for *Oath of the Tennis Court*, 1791.

Introduction

Ambrogio A. Caiani

The French Imperial experiment during the first decade of the nineteenth century cast a long shadow over subsequent European history. Napoleonic administrative integration, social reforms and cultural imperialism had made a deep impact on societies and cultures that had largely lived in isolation during the *ancien régime*. This episode made Europeans far more interconnected than they had been ever before. Societies on the old continent had resented the violent and intolerant moves to assimilate them ruthlessly into a larger imperial community.[1] The reaction against this experience was to seek specificity and fashion cultural/civic identities, that, though grounded in regional legend and tradition, were in effect new. The post-war world that emerged after 1815 was nostalgic for an irrecoverable past shattered by the *Grande Armée*.[2] Europeans realized that they had to build new social and political edifices from the ruins of the old order and the smoking embers of Revolution. What developed was not a unified monolith but a multiplicity of different models and trends.

The new borders that emerged, after the Congress of Vienna, altered completely the civic identities of Europeans. Lines of demarcation cut across the map of the continent in new and unprecedented ways. The diplomats at Vienna showed little regard for the multi-valent heritage and complex realities of the *ancien régime*. States and peoples were combined in ways that were to pose massive governmental, political and cultural challenges after 1815. Proud Ligurian republicans became subjects of the kings of Sardinia, while Belgians once governed by the Habsburgs (and then the French, for two decades) became a constituent part of a greater Netherlands. Many loyal Saxons, like the father of modern history Leopold von Ranke, became Prussians thanks to the allied victory at Leipzig. The only thing that was clear, after the great wars of Napoleon, was that a one-size-fits-all solution would not be possible, let alone welcome. Uniform legal codes, bureaucracies, languages and elite cultures were viewed with decided suspicion. Despite their best attempts the different statesmen of the Restoration could not escape the ruins and debris of the regimes they had supplanted. Post-Napoleonic polities could ignore neither the legacy of French Imperial rule and administrative reform nor the memories/traditions of their *ancien régimes*. The fall of Napoleon had created powerful centrifugal vortexes and centripetal forces that drew restored governments in opposite directions. *Ancien régime* diversity and Napoleonic uniformity represented the two extreme poles within which post-war reconstruction would take place. Neither could be ignored.

This introductory chapter is tripartite. Firstly, it will survey the current state of historiographical debates surrounding the Restoration. It will then outline some theoretical itineraries that scholars have outlined in recent years. Finally, there will be a brief description of how the chapters in this first volume contribute to, and carry forward, debates on the nature of government, monarchy and politics between 1815 and 1848. The second volume of this collection will cover topics on culture, society and religion. One of the key contentions of both volumes is the difficulty of understanding the Restoration as a unified whole. Our decision to use the plural of European Restorations was by no means arbitrary. It is only through a better knowledge of the specificities of the experience of different restored regimes that comparative frameworks and new interpretative models can emerge for a better understanding of this epoch.

Thankfully the Restoration, or post-Napoleonic period, is no longer the historiographical desert it once had been. Jacques Droz's half century of reaction and obscurantism has been replaced by a myriad of new, more sympathetic, political and cultural assessments of the *Vormärz* era.[3] In a French context, the pioneering work of Guillaume de Bertier de Sauvigny was followed by that of Emmanuel de Waresquiel. Both of these scholars highlighted that to view the French Restoration as a moment when political elites turned the clock back to 1789, and pretended the French Revolution had not happened, simply did not reflect reality.[4] In Italy Marco Meriggi, and in Germany Thomas Nipperdey, struggled against interpretations which saw these decades merely as waiting rooms for national unification.[5] There had been a concerted effort, at local and national level, among different European nations to revise unsympathetic assessments of the Restoration and emphasize that this was a much more creative episode than hitherto realized. It could be described as a laboratory where *ancien régime* legacies, and those of the Napoleonic period, were harnessed and synthesized in a quest to establish an order that, though it appealed to older pre-revolutionary traditions, was without precedent.

Scholars, working under the *aegis* of the research agendas of their home countries and regions, have shown just how sterile the dichotomy between progress and reaction can be when it comes to analysing 1815–48. They have sought to avoid the historiographical impatience that this era once elicited. The complex developments that took place around questions of representative government and social reform may seem superficially disappointing when compared with the triumph of liberal democracy, socialism and nationalism that followed.[6] Yet, the current generation of Restoration studies argues that such views are overly teleological and laden with unhelpful value judgements. Post-Napoleonic Europe challenges our most cherished convictions about the direction of history and the nature of progress. These were and remain questions which both nineteenth-century thinkers and contemporary scholars share. The challenge and reward has been to try to understand the period more on its own terms. This is certainly something that British, French, Italian, German, Dutch and Scandinavian academics, working to some extent in isolation, have accomplished over the past two decades.

Michael Broers in 1996 published a comparative and revisionist survey entitled: 'Europe after Napoleon.'[7] It shared many of the concerns of revisionist scholars but it did so from a comparative trans-European perspective. This was something that few had dared to do, and even fewer had managed to achieve. It has become a historiographical classic that traces the development of the great '-isms' of the early nineteenth century, that is conservatism, liberalism, radicalism, socialism and nationalism, across Europe. In so doing, it shows not just how vibrant political thinking and experimentation was at this juncture, but also how deeply European the process was in terms of its reach. Ultimately Broers' key insight is that the Napoleonic period had made the European continent more international and interconnected than it ever had been. The allied victory against the French Empire purported in many ways to be the triumph of particularism against universalism. The challenge that faced European states post-Vienna was how to manage vast regional diversities redolent of the *ancien régime* and conflicting political cultures on a continent still haunted by the ghost of Napoleon. This was an immense achievement for a short book of one hundred and fifty pages. It challenged scholars of post-1815 Europe to think in more comparative terms.

The gauntlet was picked up in 2000 when David Laven and Lucy Riall produced a highly original edited collection entitled 'Napoleon's Legacy', based on conference in 1997.[8] In fifteen chapters that ranged widely geographically, the authors of this volume tried to understand how the legacy of the French Empire impacted on the development of Restoration governments across Europe. What emerged from this collection was that a significant set of variables had influenced, and to an extent determined, the rhythms of governance and political culture between 1815 and 1848. These factors included: the bureaucratic edifice bequeathed by the French Empire, the extent of centralization, the relationship between state and society, the emergence of a sense of national community, new composite elites and finally the personalities of the restored monarchs.[9] Managing these variables was delicate, and as each contributor highlights, could yield very different results depending on the specific European context under consideration. The Restoration that emerged in these chapters was not just a retrograde reaction, but rather a delicate attempt to manage the post-Napoleonic order. The editors and contributors showed just how inadequate simple binaries, like progress versus reaction, could be when it came to appreciating the different strands and subtle changes that characterized Restoration politics. This volume has certainly been the most successful attempt at reconceptualizing the period, and trying to frame it in comparative terms. It has, to an extent, been strengthened by Richard Stites' posthumous narrative history of the Revolutions of the 1820s, which highlighted just how transnational revolutionary networks were in their reach across the Mediterranean and Black Sea.[10]

Few have heeded these eloquent calls for more comparative studies. The notable exception is Jean Claude Caron and Jean-Phlippe Luis' edited volume: *Rien appris, rien oublié?* (2016).[11] This collection, again, sought to understand the Restoration from its broadest European perspective. This study does bring much new, and exciting, research to light on the relationship between France, Spain and other areas of the Northern Mediterranean. There is some truly excellent work on Spanish liberalism and ecclesiastical history. Yet the fact remains that out of thirty-eight chapters only sixteen deal with non-French subjects. Equally the periodization of 1814–30 belies the reality that the Restoration is very much conceptualized in this tome according to the canons of French historiography. While the volume is a very valuable contribution to the debate, it does not really succeed in breaking out of the strictures of its national context. The Restoration here is read through French eyes, and understandably so, as the French experience is of paramount importance. After all, the Restoration of the Bourbon dynasty gave the entire epoch its name.

Yet, more does need to be done for scholars to emerge from overly Franco-centric readings of the post-Napoleonic age. Much of what happened in the Hexagon was of marginal importance to what occurred elsewhere on the continent. Each Restoration, and there were many in Europe, had its own rhythm and dynamic. To be frank, closing the Restoration period in 1830, is somewhat unhelpful. In Southern Europe the 1830s saw many important trends of government reform and consolidation continue. The Miguelist and Carlist reaction only gained political momentum and climaxed in this decade. Equally, the Revolution of 1830 in Paris irritated the wounds of 1789 but did not succeed in healing them. Elsewhere on the continent the situation was different and many of the issues ushered forth by the post-Napoleonic age only found some resolution with the 1848 Revolutions. Even this end date does not quite work for all contexts. Scandinavian scholars, from their perspective, claim this turning point is too early, and propose 1864, which ended the Schleswig-Holstein question, as a better candidate for the end of the Danish Restoration. Comparison highlights that even the superficially simple question of periodization is open to debate and enriching comparisons.

The late Sir Christopher Bayly's magisterial study 'The Birth of the Modern World' suggestively argues that there may even be a global Restoration to be explored.[12] His fourth chapter, 'Between World Revolutions', examines the final breakdown of the first European age of empire. The Americas had entered an age of post-imperial and colonial instability.[13] These regions desperately sought to build new social and political edifices, which would liberate them from the dominance of the old metropole. They would blend traditions from the imperial centre with new domestic national drives to create new polities. Bayly's superb synthesis shows that the ramifications of the European Revolutions and Napoleonic wars had truly planetary repercussions. Trade, emigration, new elites and the growth of state power unsettled old orders, not just in Paris and Vienna, but in capitals across the world.[14] For example, the meeting between Confucian traditions with imported European political and religious ideas brought the Qing dynasty into a struggle for legitimacy, and a renewed mandate of heaven,[15] which they succeeded in winning at the cost of horrendous bloodshed.[16] Bayly challenges us further by configuring the narrative of this time in a completely different way from most studies. He concludes his account with the American Civil War. This was the last great crisis in which the old eighteenth-century slave plantation economy took up arms to defend itself.[17] The war was to have important consequences in terms of government, ideology and trade globally. This has been the most ambitious attempt to re-tell a familiar story in a highly original fashion and in its planetary scope. It does put into evidence the intoxicating and magnificent potential for further inter-continental study. Yet, before heading down the road laid down by Bayly, one might suggest that more preparatory work will need to be undertaken before leaving the European heartland of Restorations. Bayly's *esprit de synthèse* is incomparable and many scholars working in a European context have published important new collections inspired by his approach.[18]

Another area of historiographical advancement that has proven very stimulating is the realm of international history. The bicentenary of the Congress of Vienna has produced some new perspectives to emerge in diplomacy and international relations. Inspired by Paul Schroeder's famous conclusion that 'for the purposes of international politics, the term "restoration" simply does not fit the Vienna settlement at all',[19] much fresh scholarship has tried to reassess diplomacy not just in 1814/15 but right up to the Congress of Verona in 1822.[20] There has been an attempt to see the period not just as one of reaction and repression, but as an effort to manage the international order in new ways.[21] The Badenese, Greek and Belgian cases have highlighted that diplomatic relations were evolving from being inter-dynastic to becoming inter-state in nature.[22] This insight highlights that a number of lessons had been learnt, by the policymakers of the Congress, after the previous century had torn itself apart with wars of succession. More interesting still has been the realization that the 'foreign' and the 'domestic' are not mutually exclusive spheres. The work of Brian Vick here has postulated that the Congress of Vienna worked in tandem with, and responded to, an international public sphere, the importance of which was increasing. This space for the exchange of ideas about international affairs could be located in salons, public spaces, publishing houses and even had its own merchandising campaigns.[23]

Ultimately the Revolutionary/Napoleonic maelstrom had created individualistic, centralist and atheistic cultural currents in Europe that deeply troubled contemporaries and statesmen. It was no accident that Friedrich von Savigny's brilliant attack against the Revolution/Napoleon's codification of laws was published during the Congress of Vienna itself.[24] The distrust of codification and its potential for disaggregation was something also noted in the Spanish conservative *manifiesto de los persas* issued in April 1814.[25] It was an appeal to sovereigns not to think just about territorial arrangements, in terms of frontiers, but to also consider the inner working of states and to find a strong post-Napoleonic settlement. The fear of social and moral disaggregation was something that deeply troubled both politicians and conservative thinkers alike throughout the period.[26] Evidence of the willingness to use international power to structure domestic affairs is nowhere more apparent than in the creation of the Free City of Krakow,[27] a highly interesting polity that existed from 1815 to 1846, and which still desperately needs an anglophone historian. This micro-state was not merely brought into existence by Vienna, but the final act of the Congress defined and drafted its Constitution in very minute detail.[28] The use of the prestige of the Concert of Europe to shape domestic politics and garner the support of international civil society has been a very fruitful area of study. It has questioned whether the Old Rankean *Primat der Aussenpolitik* is clear-cut; the Restoration period seems to suggest it was a more dynamic process than hitherto realized. The relationship between international and domestic social order was deeply intertwined.

It is becoming increasingly apparent that the goals, and reluctant interventionism, of the Holy Alliance were deeply implicated in social and domestic concerns.[29] Indeed, its international agenda was part of wider European debates about the sort of political system and the organic society underpinned by religion that needed to be established as a bulwark to repel the twin perils of radicalism and revolution. Controversially, one might even wonder whether the military invasion of Naples and Spain in the 1820s could be depicted as an early form of humanitarian interventionism.[30] Military force was used to re-impose social order on 'failed states' so that, instead of threatening collective security, they would support it.

Regardless of its ambitions, the congress system did break down by the 1830s. The multipolarity of Vienna collapsed as the great powers divided into two opposing camps: that is, the conservative signatories of the Münchengrätz convention versus the liberal adherents of the quadruple alliance of 1834.[31] The nature of this very brief cold war, though guided by international calculations, was also influenced by many internal pressures. This was especially apparent during the first Carlist Wars of the 1830s, where conservative volunteers from across Europe fought for Don Carlos whereas the liberal governments of Britain and France gave financial and logistical support to the Cristino regime. The civil war in Spain mirrored domestic ambitions of the different European powers.[32] The conservative Empires of the east sought to support informally all social systems that would sustain the new monarchical and religious order that had emerged at Vienna. The liberal constitutional monarchies of the west gave real succour to those representative governments in Southern Europe who seemed to share their own social priorities and parliamentary ambitions.

The two volumes presented here on Europe's Restorations are inspired by many of these important historiographical developments and re-evaluations. They are not only indebted to these fine revisionist studies, but also draw heavily, though by no means exclusively, on the proceedings of a conference entitled 'The Price of Peace, 1815–1848' that took place at the University of Kent's Paris campus in August 2016. They seek to make important contributions in framing the Restoration within its broadest international setting. The starting point of many chapters are specific national and local case studies. Marc Bloch, in the 1920s, wisely reminded historians that finding similarity is only one side of the coin when it comes to comparative history.[33] It is through the exploration of specificity that healthy and well thought out comparisons can be sustained. These volumes aim to push future scholars of the Restoration to think more about what is unique about their own national/regional political history and what is part of a wider trans-European story. It is an important ambition of this project to try to put historians from Northern and Southern Europe in dialogue with each other. Though these different poles of the continent have extremely different political cultures, they share more in common than one might at first suspect.

This first volume takes as its focus: Monarchies, Governments and States. While on the surface these may all seem familiar topics, there is much fruitful work to be undertaken. One area that has been brought into focus is the new relationship that monarchy and parliamentary representation established during these decades.[34] Many realized that the genie of representative government had been let out of the bottle. A balance needed to be struck between monarchical sovereignty and representative institutions. By 1815, there were three constitutional models toward which Europeans could turn: 1. The French *Charte*; 2. Polish/Norwegian Constitutions; 3. The Cadiz Constitutions of 1812. The first and third options were to have wide currency. There was some talk in these decades of the Jacobin constitution of 1793 but it was considered seriously only by small groups of extremists and would only gain mileage during the 1840s.[35] Moderates were deeply distrustful of its provisions on universal suffrage and its expensive educational and welfare policies, whereas the more recent monocameral nature and popular sovereignty enshrined in the Constitution of Cadiz, written during the Peninsular war, made it very appealing for liberals, revolutionaries and radicals.[36] This document was to become one of the key demands for the revolutionaries of the 1820s.

The Polish and Norwegian models are less well known, and this is unfortunate. They bear witness to the resurgence of composite monarchy during the nineteenth century. Sir John Elliott's concept of early modern 'composite monarchy' is of great value when it comes to interpreting the early nineteenth century.[37] In a number of instances, the Congress of Vienna bestowed several crowns on the same monarch. The examples of Norway-Sweden, Sardinia-Piedmont, Lombardy-Venetia, the United Kingdom of the Netherlands and Congress Poland all highlight the extent to which monarchs reigned over multiple kingdoms and states throughout 1815–48. The great Empires of Romanovs, Habsburgs, Hanoverians and Hohenzollerns were macro-examples of this phenomenon. Though reminiscent of early modern equivalents, these arrangements were different in both theory and practice.

Nineteenth-century composite monarchies linked 'states' together and were forged by diplomatic treaty; there was little pretence that this was the outcome of historic dynastic legitimacy. That is why these monarchical unions required in several cases new constitutional charters to establish the relationship between a reigning dynasty and a subsidiary state. In Norway popular sovereignty found its way into the text and in Poland there was much room for Tsar Alexander I's youthful liberalism to find expression. These models did not always work, and the United Kingdom of the Netherlands ultimately tore itself apart in the Belgian revolution of 1832; this was the direct consequence of the failure to establish a healthy composite monarchy.[38]

The final constitutional model, the French *Charte* of June 1814, was the most influential during these decades, because it sought to reconcile monarchical sovereignty with representative government.[39] Thanks to the work of Markus Prutsch, historians now appreciate how this constitutional charter came to be imitated on a trans-European level. This document at its most abstract was an *octroie*, that is a sanction, or free gift, from the monarch to his people. Thus, any dangerous allusions to popular sovereignty and constituent power were avoided.[40] It was a pact in which the monarch willingly shared his legislative authority with a bicameral legislature. The lower house could vote on laws, supervise public accounts and approve the annual budget. Until recently, this was seen as a purely French phenomenon, but Prutsch has shown that its impact was far broader. In the German confederation, Baden, Württemberg and Bavaria all adopted modified versions of the *Charte*.[41] Spain, eventually, accepted its own version, in the *Estatuto Real* of 1834, which abandoned the dangerous radicalism of Cadiz.[42] The experience of the Charter facilitated the gradual emergence of a new relationship between crown, ministers and parliamentary majority to emerge very slowly. How executive power would be yielded post-1815 was no foregone conclusion.

The refashioning of monarchy, new composite elites and representative institutions showed how far statesmen were willing to go to place their states on solid foundations.

An appeal was made to both the winners and losers of the Vienna settlement. The ongoing research undertaken by Matthijs Lok on the development of a *juste milieu* is bound to be instructive here.[43] No matter how intransigent reactionary statesmen wished to be, they could only achieve a stable polity by an alliance with moderate conservatives. This is certainly key when trying to understand a government like that led by Villèle from 1822 to 1827.[44] The challenge in fashioning a sustainable alliance between ultra-royalism and conservatism in France was to have disastrous consequences when it fell apart gradually in 1829. Yet, this political failure was far from universal. One need only think of how the Tories, during the 1830s and 1840s, managed to re-invent themselves as the Conservative party after their defeats in the Commons on the issues of Catholic Emancipation and the Great Reform Act of 1832.[45]

Throughout the continent, appeals were made to a public sphere and civil society composed of bureaucrats and military officers. An efficient state, that rewarded its elites and public servants with recognition and social prestige, was an important continuity that this period shared, not only with enlightened absolutism, but the Napoleonic Empire too.[46] Seigneurialism and estate-based privilege was gone forever, while Montesquieu's notion of a service nobility persisted. The old *ancien régime* non-titled nobilities of the rural world vanished, to be replaced with a service elite rewarded with titles, medals and other marks of social distinction.[47]

There is an entire history of the 'old-new elites' that emerged to govern Europe after 1815 to be written. The army, ministries and diplomatic service of Europe were populated with both the scions of old aristocratic clans and newly minted nobles.[48] Despite the rhetoric of 'age-old nobility' in this, as in many other aspects, the Restoration followed, to an extent, the Napoleonic programme to create 'masses of granite'. These restored orders realized that they could only survive if they created strong civil societies and composite elites that could recognize and sustain their right to rule. The social and political configuration of Restoration societies was emphatically not an attempt to replicate the traditional 'society of estates'.[49] Much energy would be expended to try to create a sophisticated *entente*, not just between new elites and old dynasties, but with the wider public and population.

Indeed, the thorniest question was to be the relationship between state and society. As many of the chapters in this volume highlight, restored monarchs inherited bureaucracies from the French Empire which were much more efficient and centralized than ever before.[50] They possessed a bureaucracy and powers that would have been the envy of many enlightened absolutist rulers. Many monarchs, during their exile, had promised a general amnesty and return to a past golden age of regional autonomy. They soon realized that this pledge was to be not only difficult to deliver but undesirable. The Napoleonic machinery of state made their administrators more powerful, and their revenues greater than during the *ancien régime*.[51] The implications at a grassroots level were none too pleasant. The citizen-subjects of the Restoration states faced a brave new world, where state interference in their daily lives remained as intrusive as ever.

It has been suggested that the theoretical field of post-colonial studies might prove profitable for historians trying to assess the battered and disorientated society that survived the wars of the French Empire. Gayatri Chakravorty Spivak and others have ruthlessly questioned whether 'subaltern peoples' can ever hope to recover cultures and modes of existence that were destroyed, or altered beyond recognition, by imperial and colonial power.[52] As Michael Broers has put it in his *The Napoleonic Empire in Italy*, there is a subaltern Italy to be discovered.[53] This could be broadened to a subaltern Europe that lies buried beneath the surface. The end of the Napoleonic experience was to leave Europeans with a sense of bewilderment broadly similar to that faced by twentieth-century African and Asian populations confronted with Europe's disorderly imperial retreat from the globe.

An important controversy is how far the Napoleonic Empire represented a colonial experience. This is a question that remains very open. As Broers has so ably shown, between 1800 and 1815 the populations of Europe were ravaged by French cultural imperialism, yet at the same time there was little settler colonialism.[54] One suspects that the 'imperial traumas' of the early nineteenth century in Europe, though painful, can only imperfectly parallel those later 'colonial traumas', whether they were settler-related or not, of the second half of the twentieth century in Africa and Asia. There are other potential analytical categories that could compete with post-colonial understandings of the Restoration. Recently scholars have put stress on the military and economic demobilization that followed 1815. They have suggested that the Restoration should be understood as a post-war epoch.[55] The struggle for international harmony and domestic stability in 1814/15 compares strikingly with similar processes in 1918 and 1945.[56] Whichever way one seeks to analyse the Restoration, few can ignore that this was a post-imperial time. The interconnected world of Napoleon's Empire was succeeded by states, monarchies and governments who, despite their desire to exorcize the Napoleonic and Revolutionary ghosts, were deeply influenced by them. As was stated at the beginning of this introduction, centrifugal tendencies towards localism and tradition continued to challenge the centripetal forces of the state.

The chapters in this first volume grapple with many of these subtle questions and interpretations from both a national and international perspective. In part one, Langhorne, Abbenhuis, Wirstschafter, de Graaf, Harkett and Tardy examine the emergence of an international order guided by the Concert of Europe. They highlight how the re-ordering of the European world required new solutions to meet the challenges that emerged after 1815. Concert diplomacy, interventionism, military occupation and neutrality all became essential tools with which to manage the shifting sands of the diplomatic order.

In parts two and four, the attention of the reader is drawn to the creation of new constitutional monarchies across France, Germany and Scandinavia, and to the constitutional charters created to sustain these experiments in representative government. Prutsch, Waresquiel, Ottosen, de Haan, Eckert, Mehrkens, Forsting, Frydenlund and Price examine, from very different perspectives, how monarchical sovereignty became reconciled with parliamentary institutions. Some sought to represent the reigning dynasty as emblems of national unity and powerful symbols of reconciliation. Heirs to the throne, in particular, played a vital part in this re-branding exercise. Equally fascinating is how the ambiguous and much criticized *Charte* of 1814 came to be exported across Europe. Our contributors show that defining representative monarchical government was a key priority after 1815. Many competing models existed at this time. The Bavarian and Norwegian cases show just how constitutionalism post-1815 eludes easy analysis and comparison. Each state grappled with how to fashion a constitutional settlement that would frame national priorities within wider European thinking about government.

Another key issue is how social and political identity evolved at this time. During the *ancien régime* one's status was fluid to say the least.[57] Overlapping monarchical, ecclesiastical, seigneurial, regional, judicial and trade jurisdictions meant that one served many masters, and could belong to multiple groups at the same time. The French Revolution and Napoleonic experience erased much of this old landscape and replaced it with a simplified and more individualized relationship with the state. The emergence of new states and composite monarchies left something of a cultural vacuum, and opened up the question of where one's allegiances lay. This was a question that confronted the Norwegian citizens of the Swedish king as much as it did the Ligurian subjects of the king of Sardinia. Was the *ancien régime* to be entirely forgotten, was society to be defined by the state that ruled over it or was the solution more one of cultural and linguistic national groups coming together?[58] These were open questions which new borders and sovereigns tried to answer with varying degrees of success. This a vital issue that is ably tackled in part five by Berg, Meriggi and Glenthøj.

The third part of this first volume examines composite monarchies, new elites and how politics post-Vienna were re-imagined. Schneider, de Haan, Genta, Butrón Prida, Czubaty and Bellabarba all seek to understand the nature of government where old dynasties reigned over new states. Congress Poland, Lombardy-Venetia and Norway had very different traditions of *ancien régime* statehood. New laws, systems of administration and composite elites were needed to sustain these kingdoms and regions that had little, or no, history of being ruled together. Empires like the Habsburg monarchy and Spain came to realize that it was next to impossible to return to the *status quo ante bellum*. The Habsburgs wondered how to recalibrate their rule after the dissolution of the Holy Roman Empire. Theirs was to be the composite monarchy par excellence during the Restoration. In Spain, Ferdinand VII's determination to rule as if the Peninsular war had not was to tear his kingdom apart. His neo-absolutist frame of mind managed to upset not just Cadiz-liberals but even staunchly *foral* Spain. This 'final part' highlights that, despite restored governments' best intentions, they fought many of the same struggles that they had inherited from the Napoleonic Empire. Regions had been promised autonomies and historic rights during the struggle to defeat France. Political reality often made it difficult and inexpedient to fulfil these pledges. The re-emergence of composite monarchy was one of the means through which statesmen tried to achieve a healthy balance between modern administrative practices and atavistic localism.

This first volume is closed with a magisterial conclusion by Luigi Mascilli Migliorini in which he uses the Italian concept of *instaurazione* to highlight just how fiendishly complex the process of reconstructing order was in post-Napoleonic Europe, from both a political and cultural perspective. These essays, and their profound research, constitute a call for greater collaboration and transnational comparison when it comes to the European Restorations of 1815–48. The chapters in this volume sketch out many potential research itineraries that scholars could explore in future. The second volume will examine the political cultures, religion and societies that emerged after 1815 with similar frames of reference in mind. Central to all these contributions is the realization that Europe's Restorations were characterized by many evolving dialectics. There was a constant search for a moderate compromise, *juste milieu* or middle course. The restless legacy of Napoleon, traditions of enlightened absolutism and the heritage of the *ancien régime* made the search for a viable synthesis difficult. The study of Europe, after the Congress of Vienna, will require patience both for those who toil in the archives and those who dwell in the Olympus of theory and comparative history. Hopefully, as the chapters of these collections demonstrate, the potential rewards will be great.

Notes

1. Michael Broers, *Europe Under Napoleon*, 2nd edn (London, 2014).
2. Peter Fritsche, *Stranded in the Present* (Cambridge, MA, 2010), esp. chs 1-3.
3. Jacques Droz, *Europe between Revolutions 1815-1848* (Glasgow, 1967).
4. Guillaume de Bertier de Sauvigny, *The Bourbon Restoration* (Pennsylvania, 1967); and Emmanuel de Waresquiel and Benoît Yvert, *Histoire de la Restauration* (Paris, 2002).
5. Marco Meriggi, *Gli Stati italiani prima dell'unità. Una storia istituzionale* (Bologna, 2011); and Thomas Nipperdey, *Germany from Napoleon to Bismarck: 1800-1866* (Montreal, 1996), 237-355.
6. For a deeply inspirational and Marxist account of the later period see Arno Mayer, *The Persistence of the Old Regime, Europe to the Great War* (Toronto, 1981).
7. Michael Broers, *Europe after Napoleon: Revolution, Reaction and Romanticism 1814-1848* (Manchester, 1996).
8. David Laven and Lucy Riall, *Napoelon's Legacy* (Oxford, 2000), 1-27.
9. Ibid., 6-14.
10. Richard Stites, *The Four Horsemen: Riding to Liberty in Post-Napoleonic Europe* (Oxford, 2014).
11. Jean-Claude and Jean-Philippe Luis, *Rien Appris, Rien Oublié? Les Restaurations dans l'Europe postnapoléonienne 1814-1830* (Rennes, 2016).
12. Christopher A. Bayly, *The Birth of the Modern World* (Oxford, 2004), 125-69.
13. Ibid., 128-34.
14. Ibid., 139-47.
15. Jonathan Spence, *God's Chinese Son: The Taiping Heavenly Kingdom of Hong Xiuguan* (London, 1996).
16. Bayly, *The Birth of the Modern World*, 148-55.
17. Ibid., 161-5.
18. Jürgen Osterhammel, *The Transformation of the World: A Global History of the Nineteenth Century* (Princeton, NJ, 2015); Maurizio Isabella, *Risorgimento in Exile: Italian Emigres and the Liberal International in the Post-Napoleonic Era* (Oxford, 2009); and Maurizio Isabella and Konstantina Zanou, eds, *Mediterranean Diasporas* (London, 2015); Richard J. Evans, *The Pursuit of Power, Europe 1815-1914* (London, 2016), 1-85.
19. Paul W. Schroeder, *The Transformation of European Politics 1763-1848* (Oxford, 1994), 579.
20. Mark Jarrett, *The Congress of Vienna and its Legacy: War and Great Power Diplomacy After Napoleon* (London, 2014).
21. Jennifer Mitzen, *Power in Concert: The Nineteenth-Century Origins Of Global Governance* (Chicago, 2013), *passim*.

22 Schroeder, *The Transformation of European Politics*, 575–82, 653–4 and 670–91.
23 Brian Vick, *The Congress of Vienna: Power and Politics after Napoleon* (Cambridge, MA, 2014), chs 1, 2 and 3.
24 Friedrich Carl von Savigny, *De la Vocation de Notre Temps pour la Législation et la Science du Droit* (Paris, 2006), 3–46.
25 For a full transcript in Spanish see *Manifiesto de los Persas* at https://es.wikisource.org/wiki/Manifiesto_de_los_Persas (last accessed 15 June 2018).
26 Gérard Gengembre, *La contre-révolution ou l'histoire desespérante 1789–1989* (Paris, 1989), 169–208.
27 M. Capefigue, *Le Congrès de Vienne dans ses Rapports avec la circonscription actuelle de l'Europe* (Paris, 1847), 211–28.
28 Ibid., 220–8.
29 Irby C. Nichols Jr., *The European Pentarchy and the Congress of Verona 1822* (The Hague, 1971); and Stella Ghervas, *Réinventer la tradition: Alexandre Stourdza et l'Europe de la Sainte-Alliance* (Paris, 2008).
30 Brendan Simms and D. J. B. Trim, eds, *Humanitarian Intervention: A History* (Cambridge, 2013), esp. ch. 5.
31 Linda Kelly, *Talleyrand in London* (London, 2017), 110–26; and Miroslav Šedivý, 'From Adrianople to Münchengrätz: Metternich, Russia, and the Eastern Question 1829–33', *International History Review*, Vol. 33, No. 2 (2011), 205–33.
32 Mark Lawrence, *The Spanish Civil Wars: A Comparative History of the First Carlist War and the Conflict of the 1930s* (London, 2017), chs 5–6.
33 Marc Bloch, 'The comparative history of European societies', in Marc Bloch, *Land and Work in Mediaeval Europe* (London, 1967), 44–87.
34 Roger D. Congleton, *Perfecting Parliament: Constitutional Reform, Liberalism and the Rise of Western Democracy* (Cambridge, 2011), 218–20, 425–31 and 456–8.
35 Pamela Pilbeam, *Republicanism in Nineteenth Century France 1814–1871* (Basingstoke, 1995), 108–12.
36 Marion Miller, 'A Liberal International? Perspectives on Comparative Approaches to the Revolutions of the 1820s in Spain, Italy, and Greece', in R. Clement, B. Taggie and R. Schwartz, eds, *Greece and the Mediterranean* (Kirksville, MO, 1990), 61–8.
37 Sir John Elliott, 'A Europe of Composite Monarchies', *Past & Present*, No. 137 (1992), 48–71.
38 Sébastien Dubois, *L'invention de la Belgique. Genèse d'un État-Nation* (Brussels, 2005), 328–60.
39 Pierre Rosanvallon, *La Monarchie Impossible* (Paris, 1994), 45–64.
40 Volker Sellin, *European Monarchies from 1814 to 1906* (Berlin, 2017), 8–25.
41 Markus J. Prutsch, *Making Sense of Constitutional Monarchism in Post-Napoleonic France and Germany* (Basingstoke, 2012), passim.
42 Isabel Burdiel, *Isabel II, Una Biografía 1830–1904* (Madrid, 2010), 38–44.
43 Matthijs Lok, Colloque international: 'Juste milieu – The search for a middle way between revolution and tradition', held at the Université d'Utrecht, Pays-Bas, 2004.
44 Francis Démier, *La France de la Restauration* (Paris, 2012), 646–7.
45 Robert Stewart, *The Foundation of the Conservative Party 1830–1867* (London, 1978), chs 6 and 7; and Norman Gash, *Peel* (London, 1976), 155–88.
46 Michael Broers, 'The Napoleonic Regimes', in William Doyle, ed., *The Oxford Handbook of the Ancien Régime* (Oxford, 2012), 496–8.
47 David Higgs, *Nobles in Nineteenth-Century France, The Practice of Inegalitarianism* (Baltimore, MD, 1987), 130–56; Louis Bergeron, François Furet and Reinhart Koselleck,

eds, *L'Âge des révolutions européennes: 1780–1848* (Paris, 1973); André Jardin and Andre-Jean Tudesq, *Restoration and Reaction 1815–1848* (Cambridge, 1984).
48 Dominic Lieven, *The Aristocracy in Europe, 1815–1914* (Basingstoke, 1992), chs 7–10; also recent work by Willian Godsey Jr is of particular note: see *Nobles and Nation in Central Europe: Free Imperial Knights in the Age of Revolution, 1750–1850* (Cambridge, 2009); and by the same author, *The Sinews of Habsburg Power: Lower Austria in a Fiscal-Military State 1650–1820* (Oxford, 2018); Ewald Frie and Ute Planert, eds, *Revolution, Krieg und die Geburt von Staat und Nation: Staatsbildung in Europa und den Amerikas 1770–1930* (Tübingen, 2016).
49 Bertrand Gujon, 'Distinguer et integrer? Anoblissement et élites économiques en France 1814–1830', in Caron and Luis, *Rien Appris, Rien Oublié?*, 75–90; Josef Matzerath, *Adelsprobe an Der Moderne: Sachsischer Adel 1763 bis 1866: Entkonkretisierung Einer Traditionalen Sozialformation* (Wiesbaden, 2016).
50 Laven and Riall, *Napoleon's Legacy*, 6–3.
51 Ralph Kingston, *Bureaucrats and Bourgeois Society: Office Politics and Individual Credit in France 1789–1848* (Basingstoke, 2012), 114–40.
52 Gayatri Chakravorty Spivak and Rosalind C. Morris, eds, *Can the Subaltern Speak? Reflection in the History of an Idea* (New York, 2010), ch. 1.
53 Michael Broers, *The Napoleonic Empire in Italy 1796–1814: Cultural Imperialism in a European Context?* (Basingstoke, 2005), 275–99.
54 Ibid.
55 Alan Forrest, Karen Hagemann and Michael Rowe, eds, *War Demobilization and Memory: The Legacy of War in the Era of Atlantic Revolutions* (Basingstoke, 2016), 3–26.
56 For a comprehensive survey, see Tony Judt, *Postwar: A History of Europe Since 1945* (London, 2010).
57 Gail Bossenga, 'Estates, Orders and Corps', in Doyle, *The Oxford Handbook of the Ancien Régime*, 141–66.
58 Michael Rowe, 'The French Revolution, Napoleon and Nationalism in Europe', in John Breuilly, ed., *The Oxford Handbook of the History of Nationalism* (Oxford, 2013), 127–48; For a good example see Rasmus Glenthøj and Morten Norhagen Ottosen, *Experiences of War and Nationality in Denmark and Norway 1807–1815* (Basingstoke, 2014), esp. 257–76.

Part One

New Order, New Diplomacy?

1

Neutrality, Restoration and Restraint: The Congress System at Work after 1815

Maartje Abbenhuis

When Paul Schroeder called the Congress of Vienna agreement signed in 1815 the most successful peace treaty of all time, he did so with an eye to explaining the contours of the European great power system that evolved through the nineteenth century. In that system, as Schroeder explains, the political equilibrium between the great powers was maintained in order that no one power – be it Russia, France, Prussia, the Habsburg Empire or Great Britain – would dominate. For Schroeder, the key to the 'concert system' or 'Congress system' (two terms that are largely interchangeable, although historians love to debate them) was more than a willingness to meet and discuss common concerns professed among the powers. It also reflected widespread acceptance that Europe's crises should be stage-managed collectively.[1] Hedley Bull described the inclination as a 'custodial duty' professed by the great power monarchies over the rest of Europe and as acceptance of the idea that the avoidance of war between these monarchies would benefit them all.[2] The concert system relied on the recognition of their common interest in maintaining the balance of power. The Congress of Vienna thus developed, as Andreas Osiander describes it, a 'system-consciousness' and acknowledged that the stability of one power depended, in part, on the stability of another.[3] These principles underwrote the restoration period and influenced European relations until the outbreak of the First World War in 1914.

In many respects, uncertainty drove the compromise agreements settled at Vienna in 1815. In 'restoring' Europe to the monarchies, the leaders who met at the Congress of Vienna looked both backwards and forwards: they aimed to preserve the legitimacy and right to rule of the aristocratic landed classes, who had dominated the pre-1789 era, yet also acknowledged the social and political changes that had affected Europe since the French revolution. Above all, they considered the people as politically dangerous and needing careful oversight. In 1815, it made complete sense that the best way to protect the stability of the (re-)established monarchies was to keep these states from going to war with each other. At any rate, twenty-five years of almost continuous warfare showed them that warfare was costly and calamitous, that it might encourage another Napoleon Bonaparte, or (worse) inspire the people to clamour for further revolutionary change. Restoration aimed at avoiding revolution and thus at limiting war.

The statesmen and women in Vienna worked hard to reinstate their version of continental stability.[4] They micromanaged the revision of the map of Europe, carefully assigning new territorial boundaries and off-setting competing interests. They also acknowledged the importance of war avoidance. In the aftermath of the Vienna settlement, in the period historians describe either as 'restoration Europe' or 'revolutionary Europe',[5] warfare remained a legitimate foreign policy option. But it was a carefully considered option. Carl von Clausewitz's influential work *On War* (1832) summed up the considerations best: war might be a political act and, as such, perfectly legitimate, but it was a political act with unpredictable results.[6] Therefore, in the restoration period, the choice to not go to war and to proclaim neutrality was equally valid. Neutrality, in fact, offered the European monarchies an ideal tool to manage the continental equilibrium.

This chapter focuses on the utilization of the concept of neutrality as a tool of great power diplomacy. It argues that the Congress of Vienna settlement legitimized neutrality as an effective means to manage the international system and affect international relations. The Congress, in fact, launched an 'age of neutrality', offering up war avoidance as a legitimate foreign policy option for small and large states alike.[7] In so doing, the Congress of Vienna marked a decisive break with the early modern past. For while neutrality featured prominently in the early modern period and throughout the wars fought between 1789 and 1815, it always did so as a highly contentious concept. After 1815, neutrality underwrote the stability of international relations. It was the first time, in the history of Europe at least, that principles of restraint and moderation came to dominate the ways in which the great power monarchies related to each other, and neutrality offered them a useful tool to manage those relationships.

Before 1814, neutrals had little recognized legitimacy in time of war, even if an increasing number claimed that legitimacy for themselves. After 1815, however, neutrality became embedded in the international environment in a number of key ways; first, as a means to stabilize the territorial equilibrium in Europe; secondly, as a foreign policy option that aimed at restricting and restraining the spread of war when it did occur; and lastly, as a powerful opportunity for non-belligerents to maximize their access to the open seas, to trade routes and to markets in time of war. If the restoration period (1815–49) marked a shift from the early modern to the modern world, one of its key impacts was on the global economy, evidenced by the move from a closed economic system dominated by the principle of mercantilism to an open economic system dominated by the principle of free-trade liberalism. Neutrality played a key hand in enabling the meteoric rise of Europe's industrial economies after 1815 and in Britain especially. Neutrality, then, helped to birth the modern age.

Neutrality as a tool of territorial equilibrium

The main principle guiding the reconfiguration of the map of Europe at Vienna was to balance power and to avoid contentious issues that might lead to a military conflict. This meant that all the governments in attendance had to be willing to compromise some of their vital interests. At the very least, it ensured that they had to be willing to buffer their competing interests and accept a common purpose (namely, to protect the monarchical system). There were many ways in which this was done, including by establishing small or medium-sized sovereignties that kept the great powers geographically separated from each other. For example, the newly established Kingdom of the Netherlands (including the present-day Netherlands, Belgium and Luxembourg) aimed at buffering Prussia from France and protecting the security of the Channel and North Sea for the British. Likewise, the creation of a German Confederation of States to replace the collapsed Holy Roman Empire confirmed the existence of a loose alliance of nearly forty independent principalities and independent cities, including Prussia and Habsburg-ruled Austria. Each state was a sovereign entity which acknowledged the existence of common economic and political interests across the Confederation. The Confederation's members met at regular intervals to discuss these, without binding any obligation on each other. Their existence ensured that the political interests of Prussia and Austria were balanced and kept both these powers geographically separated from France.[8]

A more decisive way to buffer came in the form of the neutralization of states and territories by great power agreement. While neutralization had been used as a means to deal with contentious regions and questions in the early modern period,[9] it was in the early nineteenth century that it was systematized as a tool of congress diplomacy and as a way of protecting the powers from going to war with each other. The Congress of Vienna neutralized three key territories: Switzerland, the city of Cracow and the tiny region of Moresnet. Each was neutralized for different reasons, but their collective neutralization spoke to the willingness of the monarchies at Vienna to compromise and to defuse potentially explosive issues.

The Swiss cantons had a long history of neutrality that pre-dated the 1815 agreements.[10] At Vienna, however, these cantons were drawn together into a sovereign state, a republic, that would not be able to take part in any future wars. The neutralization of Switzerland aimed at keeping the competing interests of the cantons (some of which were aligned with or ruled by powerful European monarchs) from affecting European politics or upsetting the geo-strategic balance of power. Switzerland was acknowledged as a volatile region, a hotbed for revolutionary ideas and liberal tendencies. As a vital trade and banking hub, Switzerland's neutralization also spoke to easing the economic relationships across the continent. In neutralizing Switzerland, then, the powers at Vienna looked to stabilize central Europe.

Of course, keeping Switzerland neutral was a harder task. Cantonal loyalties were challenged by the federalization of the country, which came to the fore during the 1847 and 1848 revolutions when the federal government used military force to suppress rebellions in seven cantons that wished to secede.[11] After 1849, however, the federal government managed to keep control over the Swiss cantons, albeit with a few crises along the way, and project a stalwart and neutral foreign policy. It was supported in these actions by the rest of the European powers, most of the time. Neutrality underpinned Swiss national identity from 1849 on, underpinning its international reputation as a nation of bankers, humanitarians and internationalists.

The neutralization of Cracow was less successful. The city was neutralized during the 1814–15 Vienna deliberations and placed under the protection of the Russians,

Prussians and Austrians. All three powers coveted the city and hoped to keep it out of their rivals' control. In neutralizing Cracow, however, they hoped to keep each other from maximizing these advantages. Still, they also imposed a condition on Cracow's neutrality, namely that the city could not harbour dissidents from neighbouring countries. In the end, the revolutions of the late 1840s swept through Cracow as it did through the rest of eastern Europe. The Habsburgs used the opportunity presented at the end of the civil unrest to incorporate the city into their empire.[12] While both France and Britain protested the development, in the midst of the upheavals of 1848, they were not in a position to force the situation.

The example of Cracow highlights how contentious neutralization could be if not all the partners to the agreement committed fully to the terms. Yet Cracow presents only one of three failed neutralization treaties in the period 1815–1914: the end to the neutralization of the Black Sea in 1871 (which was neutralized at the end of the Crimean War in 1856) was the second, and the German invasion of Belgium and Luxembourg in August 1914, the third. This last act brought with it the First World War and the entire collapse of the European concert system. It came, however, at the end of almost a century of successful neutralization policies.

When Germany invaded Belgium in 1914, it also invaded a tiny snippet of land situated on the border of Belgium, the Netherlands and Germany, with the enticing name of Moresnet (present-day Kelmis, Belgium). In 1815, Moresnet housed a profitable zinc mine of strategic interest to Prussia and the Netherlands.[13] The mine was so profitable that neither power would give up a claim to it. In order to solve the stand-off, the Vienna treaty stipulated that the mine and the 260 inhabitants of the 3.37 square-kilometre territory of Moresnet would exist outside sovereign rule. Both the Prussian and Dutch monarchies would administer the territory and make laws for its population, but could only do so with the agreement of the other. The mining company would administer the zinc distribution (and profits) to the advantage of both states. Even though Moresnet citizens were stateless and the territory became a haven for smugglers, distilleries and crime cells, its neutralization presented a suitable solution.

The neutralizations of Switzerland, Cracow and Moresnet at Vienna show up how important the alleviation of rivalry was for the great powers in 1815. That principle sat at the heart of concert diplomacy after 1815. Neutralization was, in fact, used repeatedly during the ensuing century to solve other geo-strategic rivalries both within and outside Europe, including in the Greek islands during Greece's independence struggles in the 1820s (the Ionian islands would be permanently neutralized in 1863), during the Egyptian crises in the late 1830s and early 1840s (the decision went nowhere but the Suez canal would be neutralized in the 1880s) and as a means of sending peacekeeping troops into Schleswig-Holstein in 1849.[14] When Luxembourg split from the Netherlands in the 1860s, it too was neutralized by great power agreement.[15]

Of these new agreements, the most important and most successful was the neutralization of Belgium. When Belgium seceded from the Netherlands in the 1830s during a bitter civil war that lasted almost the entire decade, the European great powers were not able to leave Belgium to its own devices. The new kingdom was too weak to protect itself against the ambitions of its great power neighbours (and the Dutch). The Treaty of London, initiated in 1830 and formalized in 1839, thus neutralized Belgium by mutual agreement of the European powers. They agreed that if any one of them invaded, all the others would come to Belgium's assistance. In so doing, they hoped to keep Belgium and north-western Europe safe from war and free from the competing claims of the Prussians and French in particular.

None of the powers expected Belgium's neutralization to succeed. The territory, a prime industrial region and one of Europe's main exporters of armaments, offered too many attractions. Yet Belgium weathered the vagaries of great power politics for nearly eighty years.[16] Its neutralization was remarkably successful.[17] It survived the 1848 revolutions with its neutrality intact and its commitment to constitutional monarchy protected.[18] Much like Switzerland, Belgium too came to embrace its neutrality as an essential part of its national identity, although domestically neutrality remained a contested idea.[19]

Of course, neutralization was not an easy solution. It required commitment from all powers to the agreement and was only sustainable if they also maintained a high degree of trust in the willingness of the others to keep their word. That commitment, as is clear from the examples of Cracow and the Black Sea, was not always present. Yet aside from Cracow, the neutralization agreements initiated during the restoration period were remarkably successful: most of them weathered the 1848 revolutionary storms and only failed when the entire nineteenth-century international system collapsed during the First World War.

Limiting wars and war avoidance: the permanence of neutrality

One of the unlooked for consequences of the neutralization agreements initiated during the restoration period was the existence of a number of governments who had to consider their neutrality as a permanent condition. These governments had a difficult task in working out how to manage their foreign affairs and their non-belligerency had to be accommodated by the great powers as well. Both Belgium and Switzerland worked extremely hard to carve out a place for their neutral voice and agency in the European political order: they did so by advocating for clearer delineations of their rights and obligations in time of war and peace and by balancing an impartial foreign policy when possible. Not surprisingly, all the great powers maintained sizeable diplomatic representation in these states.

The respect given to the neutrality of Switzerland and Belgium by the great powers also legitimated the existence of neutrality as a viable foreign policy option for other countries. With the recognition of permanently neutral states, neutrality became a permanent feature of the international system. The great powers further systematized neutrality by adopting neutrality repeatedly themselves as a voluntary foreign policy at a time when others went to war. Neutrality became such a stable foreign policy choice that many populations attached it to their national identities and internationalist values.[20] In the latter part of the century, Denmark, Finland, Norway, Sweden and the Netherlands also toyed with the possibility that they might be permanently neutralized by great power agreement.[21] They accepted the custodial duty of the great powers as effective and binding.

The key to the stability of the Congress system was the principle of restraint: the willingness not only to avoid war but also to negotiate and mediate suitable solutions to international crises. The Congress system depended on successful ambassadorial meetings and requests for multilateral discussions and solutions.[22] It also depended on the expectation that governments would eschew war if at all possible. Neutrality then became the default foreign policy position for most European countries. This is not to suggest that the restoration period was an 'age of peace'. There were plenty of wars conducted within and outside Europe between 1815 and 1849.[23] Rather, it is to suggest that warfare within Europe became less likely after 1815, and when it did occur it was usually circumscribed by the interests of the non-participating, neutral powers, many of which were great powers.

There were several consequences of this shift to neutrality. The first was that neutrality became a vibrant part of European politics. States could and did choose for neutrality in ways that did not happen in the early modern period, and neutrality politics underpinned the conduct of most wars of the time. As a result, there was also a professed need to find agreement to what the requirements of neutrals in time of war were. Where, before 1815, neutrality law was highly contested, after 1815 neutrality law became standardized (although it was never fully standardized and some key issues, such as those around blockade and contraband, continued to cause problems). Nevertheless, one of the reasons historians describe the nineteenth century as a 'golden age of international law' was due to the agency of the European powers to find agreement on the law of war and neutrality.

Another consequence of the shift was the adoption of neutrality as a long-term foreign policy option for states. Neutrality offered security to small- and medium-sized European countries, like the Netherlands and the Scandinavian kingdoms, who saw in neutrality an opportunity to protect their security at home and grow their economic and industrial empires outside of Europe. By the middle of the century, then, neutrality existed as a valid foreign policy position for all European governments. There were three types of neutral state: permanently neutral states (like Switzerland and Belgium), voluntary long-term neutrals (which included the United States of America) and occasional neutrals (who declared their neutrality when others went to war). In all the wars of the century, barring the Crimean War of 1853–6, there were more great power neutrals than belligerents. There were also numerous neutral small powers. Be they voluntary or permanently neutral, all of these states looked to protect their non-belligerency and their rights to access the global economy.

Economic opportunism: neutrality as a catalyst for the industrial revolution

The age of limited war brought into being in 1815 enabled Europeans to look outwards. It also ensured that the European economies could prosper. No longer dictated to by the wartime economic controls of the Napoleonic period nor immobilized by fear of military attack, merchants, entrepreneurs, bankers and industrialists looked to maximize their gains from the new peacetime environment. After 1815, Europeans settlers moved out of the continent, colonizing the 'New World' in unprecedented numbers.[24] They could do so in part because the seas were peaceful and free.

The peacetime conditions of the restoration period also presented an incredible catalyst for private investment in new industries, new technologies and new markets. The industrial revolution took off after 1815, bringing with it extraordinary pressures on European social, economic and political structures. It also globalized the European economy and increasingly made the economic viability of many European states dependent on their access to the global economy: to trade routes, ports, markets and sources of foreign labour and raw materials. The industrial revolution forged ahead after 1815 and in Europe, it thrived on peace.

It also thrived on security that a future war would not interrupt access to these trade routes, ports, foreign labour, raw materials and markets. It is no surprise then that the political concept of free-trade liberalism came to dominate the political ambitions of the rising middle classes throughout Europe. Free-trade liberals advocated for the rights of each individual to access the global economy unfettered by restrictive taxes, trade embargoes and local laws. These same liberals were at the forefront of political change within Europe during the restoration period: they challenged the protectionist policies of the aristocracy and drove forward plans for the establishment of constitutional monarchies and the opening up of national and imperial economies. The German Customs Union of 1833 (*Zollverein*) was one such initiative, as was the repeal of the Corn Laws and Navigation Acts in Great Britain in the 1840s.[25]

For liberals, neutrality offered protection for their global economic enterprises. Even if their country went to war, the neutrality of other states would keep vital economic highways open and their businesses thriving. And if enough powers agreed, the rights of neutrals to trade and to access the open seas unmolested could be formalized. The move to confirm the international law of neutrality was in part driven by these economic motives. As the British liberal magazine, the *Economist*, explained the advantages of neutrality in 1855: 'it permits trade to be carried without apprehending the invasion of armies'.[26] It also kept the world's ports open and commerce flowing.[27]

Of course, peace in Europe also enabled ambitious Europeans to look outwards. The acquisition of formal and informal empires advanced apace during the restoration period. Perhaps the greatest tragedy of the nineteenth-century European age of 'limited war' was that it enabled a highly successful age of 'industrial imperialism' and with it the conquest of the non-European world. While many historians claim that a drive for empire did not interest Europeans until the later decades in the century (particularly during the 1870s and 1880s conquest of Africa), there is plenty of evidence to suggest that Europeans spread their influence, their capital, their people and their ideas into the world in the restoration period. The whole nineteenth century was, as Philippa Levine rightly states, a century of 'imperial gain and aggrandisement'.[28] Much of that activity aimed at profit. A lot of it was violent and destructive.

Consider, as an example, the rise of Great Britain. The industrial revolution turned this island nation into the nineteenth century's superpower. With ready access to coal, a sizeable merchant marine protected by the formidable Royal Navy, and a pre-existing blue water empire, Britain was able to maximize its advantages and dominate the globe. Its people populated the planet, its bankers invested in new ventures (including cross-continental railway routes in the Americas and Eurasia, sheep and dairy farms in South America and Australasia, mines and plantations around the world), its entrepreneurs established new communication networks, built new factories and opened up new ports. By 1850, London was the financial capital of the world. Meanwhile, Britain had also become the 'factory of the world', turning the plethora of materials it received from across the seas into manufactured goods that fed the consumer needs of its own population and of other rising economies within and outside its empire and the European continent.

These developments had a decisive impact on the social and political make-up of British society. They also had a fundamental impact on communities around the world, in some cases changing them forever. British expansionism in the restoration period relied on protecting its security at home and the merchant marine's access to the open seas. What would become known as the *Pax Britannica* in the aftermath of the Crimean War was effectively already in place during the restoration period, namely as a foreign policy commitment to neutrality. After 1815, Britain kept out of European wars if at all possible and protected its ongoing voluntary neutrality in Europe by vouchsafing its global economic and imperial enterprises. When it did go to war, it did so in aid of these globalizing and imperial ventures. The first Opium War, fought by the British in China between 1839 and 1841, for example, aimed at forcing the Qing dynasty to accept greater access for British merchants to China's domestic economy, including in the unrestricted sale of opioids to the Chinese people. And even when Britain went to war in Europe (as it did during the Crimean War, a conflict that erupted at the end of the restoration period), British economic policies in that conflict looked first and foremost to protect open access to the seas, to its colonial settlements, to India and to sources of essential materials, which by this stage included the gold mined in Australia and New Zealand.

Britain was not the only European state that profited from an ongoing position of neutrality. Belgium prospered throughout the century as a prime industrial and trade hub, becoming one of the primary armaments suppliers for the continent. By 1850, Belgium had one of the best-performing industrial economies. The other long-term neutrals in Scandinavia and the Netherlands also prospered from their ongoing access to the global economy: the Netherlands expanded its East and West Indian empires through the century. Outside Europe, the growth and prosperity of the United States was also aided by neutrality. The Monroe Doctrine, adopted in the 1820s, aimed at keeping the United States firmly focussed on its regional interests. Outside the Americas, then, the United States remained firmly committed to a policy of voluntary long-term neutrality, keeping it from going to war for many decades.

The end of 'restoration Europe' and the rise of neutrality

The 1848 revolutions brought about fundamental political change in Europe. They signalled that the restoration experiment initiated in 1815 at Vienna to restore control of the continent to the aristocracies could not be sustained. However, where the Vienna settlements may have faltered in 1848 and 1849 on the domestic front, many of the diplomatic principles of the concert system bloomed after 1849. The tone of moderation that typified the relationship of the European powers in the first half of the nineteenth century continued to influence European diplomacy in the second.[29] The application and adoption of neutrality as a tool to manage that diplomacy blossomed alongside.

In fact, the principle of neutrality became so firmly embedded in international affairs that during the Crimean War the right to privateering was abolished and the belligerent powers looked to protect neutral trade and the right for all to access the open seas. The Declaration of Paris of 1856 formalized these radical departures from early modern warfare practices, forgoing many of the rights belligerents had jealously protected before 1815, including the right to restrict and capture neutral shipping.[30] The Declaration protected the freedom of the seas and opened them up for the movement of people, goods and capital in time of war and peace. The Declaration of Paris was, as Olav Riste describes, the 'most remarkable' of milestones and separated, as C. H. Stockton framed it, the world of war from the world of commerce.[31] In so doing, it formalized what had been standard practice in European diplomacy since 1815.

From the Crimean War on, neutrality became the bedrock on which many European states built their economic and imperial foundations. Neutrality offered the ability to avoid becoming involved the wars of others without losing the right to access the global economy, its communication networks and diplomatic mechanisms. After 1850, Europe's governments could choose their wars carefully, betting on the desire of their neighbours to remain uninvolved. Small states could vouchsafe their security by adopting long-term neutrality policies. As a result, industrial economies thrived and empires grew. Europe could thus dominate the world.

Notes

1 Paul W. Schroeder, *The Transformation of European Politics 1763–1848* (Oxford, 1994), particularly after 477; Paul W. Schroeder, 'International politics, peace, and war, 1815–1914', in T. C. W. Blanning (ed.), *The Nineteenth Century: Europe 1789–1914* (Oxford, 2000), 158–209.
2 Hedley Bull, 'Order vs. Justice in International Society', *Political Studies* 19/3 (September 1971), 269–83.
3 Andreas Osiander, *The States System of Europe 1640–1990: Peacemaking and the Conditions of International Stability* (Oxford, 1994), 186.
4 Brian Vick, *The Congress of Vienna: Power and Politics after Napoleon* (Cambridge, MA, 2014); David King, *Vienna 1814* (New York, 2009); Glenda Sluga, 'Women, Diplomacy and International Politics, Before and After the Congress of Vienna', in Glenda Sluga and Carolyn James (eds), *Women, Diplomacy and International Politics since 1500* (New York, 2015), Chapter 7.
5 Martin Lyons, *Post-Revolutionary Europe 1815–1856* (Houndsmills, 2006), especially 1–21; Schroeder, *Transformation*, 579–93; Eric Hobsbawm, *Age of Revolution, 1789–1848* (London, 1996).
6 Carl von Clausewitz, *On War*. Translated by J. J. Graham (London, 1873). Original: *Vom Kriege* (Berlin, 1832).
7 The contours for this chapter's argument are largely derived from Maartje Abbenhuis, *Age of Neutrals: Great Power Politics 1815–1914* (Cambridge, 2014) and Maartje

Abbenhuis, 'Most Useful Tool for Diplomacy and Statecraft: Neutrality and Europe in the "Long" Nineteenth Century, 1815-1914', *International History Review* 35/1 (2013), 1-22.
8   Paul W. Schroeder, 'The Lost Intermediaries: The Impact of 1870 on the International System', *International History Review* 6/1 (1984), 1-27.
9   For which: J. H. W. Verzijl, *International Law in Historical Perspective*. Volume 10 (Leiden, 1968), 23-4; M. W. Graham, 'Neutralization as a Movement in International Law', *American Journal of International Law* 21/1 (January 1923), 74-94.
10 Georges Perrin, *La Neutralité Permanente de la Suisse et les Organisations Internationales* (Paris, 1964), 15; A. Suter, 'Neutralität, Prinzip, Praxis und Geschischtsbesstein' in M. Hettling, M. König, M. Schaffner, A. Suter and J. Tanner (eds), *Eine kleine Geschichte der Schweiz: Der Budesstaat und seine Traditionen* (Frankfurt am Mein, 1998), 133-88.
11 Joachim Remak, *A Very Civil War: The Swiss Sunderbund War of 1847* (Boulder, CO, 1993).
12 C. J. Bartlett, *Peace, War and the European Powers, 1814-1914* (New York, 1996), 43.
13 L. Malvoz, *Het Neutraal Gebied van Moresnet (1816-1919)* (n.p., 1991).
14 Abbenhuis, *Age of Neutrals*, 53-62; W. Bennett Munro, 'The Neutralisation of the Suez Canal', *Annals of the American Academy of Political and Social Science* 17 (May 1901), 13-34; W. D. Wrigley, *The Diplomatic Significance of Ionian Neutrality 1821-1831* (London, 1988); W. D. Wrigley, 'The Neutrality of Ionian Shipping and its Enforcement during the Greek Revolution (1821-1831)', *Mariner's Mirror* 73/3 (1987), 345-60.
15 M. Juno, *Die Neutralität des Grossherzogtums Luxemburg* (Luxembourg, 1951); Daniel H. Thomas, *The Guarantee of Belgian Independence and Neutrality in European Diplomacy 1830s-1930s* (Kingston, 1983), 198.
16 The best overviews of Belgium's place in continental diplomacy are: Thomas, *Belgian Independence*; R. Coolsaet, *België en zijn Buitenlandse Politiek 1830-2000*, revised edn (Leuven, 2001).
17 R. Albrecht-Carrié, *The Concert of Europe 1815-1914* (New York, 1968), 11-12; M. Rendall, 'A Qualified Success for Collective Security: The Concert of Europe and the Belgian Crisis, 1831', *Diplomacy and Statecraft* 18 (2007), 271-95; Schroeder, *Transformation*, 678.
18 Thomas, *Belgian Independence*, 95-120; A. de Ridder (ed.), *La Crise de la Neutralité Belge de 1848: Le Dossier Diplomatique* (Brussels, 1928).
19 Coolsaet, *België*, especially 129-35.
20 Remco van Diepen, *Voor Volkenbond en Vrede: Nederland en het Streven naar een Nieuwe Wereldorde, 1919-1946* (Amsterdam, 1999), 16-17; N. van Sas, 'Between the Devil and the Deep Blue Sea: The Logic of Neutrality', in Bob Moore and Henk van Nierop (eds), *Colonial Empires Compared: Britain and the Netherlands, 1750-1850* (Aldershot, 2003), 33-44; O. Elgström, 'Do Images Matter? The Making of Swedish Neutrality 1834 and 1853', *Cooperation and Conflict* 35/3 (2000), 243-4; Sven Widmalm, 'A Superior Type of Universal Civilisation: Science as Politics in Sweden, 1917-1926', in R. Letteval, G. Somsen and S. Widmalm (eds), *Neutrality in Twentieth-Century Europe: Intersections of Science, Culture and Politics after the First World War* (New York, 2012), 65.
21 S. E. Cooper, *Patriotic Pacifism: Waging War on War in Europe 1815-1914* (Oxford, 1991), 56; Jukka Nevakivi, 'Finnish Neutrality' (33) and Pertti Luntinen, 'Neutrality in Northern Europe Before the First World War' (108) in Jukka Nevakivi (ed.), *Neutrality in History* (Helsinki, 1993).

22 M. S. Anderson, *The Ascendancy of Europe 1815–1914*, 3rd edn (London, 2003), 5; F. R. Bridge and R. Bullen, *The Great Powers and the European State System 1814–1914*, 2nd edn (Harlow, 2005), 4.
23 Michael Geyer and Charles Bright, 'Global Violence and Nationalizing Wars in Eurasia and America: The Geopolitics of War in the Mid-Nineteenth Century', *Comparative Studies in Society and History* 38/4 (1996), 619–57.
24 James Belich, *Replenishing the Earth: The Settler Revolution and the Rise of the Anglo-World 1783–1939* (Oxford, 2009).
25 A. Howe, 'Restoring Free Trade: The British Experience' in D. Winch and P. K. O'Brien (eds), *The Political Economy of British Historical Experience 1688–1914* (Oxford, 2002), especially 207; A. Howe, 'Free Trade and Global Order: The Rise and Fall of a Victorian Vision', in Duncan Bell (ed.), *Victorian Visions of Global Order: Empire and International Relations in Nineteenth-Century Political Thought* (Cambridge, 2007), 26–46.
26 *Economist*, 16 June 1855, 649.
27 H. Doe, 'The Long Reach of the Small Port: Influences and Connections in Small English Ports in the Nineteenth Century', in A. Gestrich and M. S. Beerbühl (eds), *Cosmopolitan Networks in Commerce and Society* (London, 2011), 133–50.
28 P. Levine, *The British Empire: Sunrise to Sunset* (Harlow, 2007), 85.
29 Cf. Chris Barber, 'Nineteenth-Century Statecraft and the Politics of Moderation in the Franco-Prussian War', *European Review of History* 21/1 (2014), 1–17.
30 Jan Lemnitzer, *Power, Law and the End of Privateering* (London, 2014).
31 Olav Riste, *The Neutral Ally: Norway's Relationship with Belligerent Powers in the First World War* (Oslo, 1965), 18; C. H. Stockton, 'The Declaration of Paris', *American Journal of International Law* 14 (1920), 357.

2

Russia, the General Alliance and the Russo-Ottoman War Scare of 1821–2

Elise Kimerling Wirtschafter

In contrast to Russia's present-day position on the political and psychological periphery of Europe, the post-Napoleonic era, at least until the Crimean War and arguably until the Bolshevik revolution of October 1917, represented a time of full integration into European society and politics – a time when the general alliance and European system stood as the cornerstone of Russian diplomacy. Russia had led the allied coalition that defeated Napoleon in 1813–14, her armies had performed heroically and honourably, and her emperor had come to be seen by his subjects and intimates as the divinely anointed saviour of Europe. Alexander I (ruled 1801–25) likewise believed that in the glorious victory of 1812 and in subsequent campaigns leading to Napoleon's dethronement, he and his people, together with their allies, had acted as the instrument of God. To Russia's monarch and diplomats, the peace settlement achieved in 1814–15 seemed equally providential. Following the struggles against Napoleon and the triumphal entry of allied troops into Paris in March 1814, Emperor Alexander possessed high hopes for perpetual peace and continuing guidance from heaven.

Generations of historians have described Emperor Alexander's religious conversion in 1812, his sense of being the saviour of Europe in 1813–14 and his commitment to an eternal peace based on the Christian principles of the Holy Alliance (1815).[1] That a Holy Alliance to preserve monarchy, encourage good governance and thwart revolution inspired Russian foreign policy in post-Napoleonic Europe became a cliché of nineteenth- and twentieth-century historiography. Attention to the Holy Alliance fits well with accounts of Alexander's religious fervour, mystical inclinations, reformist policies and idealistic moral principles. It also accords well with Church and state understandings of political authority, which invariably presented the monarch as divinely anointed and accountable to God.[2] In a letter to Alexander, dated 6 January 1816, the enlightened Russian statesman, Mikhail M. Speranskii, praised the Holy Alliance as an act that emanated not from the self-love or personal actions of the sovereign signatories, but from their having become 'the organs' of a 'pure outpouring … of Christian goodness'.[3] Such lofty moral sentiments are noteworthy, but do idealism and belief in Providence fully convey the spirit and thinking of Russia's peacemakers in 1815 and beyond?

Historians invariably temper the images of exuberance associated with the military victories of 1812–14, the signing of the First Treaty of Paris and the negotiations conducted at the Congress of Vienna with accounts of the difficulties and uncertainties caused by Russia's plans for Poland, the related question of Saxony, and Napoleon's return to France in March 1815.[4] Although Napoleon was duly defeated, this time without heroic Russian efforts, the problem of political stability in France persisted. The commitment to an enduring European peace remained strong, yet throughout the years of implementation, the preservation of peace required the unremitting attention of Alexander and his fellow monarchs, who through their personal relationships and diplomatic agents worked hard to sustain concord and consensus. Although religious conviction and Enlightenment idealism produced a beneficial diplomatic effect, peace depended most of all on vigilance, pragmatism and a willingness to act.[5] Nor could the distrust and broken promises of the Napoleonic era be easily overcome. The political leaders of all the great powers believed in allied unity and in the reality of European society; however, their most immediate task was to avoid war by monitoring each other's thoughts and actions.

This chapter describes Russian efforts to ensure tranquillity, peace and order in Europe through the prism of the Russo-Ottoman war scare of 1821–2. Based on diplomatic communications that followed the break in relations between St Petersburg and Constantinople in July 1821, it explores Russian perspectives on critical aspects of European politics. As Henry Kissinger and his interpreters repeatedly note, the foreign policy of a country or people is rooted in its historical self-awareness, memory and consciousness.[6] This insight is here developed with reference to D. P. Tatishchev's 1822 mission to the Austrian court – a mission that Alexander hoped would persuade the allies to act in concert (*concerter*) to protect Russia's treaty rights.

The backdrop to the crisis of 1821 lay in the Russian empire's military and diplomatic successes during the late eighteenth and early nineteenth centuries. Following wars in 1768–74, 1787–92 and 1806–12, Russia occupied a strong position in the ongoing struggle with the Persian and Ottoman empires to control the Balkans, Caucasus and Transcaucasia. Critical Russian interests included the internationalization of the Black Sea, free commercial navigation through the Straits of the Bosphorus and the Dardanelles, the protection of Balkan and other Ottoman Christians and of Balkan aspirations for political autonomy, and in the aftermath of the Napoleonic wars and Vienna settlement, use of the European political system to preserve peace and ensure Ottoman adherence to established treaty obligations. Although Russo-Ottoman relations stabilized after 1815 – a time when Russia committed herself to preservation of the Ottoman Empire, enforcement of recognized territorial agreements, the principle of legitimism and defence of monarchical authority – the potential for conflict remained.[7]

Tensions arose over delimitation of the Caucasian border, Russia's role as defender of Serbia's recently acquired autonomy within the Ottoman Empire, and guarantees of free navigation in the Black Sea and Straits. Forever distrustful of each other, the Russian and Ottoman empires avoided overt conflict after signing the Treaty of Bucharest in 1812. But then, in March 1821, rebellion erupted among the Ottomans' Greek subjects, and within a few months the threat of war returned. The immediate crisis resulted from an uprising among Greeks in Moldavia, led by Alexandros

Ypsilantis, who had been in Russian service. In addition, there was rebellion among Greeks in the Morea, Attica, Thessaly, Macedonia, Epirus and the Aegean archipelago; a peasant revolt in Wallachia led by Tudor Vladimirescu against the Ottoman-appointed hospodars (governors) and great landowners; and Turkish reprisals against Christian civilians in the Danubian Principalities and Constantinople that included the destruction of churches and the murder of Ecumenical Patriarch Grigorios V on Easter eve (22 April).[8] These developments, together with ongoing violations of Russia's economic and other recognized treaty rights, convinced Alexander that the Porte had decided to wage war against the Orthodox religion.

Torn between the obligation to protect Christian subjects of the Ottoman Empire and the post-Napoleonic commitment to legitimist principles, Russia consistently opposed the Greek rebellions, and by late June the revolt in the Principalities had been repressed. Still, Ottoman troops remained, and atrocities committed by Greeks and Turks continued.[9] In these circumstances, diplomatic declarations had no effect, and on 6/18 July the Russian ambassador in Constantinople, Grigorii A. Stroganov, delivered an ultimatum to the Porte, demanding: 1) restoration of destroyed and damaged churches; 2) protection of the Christian religion and the rights of Christians; 3) recognition of the distinction between innocent Greeks and those responsible for the troubles; and 4) a role for Russia in the pacification of Moldavia and Wallachia, as established by 'the spirit of existing treaties'. The Porte remained silent, and once the specified eight-day waiting period passed, Stroganov left Constantinople. Following the formal break in diplomatic relations, the danger of war loomed large, encouraged in Russia by key foreign policy and military advisers and by pro-Greek sympathies in educated society. In the end, however, after months of grinding diplomacy, the Russian monarch, who had condemned Ypsilantis from the outset, opted for peace in the interest of European unity.[10] How did this happen, and what did it reveal about Russia's relationship to Europe?

News of the Ypsilantis revolt reached the European allies during meetings at Laibach, where they had reconvened after Russia, Austria and Prussia signed the Troppau protocol sanctioning Austrian military intervention to repress revolution in Naples.[11] Having disavowed any support for Ypsilantis or for Greek rebellion against Ottoman authority, Alexander looked to his allies to act in concert in response to the crisis. Although Britain had already opposed collective intervention in Naples, as a matter of principle, Russia still hoped to win British and Austrian support in the event of war with the Ottoman Empire. The response to Russian overtures was inconclusive, though in October 1821, Metternich and Castlereagh met in Hanover to discuss measures to prevent war. The allies accepted the legitimacy of Russia's demand that the Porte should adhere to established treaty provisions; however, they rejected the idea that Russia possessed a humanitarian right to intervene unilaterally on behalf of the Greeks and other Christian peoples. Diplomatic negotiations dragged on, and only after Tatishchev's meetings with Metternich in March and April 1822 did the threat of war begin to recede.

Russian diplomatic correspondence concerning the war scare of 1821–2 is substantial, even if analysis is limited to communications between the tsar diplomat, his co-ministers of foreign affairs (Karl Nesselrode and Ioannis Kapodistrias) and his diplomatic agents in London, Paris, Vienna and Berlin.[12] There is much to be learned about the conceptual history of Russian diplomacy. This chapter's focus on Alexander I's instructions to Tatishchev is just one possibility. The impetus to send Tatishchev to Vienna was the emperor's disappointment with allied efforts to dispel what he considered the Porte's illusions. Nor had any of the allies, especially Britain and Austria, committed to strong support of Russian interests. After close to a year of diplomatic conversation and evasion, Alexander concluded that Austria had not adequately pressed upon the Porte the legitimacy of Russia's demands. Instead, the threat of war had increased: so Tatishchev was sent to Vienna to impress upon Metternich the need for (and justice of) forceful concerted action and to assess what Austria's reaction would be, if Alexander decided to go to war.

Alexander's instructions to Tatishchev were issued as a rescript dated 5/17 February 1822.[13] From the outset, Alexander emphasized that Tatishchev's mission concerned the most vital of interests – interests that the crisis in the Orient threatened and that could be protected only by 'the general alliance', as opposed to 'the exclusive combinations' of the old policy.[14] The substantive instructions began with a summary of the emperor's response, also transmitted to his agents at allied courts, to Austria's proposals of 23 December 1821 concerning Russia's claims against the Porte.[15] By the time of the mission, Austria had assumed the lead role in allied negotiations with the Porte, and Alexander made clear that at Vienna, Tatishchev spoke for his sovereign. As the instructions emphasized, even though Austria offered the most immediate possibility for allied participation in the crisis, Alexander expected cooperation from all the great powers, and he insisted that the grave matters at hand needed to be resolved collectively 'in the spirit of the alliance and for the common salvation (*salut*) of all the States of Europe'. According to the emperor, the current task of the allies was to protect the interests threatened by the crisis in the Levant, if necessary by deploying an armed force that would act for 'the general good' in the name of the alliance.[16] The interests at stake represented one element in Russia's relations with the Porte, and compromise of those interests threatened 'the order of things' enshrined in established treaties.

Having identified Russia's interests with the common European good and desire for peace, Alexander highlighted the danger posed by allied inaction and by failure to convince the Porte to change course, so that diplomatic relations with Russia could be restored. Continuation of the impasse would force Russia to act alone, a step the allies clearly sought to forestall. As if to counter allied apprehensions that Russia aimed to expand her economic and territorial interests at Ottoman expense, Alexander warned that in the event of unilateral Russian action, factions working to disrupt social order across Europe might conclude that the alliance was broken.[17] The emperor reiterated his desire to avoid war, something he believed his diplomacy had already established; however, if the Ottomans remained obstinate and the use of force became necessary, collective allied action would be more effective than any unilateral measures taken by Russia. Alexander rejected the potential claim that to address the Porte in the name of Europe accorded to the Ottoman Empire recognition as a European power. To the contrary, the purpose of collective European action would be to return the empire to the position it had occupied in the political order of March 1821, before the start of the Greek rebellions.

Alexander's instructions to Tatishchev may be read as a justification of Russian demands and a plea for allied support. Repeatedly, the emperor depicted the policy of the Ottoman government as a threat to the tranquility of Europe. Russia's calls for a formal allied guarantee to specify the actions that would be taken if the Porte refused to accede to Russian demands remained unanswered, though eventually the allies did promise moral support in the event of war. In the meantime, it was the job of Alexander's diplomats to prod the allies into articulating a unified position. Based on the events of the past nine months, the emperor assumed that without a change in the allied approach, the Ottomans would continue to violate treaty obligations. Thus if the Porte rejected the modified conditions put forward by Austria, Russia expected to employ coercive measures in the name of the alliance. Alexander understood that any movement of Russian troops into the Danubian Principalities would lead to war, even if Russia did not declare war. But backed by an allied guarantee, the nature of which was not specified, this 'war of concert' (*guerre concertée*) would quickly produce satisfactory results and would not compromise peace in the rest of Europe. Again, allied agreement in outlook and principle represented the best protection against the misfortunes caused by 'particular combinations' – just the sort of combinations that Napoleon had used in the wake of French military victories to break up multiple coalitions.

Alexander ended the instructions by comparing the act he hoped to conclude with the Troppau protocol signed by Austria, Prussia and Russia in November 1820. Russia's expectations of her allies followed directly from the actions negotiated at Troppau and Laibach. Never mind that Britain and France had not formally acceded to the Austrian intervention in Naples. They had not openly opposed it, and the rift had not violated the alliance. Similarly, if Russia acted alone to protect her interests in the Orient, this would not indicate a lesser commitment 'to the spirit of the alliance' or to the principles upon which it rested. Ongoing communication, nimble and adaptable application of eternal principles to practical realities, mutual respect for the vital interests of the great powers, and an understanding of allied unity that allowed for unilateral military action – these were the hallmarks of the post-Napoleonic general alliance.

Key to Emperor Alexander's eventual decision to opt for peace was the allies' recognition that Russia possessed a legal right to act. In February 1822, at the time of Tatishchev's mission, Russia modified her original ultimatum based on the Austrian proposals supported by Britain.[18] Henceforth, allied diplomatic communications with the Porte employed Metternich's iteration of Russia's demands: restoration of destroyed Orthodox churches, protection of the Orthodox religion, recognition of the distinction between guilty and innocent Greeks, and, finally, the evacuation of the Danubian Principalities. About a month after his arrival in Vienna, Tatishchev reported to Nesselrode (10/22 March) that because the Porte still refused to evacuate the Principalities and even demanded the return of territories ceded to Russia at Bucharest, Emperor Francis I had declared Ottoman conduct intolerable and had expressed the conviction that his fellow sovereign possessed the right to decide how Russia would obtain satisfaction. On 28 March/9 April, Tatishchev again wrote from Vienna that the Austrian government continued to act in 'a spirit of justice' and so left in the hands of the Russian monarch any decision about the use of force. Prussia had also promised to adhere to allied diplomatic measures (2/14 March), and France had acknowledged

Russia's rights once the position of the other allies became clear. In early to mid-April, Russian officials continued to expect war, but they also remained confident that should hostilities become unavoidable, allied support – no mention was made of material support – would be forthcoming.[19]

The fruits of alliance adaptability became visible by May 1822, when Ottoman troops began to leave the Principalities and Russia's diplomats could report evidence of a willingness to compromise on the part of the Porte. In a rescript of 14/26 May, Alexander congratulated Tatishchev on the success of his earlier mission and ordered him back to Vienna to represent the monarch while the allies worked to persuade the Porte to fulfil Russia's demands. Although Alexander had decided against military action, he retained the right to reconsider, and over the next few months, he relied on allied diplomacy, now entrusted to the British ambassador in Constantinople, Lord Strangford, to press for humane treatment of the Greeks and the restoration of hospodar administration in the Principalities.[20] War had been averted, but the deeper conflict had not been resolved. Only after the evacuation of the Principalities and the return of free navigation in the Black Sea and Straits would Alexander re-establish diplomatic relations with the Porte. At meetings of allied plenipotentiaries held in Vienna at the end of June, the Russian emperor reserved the right to decide on war, and in July, Russia continued to press the allies to agree on the joint action that would be taken should the Porte reject their demands. To Russia, the Porte's good intentions seemed dubious, even though by the end of 1822, the sultan had ordered the evacuation of Ottoman troops from the Principalities, restored hospodar rule and selected a new ecumenical patriarch.[21] On 15/27 November, during conferences in Verona, Tatishchev could declare that Alexander was satisfied with allied promises to take additional steps, through their ambassadors in Constantinople, to pressure the Ottoman government to accept Russia's conditions for the restoration of diplomatic relations. Going forward, the Russian government continued the pursuit of concerted action with European allies to resolve the Greek situation but demanded bilateral negotiations between St Petersburg and Constantinople on matters concerning the Principalities and Russia's treaty rights.[22]

If the diplomacy surrounding the war scare of 1821–2 reveals an effective European system capable of containing great power competition to ensure peace, this was not the result of a collective security regime founded on defined legal principles and administrative procedures. Between 1814 and the outbreak of the Crimean War in 1853 successful peacemaking resulted not from a commitment to shared governance, but from the flexibility of the general alliance and the ideal of unity that inspired the monarchs and diplomats of Europe.[23] From a Russian perspective the process of peacemaking grew out of the Napoleonic wars and the trauma of 1812. More important than any association of revolution with war was the belief that only through allied unity and the prevention of particular combinations among the great powers could peace be preserved. In the mind (and soul) of Emperor Alexander I, the desire for peace could not have been more essential or more powerful – so powerful, in fact, that it eclipsed longstanding strategic, economic and political interests. The realization of Catherinian plans for territorial aggrandizement – as recently as 1812, Russia had acquired Bessarabia from the Ottoman Empire – had temporarily been set aside. In the war scare of 1821–2, the concert of the allies did not restrain or contain Russia. Alexander remained committed to allied unity and continued to rely on friendship among the sovereigns. However, he opted for peace only after the European powers recognized Russia's legitimate demands and right to act. The allies chose peace because, more than revolution, they feared war. Although historians might conclude that the congress 'system' and the concert of great powers effectively discouraged general war on the European continent, these arrangements could not control the larger global processes that impinged upon European realities and relationships. From the Russian point of view, the Crimean War of 1853–6, in which Britain and France supported the Ottoman Empire, represented the end of the general alliance.[24]

The history of diplomatic thought and peacemaking after Napoleon's defeat offers a striking example of how European political elites, socialized and educated in the Enlightenment environment of the late eighteenth century, responded to changed historical conditions that required imaginative thinking and the recalibration of social and political expectations. The efforts of Europe's post-Napoleonic peacemakers succeeded in important respects and disappointed in others. Their policies were in some areas farsighted and in others narrow-minded and self-interested. They left behind a world dominated by great powers in the pursuit of empire and riches – a world full of violence, prejudice, cruelty and exploitation – yet they also led their respective societies into a process of accommodation to liberal democratic change and the 'culture of opposition'.[25] The overarching result of their labours, after more than two decades of war and diplomacy, was that European 'society' became a little more pluralistic and a little more civilized.

Notes

1 V. K. Nadler, *Imperator Aleksandr I i ideia sviashchennogo soiuza*, 5 vols (Riga, 1886–92); Dominic Lieven, *Russia against Napoleon: The True Story of the Campaigns of War and Peace* (New York, 2009); Marie-Pierre Rey, *Alexander I: The Tsar who Defeated Napoleon*, trans. Susan Emanuel (DeKalb, IL, 2012); Francis Ley, *Alexandre Ier et sa Sainte-Alliance (1811–1825) avec des documents inédits* (Paris, 1975); Miroslav Šedivý, *Crisis Among the Great Powers: The Concert of Europe and the Eastern Question* (Basingstoke, 2016).
2 G. M. Hamburg, *Russia's Path Toward Enlightenment: Faith, Politics, and Reason, 1500–1801* (New Haven, CT, 2016); Elise Kimerling Wirtschafter, *Religion and Enlightenment in Catherinian Russia* (DeKalb, IL, 2013); Cynthia H. Whittaker, *Russian Monarchy: Eighteenth-Century Rulers and Writers in Political Dialogue* (DeKalb, IL, 2003); Richard S. Wortman, *Scenarios of Power: Myth and Ceremony in Russian Monarchy from Peter the Great to the Abdication of Nicholas I* (Princeton, NJ, 2006).
3 M. M. Speranskii, *Rukovodstvo k poznaniiu zakonov*, I. D. Osipov (ed.) (St Petersburg, 2002), 586.
4 Henry A. Kissinger, *A World Restored: Metternich, Castlereagh and the Problems of Peace, 1812–1822* (Boston, 1957); Adam Zamoyski, *Rites of Peace: The Fall of Napoleon and the Congress of Vienna* (New York, 2007); Mark Jarrett, *The Congress of Vienna and its Legacy: War and Great Power Diplomacy after Napoleon* (New York, 2014).

5   Enlightenment thought encouraged belief in the existence of a harmonious interlocking universe based on eternal principles of reason and natural law, a belief that could be incorporated into Christian teachings about God's creation and Providence.
6   Niall Ferguson, 'The Meaning of Kissinger: A Realist Reconsidered', *Foreign Affairs* 94, no. 5 (September/October 2015), 134–43.
7   After 1815 Russia accepted the return to the Ottoman policy that in peacetime closed the Straits to foreign warships. A secret clause in the Russo-Ottoman treaty of 1799 had allowed the Russian fleet to pass through the Straits during the war. Alexander Bitis, *Russia and the Eastern Question: Army, Government, and Society, 1815–1833* (Oxford, 2006), 1–30; E. P. Kudriatseva, *Russkie na Bosfore: Rossiiskoe posol'stvo v Konstantinopole v pervoi polovine XIX veka* (Moscow, 2010), 197–215; Barbara Jelavich, *Russia's Balkan Entanglements, 1806–1914* (New York, 1991), 6–7.
8   The Vladimirescu revolt began in January 1821. After 1711 the sultan appointed Phanariote Greeks, aristocrats from the Phanar district of Constantinople, rather than local boyars, to serve as hospodars, or governors, in Moldavia and Wallachia. An imperial decree issued by Sultan Selim III in 1802 and the Treaty of Bucharest (1812) allowed Russia to approve these appointments. Richard Stites, *The Four Horsemen: Riding to Liberty in Post-Napoleonic Europe* (New York, 2014), chapter 4; Theophilus C. Prousis, *Russian Society and the Greek Revolution* (DeKalb, IL, 1994); Theophilus C. Prousis, *Lord Strangford at the Sublime Porte (1821): The Eastern Crisis*, Volume 1 (Istanbul, 2010); Theophilus C. Prousis, *Lord Strangford at the Sublime Porte (1822): The Eastern Crisis*, Volume 2 (Istanbul, 2012); Victor Taki, 'The Russian Protectorate in the Danubian Principalities: Legacies of the Eastern Question in Contemporary Russian-Romanian Relations', in *Russian-Ottoman Borderlands: The Eastern Question Reconsidered*, Lucien J. Frary and Mara Kozelsky (eds) (Madison, WI, 2014), 35–72.
9   A larger Greek crisis and much internal Greek strife continued until the establishment of an independent kingdom in 1830 and the end of civil war in 1834.
10 Bitis, *Russia and the Eastern Question*, 98–115; Charles and Barbara Jelavich, *The Establishment of the Balkan National States, 1804–1920* (Seattle, WA, 1977); Jelavich, *Balkan Entanglements*; Misha Glenny, *The Balkans: Nationalism, War, and the Great Powers 1802–2011* (New York, 2012), 16–19, 21–39; Paul Schroeder, *The Transformation of European Politics 1763–1848* (New York, 1994), chapter 13. For the text of the Russian ultimatum, see Ministerstvo inostrannykh del SSSR, *Vneshniaia politika Rossii XIX i nachala XX veka. Dokumenty Rossiiskogo ministerstva inostrannykh del* (hereafter *VPR*), second series, vol. 4 (12) (Moscow, 1980), doc. 78 (6/18 July 1821), 203–10.
11 Adopted by Russia, Austria and Prussia on 7/19 November 1820, the Troppau protocol ratified the principle of armed intervention against revolution in Naples and a general right of military intervention by coalition states in the domestic affairs of other states threatened by revolutionary movements or uprisings. Both Britain and France refused to sign the protocol but did not openly oppose Austrian intervention in Italy. *VPR*, v. 3 (11) (Moscow, 1979), doc. 186 (7/19 November 1820), 589–93; doc. 187 (7/19 November 1820), 593–4.
12 The relevant documents are published in *VPR*, vol. 4 (12); Anton Freihern Prokesch von Osten, *Geschichte des Abfalls der Griechen vom türkischen Reiche im Jahre 1821 und der Gründung des Hellenischen Königreiches. Aus diplomatischem Standpuncte*, vol. 3 (Vienna, 1867); *British and Foreign State Papers 1820–1821* (London, 1830).
13 *VPR*, v. 4 (12), doc. 153 (5/17 February 1822), 426–30.

14 Alexander's policy, according to the rescript, had been developed over the past nine months in communications between his government and allies; in a personal letter to Austrian emperor Francis I, dated 17/29 July 1821; and in another letter to British foreign secretary Castlereagh, dated 29 August/10 September 1821. See *VPR*, v. 4 (12), annotation (11/23 July 1821), 215; annotation (29 August/10 September 1821), 279.
15 The Austrian proposals are summarized in *VPR*, v. 4 (12), doc. 154 (6/18 February 1822), 430–43, a mémoire sent to Alexander's representatives at the courts of Vienna, Berlin, London and Paris.
16 The term Levant referred to the islands and coastal areas of the eastern Mediterranean ruled by the Ottomans. See Prousis, *Strangford*, vol. 1, 13. Although historians of Europe tend to use the term 'Eastern question', the documents of the era refer to 'the crisis in the Orient'.
17 At this time, all of the diplomatic principle among the allies believed in the existence of a revolutionary directorate operating from Paris that sought to foment rebellion throughout Europe.
18 *VPR*, v. 4 (12), doc. 154 (6/18 February 1822), 430–43. Metternich and Castlereagh met in Hanover in October 1821 to discuss the crisis, and in December Austria communicated to Russia proposals for modification of the ultimatum. On the Hanover meetings, see Lieven's report to Nesselrode in *VPR*, v. 4 (12), doc. 122 (21 October/2 November 1821), 330–40.
19 *VPR*, v. 4 (12), annotation (26 September/8 October 1821), 310; doc. 154 (6/18 February), 430–43; doc. 157 (28 February/12 March), 447–53; annotation (2/14 March), 454; doc. 159 (10/22 March), 454–7; doc. 164 (28 March/9 April), 470–1; doc. 165 (3/15 April), 471–4; doc. 166 (3/15 April), 474–5. Unless otherwise indicated, these documents are from 1822.
20 *VPR*, v. 4 (12), doc. 175 (14/26 May), 507–13; doc. 176 (16/28 May), 513; doc. 178 (17/29 May), 515; annotation (28 June), 536; annotation (27 July), 547. These documents are from 1822. Although Alexander preferred to see the return of hospodar rule based on the regulations stipulated in previous treaties, he had also expressed a willingness to entertain changes to the form of local government. *VPR*, v. 4 (12), annotation (13/25 September 1821), 289–90; annotation (24 February/8 March 1822), 446. On the hospodars, see also notes 8 and 21.
21 By September 1822 most of the Ottoman troops had been withdrawn from Moldavia and Wallachia. The new hospodars, or governors, chosen by the sultan, came from local boyars and princes rather than Phanariote Greeks. Still, the Porte did not consult Russia regarding the appointments. Prousis, *Strangford*, vol. 2, 11–12.
22 By February 1824 diplomatic relations were partially restored; however, again in the summer of 1825 Russia was on a path toward unilateral action against the Porte. Following an ultimatum from Nicholas I (ruled 1825–55) in March 1826, the Porte agreed to the Convention of Akkerman (October 1826) and removed the last Ottoman troops from the Principalities. In 1827 at the London Convention, Russia, Britain and France agreed to establish an autonomous Greece under Ottoman suzerainty. When the Porte refused to accept allied mediation, a combined British, French and Russian squadron destroyed the Ottoman fleet in the Battle of Navarino (October 1827). Full-scale war between the Russian and Ottoman empires raged in 1828–9 with no allied participation or support for Russia, though the allies did provide military, naval and financial assistance to the new Greek government led by Kapodistrias. Schroeder, *Transformation*, chapter 14; Jelavich, *Balkan National States*, 38–52; Jelavich, *Balkan Entanglements*, 65–89; Bitis, *Russia and the Eastern Question*, 426–9; Prousis, *Greek*

Revolution, 52–4; Prousis, *Strangford*, vol. 2, 356; Patricia Grimsted, *The Foreign Ministers of Alexander I: Political Attitudes and the Conduct of Russian Diplomacy, 1801–1825* (Berkeley and Los Angeles, CA, 1969), 259–63; Kissinger, *A World Restored*, 260–97; Jennifer Mitzen, *Power in Concert: The Nineteenth-Century Origins of Global Governance* (Chicago, IL, and London, 2013), 102–41; O. V. Orlik, *Rossiia v mezhdunarodnykh otnosheniiakh 1815–1829: Ot Venskogo kongressa do Adrianopol'skogo mira* (Moscow, 1998), 40–8. *VPR*, v. 4 (12), doc. 175 (14/26 May), 507–13; doc. 176 (16/28 May), 513; doc. 182 (9/21 June), 526–9; annotation (28 June), 536; doc. 189 (13/25 July), 543–6; annotation (13/25 November), 593; annotation (15/27 November), 599. These documents are from 1822.

23 The impact of public opinion is also relevant but must be studied in local/national context.

24 Bitis, *Russia and the Eastern Question*; John S. Curtiss, *Russia's Crimean War* (Durham, NC, 1979).

25 In a masterful study of the emergence of the modern world, C. A. Bayly describes a 'world crisis of 1780–1820' that originated in 'a growing imbalance between the perceived military needs of states and their financial capacity'. Even more consequential than the material crisis, according to Bayly, was the underlying social crisis caused by economic conflict and a 'culture of opposition' that 'had made people more skeptical of, and hostile to, established authority'. C. A. Bayly, *The Birth of the Modern World, 1780–1914: Global Connections and Comparisons* (Malden, MA, 2004), 101–2.

3

An Imperial Affair: The Allied Council of Ambassadors and the Occupation of France, 1815–18[1]

Beatrice de Graaf

Introduction

In July 1815, after the second defeat of Napoleon, Paris was a hub for allied activities – and a site of discontent and anxiety for its French inhabitants. The allied ministers sought to defuse the French spirit of revolution – not solely through treaties, but through a military occupation of France. This novel type of collective action was managed by the Allied Council of Ambassadors, consisting of representatives of the four main allied powers; Russia, Prussia, Austria and Britain. This chapter investigates the innovative, far-ranging activities of the Council, by analysing it as a project of inter-imperial collective security – indicating that it operated in a hierarchical and progressively expansive fashion regarding the identification of threats and interests, and that it became a testing ground for a series of inter-imperial security arrangements. The workings of this Allied Council, and its repertoire of measures and activities, have never been studied extensively.[2] Its minutes have been pieced together,[3] so as to offer an overview of how it attempted to organize a secure, imperial peace, for France, for Europe and for the rest of the world – and how that played out.

A legitimate occupation and imperial affair

'The war of 1815 is not a war of conquest', as the Austrian chancellor, Metternich, urged his German counterpart Hardenberg. For the allies 'the double aim' of the war was 'bringing down the usurpation of Napoléon Bonaparte' and to install a government that would guarantee order for both France and the remainder of Europe.[4] To ensure this, something new was asked for, something unheard of in seventeenth- or eighteenth-century international relations[5]: a military occupation as a joint collective action, because the danger was, as the British foreign secretary, Viscount Castlereagh, put it, 'that when the Allied Armies are removed from the Country, the System itself may fall to pieces, before it has by time been consolidated'. Hence, 'no time ought to be lost', in effecting an occupation that was to be executed by 'regularity and method',[6] and that had more in common with the occupation regime of later epochs (for example the Allied Council after 1945[7]) than with earlier efforts to restore peace.

Politically, the allied occupation did not attempt to include all of the allied coalition partners, let alone the states of Europe. It was a highly hierarchical, limited group of ministers who took their strategic aims from existing documents for the reorganization of Europe, predominantly from the so-called 'Pitt-plan' (1805)[8] and Friedrich Gentz's 1806 study on the balance of power in Europe,[9] and from the Final Act of Vienna (February/June 1815). These plans envisioned a reorganization of the European map and a hierarchy of powers: ranging from the first-rank allied powers (the four key empires), the second-rank (Spain, Portugal and the Netherlands, for example) and the third-ranked (smaller German and Italian states, including Piedmont). Other partners of the military campaign who requested membership of the Allied Council were refused and only granted indirect access to information, although they were occasionally invited to sit on subcommittees. Only four were considered 'les premières Puissances de l'Europe'.[10] Since they were the main victors, paymasters and providers of troops, protests against this directorate (from the French, but also from Spain and Portugal) fell flat. The occupation, and its managing body, the Allied Council, indeed seemed to have been perceived as legitimate by the other European powers, but it was definitely an imperial affair – as becomes clear by zooming in on the expanding scope of its activities.[11]

Igniting the allied machine

The Allied Council drew upon the management experience gained through the Central Administration in 1814: the body that dealt with allied communication, logistics and the government of the reconquered German and French lands, and which was headed by the Prussian minister Stein.[12] This Administration was a logical outcome of the *Territorialrevolution*, the geopolitical shifts and the judicial professionalization (*Verrechtlichung*) that reshaped the European continent between 1794 and 1815.[13] It combined expert knowledge of many lawyers, scholars and notables with that of allied planners and commanders, and expressed the ongoing trend of 'internal colonizing projects' not just of the eastern lands in Prussia, Poland and Russia, but also those reconquered by France. These lands that had to be *verwaltet*, managed and brought under control of new rulers and commanders. Stein's administration's first task was to serve the Sixth Coalition, to manage a supply to the troops, and to prevent retribution against civilians. Its no less important secondary task was the overhaul of administration in these lands by subjecting them to 'modern' centralized rule, as a form of *Herrschaft durch Verwaltung* ('ruling by management').[14]

While the occupation of France in 1814 was short lived, in 1815, the allies decided that a longer period was preferable. The aim was to bring back 'the people of France... to moral and peaceful habits', as Castlereagh stated in the Allied Council.[15] This time, the ministers of the four powers decided to act as a consortium without Stein. The management apparatus was more complex than in 1814. The Allied Council was the overarching political body, but subordinated to it was an executive, administrative organ, the Allied Administration – initially referred to by the Germans as the *General-Armee-Kommission*, and later as the *Vereinigtes Ministerium der alliierten Armeen*.[16] Representatives of the four major powers oversaw requests of allied governors and military commanders regarding care for troops, and settled these with the French Requisition Committee.[17] Its task was to prevent looting and mitigate chaos in the occupied French provinces, and to ensure an equal division of material support to each allied force.[18]

But the main political forum for decision-making was the Allied Council, installed once the military capitulation treaty was signed on 3 July 1815. It was designed that none of the four main allied powers would operate in isolation and that all decisions would be based on 'common and uniform principles'.[19] The Allied Council, in the minutes referred to as the *Conference des Ministres Alliés*, convened from 12 July 1815 until 1818, initially meeting every day, and later two or three times a week.[20] The Council originally consisted of Vienna's main players: Metternich for Austria; Minister of Foreign Affairs, Robert Stewart, Viscount Castlereagh for Britain; Ambassador Friedrich Wilhelm von Humboldt, Chancellor Prince Karl August von Hardenberg and General Neidhardt von Gneisenau for Prussia; and Counts Carlo Andrea Pozzo di Borgo and Karl von Nesselrode for Russia. Prince Charles-Maurice de Talleyrand, and his successor after 20 September, Armand Émmanuel du Plessis, Duke of Richelieu (the former Governor of Odessa for the Tsar who had proved himself a master of 'internal colonization' and management),[21] were summoned to join the Council (and to receive orders from them). The members knew each other well, having worked so closely together over the Vienna settlement.[22] The 'Allied Machine'[23] could now translate its imperial security ambitions into practice – starting with France.

Its four 'principles of salutary precaution' were formulated by Castlereagh, confirmed by the Allied Council, and then cemented in the Paris Peace Treaty of November 1815: first, to demilitarize the country; second, to 'de-bonapartise'; third, to de-revolutionize the political situation; and fourth, to guarantee the payment of reparations.[24] To ensure their effectiveness a series of subcommittees was created. First, the Council appointed a Military Committee, consisting of the allied commanders of the Sixth Coalition under the leadership of the Duke of Wellington. It oversaw the handling of conflicts between allied commanders, between troops, and also between French citizens (by appointing mixed judicial courts). It established a temporary military government of Paris (until the conclusion of the Paris Peace Treaty in late November). Financial matters were dealt with by an audit board. Police and intelligence issues were the province of an allied secret police force, the *Verbündetenpolizei*, chaired by the Prussian Justus von Gruner. This complex structure of committees also ensured that the autonomy of the French king, Louis XVIII and his government, remained limited.[25]

To keep allied infighting and the ongoing conflicts with the French in check, in October, Wellington was appointed as overall manager. He acted as the main conduit between the allies and the French king and government and the chair of the Military Committee and main adviser to the Allied Council. Owing to his support in 1814 and in 1815 for the return of the Bourbons to the throne, Wellington enjoyed the support of Louis XVIII.[26] He required members to send him a report at least once a week recounting their discussions.[27] In short, imperial allied rule took precedence over the rule of Louis XVIII.

Demilitarizing France: occupation as the bond of peace

To guarantee the fulfilment of the treaty conditions, the allies occupied two-thirds of France, as an 'occupation of guarantee' and as a 'bond of peace'.[28] The first task was to demilitarize the country. The Napoleonic army had to be reduced and reorganized. The Council ordered a withdrawal of all French troops to south of the river Loire and kept a check on the issue of passports.[29] Second, Wellington was to oversee an allied force of occupation in France. Altogether 1.2 million soldiers were deployed on French soil, of which 320,000 were Austrians, 310,000 Prussians, 250,000 Russians, 128,000 British as well as troops from smaller German states, Denmark, Spain and Switzerland.[30] In the autumn of 1815, the Prussians were still advocating a dismembering of France, and the separation of large parts on the eastern borders, to be absorbed into Prussia, Austria and other German states. Only after a series of notes and discussions with Wellington (the Austrians and Russians broadly agreed with the British view) did the Prussians acquiesce in the prolongation of the occupation. Eventually, the allies reduced the force of occupation to 150,000 – consisting of five cohorts: four for the main allied powers, and one for the smaller German states. This force would remain in place and occupy the territory until France had paid the yet to be determined reparations and standing arrears, including the costs of maintaining the troops.[31] Two-thirds of France was to be occupied; the British in the west, the Prussians and Russians in the north and north-east, and the Austrians in the south-east. Paris was to be liberated and left under the jurisdiction of the king.[32] Furthermore, a more long-term precautionary measure was adopted to deter new French military aggression: the creation of a physical defence line. From July 1815 onwards, Wellington oversaw the construction and expansion of a system of twenty-one forts and garrisons along three parallel lines of fortifications, ranging from the fortresses along the North Sea coast (Nieuwpoort, Ostende) via Dendermonde, Ath, Doornik, Oudenaarde, Gent and Dinant, up to the German lines of defence at Mainz.[33] This defence line, the 'Wellington-Barrier', was financed predominantly through the French reparations payments.

The occupation and ensuing 'imperial management' transformed northern and eastern France into an 'alien' country. French residents were subject to foreign troops who were there to perform their peacekeeping duties. Prussian forces had a rather bad reputation and were widely resented.[34] Christine Haynes has established how in the areas where the occupiers and the indigenous people could understand each other (as in the Alsace region), a sense of fraternity and mutual respect sometimes took root.[35] However, the pervasive sentiments were those of great distrust and rancour regarding the 'allied invasion' – a resentment that the allied reports suggested increased over time.[36] Wellington struggled with the dilemma of keeping his military forces in order while recognizing that their presence often fuelled unrest. He warned: 'If one shot is fired in Paris, the whole country will rise against us.'[37] In other words, demilitarizing the country (the first principle) clashed with the idea of stabilizing France (the second and third principles, see below). That is why, after some hesitation, the Council agreed to reduce troop levels as partial compensation for the dissolution of the *Chambre Introuvable* in September 1816. In February 1817, Wellington sent 30,000 of his troops home[38] – but only upon the condition of a reinforcement of the 'Wellington-Barrier'. In 1818 an initial series of forts was completed and manned by Dutch troops and the German Federation garrisons to serve as a replacement guarantee for the security of Europe.[39]

Notwithstanding rumours about allied disunity,[40] the occupation and the close cooperation on the Council in military matters occasioned a greater degree of understanding and rapprochement between the allied powers. Through joint troop inspections, parades, field exercises, the construction of the fortresses, the exchange of military orders, sitting on joint legal committees, the imperial powers of Europe demonstrated their united management of the French security risk.[41]

The main reason for the occupation was of course its function in enforcing the execution of the fourth principle: the payment of war reparations, back payments of individual debts and the price of the deployment of allied armies. The pecuniary indemnity for the allied powers totalled 700 million francs. In addition the expenses for maintaining a 150,000 strong allied army of occupation amounted to 360 million francs per annum.[42] On top of this came the question of French debt payments to private owners, initially amounting to a claim of over 1 billion francs.[43] After lengthy negotiations, the Allied Council decided to contact the private banking houses of Hope and Baring, in London and Amsterdam, to secure France a loan in 1817, with a second in 1818.[44] Only then could France fulfil her outstanding financial obligations and pay the required 1,893 million francs. That was less than the reparations imposed on Germany after the First World War, but in absolute terms more than any other externally imposed war debt in the nineteenth and twentieth century.[45] Thus, at the Congress of Aachen/Aix-la-Chapelle, 30 September to 9 October 1818, France was invited to accede to the Quadruple Alliance (under special stipulations) and the allies' occupying army left France in the same year. The mutual European dependency on loans and subscriptions remained and expanded. A veritable bond was forged between the European great powers' banking houses and public investors, accelerating the emergence of financial markets for investors and stock buyers, and expanding the scope of financial security/ies.[46]

Defusing the spectre of unrest and rebellion

The activities of the Allied Council did however expand far beyond military affairs and financial arrangements. The Council took a series of steps intended to unnerve resurfacing sympathies for Napoleon and his relatives – the second and third principles of salutary precaution. Since they did not feel the Bourbons could ensure that stability,[47] the first sessions of the Council's meetings were devoted primarily to ensuring (and enforcing) that Bourbon rule led to domestic stability and to removing Bonapartist sympathizers from the scene. To do so, the Prussian head of the allied 'high police', Justus von Gruner, provided daily intelligence to the Allied Council.[48] He had reformed the Berlin police, had set up a spy ring for Tsar Alexander in Prague, and was happy to be the instrument of European 'peace and tranquillity', of public order and security in Paris.[49] Upon his appointment, he hired agents to assist him. He also asked the French spy masters, Fouché and Descazes, to forward their intelligence regarding allied matters.[50] In the months that Gruner ran his agency, he had at least 14 spies at his disposal, a bureau, a series of clerks and a substantial budget to persuade others to reveal information. Gruner and his spies described the gossip on Wellington's escapades and Fouché's intrigues, on the alleged divisions between the Austrians and the Prussians, and on the magnanimity of Tsar Alexander. Exclamations such as 'Vive l'empereur!', or 'vive le petit Napoléon' could be heard regularly, as were attempts to ridicule the king and his family. Gruner even found out rumours about allied disunity were orchestrated and manipulated by Talleyrand.[51]

Gruner's initial admiration for Fouché gave way to a mounting unrest with regard to alleged Bonapartist conspiracies. The allies increasingly grew wary of rumours that an attack on King Friedrich Wilhelm III or on Louis XVIII was imminent. These reports proved to be a hoax. But the news about massacres in the French south was not. Historians still differ regarding the number of Protestants being killed – estimates vary from 1,000 to 45,000. Public order and safety was severely compromised, as was the king's authority.[52] At first reluctant, but urged by pleas from British Protestants, the Allied Council intervened and asked Louis to restore order in the south.[53] Indeed, Fouché sent a letter to the prefect of the Gard, underlining his demands for greater compliance with allied pressure on the French king and government.[54] But on 30 August, Gruner wrote to his allied masters, including to King Friedrich Wilhelm III of Prussia himself, that a second 'St Barthelemy' (referencing the trope of Protestant persecutions) was imminent.[55] The Council intervened again, this time sending the Austrian general Schwarzenberg with his troops to pacify the hitherto unoccupied Gard (a *département* in southern France).[56]

This pattern of escalating allied interference in police and political matters continued in the years thereafter. The Allied Council sent Wellington to bring the king to reason, when the ultra-royalists appeared to frustrate the occupation and the completion of the Paris Treaty provisions. In February 1816, when the *Chambre des Introuvables* threatened to reject the budget (and thus the reparation payments), Wellington, on behalf of the allies, threatened the king with the outbreak of war once again – 'Il est possible que je me trouve dans le cas de mettre toute l'Europe une autre fois sous les armes'.[57]

The dissolution of the *Chambre* in September 1816 did not placate the Council's worries over Jacobin conspiracies and revolutionary plots. From July 1815 onwards, the Allied Council worried about fugitive and émigré Bonapartists and revolutionaries continuing to foment unrest: not only in, but also outside France. In early 1816, the ministers asked Richelieu to draw up lists of 'terroristes dangereux', in order that they may be sent into exile. The Council disseminated these lists to the other courts of Europe, demanding that they identify the French fugitives and to put them under surveillance.[58] The blacklisted individuals were prohibited to settle anywhere near the border of France and were only granted passports for one of the countries represented in the Allied Council – since it was thought that only these countries were able to mobilize enough surveillance. (This measure was applied, for example, to Hortense de Beauharnais, former Queen of the Netherlands, and the estranged wife of Louis Napoleon).[59]

The Council's worries were triggered by rumours, plots and real incidents. In June 1816, Wellington's house was set on fire.[60] On the night of 10/11 February 1818, an aggrieved Jacobin from Brussels, named Cantillon, attempted to assassinate him.[61] The perpetrators were found but acquitted by French judges.[62] For the Allied Council, especially for Prussia, Russia and Austria, these attacks were linked to émigré Bonapartists from Brussels and Krakow spreading subversive pamphlets, and were perceived as an expanding network of radicals whose aim was not only the overthrow of the French, but of the imperial and monarchical European order.[63]

At that time, Gruner's secret police had been disbanded with the termination of the military rule over Paris. In his place, Metternich took over questions relating to intelligence and counterrevolutionary measures. Early in 1816, he proposed to the Allied Council the establishment of a 'European police' force. And indeed, the Allied Council, urged by Metternich and Richelieu, conveyed the impression that there was a threat of a joint military action towards the Netherlands if the new king, William I, was unwilling to adopt censorship laws and to limit the freedom of the press and so to undermine the activities of the French exiles in Brussels.[64] William and his parliament succumbed to the threat by introducing new laws concerning deportation regulations.[65] At this point, the British ministers called the Council to a halt: 'The Allied Ministers at Paris must be kept within the bounds of their original institution and not be suffered to present themselves as an European Council for the management of the affairs of the world.'[66]

The Council thus displayed a progressively expansive ambition regarding the identification and countering of transnational revolutionary threats. It initiated a number of joint memoranda, complaints, missions and measures (on passports and listing). Shortly before it turned into a 'police state', the process was stopped by the British members, who knew that Parliament would never tolerate a system of automatic military intervention on behalf of repressive regimes.

The Allied Council: expanding the scope of imperial security

From 1816 onwards, the Council stretched its remit beyond the borders of France, the Netherlands and even Europe. The ministers discussed the deployment of troops from Russia, Spain, Britain and the Netherlands to fight the Barbary Corsairs. It settled British rule over the Ionian isles.[67] And it also enabled a joint mediation intervention on behalf of Spain to repel the Portuguese invasion of the Rio Plata in 1817. This last endeavour took up a substantial number of sessions and sparked heated discussions within the Council as to its scope, institutional identity and imperial interests.

The trigger to this affair (which cannot be rendered in its full complexity here)[68] was the formal request made by the Court of Madrid to the Allied Council and to the government of France, in March 1817, to act as mediating courts in negotiating the Portuguese restitution of the territory in the Banda Oriental (today's Uruguay) – a highly strategic swath of land along the Rio de la Plata that Portugal had invaded and occupied in 1816.[69] According to Spain, the aggression demonstrated by the Court of Brazil would bring disaster not only to South America, but also to Europe. The Council accepted, and succeeded in bringing Portugal to declare Spain's formal right of property over the occupied territory. However, the Portuguese envoy Palmella came to Paris and defended the invasion as a counterrevolutionary measure, and the only means of safeguarding South America's monarchies against the advance of 'Republicks' and artiguist revolutionaries.[70] After having quelled the 'esprit revolutionnaire' in Europe, it was now high time to combat this 'malheur' not only in Europe, but in 'le monde entire', since the revolutionary uprisings in the Americas were an 'attentat contraire à la moralité des nations et à la sureté des thrones'. It had to be the 'grand but' of the European 'confédération' to fight this 'anarchie' and these 'ennemies des souverains et des peuples'.[71]

After lengthy deliberation amongst the allied ministers (and Richelieu), Portugal stepped up its bid and asked the 'court médiatrices' in Paris to come up with a concrete plan for the 'pacification of South America' as a whole. 'The greatest interest of Spain, Portugal and the whole of Europe' dictated a joint effort to put an end to the revolutionary agitation in America, 'conform to the spirit of the age', and 'with respect to the relations between the two worlds'. If the 'esprit de démogagie' was not stifled there, it would 'sooner or later' spread to Europe.[72] Wellington never saw Pozzo di Borgo and the other ministers that 'disturbed'. Subsequently, the ministers of France and Russia formally requested Wellington to accept a role as mediator between Spain, Portugal and the colonies, and practically expand his efforts in Paris to Madrid and South America.[73]

At this point, Wellington, in close correspondence and under instructions from Castlereagh, politely declined. After discussing the hazards of sending an allied expedition under the command of a 'third power' (possibly the Netherlands) to Montevideo, he explained to the Allied Council that the conflict between Portugal, Spain and the revolutionaries under Artigas was a 'bye-battle', that Spain was 'too jealous' to seriously accept European interference in her affairs, and that he could not see himself bringing such a challenge to a conclusive end.[74] Here, British unilateral imperial interests dominated over and thwarted a joint, inter-imperial effort. Since the Allied Council had been disbanded after Aachen, there was no follow-up.

Concluding remarks

The Allied Council functioned as a venue for inter-imperial cooperation and as a testing ground for its corresponding security practices and arrangements. It also gave birth to an increased sense of inter-imperial dependency. This dependency was expressed in the international mobilization of huge financial loans and public investors throughout Europe; in the attempts to function as a joint allied police force and the implementation of concrete security arrangements (black lists, uniform passports) all over Europe. It was a testing ground for Metternich's idea of creating a European police directory, as underpinned by the framework of the Holy Alliance. British opposition prevented

Metternich and the Prussians from transforming the Council into a European police directorate. But the ministers did establish some uniform standards and means of mutual assistance in dealing with unrest and uprisings. Within the societies of Europe, news about such events and incidents was reported and commented upon extensively.[75] Intelligence reports and letters of solidarity were exchanged regularly.

By means of defined institutional practices and reciprocal treaties of assistance, the Allied Council tested a series of inter-imperial security practices that were quite expansive in their ambitions.[76] After 1816, the allies' scope widened to include the whole of Europe, and far beyond – stretching to the 'other hemisphere' and South America. At the same time, critics (the radical pundits in Brussels and London for example) argued that the allied interventions contributed to greater polarization in France and elsewhere. Even Wellington felt by 1818 that it was time to leave. But after 1818, the Allied Council had left a substantial legacy; the military occupation of France was just the beginning of the large-scale imperial security projects that came later in the nineteenth century.

Notes

1 The research leading to these results has received funding from the European Research Council under the European Union's Seventh Framework Programme (FP/2007–2013) / ERC Grant Agreement n.615313. The author is currently working on a monograph about the Allied Council, with CUP.
2 Thomas Dwight Veve has studied the *military aspects* of the occupation in *The Duke of Wellington and the British Army of Occupation in France, 1815–1818* (Westport, CT, 1992). See also Thomas D. Veve, 'Wellington and the Army of Occupation in France, 1815–1818', in *The International History Review* 11 (1989) 1:98–108; Philip Mansel, 'Wellington and the French Restoration', in idem, 76–83; Enno E. Kraehe, 'Wellington and the Reconstruction of the Allied Armies during the Hundred Days', in idem, 84–97. Volker Wacker's book *Die Alliierte Besetzung Frankreichs in den Jahren 1814 bis 1818* (Hamburg, 2001) concentrates primarily on the *Prussian share* in that task. Christine Haynes is the first to systematically address the *feelings and reactions of the French population* during the occupation, Idem, 'Making Peace: The Allied Occupation of France, 1815–1818', in Alan Forrest, Karen Hagemann and Michael Rowe (eds), *War, Demobilization and Memory: The Legacy of War in the Era of Atlantic Revolutions* (London, 2016), 51–67. See also Emmanuel de Waresquiel, *Le Duc de Richelieu, 1766–1822* (Paris, 2009).
3 For the minutes of these meetings see, amongst others: National Archives, Kew (TNA). Foreign Office Files (FO) 92, 139; Geheimes Staatsarchiv Preussischer Kulturbesitz (GStA PK), Berlin. III. Hauptabteilung (HA) Ministerium des Auswärtigen (MdA) I, Politische Abteilung, Konferenz der Minister der alliierten Mächte in Paris, among others nrs. 897, 911, 1464, 1465, 1458, 1469.
4 Metternich, Memorandum to Hardenberg, 6 August 1815, Paris. GStA III. HA Ministerium der auswärtigen Angelegenheiten. I. Nr. 1461. p. 75.
5 Andreas Osiander, *The States System of Europe, 1640–1990: Peacemaking and the Conditions of International Stability* (London, 1994), 121; Mathew S. Anderson, 'Eighteenth-Century Theories of Balance of Power', in Ragnhild Hatton, D. B. Horn

and Mathew S. Anderson (eds), *Studies in Diplomatic History: Essays in Memory of David Bayne Horn* (London, 1970), 183–198.

6   Castlereagh, 'Memorandum', 13 July 1815. GStA III. HA Nr. 1461. See also Henry Houssaye, *1815. Le cent jours* (Paris, 1920), 425–426.

7   Norman Naimark, *The Russians in Germany: A History of the Soviet Zone of Occupation, 1945–1949* (London/Cambridge, 1997); Wolfgang Benz, *Potsdam 1945: Besatzungsherrschaft und Neuaufbau im Vier-Zonen-Deutschland* (München, 2012); Gunther Mai, *Der alliierte Kontrollrat in Deutschland 1945–1948: Alliierte Einheit – deutsche Teilung?* (Quellen und Darstellungen zur Zeitgeschichte. Band 36) (München, 1995).

8   William Pitt, 'Memorandum for security and deliverance of Europe', in a letter to the Russian Ambassador at London, January 19, 1805. Printed in Kenneth Bourne, *The Foreign Policy of Victorian England 1830–1902* (Oxford, 1970), 197–8.

9   Friedrich von Gentz, *Fragments upon the Balance of Power in Europe*. Translation (London, 1806); idem, 'Über de Pradt's Gemälde von Europa nach dem Kongress von Aachen', in *Wiener Jahrbüchern der Literatur* 5 (1819): 279–318, also in Gustav Schlesier (ed.), *Schriften von Friedrich Gentz: Ein Denkmal* (Mannheim, 1838), 88–156.

10 Metternich, Note, as annex to the protocol of 3 November 1815. GStA III. HA Nr. 1469, 50. See also protocol 10 August 1815, GStA III. HA I. Nr. 1461.

11 (Hardenberg), 'Etat des Négociations actuelles entre les Puissances Alliées & la France', 16–28 July 1815. GStA III. HA I. Nr. 1461, 55; Metternich, Memorandum, 6 August 1815. Sent to Hardenberg. GStA III. HA I. Nr. 1461, 75.

12 Memorandum Allied Council to Müffling, protocols 12 July 1815 GStA III. HA Nr. 1464.

13 Lutz Raphael, *Recht und Ordnung: Herrschaft durch Verwaltung im 19. Jahrhundert* (Frankfurt a.M, 2000), 17, 21–40.

14 Idem; Michael Rowe, *From Reich to State: The Rhineland in the Revolutionary Age, 1780–1830* (Cambridge, 227–8.

15 Note by Castlereagh to the Allied Ministers, 11 September 1815. T. C. Hansard, *Parliamentary Debates from 1803 to the present time* (London, 1816), 298.

16 See Volker Wacker, *Die alliierte Besetzung Frankreichs in den Jahren 1814 bis 1818* (Hamburg, 2001), 105–7.

17 'Articles arrêtés entre M. l'Intendant Général des armée & les Commissaire de S.M. T.C. sur le mode d'execution pour l'entretien, l'habillement & l'équipement des troupes', 15 August 1815. GStA III. HA I. Nr. 1461.

18 GStA III. HA Nr. 1464, protocol 14 July 1815; see the memorandum attached from Talleyrand; see also Wacker, *Die alliierte Besetzung*, 115.

19 GStA III. HA Nr. 1464, protocol 12 July 1815.

20 National Archives, London. FO 146/6, séances 14, 22, 24, 27 August 1815.

21 See De Waresquiel, *Le Duc de Richelieu*, chapters 4 and 5.

22 GStA III. HA Nr. 1464, protocol of 12 and 13 July 1815. Cited from Annex 6, protocol 13 July.

23 Castlereagh to Wellington, 13 May 1816, as cited in Niek van Sas, *Onze Natuurlijkste Bondgenoot: Nederland, Engeland en Europa, 1813–1831* (Groningen, 1985), 122.

24 Castlereagh, Memorandum, 13 July 1815. GStA III. HA Ministerium der auswärtigen Angelegenheiten. I. Nr. 1461. See also Lord Liverpool to Castlereagh, 21 July 1815, in Arthur Wellesley, Duke of Wellington, *Supplementary Despatches, Correspondence and Memoranda*. Vol. 11 (London, 1863), 47.

25 Protocol of 13 July.

26 Rory Muir, *Wellington: Waterloo and the Fortunes of Peace 1814–1852* (New Haven/London, 2015), 108–9.
27 TNA FO 146/6, séance October 1815, plus annex with instructions and objectives. Note to Wellington, signed by Castlereagh, Metternich, Nesselrode and Humboldt.
28 Christine Haynes, 'Making Peace: The Allied Occupation of France, 1815–1818', in Alan Forrest, Karen Hagemann and Michael Rowe (eds), *War, Demobilization and Memory: The Legacy of War in the Era of Atlantic Revolutions* (London, 2016), 62.
29 Protocol 17 July 1815, Allied Council. GStA HA Nr. 1464.
30 See Wacker, *Die alliierte Besetzung*, 95–8, 138–43; Andrea von Ilsemann, *Die Politik Frankreichs auf dem Wiener Kongress: Talleyrands aussenpolitische Strategien zwischen Erster und Zweiter Restauration* (Hamburg, 1996), 304–11
31 See the minutes of the Allied Council, 3rd, 10th and 13th meeting, 14 and 21 July 1815, GStA PK III. HA I, 'Konferenzprotokolle der Minister der alliierten Mächte in Paris', Nr. 1464.
32 The Prussians were deployed in Normandy, Maine, Anjou and Bretagne; the Russians in the Ile-de-France, the Champagne and the Lorraine. The British, including the Dutch and Belgians, in Thiérache, l'Artois and Flanders. The Wurtemberger and the Bavarians in the Orléanais, Nivernais, Bourbonnais and Auvergne; the Austrians in the Bourgogne, Franche-Comté, Dauphiné, Lyonnais and in parts of Provence and the Languedoc. See 'Memorandum on the temporary occupation of part of France, 31 August 1815', in Wellington, *Despatches*, Vol. 8, 253–5; see also Thomas Dwight Veve, *The Duke of Wellington and the British Army of Occupation in France, 1815–1818* (London, 1992), 11–31; Wacker, *Die alliierte Besetzung*, 141–6.
33 Cf. Wilfried Uitterhoeve, *Cornelis Kraijenhoff 1758–1840: Een Loopbaan onder Vijf Regeervormen* (Nijmegen, 2009), 289–318; H. D. Jones, *Reports Relating to the Re-Establishment of the Fortresses in the Netherlands from 1814 to 1830* (London, 1861); Veve, *The Duke of Wellington*, 93–108; Robert Gils, *De Versterkingen van de Wellingtonbarrière in Oost-Vlaanderen* (Ghent, 2005).
34 Although these feelings of resentment were exaggerated in later years: Wacker, *Die alliierte Besetzung*, 262–90.
35 Haynes, 'Making Peace', 62–3.
36 The Allied Council was made aware of this through Justus von Grüner's daily reports. Letters of Grüner and reports to the Allied Council, July–November 1815. GStA Nl Hardenberg 10a. See also ongoing reports in the protocols of the Allied Council, up until 1818. See also De Waresquiel, *Le Duc de Richelieu*, 22–3.
37 Cited in Veve, *The Duke of Wellington*, 67.
38 Veve, *The Duke of Wellington*, 109–23.
39 Although Wellington and the allies insisted on an international defensive/garrison force, the Dutch king William I refused to house foreign troops in Dutch forts. So Dutch troops manned the forts, with German troops nearby. Wacker, *Die alliierte Besetzung*, 223–31. See also 'Memorandum', discussed in the Allied Council to prepare for the Aachen Conference. FO 92/34.
40 Gruner, reports to the allied ministers, July–August 1815. Nl. Hardenberg 38 Fasz I, GStA.
41 Veve, *The Duke of Wellington*, 37–40. See for such a cooperation: 'Rapport van den Inspecteur-Generaal der Fortificaties betreffende de ontworpen grondslagen tot een algemeen systema van Defensie van het Rijk', 15 March 1816. NA, 'toegangsnummer' 2.02.01 ('Algemene Staatssecretarie en Kabinet des Konings'), inventory 5654.

42 Foreign Office, *British and Foreign State Papers: 1815–1816*. Vol. 3 (London: Ridgway, 1838), 280–91; see 292–361, for specific conventions regarding how the debt should be paid and borders drawn.
43 Richelieu to the Allied Council, 10 September 1817, protocol 13 September 1817. TNA, London, FO 146/22.
44 Letter Baring to Richelieu, 7 October 1817, Paris. Protocol of the Allied Council, 8 October 1817. TNA, London, FO 146/22.
45 Eugene N. White 'Making the French Pay: The Costs and Consequences of the Napoleonic Reparations', *European Review of Economic History* 5 (2001) 337–65, here 341, 361.
46 See also Glenda Sluga, 'The Economic History of a European Security Culture, After the Napoleonic Wars', in Beatrice de Graaf, Brian Vick (eds), *Securing Europe after Napoleon: 1815 and the New European Security Culture* (Cambridge, 2018); Jerome Greenfield, 'Financing a New Order. The Payment of Reparations by Restoration France, 1817–1818', *French History*, 30 (2016) 3: 376–400; Kim Oosterlinc, Loredana Ureche-Rangau and Jacques-Marie Vaslin, 'Baring, Wellington and the Resurrection of French Public Finances Following Waterloo', *The Journal of Economic History* 74 (2014) 4: 1072–1102; D. C. M. Platt, *Foreign Finance in Continental Europe and the United States, 1815–1870: Quantities, Origins, Functions and Distribution* (London, Boston, Sydney, 1984); Philip Ziegler, *The Sixth Great Power: Barings, 1762–1929* (London, 1988).
47 Wellington to Bathurst, 2 July 1815, in: Idem, Vol. 8, 188–93.
48 See reports by Gruner, 22 July–November 1815. In Gruner Nr. 86; Nachlass Hardenberg 10a, GStA Berlin.
49 See K. Zeisler, 'Justus von Gruner. Eine biographische Skizze', in Werner Breunig and Uwe Schaper (eds), *Berlin in Geschichte und Gegenwart* (Berlin, 1994), 81–105.
50 Especially letter Gruner to Fouché, 22 July and Descazes, 3 August 1815, Gruner Nr. 86. Gruner to Fouché, 3 August 1815. Nl. Hardenberg 10a. GStA.
51 Bericht Gruner, 13 September 1815. Nl. Hardenberg 10a. GStA.
52 Daniel P. Resnick, *The White Terror and the Political Reaction After Waterloo* (Cambridge, MA, 1966), 56–62; Charles Pouthas (ed.), *Charles de Rémusat: Mémoires de ma vie, 1797–1820*. Vol. 1 (Paris, 1958), 225–6.
53 Colonel Ross to Sir Charles Stuart, 11 February 1816, TNA FO 27/130; see P. J. Lauze de Péret, *Causes et précis des troubles, crimes et désordres dans le département du Gard et dans d'autres lieux du Midi de La France* (Paris: Poulet, 1819); letter from Wellington to Louis XVIII, February 1816, in Wellington, *Supplementary Despatches*, Vol. 9, 309–310; Document No. 104. 'Extraits des rapports du Colonel Ross, Janvier 1816', in Daniel Robert, *Textes et documents relatifs à l'histoire des Églises Réformées en France: période 1800–1830*. Vol. 37 of *Histoire des idées et critique littéraire* (Geneva/Paris, 1962), 305–11, here 307–8; Correspondance, TNA FO 27/119. See also Alice Wemyss, 'L'Angleterre et la Terreur blanche de 1815 dans le Midi', *Annales du Midi* 73 (1963) 55:287–310, here 295–6.
54 Letter Fouché to the Préfect of Nimes, 25 August 1815. Nl Hardenberg 10a, GStA.
55 Letter Gruner to Friedrich Wilhelm III, copy to Hardenberg and Allied Council, 30 August 1815. Nl. Hardenberg 10a, GStA.
56 Note Schwarzenberg. Annex to the protocol of 16 August 1815; Memorandum Schwarzenberg, 27 August, annex no. 97. GStA HA III. Nr. 1465, p. 62 e.v., 109 e.v. Schwarzenberg was dispatched again in September and October.
57 Letter to Louis XVIII, composed by Wellington and the Allied Council, 28 February 1816. TNA FO 146/6, séance 28 February 1816.

58 Minutes of the Allied Council, July–December 1816, and the first months of 1816. HA III, 1464, 1465 and 1469. See also Report by Richelieu to the Council, 19 May 1816, TNA FO 146/6.
59 Letter Allied Council to Gruner, 18 October 1815. GStA Nl Hardenberg 10a, FAsz I; Protocol Allied Council, Instructions Metternich, 15 August 1815. GStA III. HA. Nr. 1465. See also Le Prince Napoléon, *Mémoires de la Reine Hortense*. Deel III (Paris: Plon, 1927), 65–103.
60 Richard Edgcumbe (ed.), *The Diary of Frances Lady Shelley 1787–1817* (London, 1912), 202–3. Shelley refers to 'Monsieur de Cage', a phonetic rendering in English of the French name (Élie) Descazes, the French Foreign Minister and Minister of Police.
61 Muir, *Wellington*, 111–13.
62 'Attentat contre le duc de Wellington', voluminous file at the Archives de la préfecture de police (APP), Nr. APP.AA.342. Especially police reports 12–13 February. See also police reports 12 February–April 1816. AND.F.7.3839. Paris.
63 Cf. Minutes of the Allied Council, February–April 1816. TNA FO 146/6.
64 E.g. FO 146/6, séance 25 February 1816.
65 Wellington, 'Memorandum to Ministers on the Libels Published in the Low Countries', 29 August 1816, in the Duke of Wellington (ed.), *Supplementary Despatches, Correspondence, and Memoranda* [WSD], vol. 11 (London, 1858), 464–9. Van Sas, *Onze natuurlijkste bondgenoot*, 125–62; Pierre Rain, *L'Europe et la restauration des Bourbons: 1814–1818* (Paris, 1908); W. P. Sautijn Kluit, 'Dagbladvervolgingen in België 1815–1830', *Bijdragen voor vaderlandsche geschiedenis en oudheidkunde* 3 (1892) 6:307–94.
66 Castlereagh to Stuart, 22 July 1817, in C. K. Webster, *The Foreign Policy of Castlereagh, 1815–1822: Britain and the European Alliance* (London, 1924), 71.
67 Protocol 28 October 1815; Treaty of 5 November. GStA III. HA. Nr. 1469, 33.
68 See Enoch F. Resnick, 'A Family Imbroglio: Brazil's Invasion of the Banda Oriental in 1816 and Repercussions on the Iberian Peninsula', *Revista de História* 51 (1975) 101: 179–205. A monograph by Beatrice de Graaf on the Allied Council and its activities is underway with CUP.
69 Note Labrador to Council; deliberations and annex. Protocol 16 March 1817. TNA FO 146/15.
70 Allied Council, Protocol 18, 21 June 1817. TNA FO 146/22.
71 Protocol 20 July 1817. TNA FO 146/22.
72 Memorandum Palmella to the Allied Council, discussion and annexes, 21 March 1818. TNA FO 146/23.
73 Letters Wellington to Castlereagh, 23, 26, 30 March 1818. TNA FO 92/33.
74 Lengthy letters and memoranda: August 1818; 19 November 1818. TNA FO 92/33.
75 A review of the (British) *Examiner*, the (Austrian) *Wiener Zeitung*, (German) *Allgemeine Zeitung* and the (Dutch) *Rotterdamsche Courant* reveals that the 'news sky' was already quite transnational. See for a rich analysis of the European press coverage of Vienna and its aftermath: B. E. Vick, *The Congress of Vienna. Power and Politics after Napoleon* (London/Cambridge, MA, 2014), 99–111.
76 In this, it was a system of collective risk management, as provided for in Article VI of the second Treaty of Paris. See: Edward Hertslet, *The Map of Europe by Treaty: Showing the Various Political and Territorial Changes which have Taken Place since the General Peace of 1814* (London, 1875), 372–6, here 375.

4

Restoring International Order: Managing Multi-Polarity 1814–30 and the Foundation of the Concert of Europe

Richard Langhorne

The multi-polar distribution of power across the major states, which began to appear before the French Revolution and sustained the recurrent opposition to Napoleon's *imperium,* emerged in increasingly formal ways from January 1814 onwards. Experience of bringing the war to an end and creating the Vienna Settlement led to the decision to establish a managing system for international politics which was taken at Paris on 22 November 1815. The international politics of the nineteenth century were dominated by the result of that decision in one way or another until 1914. There has been a broad agreement since the mid-twentieth century that the Congress of Vienna marked a highly significant moment in the history of international politics, particularly because of the notable change in assumptions about what the purpose and method of conducting international relations should be. Attributing that significance more precisely has led to varied approaches, chiefly derived from different disciplinary origins: commentators trained in the social sciences, for example, like the unfolding diplomatic events to confirm theoretical descriptions. Historians have differing emphases, between for example high politics and social and economic pressures, as shown when the bicentenary came round in 2015, but finding out what happened and why is the starting point.[1] An earlier account by Paul Schroeder, however, remains the most clearly articulated treatment yet grand in scale and complexity. His emphasis in *The Transformation of European Politics, 1763–1848*[2] is on the importance of understanding that the conduct of international politics occurs via an international system and that the rise and decay of international systems is the stuff on which the history of international politics, itself a branch of the subject as distinct as any other branch, should be based. In this case an emerging international system that some might suggest lasted to some degree until 1941 was born out of the Napoleonic wars and the need to cope with their consequences. It is a high point in an approach that began with F. H. Hinsley's *Power and the Pursuit of Peace,* in 1957 and was also followed by Martin Wight and Hedley Bull. A somewhat extreme version of it appeared in Paul Sharp's *Diplomatic Theory of International Relations* in 2009 where the idea of an international system was pruned firmly until it became clear that the one constant factor in all international relations activities is diplomacy and its history, in whatever manifestations successive eras have developed.[3]

This chapter is concerned with two elements that were particularly significant in causing this development: first, a shift in diplomatic practice beginning in the later eighteenth century cleared the decks for a new system to be installed, and secondly a method had to be found for expressing the wish to manage international politics and this gradually emerged during the Vienna Congress itself. The first of these has not been much investigated as the shift in diplomatic practice in relation to conferences before the French Revolution and the Napoleonic wars has not seemed as interesting or dramatic as the events at the Congress itself. It was nonetheless essential to the eventual outcome in November 1815. The second is more widely understood in its consequences than in its unfolding, and in particular the fact that possibly for the first time the states at Vienna faced a danger which derived from the ideology of revolution, something they rejected in common, rather than arising from fear about the power and ambition of any individual one of them. The chapter will conclude by identifying the significant moments in the early years following 1815 when the Concert of Europe nearly failed. It survived in a more practical form after the Belgian crisis of 1830–1.

The contemporary world is multi-polar at several levels and managing its global politics is not proving successful. By contrast, at the end of the Napoleonic wars, multi-polarity established itself not just as a fact of international politics but as the source from which a system of management could emerge. It is the idea and existence of multi-polarity that most significantly connects 1815 and the centenary of the Vienna Settlement in 2015. In November 1815, the existence and recognition of multi-polarity made possible the establishment of the Concert of Europe. Its emergence was the first attempt to create a means of managing the flow of international affairs in order to minimize the risk of war and to handle its consequences if and when risk turned into reality. Since then the world has not been without an overarching international organization. The League of Nations, created after the First World War, followed the Concert system, and was an avowed attempt to improve upon it while maintaining its fundamental idea. The United Nations then ensued and it, too, was intended to repair what seemed to be the deficiencies of the League, again without deserting the original basis. All three encapsulated provisions and devices derived from what contemporaries had believed were the causes of the preceding major war. The Concert was broadly successful, the League was not. And while the UN is still in existence, it has failed to fulfil the objectives set out in its Charter and adapted itself to performing different, and some would say lesser, roles in the global system. The question for this chapter will be about why the Concert emerged when it did, what its characteristics were and why it worked, to the extent and at the moments when it did, for a hundred years – until the evening of 27 July 1914 when it finally collapsed. Here is what the great powers agreed to be the format of a mechanism for regulating the international politics and consequential diplomacy of a multi-polar system on 20 November 1815.

> To facilitate and to secure the execution of the present Treaty, and to consolidate the connections which at the moment so closely unite the Four Sovereigns for the

happiness of the world, the High Contracting Parties have agreed to renew their Meetings at fixed periods, either under the immediate auspices of the Sovereigns themselves, or by their respective Ministers, for the purpose of consulting on their common interests, and for the considerations of the measures which at each of these periods shall be considered the most salutary for the repose and prosperity of Nations, and for the maintenance of the Peace of Europe.[4]

It could almost be a description of the UN Security Council – certainly it was a Great Powers Charter. Nothing like it had been seen before, no previous distribution of power across states had been recognized as sufficiently stable to be amenable to regulation in such a way; and it had been the French Revolution and its aftermath that had created a previously unimaginable motive for doing so. How did the powers reach such a remarkable outcome?

There are two significant factors to consider: first were earlier evolutions in diplomatic practice which had laid some groundwork and, secondly, the more immediate experience of creating an effective alliance against Napoleon and maintaining it against all the odds of capricious rulers and the truly awful communications, made worse by the unusually bad winter of 1813/14.

First, the earlier groundwork: by the time of the French Revolution, diplomacy was visibly emerging from the morasses of stultifying procedure, precedence and other sources of often childish disagreement which were in part a legacy from the deeper past of the Middle Ages. They were also partly a legacy of the establishment of resident ambassadors living in dedicated embassy buildings in a foreign capital. The first was centred on determining that ambassadors really had been given full powers to negotiate, and agreement on this tricky matter – genuinely tricky in an age of slow communications – could take months and could ultimately fail. The second arose from deciding how to create an order of precedence when, for the first time, the arrival of the resident meant that rulers had more than a very few ambassadors to deal with at the same time. Furthermore, this troupe of envoys brought with them staff, armed guards, relatives who could claim diplomatic immunities and privileges, chiefly involving the non-payment of debts. It is obvious too that any order of precedence would contain a great deal of signalling about the relationship between different rulers both vertically – with the local one – and horizontally vis-à-vis the representatives of the others. Sorting all this out was not finally completed until during and after the making of the 1815 settlement. Much of the gradual abandonment of these competitive displays of relative power occurred during the second half of the eighteenth century and it happened because of a decline in warfare following the Peace of Paris of 1763. The rough-and-ready equality of the nascent great powers, Russia, Britain, France, Austria and Prussia, made the emergence of any new hegemon improbable and at the same time increased the nervousness of rulers about their security, each fearing each other almost equally: in the place of unwinnable wars, there came an increase in the significance of diplomacy. In turn, the delaying tactics which had characterized earlier years began to be abandoned by mutual agreement, so that negotiations began with a general statement that discussions would proceed informally until agreement was reached and only then were matters formalized in a more traditional way. Progress at this level can be roughly measured by comparing developments at the congresses of the late seventeenth century with the making of the Peace of Teschen in 1779.

The Congress of Nijmegen (1676–9) was a lengthy and diffused set of negotiations which led eventually and separately to treaties of peace between France and the Netherlands, France and Spain, and France and the Empire. The mediation of the English was partly to blame for the length of the negotiations since Charles II's relations with France were not straightforward. Matters of precedence were as usual, perhaps even more than usual, much to the fore. The signature of peace between France and Spain required the three ambassadors on each side to enter the room simultaneously, to sit simultaneously in six identical chairs, and finally to sign the documents simultaneously, with no doubt identical pens.[5] However, in one respect, the Congress of Nijmegen seems to have made progress in that it decided to ignore what had tended to be a very vexed question at meetings of this kind: it declared that titles assumed or omitted by any ruler did not prejudice the rights of anyone. In this particular case, the Emperor had called himself the Duke of Burgundy, the King of Spain had called himself King of France, the Duke of Lorraine had called himself Count of Provence.[6] Sometimes, such claims were purely symbolic, as at the Congress of Oliva, where King Charles X of Sweden had demanded recognition as King of the Vandals.[7] To have agreed to sidestep such problems was plainly an advance.

The Congress of Ryswick in 1697 resorted to the use of a round table, apparently for the first time, in order to prevent days of dispute about who sat where. The Congress of Carlowitz (1699) was in all respects a remarkable occasion. It marked an important stage in the rise of Russia and the decline of Turkey, and succeeded in arranging an adjustment of territory which took account of these shifts as they affected the Emperor, Russia, Poland, the Venetian Republic and the Ottoman Empire. A considerable area round the ruined castle of Carlowitz on the Danube was neutralized for the purpose of the meeting, and a temporary conference village was specially constructed, with a carefully designed negotiating hall, with four sets of doors so that the delegations could all enter simultaneously at the sound of a horn. Places at the table, however, caused disputes, and the conference decided in the same style as had been used over the question of titles, that place should specifically be declared to be of no significance. After the initial formal meetings involving the exchange of full powers, and the fulfilling of the whole ponderous mechanism of diplomatic etiquette, the first session took place on 13 November 1699. On the next occasion it was decided to abandon strict diplomatic ceremony, and the discussions remained informal until the signature of the treaties in January 1700.[8]

During the eighteenth century the habit of formally deciding to abandon formalities grew stronger and by the end of the 1770s, a war which was only designated as such because the diplomatic vocabulary did not yet include the word 'crisis', ended in a completely informal way. The so-called Congress of Teschen was assembled to make peace at the end of the 'War' of the Bavarian Succession. It was an interesting episode from several points of view. It was hardly a war in the accepted sense, powers showing the greatest possible reluctance to begin let alone persist in actual fighting. The conflict, which was largely between Austria and Prussia, was brought to an end principally by the intervention of Russia, who achieved it partly by threatening the use of force, and partly by employing a vigorous mediation in conjunction with France. Lively negotiations produced a possible draft peace treaty by February 1779, and it was agreed to summon a ratifying Congress at Teschen in Austrian Silesia on 10 March 1779. The plenipotentiaries were instructed, on the suggestion of Catherine the Great, to negotiate a peace without any formality or etiquette, and the first meeting of the Congress proceeded at once to inspect copies of the previously negotiated settlement. No other general meetings were held except for the final session on 24 April, and discussions were held as a part of a daily social life, much of it apparently in coffee houses, and at informally arranged conferences.[9]

Rousseau, who regarded the old ways with contempt, described it all amusingly and succinctly, complaining particularly about the pointless childishness of procedural wrangling; but not long after he wrote, the characteristics he mocked had essentially disappeared.[10] What emerged, expressed in a more analytical way, was a step change in the relationship between rulers – the users of diplomacy – and the diplomatic system itself. The straightforward notion that, in the words of Ermolao Barbaro, the diplomat existed to pursue only the interests of his principal and to do and say anything that assisted in that purpose was the doctrine that had supported the whole apparatus of diplomacy since it became the sole property of the state during the sixteenth century.[11] No part of the machinery of diplomacy supported the idea that diplomacy might be required to promote cooperation as well as competition. A whole system of representation had evolved, effective departments of government to manage the formation and conduct of policy had been built up, but there was as yet no way of expressing a desire by the chief users to cooperate and manage the international system collectively. On the other hand, a clearing of the decks of outmoded practice had occurred and the casual way in which the War of the Bavarian Succession was both conducted and ended indicated that by the late eighteenth century diplomacy was ready to move on once the motive became strong enough. What made it strong enough was the experience of the French Revolution followed by the struggle against Napoleon and the result was to be the establishment of the Concert of Europe.

The extraordinary diplomatic developments of 1813–15 began in London. On New Year's Eve 1813, the British Cabinet took the unprecedented decision to send the foreign secretary, Robert Stewart, Lord Castlereagh, to Switzerland, there to join the ministers and rulers of the other powers allied against Napoleon. The reason was that in the late autumn of 1813, the four powers of the last coalition against Napoleon were having to face the likelihood that he would seek a negotiated peace settlement at any moment, and long distance from wherever that happened would mean exclusion from it. Duly, in early 1814, Castlereagh arrived in Basel.

The background to the attitude of the allies in such a situation was plainly important, because it was to determine the form in which a famously successful attempt at European hegemony – a Napoleonic unipolarity – was to be broadened into a new pattern of power which accurately reflected the conditions revealed by the end of the war; and in this case, as in no other so far, this pattern was to involve the creation of a formal relationship between five powers. The powers concerned were Russia, Britain, Austria, France and Prussia. Their rough equality of power – or, perhaps even better, influence – had been a fact since the early eighteenth century. The Revolutionary wars had been, in a sense, only an interruption in the process, much as the period 1919–45 would be in the creation of the bipolar system between 1890 and 1955; and one of the most important lessons that the European powers had learnt from Napoleon's attempt to buck the trend was that they rejected his version of a French-dominated European structure more than they feared the possible pretensions of each other. And they were greatly helped towards this understanding by the recognition arising out of the wars that the power of Napoleon had not been directly related to the intrinsic power of France so much as to the power released for a time by the international appeal of the ideology of the Revolution. Once Napoleon was seen to be more French Emperor than Revolutionary Liberator his extraordinary role was compromised and his sources of power restricted. It was thus an important aspect of the creation of a new European international system that the emerging great powers feared a set of ideas more than they feared each other as states: they had acquired a common motive on which to base practical measures designed to prevent further eruptions of warfare.

If the Austrian chancellor, Kaunitz, had been the first to propose radical responses to the threat created by the French Revolution in 1791, the origins of an attempt to organize a new system can most clearly be seen in an exchange between William Pitt, the prime minister of England, and Alexander I, Tsar of Russia, which occurred in 1805. In this striking document, Pitt listed three things which had to be achieved in order to secure a programme for what he called a 'concert' of powers. They were: to reverse the enlargement of France; to reconstruct the areas thus released in such a way as to create viable states able to fend off any further French attempts at encroachment; and, thirdly, 'to form, at the restoration of peace, a general agreement and guarantee for the mutual protection and security of different powers, and for the re-establishing a general system of public law in Europe'. Later in the paper, Pitt described what he envisaged in greater detail thus:

> Supposing the Efforts of the Allies to have been completely successful ... His Majesty [George III] would nevertheless consider this Salutary Work as still imperfect, if the restoration of peace were not accompanied by the most effectual measures for giving solidity and permanence to the System which shall thus have been established. Much will undoubtedly be affected for the future Repose of Europe by these Territorial Arrangements, which will furnish a more effectual barrier than has before existed against the Ambition of France. But in order to make this security as complete as possible, it seems necessary, at the period of a general Pacification, to form a Treaty to which all the original Powers of Europe should be Parties, by which their respective Rights and Possessions, as they then have been established, shall be fixed and recognized, and they should all bind themselves mutually to protect and support each other, against any attempt to infringe them – It should establish a general and comprehensive system of Public Law in Europe, and provide, as far as possible, for repressing future attempts to disturb the general Tranquillity, and, above all, for restraining any projects of Aggrandizement and Ambition similar to those which have produced all the Calamities inflicted on Europe since the disastrous era of the French Revolution.[12]

The significance of this text lies principally in the terminology used by Pitt to describe the objectives of the coalition. One was, inevitably in the circumstances, to bring down France – and it is clear that he recognized the particular importance of what the Revolution had stood for – but, more surprisingly, the principal objective appears as almost a negative – to restore the status quo ante in terms of the distribution of power, and to arrange for its protection. It must be doubtful if any earlier period would have comprehended such a war aim, even during the period of coalitions against Louis XIV. It is particularly surprising in view of the fact that the pre-Revolutionary period had not been characterized by any general acceptance of its stability. Indeed, if after 1763 there had been a marked reduction of warfare in Europe, there had been no reduction in efforts to test or change the status quo by other means, particularly by diplomacy, or in other areas – for example, the Ottoman Empire. It was evidently the persistence of a fundamental opposition to Napoleon's imperium, however often coalitions against him collapsed, which had given notice that the distribution of power was so arranged that neither the efforts of other powers, nor the Revolution, nor the power of Napoleon's generalship, could shift it. The interest of all came to lie in finding the most reliable way of defending what quite clearly could not be changed, even by laying out the most expensive resources.

There is, here, an instructive comparison to be made between the events of 1813–15 and those of 1945–7. In both cases, a great war had produced a practical resolution of the difficulties that had caused it – unlike the catastrophe of 1914–18 – but in the first case, the circumstances of the end of the war produced in the parties a clear perception of the real distribution of power. It had been around for some time, and it had survived the attempts of the Revolution and Bonapartism to alter it. But in 1945, the change came extremely suddenly: in practice, one system, after a run of some two hundred years, gave way to another in the space of six years and in circumstances of the greatest possible physical, political and economic disruption. The origins of the Cold War are to be found in this confusion. Unlike the powers of 1814, the new superpowers did not have a shared view of what the new distribution of power actually was, nor a sense that it was stable. Thus, instead of being able to build a settlement on new foundations, they set about testing the ground in order to discover where the footings actually were, and to find out how enduring they appeared to be. The results were dramatic and unpleasant, and lasted in their most compelling forms until the mid-1950s. Thereafter, reluctantly, for ideological reasons, but definitely, the powers accepted the validity of the status quo, and acquired a joint interest in maintaining what it was evidently ineffective to try to change.

The effects of the very different assessment made by rulers and statesmen in 1814 first became apparent in February, after the arrival in Basel of Lord Castlereagh. The motive for his unprecedented mission away from England while in office was wholly practical and not in the least disinterested. It had been evident since the Battle of Leipzig in late 1813 that Napoleon might seek a negotiated settlement at any moment. Indeed, any rational observer might have supposed that the sooner he did so, the better an outcome he might expect to achieve. As already noted, the Cabinet in London on the last day of 1813 decided that it would be dangerous to be cut off from any negotiations by distance, exacerbated by winter weather, and instructed Castlereagh to go to Europe so as to be able to join Metternich, Hardenberg of Prussia and Alexander I of Russia in receiving any approaches from Napoleon and generally to see to the political business of holding the coalition together until Napoleon gave in. His absence was expected to last for six weeks; he was effectively to be away for nearly two years. Napoleon, however, regarded his own position as being conferred by military success and unlikely to survive the humiliation of having to accept a negotiated peace. He fought on until the bitter end and, erratically, Castlereagh and his colleague ministers followed the campaign, in circumstances of the greatest physical discomfort, until it ended at Paris in May. They then had to proceed to Vienna, deal with the return of Napoleon, and renegotiate the peace with France in November 1815. For most of this time, the allied ministers stayed together, having been joined by the French foreign minister, Talleyrand, from early 1815, after allied divisions over the future of Poland had allowed the French to play a great power role for the remainder of the Congress.

Both Metternich and Castlereagh found the personal proximity of foreign ministers useful. Metternich was the more emotional: 'Castlereagh has arrived and is behaving like an angel,' he said early in their acquaintance. The object of this encomium was more precise, having already while en route to Basel commented that he expected difficulties to arise 'from the want of an habitual confidential and free intercourse between the ministers of the great powers as a body'.[13] He discovered great virtues when the situation was remedied. On 2 February 1814, he wrote, 'You must all be aware how deep was the distrust and alarm which existed some days ago as to supposed divergences of opinion, which it was feared were irreconcilable in themselves, and how soon these differences disappeared when the allied ministers were ordered to enter upon their discussion. To such a degree did this happen, that every individual question which they have been called upon to deliberate has been decided, not just unanimously, but with cordial concurrence.'[14] At the next serious meeting, at Châtillon, it was recorded that Castlereagh had been prepared to deal with business 'only in conferences of the four ministers'.[15] It is perhaps not therefore surprising that shortly afterwards, meeting in a dingy café and sitting at whist tables, Metternich and Castlereagh agreed that the stakes had never been higher when they drafted the Treaty of Chaumont. They were certainly taking risks. It was agreed that they were representing Europe as a whole and they were prepared to write down that it would be necessary to arrange a form of supervision for international politics for twenty years after the conclusion of peace. The means of achieving this would be decided by the four powers concerting together.

Despite these revolutionary developments, it remained the case that they were no nearer actually finding a means of organizing the management of the international system than Pitt had been, however generalized among the 'great powers' the wish had become, and however frequently that new description of the allies was now in use. There was a hint in an extraordinary article that Metternich published just before the opening of the Congress of Vienna of the way things were to develop. He was trying to explain, when peace with France had already been made at Paris in May, what the authority and justification was for a separate and additional meeting in Vienna in the autumn, no doubt, partly at any rate, for the consumption of the smaller powers. Their position had been seriously undermined by the united determination of the great powers to remain those, as Castlereagh had said, 'with whom the conduct of business must practically rest'.[16]

'The Powers which made the Treaty of Paris,' wrote Metternich, 'will determine the meaning which they wish to attach to the word congress, and will also decide the form which would seem most appropriate for reaching the goals they have set themselves. They will use this right of determination equally to the advantage of the interested parties, and thus to the good of Europe as a whole, and the plenipotentiaries at Vienna will deal with matters in the most efficient, prompt and confidential way. Thus the congress is brought into being of itself, without having received any formal authority, there being no source which could have given any.'[17] It was to be another year before the logical result of these developments appeared.

Meanwhile, the preoccupations of negotiating the territorial settlement and arranging for appropriate rulers – in particular the problem of securing suitable rights for the king of Poland in the face of the Tsar's determination, backed by overwhelming force, to be king of Poland himself – prevented serious consideration of the future management of the international system. Pitt's idea of a general Treaty of Guarantee was widely assumed to be the likely mechanism; but as time went on, both the British and the Russians grew less satisfied with it. The Tsar produced the Holy Alliance as an alternative, and it began to look as if the London Cabinet would be forced by Parliament to reject any forward obligations to defend the European settlement at all. The return of Napoleon further delayed proceedings and the decision of Waterloo, followed by the negotiation of the second Treaty of Paris, produced an emergency. The powers now knew that they wished to defend the status quo in Europe against adventurism, and specifically against revolution. They also knew that they felt that the distribution of power was stable enough and balanced enough to permit a cooperative method of defence to be employed; and on top of that they had established the practice, if not the right, of the great powers to supervise the international system as an oligarchy: but they had not yet found a way of organizing multi-polarity.

In the end it was, as is so often the case, no great principle, still less any great emotion, which provided the answer, but the declaration of what had become standard, comfortable practice. The strange situation which had brought about the constant association of the allied foreign ministers had continued for so long (February 1814 to November 1815) that its novelty had worn off, and the cooperation which had provoked the exaggerated adulation of Gentz after the Vienna Congress had by late 1815 simply become too convenient to abandon. Gentz had claimed that the Congress had 'united all the states by a federative bond under the direction of the five principal powers.'[18] The obligations of the Treaty of Chaumont and the expectations of the signatories of the Vienna Settlement were to be fulfilled by a last-minute addition to a part of the second treaty of Paris of 20 November 1815. This clause, as has been seen, provided for the establishment of regular conferences in peacetime, which were to have as their agenda no less than those 'measures ... which shall be considered the most salutary for the repose and prosperity of nations, and for the maintenance of the peace of Europe'. There was an irony in this outcome: to restore order internationally had required a revolution – or, as Paul Schroeder would have it, a transformation – in the conduct of international affairs – something sufficiently clear to Metternich that he found some awkwardness in explaining it away.[19]

Initially these meetings were known as Congresses, which began in 1818, at Aix-la-Chapelle (now Aachen in Germany), continued with successive sessions at Troppau (Opava, Czechia) and Laibach (Ljubljana, Slovenia), and ended with Verona in 1822, and became known as the Congress System. No doubt inevitably, this first stab at the creation of a genuine international organization, well based as it was upon the realities of power and the experience of statesmen, did not survive for long in its original form. It did not, however, collapse beyond recall, as later the League was to do. In the face of the emergency caused by the revolt of the Belgians in 1830, and their determination to modify a crucial provision of the 1815 settlement by dissolving the united Netherlands into two states, the great powers gradually took charge of the crisis and evaded what could easily have developed into a general war. The means of doing so turned out to be based on a modification of the idea set out in 1815. It had been intended that congresses of the powers would be both regular – i.e. meet whether there was a problem or not, which encountered British objections – and have a duty to protect the settlement against all change. This produced a stasis based principally on the inability of the member states to agree about whether revolutions or nationalist manifestations were to be suppressed by armed intervention, a view broadly supported by Austria, Russia and Prussia, or whether their consequences were to be controlled if they spread more generally, a view shared by Britain and France.

In 1830, however, the profound pressures that had propelled states into the activity of meetings surfaced once more. The first truly major crisis of the post-war era emerged from a revolt against Dutch rule by the Belgians. The Netherlands had become separated in the seventeenth century when the Protestant north acquired independence and the southern provinces remained under Hapsburg rule. They had been reunited in 1815 under the rule of the king of Holland. At the strategic level, the creation of a united Netherlands had been designed to produce general security along the coast opposite Britain and to be a barrier against any French attempt to restore French rule in the French-speaking areas. These factors alone would have produced objections to allowing the Belgians to secede; but there were matters of principle also. The Vienna Settlement had been made with the restraint of revolutions and nationalist ambitions very much in mind. It was clear that the Brussels revolt had been sparked by the revolution in Paris in 1830 and was as much an objection to the nationality of the king of Holland's administrators in Brussels as to his rule per se. To allow the Belgians to secede unilaterally would have compromised the strategic and political principles of the Vienna Settlement and there was no doubt of the practical possibility of both sides being assisted militarily. The settlement had made Prussia a neighbour and France had always been so, which presented the very real prospect of the former supporting the undoubted rights of the king of Holland as he had requested and the latter helping the Belgians to resist.

The acute danger which this represented produced results. The king of Holland had appealed to the powers expecting that his rights would be upheld by a Congress at which he would be present following the rule laid down at the Congress of Aix-la-Chapelle in November 1818. The chain of events that followed seems to have been largely accidental.

The powers could not agree where a conference would be held and in any case had to meet somewhere to decide whether to respond to the king of Holland's appeal. London was chosen for this purpose and the meetings began on 4 November 1830. The embassies there were particularly well staffed at the time because of an ongoing crisis in the Near East and this may help to explain why the conference did not set a place and a date for a new Congress, but proceeded to deal with the issue itself. Sheer urgency is the most likely motive, as the Belgians had virtually expelled the Dutch by this time. In this case, the consequences were far more important than the reason why events happened to turn out as they did. Nonetheless perhaps the most important was indeed urgency, which dictated that the ambassadors in London at the time, and not special plenipotentiaries or rulers, represented the great powers. The British foreign secretary, Lord Palmerston, took the chair. Urgency also meant that no discussion took place about the limits of the conference's authority. Metternich, who sent persistent objections from Vienna about the existence and activities of the conference, complained that its basis derived only from the broad object 'La Belgique s'est revoltée, il faut arranger l'affaire'[20] and that this allowed far too much independence and, moreover, that he had never known whether the conference had powers of intervention, mediation or arbitration.[21] Because of this, the conference responded to circumstances and not principles.

Palmerston demonstrated this change very clearly. At the beginning he wrote '... we are not conquerors disposing of subjugated kingdoms, but Powers looking after our security and mediating between contending parties'.[22] Six months later, when much water had flowed along the dykes, his tone was different:

> The Conference is tired of conferring and the mediators can mediate no longer; all things have their ends and the patience of the five powers has reached its limits. We have interests of our own to consult which prescribe the preservation of peace, and a general war can only be prevented by putting an end to the local contest between Holland and Belgium. If the Belgians should refuse their consent to these articles we should immediately take steps to compel their acquiescence.[23]

It was Palmerston, too, who expressed an important fact about the flexibility which the representatives at London displayed. After chairing the meetings, he remarked that 'The only use of a plenipotentiary is to disobey his instructions. A clerk or a messenger would do if it is only strictly necessary to follow them.'[24]

There is no question that this conference made a new device available to diplomacy. It established a precedent for the holding of conferences when and where required, using the local ambassadors chaired by the local foreign minister. It also made it possible, subject always to the ultimate agreement of the parties, for such meetings to modify the public law by peaceful means, in the interests of defending its broad integrity against all comers.

To understand why this was so, it is only necessary to list what the London meetings did: they used coercion against sitting monarchs, in this case both the king of Holland and the king of the French; they created a new state of Belgium; they neutralized it and decided its borders; they wrote its constitution and appointed its monarch. It was an extraordinary and unprecedented achievement.

Palmerston was pleased: 'Conferences and elephants', he wrote, 'have the same period of gestation, twelve months with a fortnight occasionally over their time; in sagacity we know the resemblance holds good.' He was wrong about the gestation period, which is 645 days, but nonetheless conferences got quicker as time passed and the sentiment was confirmed.[25]

The mechanism seems to have been favoured by its non-compulsory nature, by the abandonment of the idea of holding regular meetings whether or not there was an immediate reason for one and by the practice of not involving rulers or heads of government for most of the time – Berlin in 1878 being a very obvious exception. The device was thereafter used or not used for the rest of the century according to the wishes of the great powers, as any system will be, but it was a measure of its successful practical application that there grew up an expectation that it would be used, and that failure to do so represented a defeat for Europe. How well it worked depended on the stability of a roughly equal distribution of power across the major states and a persistently clear idea about where geographically its authority stopped.[26] Insidious failure on both these counts after 1890 began to undermine the Concert system and, notoriously, collapse came in July 1914.

Notes

1 The bicentenary in 2015 induced several related studies: for example, Mark Jarrett, *The Congress of Vienna and its Legacy* (London, 2013), a cheerful narrative and illustrated account; Brian E. Vick, *The Congress of Vienna: Power and Politics after Napoleon* (London, 2014), an excellent discussion of the Congress itself which emphasizes the public sphere, less than the political contexts and attitudes surrounding it; Jennifer Mitzen, *Power in Concert: The Nineteenth Century Origins of Global Governance* (Chicago, IL, 2013) uses the Congress and its aftermath as a lesson in how it has been and can still be possible to have important areas of public life managed by a group of states thus evading the need to establish a global government to manage globalization.
2 Paul W. Schroeder, *The Transformation of European Politics 1763–1848* (Oxford, 1994).
3 F. H. Hinsley, *Power and the Pursuit of Peace* (Cambridge, 1957); Paul Sharp, *Diplomatic Theory of International Relations* (Cambridge, 2009).
4 Richard Langhorne, 'The Development of International Conferences 1648–1830', in Christer Jonsson and Richard Langhorne (eds), *Diplomacy* (London, 2004), II, fn. 44, p. 304.
5 H. Vast, *Les Grands Traités du Règne de Louis XIV*, 3 vols (Paris, 1893), II, 38.
6 Ibid., II, 33 'Le Congrès finit par declarer que les titres prit ou omis, de part et d'autre, ne pourront ni nuire, ni prejudicier à qui que ce soit.'
7 C. G. de Koch and F. Schoell, *Histoire Abrégée des Traités de Paix entre les Puissances de l'Europe depuis la paix de Westphalie*, 4 vols (Brussels, 1838), IV, 117.
8 Ibid., IV, 355; and see also J. W Zinkeisen, *Geschichte des Osmanischen Reiches in Europa* (Gotha, 1857), 209.
9 Koch and Schoell, *Histoire Abrégée des Traités de Paix*, I, 434.
10 'Il se forme de temps en temps parmi nous des espèces de diètes gènèrales sous le nom de congrès, où se rend solennellement de tous les Etats de l'Europe pour s'en retourner de même; où l'on s'assemble pour ne rien dire; où toutes les affaires publiques se

traitent en particulier; où l'on délibère en commun si la table sera ronde ou carrè, si la salle aura plus ou moins de portes, si un tel plénipotentiare aura le visage ou le dos tourné vers la fenêtre, si tel autre fera deux pouces de chemin de plus ou de moins dans une visite, et sur milles questions de pareille importance, inutilement agitées depuis trois siècles, et très-dignes assurément d'occuper les politques de nôtre.' E. Satow, *A Guide to Diplomatic Practice* (London, 1922), 2.
11 'The first duty of an ambassador is exactly the same as that of any other servant of a government, that is, to do, say, advise and think whatever may best serve the preservation and aggrandizement of his own state', quoted in V. E. Hrabar (ed.), *De Legatis et legationibus tractatus varii* (Dorpat, 1906), 66.
12 Pitt's Memorandum on the Deliverance and Security of Europe, 19 January 1805, in H. W. V. Temperley and L. M. Penson, *The Foundation of British Foreign Policy* (Cambridge, 1938), 18.
13 C. K. Webster, *The Foreign Policy of Lord Castlereagh* (London, 1931), I, 199.
14 Ibid., 209.
15 Ibid., 212–13.
16 Ibid., 337.
17 Printed in d'Angeberg (L. J. B. Chodzko), *Le Congrès de Vienne et les Traités de 1815* (Paris, 1863), author's translation, 362–4.
18 Quoted in F. H. Hinsley, *Power and the Pursuit of Peace* (Cambridge, 1963), 197.
19 Schroeder, *The Transformation of European Politics*, 34 and note 17.
20 Metternich to Trautmannsdorf, 13 November 1832 in Metternich, *Mémoires*, V, 406–11.
21 Webster, *Palmerston*, I, 107.
22 Ibid., 108.
23 Ibid., 108.
24 D. Southgate, *The Most English Minister* (London, 1966), 39.
25 Webster, *Palmerston*, I, 111.
26 The defined area of operation was extended to include the Ottoman Empire at the Paris Peace Conference of 1856 and then Africa at the Berlin conference of 1884/5; but the need to deal with the China crisis of 1895–1905 was unable to evoke a similar response because two of the significant powers involved – Japan and the USA – did not belong to the European system and, at least in the US case, did not wish to.

The Art of Diplomacy: Jean-Baptiste Isabey at the Congress of Vienna

Daniel Harkett*

Let's begin with a watercolour (plate 1). It's a study of costume – the outfit of an inspector general of artillery, to be exact – made by Jean-Baptiste Isabey for a volume of images documenting Napoleon Bonaparte's coronation, including the costumes worn by the event's participants.[1] The image is a fantasy, of course; we see the inspector in full ceremonial garb walking with a dancer's step on the battlefield as if he were a dandy on a fashionable Parisian street. What seems to have interested Isabey – or what appears to animate his image, to rescue its viewer from boredom – is the effect of the breeze: the smoke blown into the image from the left; the coat lifted by the same breeze in conjunction with the walker's movement to reveal the finery underneath; and the feathers in the hat, themselves the colour of smoke, pushed across the face so as to half obscure it, a movement echoed by wisps of greyish, curly hair.

Isabey was, in so many ways, a painter of lightness. In his many portraits, often executed in the fluid medium of watercolour, he accentuated the serpentine play of gauzy fabrics, which float around his subjects, suggesting an affinity between them and the clouds that frequently serve as the only setting in closely cropped compositions (plate 2). Hair, too, was a particular interest of his. Isabey was a connoisseur of curls, a lover of follicular eddies and swirls. Even when painting men in heavy uniforms, Isabey found in hair a feathery counterpoint (plate 3).

In 1814, Isabey brought his lightness to the Congress of Vienna, the conference at which the victors in the war with Napoleon, along with representatives of the restored Bourbon monarchy in France, attempted to reach agreement on the form of post-Napoleonic Europe.[2] Already familiar with the city and the Habsburg court from a previous visit in 1812, Isabey was invited to the Congress by Charles Maurice de Talleyrand-Périgord, French foreign minister and chief French negotiator, and was charged by him with creating a representation of the event.[3] Isabey, then, had to find an answer to an intriguing question: What does a peace conference look like?

Isabey's portrait studio

When Isabey arrived in Vienna in late September 1814, he took lodgings in the district of Leopoldstadt, the most fashionable part of the city.[4] Close to the well-known Café Jüngling and the promenading route to the Prater, the public park, Isabey set up a portrait studio that became a popular destination for many connected with the Congress. Isabey hung works in various states of completion on the studio walls, where they could be seen by those coming to sit for a portrait (like the one in plate 3) and by other visitors. One of those visitors, the French aristocrat, Auguste de La Garde-Chambonas, wrote in his memoir: '[Isabey's] studio, which was entirely covered with sketches, drawings and unfinished portraits had the appearance of a magic lantern where members of high society brought together by the Congress appeared in turn.'[5] The painter also kept an album in his studio, in which visitors wrote tributes to his talent, linking themselves together in shared admiration.[6] Isabey's studio thus became an environment in which elite members of post-revolutionary European society could understand themselves as a coherent group. It offered participants in the Congress of Vienna a spectacle – a magic lantern show – of elite community.

Did La Garde-Chambonas's metaphor of a magic lantern, a device that projected images without substance, also suggest that the unity created by Isabey's painting programme was illusory? Perhaps. At least one visitor to Isabey's studio, Alexandrine du Montet, was sceptical of whether the artist's images would stand the test of time. She found the colours already weak and complained about Isabey's flattery of his sitters as well as the softness of his forms. The princesses of Europe, she said, were lost in 'waves of muslin'.[7] Art historian Udo Felbinger has suggested that Isabey changed his technique to meet the burgeoning demand for his work in Vienna, moving away from his painstaking process of painting miniatures on ivory to use quicker methods. The results, however, were works with less durability that have now lost their original lustre, a tribute to the baronne du Montet's perspicacity and a sign of the fragility of Isabey's project.[8] Nevertheless we can say that Isabey's portrait practice met the imagined needs of the assembled dignitaries, at least temporarily, so crowded was his studio. This was a group dedicated to redrawing the boundaries between nations but one claiming the collective right to do so, a group that found class solidarity by taking up fictive residence in Isabey's ethereal world. That world, constituted by a group of finished portraits, sketches and album notes – a world that intersected with Isabey's studio and claimed it as a dream space – was one answer to the question of what a peace conference might look like.

Isabey, diplomat

Although on the face of it a supplement to the official spaces of the Congress, Isabey's studio was imagined as a place where diplomatic work was done. Isabey himself promoted this idea, writing later that sovereigns, princes and negotiators, whose interactions were governed by strict regulation elsewhere, found 'a thousand plausible pretexts for exchanging ... confidences' in his studio.[9] Isabey also suggested that in

Vienna he operated like a diplomat, deploying wit, flattery and a knowledge of ceremonial procedure to complete his portrait commissions successfully.[10] Other commentators recognized his skills and celebrated them. 'He is the Congress in the form of a painter,' said Charles-Joseph de Ligne.[11]

Indeed, what is remarkable in the anecdotal accounts of the Congress is the way Isabey emerges as an intensely desired figure: participants wanted to be close to him and enjoyed the prospect of being the object of his gaze. His studio album was one place where those desires were acknowledged. The Russian princess Catherine Bagration, for example, wrote there that Isabey had 'a pleasing appearance, good manners and a natural eloquence', such that he is highly 'sought after'.[12] But she was most concerned that he remembered her; she hoped that at a future moment he would return to the album and see her inscription, leaving her unforgotten. Isabey became a conduit of desire in Vienna, a figure who attracted the libidinal energies of the Congress's participants and redirected them into forms of collectivity, such as the experience of his studio and his album. What are diplomats, after all, but managers of desire?

Given Isabey's artistic and social skills, it is not surprising that he was called upon to assist in the staging of the *tableaux vivants* that formed part of the Congress's festivities. On several occasions, members of the social elite present in Vienna performed – that is, reproduced with their bodies – the compositions of European history and genre paintings, both old and new, for an audience of their peers. These performances of paintings that were intended to teach virtue offered guides to action and comportment. It is not hard, for example, to see the relevance to those at the Congress of Charles Le Brun's *The Queens of Persia at the Feet of Alexander* (1660–1, Château national et musées de Versailles, Versailles), one of the performed pictures, which represents a leader showing mercy after a military victory.[13] But more important than the lessons themselves, which were hardly novel, was the shared experience of them, an affirmation of values held in common by performers and spectators.

Just as Isabey's management of his studio was read as a kind of diplomatic practice, so the process of creating the *tableaux vivants* substituted for and spectacularized the formal negotiations. In one absurd sequence of anecdotes, which circulated among those in attendance in Vienna, a planned *tableau vivant* representing gods and goddesses on Mount Olympus was thrown into disarray. It seems that a princess, nervous about appearing vain, refused at the last minute to appear as Venus, while a prince would not shave his moustache in order to play the part of Apollo. Isabey, it was said, solved the first problem by arranging for Venus to be seen only from the back, while the Austrian empress, Maria Ludovika, successfully applied some unspecified pressure on the prince to ensure he changed his mind and appeared without his whiskers.[14] A clever trick, a timely assertion of power: these are elements of diplomatic practice, like the ones Isabey used in his studio.[15] And, like Isabey's portrait practice, the *tableaux vivants* represented an orderly management of desire, which was palpably present for viewers. La Garde-Chambonas, for example, was as interested in the beauty of the bodies that recreated *The Queens of Persia* as in the work's moral message, noting that the final picture was 'at the same time heroic and voluptuous'.[16] Watching the *tableaux vivants* in Vienna, and listening to the gossip about them, was thus to witness the production of aesthetic, moral, social and diplomatic order. A peace conference could look like a performed picture.

Representing the negotiations

While all of this was going on – the portrait painting in the studio, the performances of *tableaux vivants* – Isabey was working on creating a drawing of the negotiations themselves, which would eventually be turned into a print. The artist's task was a difficult one. How was he to find form for a multifaceted process that contained little obvious drama, but whose outcome would be enormously significant? Isabey himself wrote of the challenges of selecting the right moment and of organizing a crowd of similar-looking figures without the result appearing monotonous.[17] Isabey's anxieties may be common among artists undertaking group portraits, but an image of a diplomatic group was especially testing.[18] Diplomats were and are not supposed to be demonstrative for fear of giving something away or upsetting a fragile set of possibilities. As a critic noted when Isabey's final drawing of the Congress was exhibited in Paris at the Salon of 1817, the Vienna plenipotentiaries were 'enslaved' by the laws of etiquette and habituated to observing distrustfully rather than expressing themselves freely. How might one represent these 'impenetrable physiognomies'?[19]

One potential model for Isabey was an image Talleyrand had used, according to nineteenth-century commentators, when he invited the painter to join the French legation. 'You will paint the congress,' said Talleyrand to Isabey, supposedly, while pointing to a print after a painting – which Talleyrand also owned – by the seventeenth-century Dutch artist Gerard ter Borch (plate 4).[20] (Isabey did paint individual members of the Congress but probably always intended his drawing of the negotiations to be a preparatory work for an engraving, like the one Talleyrand indicated, rather than a painting.) Ter Borch's picture shows representatives from Spain and the Dutch Republic swearing an oath to uphold the Treaty of Münster (1648), which brought an end to an eighty-year conflict between Spain and its rebel provinces. The treaty was part of a larger European peace settlement, the Peace of Westphalia, which served as a precedent for attempts to construct a new European order after the fall of Napoleon. Indeed Ter Borch's painting hung in the very room in Talleyrand's residence where the first Treaty of Paris (1814), a rough draft of the Vienna agreement, was signed.[21]

Alison McNeil Kettering argues that Ter Borch's goal when making his picture was to secure the agreement itself.[22] He chose to represent the very end of the diplomatic process, when the two sides gave assurances that the terms of the ratified treaty would be observed. Carefully describing the scene – including the panelled walls of the council chamber, the candelabrum with its sculpted figure of the Virgin Mary, the documents themselves and the precious containers in which they will be kept – Ter Borch provides visual evidence that the agreement took place and positions his viewer as an eyewitness, a guarantor of sorts.[23] The fixity of the composition, with its rows of closely packed figures, supports Ter Borch's assertion that the agreement has a solid basis and that it will last.

Despite Talleyrand's attachment to Ter Borch's image, Isabey seems to have interpreted it as a counterexample rather than a model. Instead of focusing on a conclusion, Isabey became interested in the process of the peace conference, especially what was going on behind the official negotiations – the unconscious of the Congress, if you will. An initial pen and ink sketch set the terms of the final drawing (plate 5). Isabey places the viewer in the Austrian foreign minister Klemens von Metternich's official residence on the Ballhausplatz in Vienna, where the discussions took place. A session has just ended and the participants, representatives of the eight powers that had signed the Treaty of Paris, are conversing casually.[24] They do so in the company of a painted portrait of an Austrian emperor (either the reigning monarch, Francis I, or his predecessor Leopold II) and a bust of the celebrated eighteenth-century Austrian diplomat, Wenzel Anton von Kaunitz-Rietberg.[25] Visible through the open door is a portrait of the eighteenth-century Austrian empress, Maria Theresa. Although Maria Theresa's presence signals her importance as a historical European leader and might indicate that women had a role to play in the peace process, she is separated from the room where the negotiations are taking place. Isabey suggests that the official business of the Congress was the province of men, in contrast to the mixed gender sociability of the portrait studio and the performances of the *tableaux vivants*.

Isabey's sketch of the Congress is strikingly informal. No rigid ceremonial, as in Ter Borch's picture, here. Instead, Isabey represents off-duty diplomats engaged in small conversations, conducted arm-in-arm, with hands on shoulders, or with heads held close (plate 6). Together the interlaced figures form a circuit of homosocial desire, one that the Byronic figure at the centre of the composition, languorously draped over a chair, invites the viewer to join. Although separated by nationality and national interest, these negotiators share a commitment to sociability and fraternal intimacy. It is this, Isabey suggests, that might serve as the foundation for a political agreement.

When looking for a way to represent the Congress, Isabey perhaps drew on a model from closer to home than Ter Borch's image: the artist's studio. In the 1790s his friend and fellow painter Louis-Léopold Boilly had famously represented Isabey's own studio as a vibrant space of homosociality (plate 7).[26] The image even has some compositional similarities to Isabey's Vienna drawing when we consider the lateral arrangement of conversational groups, the figures gathered around a table, the central seated figure and the portfolio left resting against the chair in the studio, which reappears as a diplomatic bag at the Congress. The extent to which Isabey consciously used Boilly's painting as a template is difficult to judge but it is clear that the two works share a sensibility, a feeling that communities form through small acts of intimate exchange. By imagining Isabey's studio as a place where male artists could take pleasure in each other's company, Boilly situated it and Isabey himself at the heart of a larger revolutionary artistic culture that organized itself representationally by emphasizing fraternal bonds.[27] At the Congress of Vienna, Isabey found in this visual code a solution to the problem Talleyrand had set him. Just as his portrait studio came to function as a useful diplomatic space, so it turned out that artists' habits of self-representation could serve the diplomatic cause too.

The diplomats at the Congress seem to have enjoyed the fantasy Isabey imagined for them because they, as the artist tells us, approved his first drawing before he proceeded with the project.[28] With most of the figures in the first sketch generic stand-ins for the actual negotiators, Isabey then set about establishing the likenesses of the figures to be represented. Doing so once again required him to blend his artistic and diplomatic skills. The Duke of Wellington, a new addition to the picture after his arrival at the Congress in February 1815, complained about being shown in profile before Isabey flattered him into approval by comparing his profile to that of the illustrious French king Henri IV.[29] Likewise, Isabey used his wit to win over Wilhelm von Humboldt, a member of the Prussian delegation, who was initially reluctant to sit for him.[30] In the final drawing, Isabey gives particular prominence to Metternich, the diplomatic host of the Congress, who is standing and framed by the doorway on the left; Lord Castlereagh, the British foreign secretary, seated in the chair at the centre; and, of course, Talleyrand, seated on the right at the table, looking out at the viewer (plate 8).

As Isabey introduced likenesses to his image, he made many other changes that, he perhaps thought, rendered the picture more suitable for public consumption. He altered the dress of his subjects, replacing their generic suits, which emphasized their commonality, with ceremonial clothing that differentiated the figures and stiffened their poses. Numerous studies for these uniforms survive, showing the care Isabey took to get them right. In the studies, the details of the figures' new clothing and their spreading, dark tonality create a reverse Pygmalion effect; bodies lightly sketched in pencil harden before our eyes (plate 9). If we look closely at the finished drawing, we can also see that Isabey reduced the expressiveness of the figures and subtly distanced them from one another, attenuating the eroticism of the earlier sketch (plate 10). On the right of the image, for example, the figure reaching extravagantly across Talleyrand now gestures more modestly. Hands that rested on shoulders have been withdrawn. The angle of the head of Friedrich von Gentz, an adviser to Metternich who stands behind Talleyrand, has been changed so he no longer nuzzles the man standing next to him while they read a document together. The new heaviness of the figures is matched by the heaviness of the illusionistic frame of the final image, which features portraits of monarchs, coats of arms of those involved in the negotiations and emblematic representations of truth, prudence, wisdom and justice – all imagined to have been carved in stone.

What, then, is the relationship between Isabey's first sketch of the Congress and his final drawing? Perhaps it is analogous to another set of images, a sketch and a drawing made by Jacques-Louis David as he developed his picture, *The Oath of the Tennis Court*, during the Revolution. The work, never completed, was intended for the meeting room of the National Assembly. It was to be an inspiring group portrait of the members of the Third Estate of the Estates General swearing an oath not to disband until their demands were met.[31] David's drawing, a detailed plan for the final painting, depicts bourgeois men in everyday dress reproducing the resolve of ancient heroes in a noble cause (plate 11). This act of reproduction was cued by David himself when he exhibited the drawing together with his *Oath of the Horatii* (1785, Musée du Louvre, Paris) at the Salon of 1791.[32]

When David started work on the final painting, he created a sketch in which he planned his revolutionary heroes first as nudes – the idealized, classical bodies academic artists learned to produce by studying ancient sculpture and participating in life drawing classes (plate 12). David thought of these nudes as the foundation stones for revolutionary representation; they are, in the words of art historian Ewa Lajer-Burcharth, visual signifiers of 'a certain subjective ideal, exemplary in both its moral and physical perfection – the revolutionary subject as maleness par excellence'.[33] The clothed figures in the completed picture, which we can imagine with the help of the detailed preparatory drawing, would have been built on the armature of the nudes, which would have still been present beneath layers of paint. The final figures would have been inflected nudes, or ideals made to look contemporary. Isabey, who trained in David's studio, at times developed pictures in this way as well. A study for *Napoleon Visiting the Oberkampf Manufactory, at Jouy, June 20, 1806* (1806, Bibliothèque nationale de France, Paris), for example, consists of four figures posed as they will be in the final painting, but nude.[34] In Isabey's first Vienna drawing, we can find traces of the approach he learned from David. The figures' tightly fitted clothes at times suggest the presence of muscular, classical bodies underneath. The shading and the marked creases on the jacket of the figure seated on the far right, for example, map a physique that would not be out of place among Michelangelo's ignudi (plate 6).

But the figures in Isabey's preliminary drawing are not nudes. If David imagined the classical nude as the basis for the revolutionary body, Isabey suggests in his preparatory work that the contemporary clothed figure was the starting point for an image of post-revolutionary peace. Further, unlike David's revolutionaries, who reach purposefully into the air, Isabey's diplomats are caught in a contingent moment. Their intimate and unpredictable conversation contrasts with the synchronous acts of public oath-taking in David's image. Isabey did draw from revolutionary visual culture when he made his picture but looked to Boilly rather than David, the lightness of nimble social performance being more important than the weight of the classical tradition. Even if Isabey decided that his final, public image needed to include documentation of ceremonial dress and a heavy, allegorical frame, it remains a picture of intimacy. For all the differences between Isabey's pair of images and David's, however, what they share – and what makes it instructive to consider them together – is their use of an ideal as a substructure. Underneath the final work is, or would have been, a vision of the ideal political subject, whether David's self-contained classical hero, acting in parallel with others, or Isabey's relational wit, participating in a process of social exchange.

By March 1815 Isabey's final drawing was complete but its display and reproduction were disrupted by Napoleon's return from Elba. Although the Congress continued, Isabey went back to Paris to rejoin his former patron, and subsequently fled to London after the Hundred Days were over.[35] The drawing was eventually exhibited in Paris at the Salon of 1817 and then at an exhibition of Isabey's works in London in 1820, where King George IV purchased it.[36] Jean Godefroy reproduced it as an engraving in 1819, which was supplemented by a lithographed key Isabey made himself. The subscription for the engraving – a means of advancing the capital required to pay Godefroy's considerable fee of 40,000 francs – had been started in January 1815. The list of subscribers, which included monarchs and members of the European aristocracy, was another material trace and performance of the sociability of Vienna, like the album Isabey had kept in his studio.[37]

When Isabey's final drawing was shown in Paris at the Salon of 1817, the critic François Miel acknowledged the challenges Isabey had faced when planning his picture of the peace conference but praised him for overcoming them, echoing the way the artist had been characterized in Vienna. A 'man of wit' ('homme d'esprit'), Isabey had cleverly chosen a relaxed moment in the negotiations, which allowed for the representation of a variety of expressions, even if his figures continued to display a certain rigidity. Although generally pleased with the picture, Miel noted that he found his eye too much attracted to the figures' legs, whose bright silk stockings he described as 'more elegant' as clothing than advantageous in a picture. It is an odd observation that upends the picture's informational hierarchies and returns us to the eroticism of the first drawing.[38] The legs, notionally insignificant, changed the least as the picture evolved. They carried with them traces of the libidinal energies that Isabey attempted to marshal and sublimate while in Vienna, that needed to be tamed for the final picture, but that continued to grip viewers.

Brought to Vienna to represent the Congress, Isabey imagined the peace conference in multiple ways. It could be a collection of portraits in his studio, an album with notes from visitors, a *tableau vivant* or a picture of men chatting around a table. Although different materially and in their gender politics, these responses to the question of what a peace conference might look like all suggest that Isabey and other attendees saw peace in sociability. Isabey himself seems to have been indifferent to the larger political questions of the Congress, questions of who should rule where and how. Or, at least, he was willing to move fluidly from working for Napoleon, to creating a sympathetic representation of the Vienna negotiators, to working for Napoleon again. Unlike Ter Borch's picture of the Treaty of Münster, Isabey's image takes no position on the Vienna agreement itself; it is a picture of a process rather than a conclusion. Isabey's investment was not in the restoration of particular regimes, but what we might think of as the everyday restoration of intimacy, connections between people that are always in danger of being lost, especially in times of political discord and military conflict.

After Waterloo, members of the elite in France also sought the restorative power of sociability by reviving and reinventing the forms and practices of the salon, to which Napoleon had been hostile. In salons, both men and women invested shared intimate experience with reconciliatory potential in the wake of revolutionary trauma. Isabey modelled a role for artists in that kind of undertaking in Vienna, and it was taken up in various ways in France by Virginie Ancelot, François Gérard, Marie-Éléonore Godefroid, Horace Vernet and others.[39] These artists became hosts, participants and suppliers of imagery in the Restoration's salon culture. They, like Isabey, were to use their compositional skills to make social groups as well as pictures.

Notes

* I presented a version of this essay at the Society for French Historical Studies conference in April 2017 in Washington, DC. I am grateful to Juliet Bellow, Hollis Clayson, Lela Graybill, Keren Hammerschlag and Daniel Sherman for their comments then. I am also grateful to the Institut national d'histoire de l'art in Paris for the *chercheur invité* fellowship that allowed me to complete the research and writing in the summer of 2017.

1 François Pupil, *Jean-Baptiste Isabey (1767–1855): Portraitiste de l'Europe* (Paris, 2005), 134.
2 Recent overviews of the conference include Antoine d'Arjuzon, Pascal Éven and Isabelle Nathan (eds), *Le Congrès de Vienne ou l'invention d'une nouvelle Europe* (Paris, 2015) and Sabine Grabner, Agnes Husslein-Arco and Werner Telseko (eds), *Europe in Vienna: The Congress of Vienna 1814/15* (Munich, 2015).
3 Mme de Basily-Callimaki, *J.-B. Isabey, Sa Vie – son temps, 1767–1855* (Paris, 1909), 131; Auguste de La Garde-Chambonas, *Souvenirs du Congrès de Vienne, 1814–1815* (Paris, 1901), 113; Edmond Taigny, *J.-B. Isabey, Sa Vie et ses oeuvres* (Paris, 1859), 37.
4 Cyril Lécosse, 'Jean Godefroy (1771–1839), d'après Jean Baptiste Isabey (1767–1855) *Le Congrès de Vienne*, 1819', in Emmanuel de Waresquiel (ed.), *Talleyrand, ou, Le miroir trompeur* (Paris, 2005), 111; Basily-Callimaki, *J.-B. Isabey*, 160.
5 'Son atelier, entièrement tapissé des esquisses, de ses dessins, de ses portraits ébauchés, semblait une lanterne magique où apparaissaient tour à tour les notabilités réunies en ce moment au Congrès.' La Garde-Chambonas, *Souvenirs*, 114.
6 Ibid.; Basily-Callimaki, *J.-B. Isabey*, 172.
7 'toutes les princesses de l'Europe sont entourées, emmaillotées, voilées dans des flots de mousseline et dissimulées dans les roses'. Alexandrine du Montet, quoted in Basily-Callimaki, *J.-B. Isabey*, 185.
8 Udo Felbinger, 'French Art in Vienna at the Time of the Congress', in Grabner, Husslein-Arco and Telesko, *Europe in Vienna*, 167.
9 'Pendant la durée des conférences, mon petit gîte, tout modeste qu'il était, fut le rendez-vous de bien des têtes couronnées; les souverains, les princes qui n'étaient pas tenus de siéger au congrès, les plénipotentiaires mêmes, qui n'osaient se rendre visite chez eux officiellement, pour ne pas éveiller des susceptibilités rivales, avaient, en se recontrant dans mon atelier, mille prétextes plausibles pour échanger des communications ou des confidences. Ma maison fut, en quelque sorte, les coulisses du congrès.' Quoted in Taigny, *J.-B. Isabey*, 38. Taigny and Basily-Callimaki both quote from notes Isabey made about his experiences at the conference later in life. The current whereabouts of those notes is unknown. See Taigny, *J.-B. Isabey*, 7–8 and Felbinger, 'French Art in Vienna', 171n21.
10 Ibid.
11 'Isabey, c'est le Congrès fait peintre.' Quoted in La Garde-Chambonas, *Souvenirs*, 112.
12 'Avec un extérieur agréable, des formes polies et une éloquence naturelle, Isabey a tout ce qu'il faut pour attirer l'envie et la désarmer ... il est recherché dans tous les cercles.' Quoted in Basily-Callimaki, *J.-B. Isabey*, 172.
13 In addition to *The Queens of Persia*, the other paintings that La Garde-Chambonas mentions being performed in Vienna are *Louis XIV aux pieds de madame de La Vallière* by 'un jeune artiste viennois', Guérin's *Phédre et Hippolyte* (1802, Musée du Louvre, Paris) and *La Conversation espagnole*, presumably Carle Van Loo's picture of 1755 (The Hermitage, Saint Petersburg). La Garde-Chambonas, *Souvenirs*, 133–4 and 216.
14 Ibid., 136–7; Basily-Callimaki, *J.-B. Isabey*, 168–71.
15 La Garde-Chambonas describes the discussions about the Mount Olympus tableau as 'une négociation bien autrement délicate et difficile que celles qui se traitent habituellement entre les sommités diplomatiques'. La Garde-Chambonas, *Souvenirs*, 136.
16 'à la fois héroïque et voluptueux'. La Garde-Chambonas, *Souvenirs*, 217.

17 'Le sujet, par lui-même, laissait peu de place à l'imagination. La grande difficulté était de grouper un grand nombre de personnages dans un espace restreint, dans des attitudes à peu près semblables, sans tomber dans la monotonie, et de donner aux physionomies une expression appropriée au rang at au caractère des individus, sans altérer la ressemblance. Un autre embarras était de décider à quel moment de la séance je peindrais les plénipotentiaires.' Quoted in Taigny, *J.-B. Isabey*, 38.
18 For further discussion of the challenges of group portraiture, see Bridget Alsdorf, *Fellow Men: Fantin-Latour and the Problem of the Group in Nineteenth-Century French Painting* (Princeton, NJ, 2013).
19 'il n'est pas aisé d'arranger, suivant les règles de la peinture, des hommes asservi par état aux lois de l'étiquette, de donner du mouvement à des figures qui s'entr'observent avec une attention presque défiante, de rendre expressives des physionomies ministériellement impénétrables.' E. F. A. M. Miel, *Essai sur les beaux-arts, et particulièrement sur le Salon de 1817, ou examen critique des principaux ouvrages d'art exposés dans le cours de cette année* (Paris, 1817 and 1818), 123–4.
20 According to Taigny (*J.-B. Isabey*, 37), Talleyrand motioned toward the print after Ter Borch's work and said to Isabey, 'vous peindrez le congrès: vous êtes de la légation.' La Garde-Chambonas (*Souvenirs*, 113) and Basily-Callimaki (*J.-B. Isabey*, 160) tell similar versions of the story.
21 The British painter David Wilkie visited Talleyrand in June 1814, shortly after the Treaty was signed, and makes this claim. Allan Cunningham, *The Life of Sir David Wilkie*, vol. 1 (London, 1843), 425.
22 Alison McNeil Kettering, *Gerard ter Borch and the Treaty of Münster* (Mauritshuis, 1998), 17.
23 For all the realist rhetoric, McNeil Kettering notes that Ter Borch of course took liberties with his composition. At the event itself, for example, the Spanish delegation swore the oath of ratification first, followed by the Dutch. Ter Borch shows the two sides swearing the oath simultaneously. McNeil Kettering, *Gerard ter Borch*, 16–18.
24 'Un autre embarras était de décider à quel moment de la séance je peindrais les plénipotentiares. Seraient-ils en délibération? Saisirais-je plûtot l'instant où la causerie familière suit la clôture des discussions? Je m'arrêtai à ce dernier parti.' Isabey, quoted in Taigny, *J.-B. Isabey*, 38.
25 Traditionally, writers have identified the Habsburg monarch as Francis I, the reigning emperor at the time of the conference. See, for example, Basily-Callimaki, *J.-B. Isabey*, 189. In his description of Isabey's final drawing, written in 1817, the critic Miel (see n19) notes the presence of a picture of 'l'empereur d'Autriche,' which implies it is the current ruler. Werner Telesko has recently claimed, however, that the represented figure is Leopold II and that his inclusion underlines the role of Austria in European peace efforts that preceded the Napoleonic era. Werner Telesko, 'Jean-Baptiste Isabey's Picture of the Congress of Vienna', in Grabner, Husslein-Arco and Telesko, *Europe in Vienna*, 131.
26 On Boilly's picture, see Susan L. Siegfried, *The Art of Louis-Léopold Boilly: Modern Life in Napoleonic France* (New Haven, CT, 1995), 96–101 and Abigail Solomon-Godeau, *Male Trouble: A Crisis in Representation* (London, 1999), 55.
27 On artists, fraternity and representation in the revolutionary era, see Thomas Crow, *Emulation: Making Artists for Revolutionary France* (New Haven, 1997) and Solomon-Godeau, *Male Trouble*.
28 'Mon croquis fut agréé.' Isabey, quoted in Taigny, *J.-B. Isabey*, 38.
29 Ibid.

30 La Garde-Chambonas, *Souvenirs*, 387.
31 Antoine Schnapper, *Jacques-Louis David, 1748–1825* (Paris, 1989), 249.
32 Philippe Bordes, *Le Serment du Jeu de Paume de Jacques-Louis David* (Paris, 1983), 69.
33 Ewa Lajer-Burcharth, *Necklines: The Art of Jacques-Louis David after the Terror* (New Haven, CT, 1999), 106.
34 The study is reproduced in Pupil, *Jean-Baptiste Isabey*, 120.
35 Taigny, *J.-B. Isabey*, 40–1; Lécosse, 'Jean Godefroy', 111.
36 Edmund Schilling and Anthony Blunt, *The German Drawings in the Collection of Her Majesty the Queen at Windsor Castle, and Supplements to the Catalogues of Italian and French Drawings* (London, 1971), 211.
37 Felbinger, 'French Art in Vienna', 170.
38 'Les parties inférieures sont bien modelées, mais on trouve que dans plusieurs figures elles ne sont pas exemptes d'une certaine roideur; on sent aussi que l'oeil est trop attiré vers les jambes. Le premier de ces défauts tient à la forme de l'habillement moderne; le second, à l'éclat des bas de soie, chaussure plus élégant dans une toilette qu'advantageuse dans un tableau.' Miel, *Essai sur les beaux-arts*, 124.
39 For further discussion of the relationship between art and sociability during the Restoration, see: Daniel Harkett, 'Delphine Gay and the Paris Salon', in James Kearns and Alister Mill (eds), *Painting for the Salon/Peindre pour le Salon, 1791–1881* (Oxford and Berne, 2015), 73–92 and Daniel Harkett, 'Mediating Private and Public: Juliette Récamier's Salon at L'Abbaye-aux-Bois', in Temma Balducci and Heather Belnap Jensen (eds), *Women, Femininity, and Public Space in European Visual Culture, 1789–1914* (Farnham, 2014), 47–64.

6

Cosmopolitan Conspirators: The Conspiracy against the Holy Alliance during the French Intervention in Spain

Jean-Noël Tardy

The series of revolutions across southern Europe which began in 1820 (first in Spain, then in Piedmont and Naples, and lastly the wave of conspiracies which swept through France) might provide grounds for believing in the existence of a revolutionary 'Liberal International'.[1] The idea of an international conspiracy of liberal revolutionaries began as a central theme of ultra-royalist propaganda, but it was also taken at face value by many police authorities across Europe. Two modern historians, José Luis Comellas Garcia-Llera and, later, Marion S. Miller, have argued for the existence of a Liberal International, not as a single well-defined organization, but as a network of close-knit relationships among liberals in the various European countries, especially those of southern Europe.[2] We do indeed find exiled Italian revolutionaries in Paris, London, Madrid and Barcelona being supported by local liberal élites. Model constitutions and reformist political ideas also circulated from country to country, particularly from Spain to Italy, where Spanish resistance to the Napoleonic Empire and subsequently to the absolutism of Ferdinand VII were inspirational to Italian revolutionaries.[3] A 'Holy Alliance of Peoples' to counter the Holy Alliance of monarchs was a powerful and stirring idea for liberals: French as well as Italian Carbonari formed a corps of volunteers to defend the Spanish constitutional regime in 1823, as a French army prepared to intervene in favour of the Spanish Bourbons. The presence of foreign volunteers on Spanish soil raises the question of whether an active international activism existed, if not quite a fully fledged 'International movement'. More fundamentally, the proliferation of international contacts intent on forging relationships to counter the Holy Alliance casts a new, transnational light on the underground opposition to the restored Bourbons within France.[4]

Cosmopolitanism, nationalism and international organizations

The nation-state was not the only setting for intellectual and political life in post-revolutionary Europe. Indeed, in those areas where French influence had been most marked under Napoleon, the concept of the nation-state was still a very new idea. Accordingly, the birth of cross-border political networks was a continuation of the cosmopolitan attitudes prevalent in the eighteenth century, which were inseparable from the development of the transnational civil society linked to the Enlightenment, often centred on salons and, above all, Freemasonry. French expansion during the Revolution and the Empire, and the contradictory reactions to it – of foreigners enlisting in the *Grande Armée* on the one hand, or the birth of anti-French patriotic societies on the other – made this, at once, a time of increasing international association, and also a crisis of the cosmopolitan ideal. The Congress of Vienna and the Holy Alliance most feared the international dimension of the Revolution which, in turn, made cooperation among governments and police authorities an issue of crucial importance to the future European order. It is clear that both solidarity among the monarchs and solidarity among their enemies have been over-estimated. Few revolutionaries really had international reputations or truly international networks. Nevertheless, there was the example of that most flamboyant heir to the cosmopolitanism of the Enlightenment: General Lafayette, 'the hero of two worlds', and embodiment of international liberalism since his American adventure in the 1770s. He fully subscribed to the cosmopolitan ideal of Enlightenment Freemasonry; he had a social network far beyond the borders of France; he very readily welcomed anyone recommended to him to Paris or his country estate, La Grange. Many of his guests were British or American: the British social and political thinker, Jeremy Bentham, the popular American author, James Fenimore Cooper and others stayed with the Lafayettes, and the English writer and intellectual, Frances (Fanny) Wright, travelled extensively with the general in the 1820s.[5]

Philippe Buonarroti was another central figure in this cosmopolitan world. He exemplifies a new political figure, one which was to have a great future: the professional revolutionary. A Tuscan who had become a French citizen during the Revolution, he committed himself to the revolutionary struggle, first with the Jacobin Republic of 1792–4, and then, after the fall of Robespierre in 1794, with Gracchus Babeuf in a major conspiracy to overthrow the less radical Directory of 1795–9. The Directory imprisoned him, and the successor Napoleonic regimes kept him under surveillance. His political activities operated in the shadows, and his recruiting ground was Freemasonry. He developed an ideology of cosmopolitanism and social egalitarianism. Buonarotti's importance has sometimes been over-estimated, but he still developed networks among those opposed to the restored autocracies, often extending his influence by infiltrating other organizations. Although its numbers were always small, his own organization, with its core ideology of egalitarianism, was the closest example in post-Napoleonic Europe to a coherent 'International', as later Marxist regimes defined it.[6]

Other opposition figures also had both direct relationships and shared political cultures that extended beyond a single country. An important example is found among former French administrators of territories conquered under Napoleon. The careers of three such men are particularly noteworthy: one was Pierre-Joseph Briot, a Jacobin who had accepted and served Napoleon; he became an administrator of the Abruzzi, in the Napoleonic satellite kingdom of Naples, but retained his republican beliefs and favoured popular emancipation. It was probably Briot who introduced the Carbonari sect into the kingdom in the last years of Napoleonic rule, but he failed to keep its membership under control, as its opposition to Napoleonic rule became increasingly overt, in direct contrast to the secretive tactics at the heart of Carbonarism.[7] The Marquis Voyer d'Argenson is another such figure. A French noble and supporter of the ideals of 1789, he served as the Napoleonic prefect of Antwerp in Belgium (then French territory) but resigned in protest against the abusive authoritarianism of the Napoleonic police. Joseph Rey of Grenoble had been a young deputy prosecutor at Piacenza, in the Italian department of Taro, then annexed directly to France, in 1807, but later turned to Utopian socialism in his disillusionment with Napoleon.[8]

Exiles were prominent among those most likely to become international conspirators after 1814. The restored Bourbons in France exiled many political opponents, while for others, voluntary exile was the wiser course of action in these years. Among their ranks were the regicides, deputies of the revolutionary National Convention who had voted for the execution of Louis XVI and Marie Antoinette in 1793. There were also politicians who compromised themselves by supporting Napoleon during the Hundred Days. While the regicides probably posed no serious threat to the Restoration, the same was not true of the younger generation of exiles. One of the first political manoeuvres of those liberals most opposed to the regime of Louis XVIII was an attempt to replace him with the Dutch Prince of Orange, who had shown sympathy for French liberals proscribed by the Bourbons. In 1819, Claude de Corcelle was one of the most committed advocates of this solution. After 1821, the failure of the Carbonari conspiracies made exiles of many leading prominent Italian and Spanish liberals, including the Comte de Santa-Rosa and General Pepé. They found warm welcomes in the Parisian salons, and the circle around Lafayette. Other, more obscure Italian revolutionaries found refuge in Marseille or Corsica, if under close police surveillance, which led some to consider leaving for Catalonia or the New World.

The proliferation of revolutionary associations kindled hopes of setting up an umbrella organization for all European opposition groups. Some believed Freemasonry could provide the catalyst for coordination, but the revolutionaries were disappointed by the cautiousness of the French Grand Orient Lodge, which had been closely integrated into the Napoleonic regime, and then advocated submission to the Bourbons after 1814. Consequently, revolutionaries made use of Freemasonry only as a recruiting pool or, occasionally, as cover from the attention of the authorities. Joseph Rey attempted to foster closer links among European liberals through the 'Union', which his memoirs reveal was inspired by the German *Tugenbund*. He was in touch with Swiss, German and Italian liberals, and tried to extend his organization to Germany from 1816 onward, with the further aim of convening a congress of European secret societies in Switzerland, and forging a union among them in implicit memory of the legendary Swiss national hero – and anti-Austrian rebel – William Tell. However, Rey's involvement in the Carbonari conspiracy of 1820 put an end his efforts and obliged him to leave France for London. Subsequently, he lost much of his influence.[9]

The upholders of the Vienna settlement, including Metternich himself, firmly believed in the existence of a pan-European revolutionary organization, and they saw it in the Carbonari. Metternich's police called for international cooperation to counter this revolutionary peril, and France was one of the governments most receptive to this.¹⁰ In reality, the origins and workings of the French Carbonari belie this belief in international conspiracy, and reveal how complex – yet limited – such transnational dealings actually were. Italian Carbonarism was undoubtedly a borrowed and refashioned form of the organizations and rituals of the forest Carbonari or *Bons Cousins Charbonniers*, an apolitical mutual aid society – originally of charcoal-burners – under the symbolic patronage of a legendary religious figure, St Theobald. It is probable that Pierre-Joseph Briot spread its constitution throughout Italy, and that Italian radicals opposed to Napoleonic rule appropriated it; some, like the Marquis de Attellis, went so far as to deny any French influence in the secret society's origins.¹¹ After 1815, Carbonarism evolved into an organization of Italian liberals hostile to the Vienna settlement. According to the French Carbonari, the Italian example played a large part in their own organization, which was founded in late 1820. Two young men involved in the conspiracy of August 1820, Dugied, a wine merchant, and Joubert, a customs clerk, went to Naples to fight for the insurgents and were apparently initiated into the Carbonari. Dugied subsequently brought the Italian constitution home with him. Nevertheless, the two organizations were clearly very different: the French activists, Bazard and Buchez, changed the Italian text completely. Italian Carbonarism had many degrees of membership, implying an initiation process; conversely, the French Carbonari kept only its basic distinctions, such as the President and Deputy of the *vente* (cell), who handled all communication upwards and downwards within the chain of command of the organization. The links between the two secret societies were tenuous as well, except along the frontiers, where there were many Italian exiles. The Italian Carbonari were astonished that their recognition signs were not used by the French society: 'federal Carbonarism', which developed after the revolutions of 1821–2 within the French secret society, tried to reintroduce secret signs to facilitate contact in more repressive circumstances. In Marseille, it was Italian refugees who established the organization, and so the French Carbonari here followed Italian, rather than French, practice.¹² French Carbonarism was hardly an international organization. Only Switzerland was really integrated into a wider network, because of the unique fact that Swiss Carbonarism was dominated by Buonarroti, who subordinated it to his ideology and his own organization, the Society of Perfect Sublime Masters.

1822–3: The fight against French intervention in Spain; a reverse for international liberalism

The liberal conspirators' reaction to the intervention of the Holy Alliance in Spain perfectly illustrates the close-knit relationships among European opponents of the Vienna settlement. However, it also reveals the extent to which their interests diverged from each other, for either ideological or patriotic reasons. Portuguese and Spanish liberals, Italian refugees, British radicals and French liberals were all violently opposed to this reactionary intervention by Louis XVIII's government. The French believed it would be possible to turn the army against the Bourbons if it could be confronted by a corps of volunteers in uniform bearing the eagle of the *Grande Armée*. Many secret societies across Europe sprang into action, claiming to be strong enough to oppose the invasion of Spain: French Carbonari, Buonarroti's 'Sublime Perfect Masters', the 'European Constitutional Brothers' of General Pepé, Cugnet de Montarlot's 'Order of the Sun' were all competing organizations, if sometimes in alliance. None of them could fairly claim to be the conspiracy's sole organizing intelligence. The French Carbonari played an essential role, but their actions were necessarily limited; their representative in south-western France was General Laffitte, whose task was to coordinate attempts to 'turn' the French army.[13] The radical newspaper *L'Ami des peuples* ('Friend of the Peoples') reported that an appeal had been made in the Masonic lodges for volunteers to go to Spain, and that each lodge was asked to provide two men.[14] If such an appeal was made it had little success: most of the French volunteers who fought in Spain were exiled Carbonari in Brussels or London, already pursued by their own police. The cells of south-western France (Bordeaux, Toulouse, Bayonne) played an important part in spreading liberal propaganda in the army, making contact with officers and NCOs; but that was only the French part of the conspiracy, and more contact was needed with other forces possibly prepared to oppose the expedition.

When General Pepé went to London to rally British radicals to his 'Constitutional Brothers', he encountered the mistrust which a 'foreign' secret society can arouse.[15] The British were unwilling to join forces with an organization which sought them to commit themselves to action without any opportunity to debate its leaders' decisions in public. Only General Wilson was ready to take up arms again on Spanish territory familiar to him from the Peninsular War. Pepé found another keen partner in Lafayette.[16] With such allies, it was now possible to contemplate real action in Spain. The work of coordination was left to men who were active but less prominent, and for that reason more vulnerable to prosecution. They were a remarkably cosmopolitan group,[17] including two businessmen, one French (Martial Sauquaire-Souligné) and the other English (John Bowring), a diplomat (the Chevalier d'Oliveira, Portuguese chargé d'affaires in France) and two former Napoleonic army officers already compromised in conspiracies, Colonel Fabvier (a Frenchman) and Colonel Asinari di San Marzano (a Piedmontese). Martial Sauquaire-Souligné relied on his project for a European subscription loan, which enabled him to correspond with the most influential liberal leaders and receive their emissaries. Dr Bowring was a young merchant and intellectual, who, like many British radicals, combined political radicalism with advocacy of free trade; he was a friend of Bentham, and translated his works into French. He frequently visited Paris, Lisbon and Madrid, his travels made easier by his remarkable aptitude for languages, a dozen of which he spoke fluently. He was also a romantic, fascinated by the legends and popular cultures of the various lands he visited. Bowring moved from country to country; he carried Sauquaire-Souligné's correspondence to Portugal and Spain; in London, he worked with the charismatic General Sir Robert Wilson. The Portuguese liberals had reason to fear the Holy Alliance: Sauquaire-Souligné sought to involve them financially in his projects[18] through his agent in Lisbon, Colonel Freire. Above all, he succeeded in winning over the Portuguese chargé d'affaires in France, Dr João Francisco d'Oliveira, who sheltered the conspirators in the embassy and saw to all their correspondence. His superior, the foreign minister, was the great liberal theoretician Silvestre Pinheiro Ferreira.[19] Cautiously, he did not invest the millions entrusted to him. The Spanish government, too, was prudent: the contact there for the French Carbonari was an obscure secretary of the Duke of Santo-Lorenzo.[20]

An important reason for the failure of the international conspiracy was the unenthusiastic welcome which the liberal regime in Spain gave to the underground manoeuvres of the French liberals. With just a handful of exceptions, even the most revolutionary of the Spanish liberals shunned Carbonarism when Italian exiles tried to establish it in their midst. They rallied instead to the *Comuneros*, an organization with wholly Spanish roots and traditions, or they turned to Freemasonry. The Spanish government did not trust the emissaries from the Carbonari. Their national parliament, the Cortes, believed until the last moment that war could be avoided; moreover, the government did not approve the conspirators' manoeuvres in support of the Colombian secessionists from the Spanish empire. The money provided to General Laffitte came from the Carbonari's emissary, Don Francesco-Antonio Zéa, and was conveyed from London to the Pyrenees by Colonel Pisa, the Italian aide-de-camp to General Pepé.[21] Zéa, the vice-president of the Colombian rebel leader Simon Bolivar, came to Europe in June 1820 on a mission to gain recognition for Colombian independence, and to ensure its financial future. He persuaded some liberal bankers to lend two million pounds to the new Colombian Republic, and was in touch with Lafayette, who promised Spain 50 million francs on condition that Colombian independence was recognized. It appears that Mexico promised a similar amount. To negotiate the diplomatic transaction, Pepé went to Madrid bearing letters from Lafayette and, to establish his credentials, the latter's correspondence with the foreign ministers of Colombia and Mexico. (Fanny Wright travelled from Paris to Dover to deliver these letters in person.)

The French foreign minister alerted his British counterpart, who had Pepé arrested as he set out for Madrid. However, the Italian general was protected by British radicals, who persuaded the authorities not to cause a scandal by searching him. According to his memoirs, once in Madrid, Pepé managed to arrange an interview with the most influential members of the Cortes at the house of General Riego, a leading figure in the Spanish government. This caused some difficulty, because the Russian and British ambassadors were putting pressure on the Spanish government to temporise their policies. Pepé explained Lafayette's proposal, and argued that the 100 million francs from the new South American countries could finance the defence of Spain and the organization of a corps of French volunteers; but the Spaniards, led by the deputy Galliano, refused to recognize the independence of Mexico or Colombia – for fear, they claimed, of further alienating pro-imperial opinion in Spain.[22] Pepé also had difficulties among the Italian refugees. In Barcelona, he encountered a more radical rival, de Attellis, who had already opposed him during the revolution in Naples.

The police seriously disrupted the organization set up by Sauquaire-Souligné. On 5 October 1822, Bowring was arrested at Calais on his way to London.[23] Then De Oliveira decided to return to Lisbon, but as he was embarking at Le Havre on 15 November, his baggage was opened by the French authorities, and his papers seized. That search confirmed the suspicions of the police: they found many letters from Sauquaire-Souligné, who had fled as soon as John Bowring's arrest became known, leaving France first for London and then for Lisbon. Lafayette soon lost control of the international conspiracy to other activists, foremost among them the French deputy in the National Assembly, Manuel, an important leader of French Carbonarism, and Lafayette's rival. Manuel's methods were pragmatic; he believed that both veterans and the French people, as a whole, were more likely to revolt in the name of Bonapartism than of international revolution. In contrast, Lafayette never disguised his dislike of the Napoleonic regime.[24] After Sauquaire-Souligné's flight, the organization of the French volunteer corps fell to an officer who had been particularly involved in resistance to the Bourbons, Colonel Fabvier,[25] who had worked persistently in the liberal underground since the Carbonari conspiracy of August 1820. In Paris he had sympathized with the Italian refugees, Carlo Asinari di San Marzano in particular, and was one of the first to join in recruiting soldiers to fight in Spain. In a note to the Spanish government, he strongly recommended the choice of General Laffitte as the main agent for the operation.[26] Fabvier was not, strictly speaking, a Carbonaro. He declined to be initiated, and even more vehemently refused to obey students with no military experience. He did take part in the project coordinated by Sauquaire-Souligné, since he travelled to London in August 1822 and there met Robert Wilson and the French exiles.

Appalled at the situation of those sentenced to death in Poitiers and Paris for their part in the conspiracy, he did all he could to save them, and at that point worked with John Bowring to smuggle the famous 'Four Sergeants of La Rochelle' to Britain. The operation failed, and Fabvier was again put on trial. He was acquitted on 28 November 1822,[27] but by the time he was freed, the 'Four Sergeants' had been executed. Deeply moved by their deaths, for which he blamed the amateurism and boastfulness of the Carbonari, he threw himself body and soul into the Spanish venture. With the utmost secrecy, he left for London in early December, eventually reaching Santander. He kept his distance from Carbonarism and its leaders, Commandant Caron and General Lafayette. His particular complaint about Caron was his association with the *Comuneros*, the most extreme of the Spanish revolutionary groupings.[28] Fabvier tried to rally known Bonapartists like General Piat and General Gourgaud to the resistance; he also wanted to gain control of the volunteer battalion in Catalonia, the self-styled 'Sacred Battalion', or 'Napoleon II Battalion', and to persuade its men to enter the Basque country, to oppose the French invasion.[29] In liaison with Manuel he manoeuvred against Lafayette, whose authority he was unwilling to recognize. His pragmatically grounded organization had no special rites or practices, although its members were referred to by numbers in its correspondence. The police then intercepted General Piat's coach. The Duc d'Angoulême, the Bourbon prince commanding the French invasion, confirmed Major-General Guilleminot in his post, despite his being suspected of involvement in the plot; but this was enough to ensure the French troops stayed loyal to the Bourbons. The Spanish affair turned into a disaster for the conspirators: French regulars fired on the French volunteers who awaited them on the Bidassoa, flying the revolutionary standard, the Tricolour. Fabvier knew the game was lost. He knew that French regular troops, even those hostile to the Bourbons, would not desert once they were engaged against foreigners. The Spanish debacle showed there was no real 'Liberal International' beyond a shared sentiment of hostility to the Vienna settlement and plentiful, but competing, initiatives by networks of conspirators.

After Revolution and Empire, Europe was fertile ground for international political conspiracies; but while some underground organizations managed to gain a considerable influence nationally (the Italian and French Carbonari in particular, to the point of looking in the latter case like a centralized clandestine party, present almost throughout the country), no organization succeeding in embodying insurrectionary liberalism across Europe. The proliferation of initiatives, and the divisions among revolutionaries, expose how illusory these enterprises were. However, they also bear witness to the strength of this 'cosmopolitanism of action', an expression subsequently applied to the revolutionary situation of the 1830s.[30] It is that cosmopolitan outlook, inherited from the eighteenth century, which was championed by both Lafayette and Philippe Buonarroti, whatever their ideological differences. Buonarroti, companion of Babeuf, found his influence increased when the Jacobins were rehabilitated after the July Revolution of 1830. However, if his universalist Carbonarism borrowing Masonic and revolutionary symbolism is compared with the later nationalism of Mazzini, the metamorphosis of a European revolutionary movement emerges, which henceforth championed emerging national identities, and the right of peoples to self-determination.

Notes

1 The use of the term 'International' reflects the posited proto-relationship between the activities of revolutionaries in this period with those of Marx and Engels, in their attempts to coordinate socialist revolution through cooperation among socialist movements, internationally, through the First International, created in London in 1864. It was followed by a more moderate Second International of socialist and labour parties founded in 1889, Lenin's Soviet-sponsored Third International of 1919, and the Trotskyite Fourth International of 1938. All sought to coordinate left-wing movements on an international scale.
2 José Luis Comellas Garcia-Llera, *El Trienio constitucional* (Madrid, 1963), 397; Marion S. Miller, 'A "Liberal International?" Prospects on Comparative Approaches to the Revolutions in Spain, Italy, and Greece in the 1820s', in Richard W. Clement, Benjaimin F. Taggie and Robert G. Schwartz (eds), *Greece and the Mediterranean* (Kirksville, 1990), 61–8.
3 Pierre-Marie Delpu, 'Fraternités libérales et insurrections nationales: Naples et l'Espagne, 1820–1821', *Revue d'histoire du XIXe siècle*, 49/2 (2014), 195–213.
4 On exiles, Maurizio Isabella argues for the idea of a European and transatlantic civil society animated by a liberal ideal going beyond state borders: Maurizio Isabella, *Risorgimento in Exile: Italian Emigrés and the Liberal International in the Post-Napoleonic Era* (Cambridge, 2009), 22–3. See also Delphine Diaz, 'Une "internationale liberale" à l'epreuve de l'exil? Exiles européens en France sous les monarchies censitaires', in Eric Anceau, Jacques-Olivier Boudon and Olivier Dard (eds), *Histoire des Internationales: Europe, XIXe–XXe siècles* (Paris, 2017), 41–68.
5 Lafayette's network of intellectuals is central to the study by Lloyd Kramer: *Lafayette in Two Worlds: Public Cultures and Personal Identities in an Age of Revolutions* (North Carolina, 1996). On Fanny Wright, see Kramer, *Lafayette*, 154–71.
6 See Armando Saitta, *Filippo Buonarroti, contributi alla storia della sua vita e dal suo pensiero* (Rome, 1950). Arthur Lehning, 'Buonarroti and his international secret societies', *International Review of Social History* (1957) 112–40, and in Arthur Lehning,

From Buonarroti to Bakunin: Studies in International Socialism (Leiden, 1970); Jean-Marc Schiappa, *Buonarroti l'inoxydable (1761–1837)* (Paris, 2008).

7   The idea that it was Briot who brought Carbonarism is argued for in Francesco Mastroberti, *Pierre-Joseph Briot, un giacobino tra amministrazione e politica* (Naples, 1998).

8   Nicolas Boisson, *Les figures de Joseph Rey (1779–1855): conspirateur libéral, philosophe et socialiste utopique* (Grenoble, 2001), 125, note 65.

9   Joseph Rey, 'Notice historique sur les sociétés secrètes qui ont existé in France pendant la Restauration', *Le Patriote des Alpes*, 18 November 1847.

10 Donald, E. Emerson, *Metternich and the Political Police: Security and Subversion in the Hapsburg Monarchy, 1815–1830* (The Hague, 1968), 52.

11 *The Ottimestre Costituzionale delle Due Sicilie autenticamente documentato, da servire alla storia di quel regno*, by Orazio de Attellis, Marquis of Santangelo, National Library of Naples, mss cc. 28–9.

12 Archives Nationales de Paris (ANP), BB30, 239, Ducros' account.

13 Jean-Noël Tardy, *L'Âge des ombres: Sociétés secrètes et conspirations au XIXe siècle* (Paris, 2015), 158 sq.

14 'Causes secrètes de la Révolution de 1830. Revelations officielles sur the fameux comité-directeur et les carbonari de Paris', *L'Ami des peuples*, September 1830.

15 Gugliemo Pepé, *Memoires du général Pepé sur les principaux événements politiques et militaires de l'Italie moderne*, 3 vols (Paris, 1847), vol. 3, 343 ff.

16 Pepé, *Mémoires du général Pepé*, 374 ff.

17 See trial documents in Jacques Nicolas de Broe, *Requisitoire de M. de Broé, avocat general, prononcé le 7 février 1824 devant la cour d'assises de la Seine, dans le procès contre Sauquaire-Souligné et autres et la femme Chauvet* (Paris, 1824).

18 Letter from Sauquaire-Souligné to Pinheiro-Ferreira in de Broe, *Requisitoire*, 22.

19 Viscount de Santarem, 'Notice biographique sur M. Pinheiro-Ferreira', *Revue de droit français et étranger*, iv (1847), 75–81.

20 ANP AB XIX 3566 Notes.

21 The saga of Zéa's 50,000 francs and their journey to General Laffitte seems romantic, to say the least; yet the multiplicity of sources mentioning the money leaves no doubt it really existed. The main source is General Pepé: Pepé, *Mémoires*, vol. 3, 376. However, there are also the references to a connection with Zéa, wrung from three Carbonari conspirators – artillery lieutenants Peugnet, Trolé and Gaillardon, under very hard questioning: Services Historiques de l'Armée de la Terre (SHAT) C18/46, *Interrogatoires des accusés dans l'affaire des artilleurs de Strasbourg*. The 50,000 francs were mentioned at the Carbonari Congress of Lyons: ANP AB XIX 3566 Notes. The account given here is based mainly on the *Mémoires* of General Pepé.

22 See under 'Zéa' in the *Biographie Universelle, ancienne et moderne* (Paris, 1828), vol. 52, 171–4.

23 John Bowring, *Details of the Arrest, Imprisonment and Liberation of an Englishman by the Bourbon Government of France* (London, 1823), 9.

24 ANP F7 6664 Interrogation of Husson, on whom see Laurent Nagy, 'L'émissaire de la Charbonnerie française au service du Trienio Liberal', *Historia Constitucional*, 15 (2014), 223–54.

25 Fabvier's role may be traced in detail from his papers in Departmental archives of Meurthe (ADM) Fonds Fabvier 16J (8) and the study by Antonin Debidour, *Le général Fabvier, sa vie militaire et politique* (Paris, 1904), 189–252.

26 ADM Fonds Fabvier 16 J 8, Note to the Spanish government, 23 January 1823.

27 ANP F7 6659, the Dentzel-Fabvier affair.
28 ADM, Fonds Fabvier, 16 J 8. Journal de Fabvier, 11 January 1823
29 See Debidour, *Le général*, 217; on the Napoleon II batallion: Walter Bruyere-Ostells, *La grande armée de la liberte* (Paris, 2009), 86–7.
30 Emmanuel Fureix, 'Introduction', in Sylvie Aprile, Jen-Claude Caron and Emmanuel Fureix (eds), *La liberté guidant les peuples: Les révolutions de 1830 in Europe* (Seyssel, 2013), 27.

Part Two

Charters and Constitutional Monarchy

Louis XVIII and the Charter of 4 June 1814: Time, Memory and Oblivion

Emmanuel de Waresquiel

The end of a moment of crisis, whether the wars of religion in the 1600s, the wars of conquest of the Revolution and Empire after 1814, or the great twentieth-century global conflicts in 1919 and 1945, is particularly revealing. It obliges states as well as individuals to innovate, facing them with often contradictory choices over whether to revive former powers and the political and social systems that had caused or endured these crises, over rupture versus restoration. These endings are also important because of the fragile and volatile contexts that shape them, where the weight of the past, lack of legitimacy and the intensity of political and social divisions form major obstacles to be overcome.

With the country militarily defeated after almost a quarter of a century of European warfare and with the Empire, the heir of the Revolution, on the point of collapse, France experienced a period of this type in 1814. Never had the question of how to 'end the revolution' been more acute. The choices made in that year – restoration through the recall of the Bourbon dynasty that had ruled before the Revolution, but also consolidation of that same Revolution by preserving its main political and social gains – mark an effort of reconstruction that was profoundly original and in a sense, unique.

The Charter conceded by Louis XVIII to the nation on the 4 June 1814 did not reflect every aspect of this profound experience, but it did provide a foundation and a meaning to the new regime that it inaugurated. For better or for worse, it gave the country a constitutional framework despite the minor modifications of August 1830 – to say nothing of the suppression of its preamble – right up until February 1848. Its longevity bears out Napoleon's aphorism that the best constitutions should be preferably 'short and obscure ... so as not to impede the action of government'. The antique word 'Charter' masked in reality an unprecedented, incomplete, supple and paradoxical undertaking.[1]

What does one behold in the preamble and 76 articles of a text which sought to resolve a quarter century of crisis, civil and foreign war: an attempt at reaction, a proof of transition or the expression of a transaction? Judged as a transition, the Charter of 1814 is gloomily silent and littered with ambiguities. In its text the past, like a rabbit in a hat, disappears to reappear in a new and unexpected form. At its unveiling in 1814, the Charter was greeted less as a transition than as a transaction, between two different versions of the past – the old régime and the Revolution – between liberty and order, between birth and merit, between glory and peace, and more generally between the old and the new. Here, at first sight, lies the spirit of the text: a transaction with an aura of reconciliation. The concept of reconciliation, quite logically, lay at the heart of the king's speech of 1814 and in his public interventions Louis XVIII constantly repeated his wish to 'reconcile all my children'. As the preamble to the Charter put it: 'Our dearest wish is that all Frenchmen should live as brothers.' At least until 1820, if not to the end of his reign, Louis never swerved from this policy. He wrote in this sense to his brother in January 1818: 'The system I have adopted and which my ministers are following unswervingly is based on the maxim that one should never be the king of two peoples, and all my government's efforts aim to ensure that these two peoples, whose division is only too obvious, end by becoming one . . .'[2]

This explains why at the moment of its proclamation the Charter enjoyed a widespread support that rested on being capable of several interpretations. Napoleon's former prefect Prosper de Barante summed this up in a report to the king of July 1815, just after the Hundred Days. In his eyes the Charter had been 'handed down by the king' and 'dictated by opinion' in equal measure. At the outset the Charter was welcomed just as much by the heirs of the Revolution, at least that of 1789, as by the moderate supporters of the former monarchy, if not those who, in the words of the deputy Felix Faulcon, had 'learned nothing and forgotten nothing' in emigration. One must also remember the climate of relief, expectation and euphoria generated by the return to peace, in which the Charter was framed, to understand the widespread acceptance it gained, with the exception of a few adherents of the old régime who refused to accept the principle of a written constitution. Furthermore, as Barante shrewdly noted, there was far less inclination to give written constitutions the importance – that 'dignity of theory' – they were later accorded. 'It appeared to everybody simply a formality required by circumstances, and not destined to outlive them long.'[3] There was also little familiarity with modern parliamentary mechanisms, those 'institutions so successfully worked out by a neighbouring people' in Talleyrand's words.[4] Their workings in England were often cited, but rarely analysed in great detail. Hence, following the example of the senatorial constitution, the principle of two chambers was adopted, because it seemed self-evident, like 'the air one breathes'. 'One could say that at certain moments, there are some ideas that spread like epidemics', commented the baron de Vitrolles.[5] Many royalists were satisfied that the Charter had been freely conceded by the king, since this preserved the essence of his prerogative, while liberals approved it because it recognized, especially in the first section of the text concerning the 'public law of the French', the gains of the Revolution. It was in this sense that Guizot speaks of the Charter as 'a peace treaty after a long war, a series of new articles added, by common accord, to the original pact between nation and king'.[6]

But was this the intention of its chief author, Louis XVIII? The idea of transaction and common accord presupposes a negotiation, which was far from the case. As we have seen, during his interminable exile Louis XVIII never renounced the 'dignity' which flowed naturally from his dynastic and hereditary rights. Even before leaving London for Paris in April 1814, he had no intention of having his policy dictated to him. In the light of the monarchical tradition, divine right and 'ancient constitution of the kingdom' to which he was the heir, it was clear that he would reject the idea of imprisoning himself within a constitution written in Paris by a commission of the old imperial senate, which Talleyrand shrewdly described as 'a slip-knot'. He must have remembered the example of his brother Louis XVI, reduced by the constitution of 1791 to the rank of 'first official of the nation'. In a letter to his cousin Ferdinand VII of Spain, he later explained that he had refused to become king 'by the grace of the senate' and had instead preferred to concede a constitution to his peoples himself because this was 'the spirit of the age' and that it was better 'to give it rather than receive it'.[7] Rivarol was right to say that 'if one wants to avoid a revolution, it is better to plan and carry it out oneself'.

On 2 April, the conservative senate, illegally convoked by Talleyrand, voted to depose Napoleon and his family. On the sixth, it published a liberal constitution whose second article freely called to the French throne 'Louis-Stanislas-Xavier, brother of the last king, and after him the other members of the House of Bourbon, in the traditional order'. Napoleon was removed from power for having 'violated the social pact'. For the senators, this was a continuous chain that stretched from the constitution of 1791 to the consular and imperial constitutions of the years VIII, X and XII. In this sense the deposition of Napoleon is very similar to that of James II in 1688, during the English 'Glorious Revolution'. Also in this sense, the ephemeral senatorial constitution of 6 April was a way for the senators to revive the sacrosanct 'national and constitutional pact'.

In just a few days, all of this was brushed aside. By rejecting the senatorial constitution, Louis was in a way committing an act of usurpation – against the nation but also, more surprisingly, against the old monarchy itself. At the time, the word usurpation was used to refer to Bonaparte, but it quickly rebounded on his successor. In the absolutist logic of the most diehard royalists, Louis XVIII did not have the right to make himself into a constituent power, a power that the partisans of absolute monarchy regarded as a monstrous offspring of the Revolution, an attack on divine right and a Pandora's box of disorder.[8] Nonetheless, shortly after arriving in France and on the eve of entering Paris, Louis signed the declaration of Saint-Ouen in which, while accepting the bases of the senatorial constitution, he judged it 'precipitate', refused to recognize it as 'the fundamental law of the state', and promised in its place 'a liberal constitution ... carefully thought through'. This would emanate entirely from him and simply be 'put before the chambers'.[9] In this way Louis XVIII embarked on a form of 'royal revolution' rather similar to that which his brother Louis XVI had attempted unsuccessfully in May 1789. Far more than a return to the past, a transitional text or the expression of some transaction, the Charter here appears what one might term a *genuine reformulation of the old monarchical absolutism*.

On 6 May, Louis appointed three commissioners. These were the abbé de Montesquiou, agent general of the clergy in 1785, who had worked for one of his spy networks in Paris during the Consulate, joined the provisional government in April 1814 and was currently minister of the interior, comte Ferrand, who had previously served in the émigré army of the prince de Condé and was now minister of state and director of the post office, and comte Beugnot, a former deputy to the legislative assembly, prefect under the Consulate and councillor of state under the Empire, who was now director-general of the police. Dambray, the chancellor and keeper of the seals, headed the royal commission. Leaving aside their differing trajectories under the Consulate and Empire, it is striking, and hardly coincidental, that all sprang from the world of the *parlements* of the old régime. Dambray, the son-in-law of Barentin, the chancellor of France in 1789, had been successively advocate general of the *cour des aides* and then of the *parlement* of Paris, Ferrand a councillor in the *chambre des enquêtes* of the *parlements* of Rouen and then Paris and Beugnot, who in contrast to the other two came not from the robe nobility but from the office-holding bourgeoisie, had been an apprentice lawyer, also at the *parlement* of Paris. In this light one can assume that all three knew intimately the juridical corpus of the *ordonnances* and royal edicts of the old monarchy. All, with the possible exception of Beugnot, were equally careful to preserve the monarchy's old parliamentary traditions, described by Ferrand in his speech before the Charter's reading on 4 June, as 'salutary checks and balances which, under different names, have always existed in our constitution'. These 'checks and balances', he went on to emphasize, made the royal authority 'a power which always protects but never oppresses'.[10] This, as we shall see, was significant, as were also the old family and *parlementaire* rivalries that divided them, most obviously that between Dambray and Ferrand, who was furious that the former had been preferred to him as chancellor.[11]

On 18 May Louis appointed eighteen legislators chosen by Ferrand and Sémonville, another member of the senate, and drawn equally from the legislative body and senate of the Empire, to discuss the articles of the proposed Charter on the basis of a first draft drawn up by the abbé de Montesquiou and approved by the king. Little is known of these discussions, which only lasted a few days, from 22 to 28 May 1814, apart from the accounts given by Beugnot and Ferrand in their memoirs, and by the future ultra-royalist deputy Clausel de Coussergues in 1830.[12] However, Ferrand and Beugnot both insist that every time the commission departed from the original draft and proposed new articles, particularly if these concerned the royal prerogative, Louis was consulted by the commissioners and decided the issue himself. His manuscript corrections in the margins of some articles in a first version of the text confirm this.[13] Seventy-six articles were drawn up, divided into eight sections; there was no time to add the planned articles regulating future elections to the Chamber of Deputies, which were postponed until the next legislature. Since the king was determined that the Charter be enacted in the presence of the allied monarchs with whom he had just signed the Treaty of Paris and who were on the point of departure, the royal session scheduled for 10 June was brought forward to the fourth.

On 2 June, Louis ordered Fontanes, the former grand master of the imperial university, to draft a preamble to the Charter, but this was judged too literary and was passed to Beugnot who completed it in just a few hours, during the night of 3–4 June, with the help of the general secretary of the police department, Victor Alexandre Masson. In 1808, Masson had been Beugnot's subordinate as secretary general of finance of the grand duchy of Berg, then chief of the funding department of the police ministry. That a specialist in public finance should have collaborated in drafting the juridical and political basis of the future constitutional charter of 1814 is not the least of its paradoxes. There are other even more astonishing ones. Beugnot relates in his memoirs that when he presented his text to the king on the morning of 4 June Louis, concerned not to be late for the session at the Palais-Bourbon and glancing at the clock, decided there was no time to read it. 'Might I observe to the king,' Beugnot ventured, 'that the preamble to the Charter is new and should be submitted for his approval?' 'Yes', replied Louis, 'but we have confidence in you, and I know that you're a past master at this sort of thing.'[14]

Beugnot was certainly a past master at the art of improvisation. Talleyrand had already asked him to compose, for insertion into *Le Moniteur*, the banal speech that the comte d'Artois, Louis XVIII's brother, had made on his entry into Paris on 13 April. It was he who came up with the famous phrase prepared for the prince: 'No more divisions; peace; finally, I am seeing France again, and nothing has changed, except that there is now one more Frenchman!'[15] Apart from his juridical knowledge and experience of the upper echelons of the imperial administration, Beugnot had a reputation for wit. He was also credited with great pragmatism, which is significant in view of subsequent events. Since the Revolution, he had served each succeeding regime without demur, changing his views markedly in the process, particularly on the religious question, all the while fulfilling his duties with unvarying enthusiasm.[16] 'He had a flexible backbone', recalled the duc de Broglie in his memoirs. 'In a word, he belonged to the tribe of civil servants.'[17] Vitrolles, who was secretary of state of the first ministry of the restoration and dealt with him often, added: 'Never did anyone so tall manage to bow so deeply.'[18] It is however clear that the broad outlines of the preamble had been discussed previously by the king and the commissioners.

The first question raised during the Charter's drafting was how it should be promulgated. Should it be formally debated and by whom, or would a simple public declaration by the king to the French nation suffice? On this point, the royal commissioners were divided. Ferrand, rightly questioning the representative legitimacy of the former imperial legislatures, insisted that the text be submitted to electoral assemblies. For the others, any discussion with representatives of the nation was unacceptable. Ultimately, it was the opinion of chancellor Dambray backed by Beugnot that prevailed. The report submitted to the king on 2 June, which certainly echoed Louis XVIII's views, is very clear on this point.[19] If the electoral assemblies or the two imperial chambers were permitted to discuss the text, this would amount to recognizing that their authority pre-dated Louis'. But the Charter emanated from the king. For Beugnot, the idea of a joint session of the two imperial chambers convoked at the Palais-Bourbon to debate the text was nonsensical. The nation certainly needed to be represented in some form or other, but this could only be passively. The king, not the nation, was sovereign, and it was he who freely granted it its rights. Hence the only possible method of promulgating the Charter, which clearly stated the precedence of royal sovereignty over that of the nation was that of concession. Beugnot stated this succinctly in his report: '[This] plan has the rare merit of absorbing the revolution in the monarchy; all the arguments against it and which would allow the senate or the legislative body a deliberative role would in contrast absorb the monarchy in the revolution.'

The essence of the text of 4 June 1814 lies at the end of the preamble, in its conclusion, which revived the formula of the old royal *ordonnances*: 'For these reasons, voluntarily and by the free exercise of our royal authority, we have granted and grant to our subjects, on behalf of our successors and ourselves, the following constitutional Charter.' Beugnot insists clearly and repeatedly in the preamble upon the 'rights' and 'prerogatives' of the crown. The source of the Charter was the king's will alone. Speaking of 'his' peoples, Louis XVIII stated: 'We have hoped that, instructed by experience, [they] will be convinced that only the supreme authority can give the institutions which it creates the force, permanence and majesty with which it is itself endowed.' On this point, there was complete agreement between the king and the commissioners.[20] The thesis of royal sovereignty was thus fully reaffirmed. 'Supreme authority' rested with the king. Sovereignty and legitimacy were one and the same thing.

The very term 'Charter' used in the preamble, in preference to 'Ordinance of Reformation' and in the opposite sense to 'Constitutional Act', reinforces the theme of concession. Here again, Beugnot is the best guide. The word, taken once more from the old vocabulary of the monarchy, clearly reflects the idea of a new institution, and not a simple reform of abuses, implemented by the will of the sovereign.[21] This is thus a constitutional charter, rather than a constitution harking back to the Revolution and to the concept of a contract between king and nation.

But what was the basis of the royal sovereignty described in the text? Once again, one must read the preamble and note its silences. Neither hereditary nor divine right is mentioned explicitly. Nothing is said of the fundamental laws of the monarchy, its hereditary principle, its rules of succession or its transmission from male to male in order of primogeniture. There is also nothing on the ultimate origin of royal sovereignty, which is only mentioned once and in passing at the beginning of the preamble, when the king invokes 'divine providence' to explain his return to his kingdom. There is a similar silence in the body of the Charter and in the second section concerning the 'forms of the king's government'. In this area, Stéphane Rials writes of the 'incompleteness of the Charter'.[22] The Charter is presented not as an all-embracing constitution and sole repository of the supreme law, but as a sort of additional act to the pre-existing fundamental laws of the old monarchy, a logical mechanism since Napoleon was to imitate it during the Hundred Days.[23] As the abbé de Montesquiou warned during the first meeting of the commission drawing up the Charter, it would be dangerous to bring up the origins of royal power. To discuss a 'principle whose roots lie in the distant past' would in a sense be to 'put it back into question'. That was self-evident. The same applied to divine right. To explain what was obvious and sacred would be to weaken it in equal measure. It would probably also give rise to endless polemics. It was better not to speak of what could provoke anger, just twenty-five years after the Revolution. This was what Faget de Baure argued on 22 May: 'One should not carelessly rake over the origins of peoples and kings, since there are sacred monuments that must not be touched.'[24] Indirect reference to the divine origin of royal power is made in article 74 of the Charter which connects it to the 'solemnity of [the] coronation'. Yet the purpose here is to remind the king that he is taking his oath to the Charter before God. This is a further paradox, and by no means a minor one. How does one accept the rights of man, or any positive right, in the context of the immanence and transcendence of God of whom one is the representative on earth, crowned as the 'lord's anointed'? This fiction, nonetheless, is maintained.

Significantly, all the official portraits of the time show Louis XVIII in his coronation robes – even though ultimately he was never crowned – clothed in the great robe with its fleur-de-lys and equipped with the attributes of his divine power: the sceptre, the hand of justice and the closed crown. It would be the same with his brother and successor, Charles X.[25]

In contrast, the preamble to the Charter constantly invokes the historic rights of the crown. Here Louis deliberately placed himself in the ancient traditions of the monarchy. He invoked in turn 'the kings, our predecessors' and 'the venerable monuments of past centuries', while emphasizing their continuing adaptation 'to changing times' and to 'the people's wishes'. In this context, the Charter is at once a new institution and the product of an ancient heritage, from the first communal liberties conceded by the Capetians in the twelfth century to the legislative and administrative construction of the kingdom under the Valois and the Bourbons. No-one at the time seems to have noticed the strange paradox of this brief historical résumé of ten centuries at the heart of the preamble. It begins by recalling the Fields of March and May of the first Frankish and Carolingian kings, the communal charters of Louis VI, Louis IX and Philip the Fair, and ends with the chambers of the Third Estate of the Estates General convoked under the Valois, those chambers 'which have so often given at once proofs of their zeal for the people, of their fidelity, and of their respect for the royal authority'. The Estates General of Tours in 1484, during the minority of Charles VIII, and Philippe Pot's opening speech about the political rights of the people as the Third Estate sat as an order for the first time, are not explicitly mentioned, but everybody must have had them in mind.

The preamble moves on to the great royal administrative reforms of Louis XI through to those of Louis XIV, building up the royal authority. The choice of rulers mentioned in this short passage, Henri II, Charles IX and especially Louis XIV, leaves no doubt about the author's intentions. Only their names are invoked, but the ordinances with which they are naturally associated are clearly present in the subtext: that of 1467, by which Louis XI made permanent the offices of the royal administration, those of 1551 and 1566 (the ordinance of Moulins), and especially those of 1665 and 1673, by which the French monarchs unified the kingdom's judicial system as they reduced the powers of the *parlements*. This particularly applies to Charles IX's ordinance of 1566 and Louis XIV's of 1673, which limited the *parlements*' powers of remonstrance, while the ordinance of 1665 had deprived them of the title of 'sovereign courts'.

This reminder of how the monarchical state was built legitimized and reinforced the sovereign's dynastic rights. 'Our first duty towards our peoples is to preserve the rights and prerogatives of our crown.' As the comte de Jaucourt shrewdly wrote to Talleyrand a little later, during the Hundred Days, just as to many Napoleon appeared to have been elected – not least by plebiscite – the king was attempting to escape the control of the nation and speaking too often of his own rights. He was not, as a captain of the former imperial army wittily observed, 'the manager of a large public property'.[26] All this, concluded Jaucourt, 'shocks and repels'.[27]

It is clear that, in Jaucourt's eyes, the Charter was not the result of any pact between the king and the nation's representatives. Louis XVIII considered himself neither enthroned nor restored in 1814. He was and remained king from the moment the dynastic laws of the house of Bourbon made him so. His sovereignty pre-dated all others, that of the people as well as that of the nation. His sovereignty existed wherever he himself resided, whether in France or abroad. Because his sovereignty merged with his legitimacy, he had been king during his exile and was to be so again in Ghent during the Hundred Days.

Arriving at this point required resort to a fiction, that of monarchical continuity, and this could only be achieved by sleight of hand, since the great omission of the Charter's preamble was obviously the Revolution. When this is invoked, it is always indirectly, sketchily and negatively. 'Important alterations' during the previous half-century, or 'fatal errors', are successively mentioned, and a political lesson drawn from them: 'When violence extorts concessions from a weak government, public liberty is endangered as much as the throne.' In the more recent past, the preamble does briefly refer to 'the ever-increasing progress of enlightenment' and 'the changes that this progress has made to society'. But the liberties of the kingdom predate these developments and are never associated with the Revolution. Everything is linked. The legislative chambers created by the Charter are emanations from the monarchy's ancient past. The lower chamber derives from that of the Third Estate; the upper from the ancient peerage of France, from the great vassals of the crown under the Capetians, and then beginning in the sixteenth century from the dukes and peers of the Valois era. The aim is to reconcile 'the past and the present', to 're-forge the chain of time', as if the Revolution was merely a parenthesis in the historical continuity of monarchy. It was thus logical to date the preamble from 'the year of grace 1814', and the declaration of Saint-Ouen from the 'nineteenth year' of Louis XVIII's reign. These 'nineteen years' were seized on by cartoonists who depicted the king leafing through the first – blank – eighteen years of his rule. This mattered little. 'The dead invest the living. The king is dead, long live the king!' The reign of Monsieur, comte de Provence begins in 1795, with the official news of the death of his young nephew Louis XVII, the son of Louis XVI, as if the Revolution, the Republic and the Empire had never existed.

In the same logic, this reinvented continuity necessitated contortions of memory. While the monarchy's past was to be remembered, that of the Revolution was to be forgotten. The king's sovereignty as well as his legitimacy depended on this. Wisdom, politics and prudence also dictated it. 'We have effaced from our memory, as we would wish to efface from history, all the evils that have afflicted our country during our absence.' And in the same vein: 'The dearest wish of our heart is that all Frenchmen should live as brothers, and that no bitter memory should ever trouble the security that should follow the solemn law that we grant them today.' Here Louis placed himself in another monarchical tradition, that of the great edicts of pacification aimed at ending civil and religious war. Particularly relevant here was the edict of Nantes signed by Henri IV in 1598 after nearly forty years of warfare between Catholics and Protestants. The edict's first article expressly demands that 'the memory of everything past ... remain extinguished and suppressed as if it had never happened'.[28] At the time people did not speak of *oubli* (forgetting) but of *oubliance*. In 1814 as in 1598, national reconciliation, the revival of the 'great family' of the French could not be imagined without a profound process of amnesia. To each his *damnatio memoriae*. In 1793, the

Convention's representatives on mission had tried to expunge the memory of the monarchy. In 1814, it was the Revolution's turn to be expunged. A great aberration, an eminently French paradox, had been brought to an end.

In this way, and thanks to this exercise in selective memory, the rights of the king, announced in the preamble, could clearly be spelt out in the Charter's main text. His person was inviolable and sacred. To him alone belonged the executive power (art. 13). He was the supreme head of state, commander-in-chief of the armed forces, he declared war and directed diplomacy. He proposed, sanctioned and promulgated the law (art. 16 and 22). From him emanated all justice (art. 57). He could also draw up the regulations and ordinances 'necessary for the execution of the laws and the security of the state'. This was the thrust of article 14, which would end by overthrowing the elder branch of the Bourbons in 1830, when Louis XVIII's younger brother, in Lamartine's words 'breaking his oath in good faith',[29] mistook a simple regulatory power for a temporary dictatorial one, and felt empowered to suspend the Charter faced with the opposition of the Chamber of Deputies.[30] If one only reads this section of the Charter, the king, far from being the 'neutral power' in which Benjamin Constant, despite launching the concept in May 1814, only half believed, concentrated in his person the executive, legislative and judicial powers, just as he had before 1789.[31]

However, and it is here that the text's complexity resides, the rights of the monarch, 'providence' and heredity are not incompatible with the 'rights of the nation'. Louis XVIII knew how to make concessions at the moment when, from a position of strength, he did not feel these were being extracted by force. He was just as ready to amend his royal prerogative, as long as this remained preponderant. Firm on principles and on what he considered essential, he knew, as a pragmatic realist, a child of the Enlightenment and a shrewd politician, how to adapt to necessity and circumstance. As such, he both confirmed and resolved the theory of Ranke, in whose *Essay on the French Restoration* all restorations are confronted by the difficulty of reconciling the recent and the ancient past. Pasquier describes the king, perhaps a little too enthusiastically, as 'a liberal, accepting the necessities of the time' and 'a sincere supporter of parliamentary government'.[32] To Lainé, the president of the Chamber, Louis appeared in the last months of 1814 as a crucial defender of liberty in the face of all the advocates of the old régime who were using him to criticize his government: 'The French don't know me, they don't know that I'm more attached than anyone to the Charter I've given them, that in my eyes it is the palladium of the monarchy'.[33] The king's use of the word 'palladium' is revealing. In this sense, the Charter was the safeguard of the monarchy. The Charter's purpose in his eyes was to absorb the Revolution into the monarchy and not, naturally, to dissolve the monarchy in the Revolution. The king's favourite and minister of police Decazes encapsulated this in the aphorism that opened his important speech of 15 December 1817 to the Chamber of Deputies: 'Monarchize the nation, nationalize the monarchy...'

Following this basic principle, Louis XVIII, king by right, accepted limits to his sovereignty, shared legislative power with two chambers on the English model – one elected on a property franchise and the other nominated, initially for life: the Chamber of Deputies and the Chamber of Peers – and accorded them indirect initiative in legislation (art. 19 and 20). He even agreed to go further than the constitution required in recognizing the powers of parliament, beginning with the presentation of the first proposed budgetary law of his reign in July 1814. He authorized the chambers to discuss not only the tax revenues, as the constitution allowed, but also government expenditure ministry by ministry, of which the constitution said nothing. Historically, the budget of 1815 is the first 'modern' French budget. Furthermore, after the Hundred Days, the king's powers would be substantially revised and limited by a whole series of constitutional ordinances, from the creation of a unified ministry on 9 July to the reorganization of the Council of State on 23 August. But the concessions stopped there. Even during the most liberal period of the restoration, the principle of ministerial responsibility to the chambers, only just conceived, and still imperfectly, by Benjamin Constant, was far from being accepted. In a famous speech to the Chamber of Deputies of 3 January 1816, Elie Decazes limited the role of ministers to that of first secretaries of a king who alone decided policy and who charged them solely with its execution. 'The Charter does not permit minsters to present any draft law except in the king's name; not only is this their function, but their duty; they can propose nothing in their own names, and if they are responsible, it is simply for the execution of laws that they have proposed in the king's name.'

If in 1814 Louis tacitly agreed to amend his legislative powers, this did not make his régime a parliamentary one, but rather one that could be termed, following Stéphane Rials, a 'limited monarchy' tempered by the chambers. It was not this that most impressed contemporaries, but instead the Charter's acceptance of the Revolution's principal social achievements.

Despite never being mentioned in the preamble, the Revolution, with its juridical, political and social conquests, was nonetheless present almost in its entirety. By the same token the old régime, with its orders and privileges, disappeared a second time in a puff of smoke. The 'public rights of Frenchmen', somewhat neglected since 1789 and never evoked in the constitutions of the Empire, came right at the beginning of the text: equality before the law (art. 1), of taxation (art. 2), eligibility for public office (art. 3), and justice (art. 62), liberty of the individual, of assembly and of the press, even if 'laws to repress the abuse of this liberty' were mentioned (art. 8), religious freedom, even if Catholicism remained the official religion in accordance with the royal ordinance of 1685 (art. 5 and 6), inviolability of property, including that termed 'national' and resulting from the sale of church and noble lands during the Revolution (art. 9), the introduction of juries (art. 65) and the immovability of judges (art. 58) and last but by no means least, the Napoleonic civil code (art. 68).

Louis also took the very shrewd decision to restore certain liberties trampled underfoot by Napoleon. Conscription was abolished (art. 12) and confiscations declared illegal (art. 66). The public debt was also guaranteed (art. 70), which had previously been far from the case, and meant that the Empire's creditors would be paid. Finally, nobody could be disturbed on account of their previous opinions or votes.

From this point of view, the Charter inaugurated a regime that was without doubt the most liberal and tolerant in Europe at the time. Even in England, Catholics still had no political rights and in London it would have been unthinkable to make a Catholic a minister, in the way Protestants like Guizot, Portal and Jaucourt soon would be in Paris. This fact can never sufficiently be underlined. These advances in themselves were a small revolution. As Mme de Staël emphasized, writing of the first restoration, 'no confiscations, no exiles, no illegal arrests took place for ten months: what progress after fifteen years of tyranny! England had barely achieved this noble and happy state thirty years after the death of Cromwell.'[34]

It is equally true that the monarch's sovereign power emerged strengthened from this constitutional test, especially in comparison to that which the constitution of 1791 had assigned his brother. In 1791, it was the national assembly that had dominated and held sole legal power in the sacrosanct name of separation of powers. The royal veto grudgingly voted was simply a poultice applied to a wooden leg, and a dangerous remedy to boot. As to executive power, Louis XVI had lost all control over an administration which depended at all levels on election. In contrast, in 1814 the king inherited all the administrative centralization of the Consulate and Empire. Fouché commented drolly that the king had been happy to sleep in Napoleon's bed.[35] Prefects were a useful instrument for the exercise of power. On this level, the Revolution and Consulate completed what the monarchy had failed to do faced by the resistance of the intermediary bodies – social groups, provinces and towns – buttressed by the famous ancient 'liberties' of the kingdom: the dream of a rational, uniform and centralized administration, entirely under the government's control and solidly established on the ruins of the old orders, privileges, rights, customs, franchises and liberties of all kinds. Considering that the job of administration is to impose the 'will of the state' based on the constitution, the dilemma resulting from the Charter's complete silence about this Bonapartist element becomes acute. In the eyes of the king, this element had the merit of existing, and no more. When the nobility of Toulouse welcomed his nephew the duc d'Angoulême in April 1814, praising the merits of the former Estates of Languedoc, Angoulême replied to his stupefied audience that he much preferred the new departments to the old provinces.[36]

Among the émigrés who had left the country at the beginning of the Revolution and had just returned, the most lucid, such as the highly competent duc de Richelieu who had governed the southern provinces of the Russian empire for the Czar, could hardly fail to notice the changes operated by the Revolution in the French administrative machine: 'The bureaucracy is ten times worse than in Russia. The various ministries receive over ten thousand letters a day. I haven't yet seen anybody who doesn't think themselves capable of filling any administrative post as long as it is lucrative, and almost all of them are.'[37] The administration was so powerful that it had become the Garden of Eden for everyone who wished to get on, which was difficult since the king had noted its effectiveness and only changed very few civil servants in 1814, on the wise principle that the competent, disciplined men miraculously trained up by the 'usurper' should not be dislodged. Thanks to the king, the same governing class stayed in power, happily jumping, in the picturesque phrase of Benjamin Constant, 'onto another branch'. Only a few regicides, who were not otherwise disturbed, were discreetly shifted from their imperial functions (Chamber of Peers, *académie française*, *conseil d'État*, court of appeal). No political change has ever been as mild as that of the first restoration.

To take just one example, that of the prefectoral corps, of 43 new prefects appointed, 31 were former imperial prefects or sub-prefects who had been moved or promoted.[38]

The old régime's share was just seven former émigrés and two ultra-royalists.[39] When during the Hundred Days (14 April 1815) Napoleon gave the order to compile a list of all former émigrés who had been favoured for administrative jobs, this proved extremely disappointing. Of the 147 sub-prefects and *secrétaires généraux* appointed, promoted or moved under the first restoration, only 25 former émigrés were found. It was the same for the judges who, apart from those appointed during the first restoration, had very largely remained in place.

Beyond the very specific situation which he inherited, Louis followed the example of Louis XIV in deciding that he would be better served by the representatives of a successful bourgeoisie dependent on the government for what fortune it still had to make than by 'his' old nobility, less ruined by the Revolution than generally thought and which he distrusted for the independent and *frondeur* traditions it had displayed in the years before the Revolution. His verdict on the nobility in his *Commentaries on the grievances of the nobility of Poitou to the estates general of 1789*, accusing it of deep hostility to the royal prerogative, is unanswerable: 'How can a nobility which degrades the crown and breaks the sceptre of its king complain when the bourgeois deprive it of its titles and prerogatives? Can those who have respected neither the throne nor the altar demand respect from their inferiors?'[40] It was a case of the biter bit. Louis' aversion for the kingdom's second order goes a long way towards explaining the dislike, even hate, he aroused in the most extreme royalist circles. The king only made two exceptions to this rule, for his court and his household guards.

Unsurprisingly, it was these ultra-royalists who led the assault. They first attacked the personnel, then swiftly moved on to the substance of the new institutions. Joseph Fiévée, for example, regretted in his *Correspondance politique et administrative* that the Revolution had 'dispersed the [intermediary] bodies of the state, the corporations, the institutions'. It had left nothing in the land 'but isolated individuals'. In Fiévée's view, liberties were not simply the business of the chambers. 'Should we be building an edifice with no foundations?', he asked. 'Sooner or later the sovereign power will be destroyed in its fall ...' Fiévée also championed the old, independent and hereditary municipal and provincial bodies which he considered 'the foundation-stones of monarchical liberties'.[41] All the rancour of those royalists who harked back to an increasingly idealized old régime is encapsulated in a reflection of the deeply ultra baron de Frénilly on the king's return: 'I never thought there would be any contradiction between restoring the legitimacy of persons (the Bourbons) and the legitimacy of things, between replanting a dynasty and replanting the old institutions ... What a blockhead I was!'

The monarch's new position of strength was thus based on the new state structures inherited from the Revolution and Empire and equally, if not more, on the character of the king himself, whose ambition and taste for power are an established fact. Paradoxically, it was the very fact that the Revolution had put the king in such a strong position that made the 'reconciliation' of 1814 possible. This made it possible to forget the successive failure of the reforms attempted by Louis XVI in 1774–5, 1787–8 and 1789, while completing their work. The personality of Louis XVI's brother counted for a great deal in this fragile success, which furthermore was swiftly subjected to the political and social shock of the Hundred Days. For this reconciliation rested not only on the coexistence of the king's rights and those of the people, it was forced to survive in the difficult context of a country where traditionally the law was valued more than rights, and principles more than practice.

The question of sovereignty in particular was to poison debate because of its conceptual power and the brutality of its displacement at the beginning of the Revolution. In 1789, sovereignty had been neither shared nor limited, but had been conquered by force by the Third Estate deputies to the Estates General. The very power with which the absolute monarchy had endowed it, and the conditions of its transfer, ensured that for many years it retained a greater symbolic and theoretical force than in any other European state. After 1789, no middle way between the sovereignty of the king and that of the people was possible in France.

In conclusion, as already emphasized, reconciliation entailed forgetting the Revolution. It was by respecting this voluntary process of forgetting that the restoration of the Orange dynasty was consolidated and perpetuated after 1815 in the Netherlands. However, in order to forget one must also forgive. 'Forgetting' and 'forgiveness' cannot exist without each other. From the first, the restored regime announced 'pardon'. In his brief speech before the reading of the preamble, Louis explicitly invoked the testament in which his brother had pardoned his 'enemies'. 'It is with eyes fixed on this immortal work, and imbued with the sentiments that dictated it ... that I have drawn up the constitutional Charter which you are about to hear.'[42] The testament written by Louis XVI in the Temple on 25 December 1792, in the middle of his trial, would be reissued at least thirty times up to the end of the restoration. It became the keystone and foundation of the regime. And indeed, article 11 of the Charter did stipulate that nobody should be disturbed on account of their opinions or previous votes.

Yet the pardon and forgetting prescribed by a monarchy which by this act took on a quasi-sacrificial dimension, was necessarily reinforced by the memory of the martyr-king. It was here that the ambiguity of this pardon became clear. From the start of his reign, Louis XVIII sometimes encouraged and generally allowed his most extreme supporters to celebrate their 'martyrs' and to develop a policy of 'expiation' of the 'crimes' of the Revolution, which threatened to envelop his regime in a cloud of funeral incense unbearable to anybody who had participated in or benefited from the upheaval of 1789.[43] The official reburial of the bones of Louis XVI and Marie Antoinette at the basilica of St Denis on 21 January 1815 was the key moment in this process. The regicide of 21 January 1793 had been forgotten by nobody. Then, after the trauma of Napoleon's return in March 1815, the focus shifted imperceptibly from regicide to the regicides themselves. In the royalist rhetoric which accompanied the discussion of the draft amnesty law for those involved in the Hundred Days, the regicides, in La Bourdonnaye's words those 'monsters ... stained with the blood of their king', stood as twice guilty: 'parricides' in 1793, criminals in 1815. They no longer deserved what was primly termed the 'benevolence' of the king. As a result, approximately two hundred ex-deputies to the Convention were exiled from the kingdom for life by the law of 12 January 1816, while another law of 19 January made 21 January an obligatory day of mourning for Louis XVI. As Chateaubriand rightly remarked, after the Hundred Days 'regicide' became the central issue of the régime. Thus, very swiftly, the Revolution it wanted so much to forget re-emerged everywhere, underlying every speech and debate, attacked by one side, defended by the other.[44]

The climate rather than the actual laws created by the régime, especially the freedom of expression it granted and the powerful revolutionary memories this revived, became an apple of discord, profoundly dividing the 'old' from the 'new' France. If Louis XVIII had carefully managed the practicalities of his restoration, he had not sufficiently appreciated its symbolic aspects, always so important in France. Thus, the spirit of reconciliation of June 1814, reflected by his own personality as much as by the country's desire for peace, did not survive him.

Time, and the reinterpretations of history, have served this spirit little better. By making the present disappear in favour of the past, the Charter in some sense summoned up the magic of a fairy story. To my knowledge, no other French constitutional text is based so little on contemporary circumstances. One cannot retreat into the past with impunity. A last look at the Charter's preamble reveals the dangers of this trap. Its words are exclusively concerned with the monarchy's past. Its main theme is history, and this could be interpreted in any number of ways over the course of the nineteenth century. By emphasizing fidelity to 'the old conception of the kingdom', Louis XVIII confused rather than clarified matters. One searches the Charter in vain for a definition of royal power adapted to the era in which it was written. As Pierre Rosanvallon puts it so well: 'The reference to monarchical tradition was a means of avoiding a definition of constitutional monarchy.'[45] But what past was being evoked, that of the construction of royal power, or of the birth of liberties; the domination of the two privileged orders of the kingdom, or the growth in power of the Third Estate? As Guizot put it, these differing interpretations swiftly created 'conquered' and 'conquerors', a 'king' and a 'nation'. This made the resulting divisions all the more profound.

By allying with those 'conquered' by the Revolution from the early 1820s, and by overtly opposing the nation from 1829, the royal authority eventually dissipated all the ambiguities surrounding its founding Charter. In the last years of the restoration, these ambiguities were transformed into absolute incompatibilities. From that point on, the text of the Charter itself became the point at issue. For the liberals, its concession was no longer anything more than one moment in a vast process of national adhesion to the Charter that made it essentially a contract. In their view, the Charter now belonged to the nation much more than to the king. For their royalist adversaries, on the other hand, the essence of the Charter lay solely in its concession.[46] It was 'a gift of the monarchy, the sole source of French liberties', a pure 'concession of the royal authority', explained the ultra deputy Félix de Conny to the chamber on 15 March 1830. The monarch could just as easily therefore withdraw it from the nation.[47] It was here that article 14, permitting the king to make ordinances for the safety of the state, intervened. What resulted from this, and how the conflict ended in the revolution of July 1830, is well known.

Yet ambiguities, for as long as they last, have the merit of nourishing controversies and enriching debates. They were particularly dense, original and numerous between 1814 and 1830. Imperfect as it was, the Charter of 1814 profoundly and durably marked the country's institutional, political and social experience.

Translation by Prof. Munro Price

Notes

1. The Charter has of course been analysed on several occasions by Paul Bastid, *Les institutions politiques de la monarchie parlementaire* (1954); Jacques Godechot, *Les constitutions de la France depuis 1789* (1979); Stéphane Rials, *Révolution et contre-révolution au XIXe siècle* (Paris: Albatros, 1987) and Pierre Rosanvallon, *La monarchie impossible. Les chartes de 1814 et 1830* (1994), to cite only the best-known twentieth-century historians. See also the very iconoclastic argument of Volker Sellin: *Die geraubte Revolution. Der Sturz Napoleons und die Restauration in Europa* (2001).
2. Letter of Louis XVIII to his brother, 29 January 1818, cited by Ernest Daudet, in *Louis XVIII et le duc Decazes, 1815-1820* (Paris, 1899), 259.
3. *Souvenirs du baron de Barante* (Paris, 1898), vol. 3, 39.
4. Talleyrand's speech presenting the Senate delegation to the king at Saint-Ouen, 2 May 1814, in *Mémoires et correspondances de Talleyrand* (Paris, 2007), 433.
5. *Mémoires du baron de Vitrolles* (Paris, 1884), vol. 3, 238.
6. François Guizot, *Mémoires pour servir à l'histoire de mon temps*, vol. 1, 34.
7. Cited by Philip Mansel in *Louis XVIII* (Paris, 1982), 192.
8. Villèle writes in his memoirs, written after the 1830 revolution, of 'the usurpation of the constituent power by the monarchy', which only served to 'prepare new usurpations for the future, through riots, assemblies and provisional governments ...' (vol. 1, 251–2). See also marquis de Villeneuve, *De l'agonie de la France ...* (Périsse frères, 1839), vol. 2, 378: 'Louis XVIII and his Charter were everywhere like an insatiable force of usurpation ...'; the usurpation of property confiscated by the revolution and not restituted; usurpation of noble rights by the chamber of peers, etc. Cited by Oscar Ferreira, 'Louis XVIII dans la Charte de 1814. Prisons imaginaires', *Jus Politicum* no. 13, January 2015. The author is the only one to my knowledge to describe the Charter as the essential instrument of an inevitable transition: from the old monarchical absolutism to modern despotism.
9. On the declaration of Saint-Ouen, partly drawn up during the night of 2-3 May 1814 under the king's supervision by the baron de Vitrolles and the marquis de La Maisonfort who took all the credit for themselves, see their respective memoirs: *Mémoires et relations politiques du baron de Vitrolles* (Paris, 1884), vol. 2, 172–3 and *Mémoires d'un agent royaliste* (Paris, 1998), 222–3. See the full text of the declaration, in *Déclaration du roi Louis XVIII donnée à St-Ouen le 2 mai 1814 sur la nouvelle constitution française ... par L. Rondonneau. A Paris, mai 1814, de l'imprimerie de Doublet.*
10. Ferrand's preliminary speech is published by Pierre Rosanvallon, as an appendix to *La monarchie impossible*, op. cit., 247–9.
11. *Mémoires du comte Ferrand, ministre d'Etat sous Louis XVIII* (Paris, 1897), 68–9.
12. *Mémoires du comte Ferrand* already cited; *Mémoires du comte Beugnot* (Paris, 1868), vol. 2, 169–271; Clausel de Coussergues, *Considérations sur l'origine, la redaction, la promulgation et l'exécution de la Charte* (Paris, 15 June 1830). Clausel was also a member of the Court of Appeal.
13. See Pierre Rosanvallon, *La monarchie impossible. Les Chartes de 1814 et de 1830* (Paris, 1994). Appendix XIV: 'Correction apportées au premier projet de la Charte (projet A)', 222–5.
14. *Mémoires de Beugnot* (Paris, 1868), vol. 2, 262.
15. *Mémoires de Beugnot*, op.cit., vol. 2, 130.

16 He had defended refractory priests against the deputy Albitte in the Legislative Assembly in 1791, and pursued them at the beginning of the Consulate as prefect of Rouen, on the instructions of Fouché. See his letters to the minister of police in my *Fouché* (Paris, 2014), 351.
17 *Souvenirs du duc de Broglie* (Paris, 1886), vol. 1, 259.
18 *Mémoires du baron de Vitrolles* (Paris, 1884), vol. 1.
19 See Beugnot's report in Pierre Rosanvallon, op.cit., appendix XVIII, 241–3.
20 See *Mémoires du comte Ferrand*, op.cit., 81.
21 *Mémoires de Beugnot*, vol. 2, 250–1
22 See Stéphane Rials, *Révolution et contre-révolution*, 101.
23 The expression was used by both Bonapartists and royalists. For example, on 3 January 1825, the ultra-royalist newspaper *Le Drapeau Blanc* described the Charter as 'an additional act to the fundamental laws of the kingdom'.
24 *Mémoires de Beugnot*, vol. 2, 173. However, the declaration of Saint-Ouen opens with the traditional formula used before 1789: 'Louis, by the grace of God king of France and Navarre, to all who will see these present letters, Greetings.'
25 On the portraits of the two kings of the restoration in coronation robes, see my article 'Portraits du roi et de ses élites sous la restauration et la monarchie de juillet', *Versalia*, no. 9, 2006.
26 *Souvenirs historiques du capitaine Krettly* (Paris, 2003), 151.
27 *Correspondance du comte de Jaucourt avec le prince de Talleyrand* (Paris, 1905). Ostend, 27 March 1815, 250.
28 See on Google the text of the edict of Nantes established by the *Ecole des Chartes*, under the direction of Bernard Barbiche, under the heading 'L'édit de Nantes et ses antécédants (1562–1598).'
29 *Oeuvres de Lamartine* (Brussels, 1838). 'Sur la politique rationnelle', 382, note.
30 On the different interpretations of the article 14, see the third section of Oscar Ferreira's article 'Un dictateur dans la Charte? L'article 14 et la libération du roi', in 'Le roi dans la Charte de 1814. Prisons imaginaires', *Jus Politicum*, no. 13, January 2014.
31 Benjamin Constant, *Réflexions sur les constitutions, la distribution des pouvoirs et les guaranties dans une monarchie constitutionnelle* (Paris, [end of May] 1814.
32 *Mémoires du chancelier Pasquier* (Paris, 1893), vol. 2, chapter XX?
33 *Mémoires et journal de Jean-Pons Guillaume Viennet, 1777–1867*, ed. R. Trousson (Paris, 2007), 256.
34 Germaine de Staël, *Considérations sur la Révolution française* ed. J. Godechot (Paris, 1983), 493.
35 The witticism is cited by Taine in *Les origines de la France contemporaine* (Paris, 2011), 1402: 'It's the bed of Louis XIV, but wider and more comfortable, enlarged by the Revolution and Empire ...'
36 *Mémoirs et correspondence du comte de Villèle* (Paris, 1888), vol. 1, 248. The prefect of Nantes, Prosper de Barante, commented very shrewdly about the duc d'Angoulême, whom he welcomed to his department in July 1814: 'He did not share the old émigrés' repugnance for the imperial regime ... This equality of obedience, suppression of aristocracy, regularity of administration and command, all suited him well. A sort of instinct or confused insight told him that this was a good basis for absolute power.' *Souvenirs du baron de Barante* (Paris, 1898), vol. 2, 74–5.
37 E. de Waresquiel, *Le duc de Richelieu* (Paris, 1991), 213–14. Letters of the duc de Richelieu to his friend the abbé Nicolle in Odessa, January 1815.

38 An exhaustive list of the prefectoral changes can be found in Jean Tulard, *Les vingt jours* (Paris, 2001), 47–52.
39 There is a good study of the movement of prefects in Charles Pouthas, *Guizot pendant la restauration* (1923).
40 'Réflexions critiques écrites en 1799 par le roi Louis XVIII à l'occasion des Réflexions sur les cahiers de la noblesse du Poitou aux Etats généraux de 1789, publiées par M le chevalier de la Coudraye', in Martin d'Oisy, *Manuscrit inédit de Louis XVIII précédé d'un examen de sa vie politique jusqu'à la Charte de 1814* (Paris, 1839), 375.
41 Joseph Fiévée, *Correspondance politique et administrative* (Paris, 1815). First letter, Nevers, 21 May 1814; third letter, Nevers, 9 June 1814, 2, 13 and 91.
42 The king's speech is not reproduced in Godechot. See AP, 2e série, vol.12, 32.
43 On this subject see the very illuminating thesis of Emmanuel Fureix, 'Mort et politique à Paris sous les monarchies censitaires: mises en scène, cultes, affrontements', doctoral thesis under the direction of Alain Corbin, Paris I, December 2003.
44 'The deaths of the king and of the royal family are the real crime of the Revolution'. Chateaubriand, *De la monarchie selon la Charte* (1816). On this point, Mona Ozouf underlines the growing use of the word 'regicide' in ultra-royalist speeches during the restoration: 'Régicide, la loi électorale; regicide, la Charte; toute constution, dira un prédicateur parisien, est un regicide . . .', in 'Ballanche: l'idée et l'image du régicide', *L'homme régénéré. Essais sur la Révolution française* (Paris, 1989). See also the article of Emmanuel Fureix, 'Regards sur le(s) regicide(s). Restauration et recharge contre-révolutionnaire', in *Siècles*, 23/2006: 'Mémoires et miroirs de la Révolution française', 31–45; and my own forthcoming article, 'Joseph Fouché et la mémoire révolutionnaire'.
45 Pierre Rosanvallon, *La Monarchie impossible*, op. cit., 58. See also Oscar Ferreira's excellent article, 'Le roi dans la Charte de 1814. Prisons imaginaires', in *Jus Politicum*, no. 3, January 2015.
46 The law of 22 March 1822 made criticism of the Charter's concession a crime.
47 See the two opposing speeches of Agier and Conny to the Chamber of Deputies during the debate of 15 March 1830, cited by Pierre Rosanvallon in *La monarchie impossible*, op. cit., 97.

8

Constitutional Monarchism in Post-Napoleonic Europe

Markus J. Prutsch

Introduction

The challenges of the post-Napoleonic age were manifold, ranging from economic consolidation, via social integration to political reconciliation. An overarching concern was the legitimacy of rule and rulers; more particularly: the question how after the experiences of the Revolution the issue of 'sovereignty' could be tackled, and regimes be legitimized and put on a solid basis.[1] Perhaps the main problem in this regard was how to reconcile European princes' claims to preserve their monarchical sovereignty with post-revolutionary societies' expectations, in particular their hopes for a constitutional state. At the Congress of Vienna – and in contrast to the widespread perception of the age after 1814 as having been 'reactionary' – it was generally felt that the Spanish approach of rigid neo-absolutism was denying the *zeitgeist* and was therefore not a long-term solution.[2] In comparison, the example of the French Restoration under Louis XVIII (1755–1824), who was willing to provide constitutional guarantees in order to achieve a lasting settlement, seemed a more appropriate and reasonable solution. It therefore comes as no surprise that the Bourbon Restoration project in 1814 was, as the Revolution itself had been, an act of great importance for Europe: an act which might now serve as a key to overcoming the revolutionary epoch permanently.

The *Charte constitutionnelle* ('Constitutional Charter') played a pivotal role within this context, laying the foundations for the new regime and putting forward possible solutions to bridge the diverging aspirations of rulers and post-revolutionary societies.[3] Indeed, the new system made the monarch the dominant political power and declared him the sole holder of the *pouvoir constituant*, while at the same time restricting the sovereign by a written constitution which provided civil liberties and allowed citizens to partake in the political and legislative process. For this reason, the 'constitutional monarchism' exemplified by the French *Charte*, which might also justifiably be termed 'monarchical constitutionalism',[4] has frequently been considered to be a central model for post-Napoleonic Europe.

It is, however, worth ascertaining how far this claim holds true. With this in mind, the following questions are to be answered:

1. How far can the *Charte constitutionnelle* and the concept of 'constitutional monarchism' be claimed to have been a constitutional innovation?
2. What role did constitutional monarchism play as a model in nineteenth-century Europe?
3. What were the prospects of institutionalizing constitutional monarchism in the longer term, and how can its status be assessed within the context of European constitutional developments?

The *Charte constitutionnelle* of 1814

Wise enough to realize that 'the restoration of the ancient line can mean any thing [sic] else but the restoration of the ancient constitution of the monarchy',[5] in spring 1814 Louis XVIII managed to reinstate the Bourbon dynasty with no intention of going straight back to the *Ancien Régime*. He withstood the temptation to restore the monarchy with all its previous powers. Instead, the *Charte constitutionnelle*, which had been set up under Louis' personal direction as the new constitution of the country and was formally proclaimed on 6 May 1814, incorporated the legal achievements of the previous decades and established a modern representative system involving the French nation in the political process. In this respect, the *Charte* included many of the liberal aspirations laid down in the constitutional draft prepared by the French Senate in the wake of Napoleon's deposition, which had been intended as the legal grounds for the restoration of the Bourbon monarchy. At the same time, however, the *Charte* was based on a completely different ideology than the 'Senatorial Constitution', namely on the doctrine that the *pouvoir constituant* and all state authority resided in the person of the king, thus, at least theoretically, rejecting a separation of powers. The most obvious expression of 'monarchical sovereignty' was the way the *Charte* was enacted, namely by royal *octroi* (sanction) neither voted upon by a parliament nor confirmed by a popular plebiscite. The affirmation of the 'monarchical principle'[6] was the demarcation by which the new constitution was clearly distinguishable not only from its revolutionary predecessors, but from the English constitutional system as well. Rather, the *Charte* was in the tradition of Samuel von Pufendorf's (1632–94) panegyric for a *monarchia limitata*, which he had sharply differentiated from *res publica mixta* in *De jure naturae et gentium* (1672)[7] by resorting to Hugo Grotius's (1583–1645) concept of 'limited monarchy'.[8] For Pufendorf, the *res publica mixta* and the division of sovereign power exemplified the *res publica irregularis*. The only 'regular' polity was the *monarchia limitata*, in which the monarch was bound by certain laws and the consent of the nobles and the representatives of the nation, but still continued to embody undivided sovereignty. In point of fact, Pufendorf vehemently denounced the idea that supreme sovereignty must be crippled in a limited monarchy, even if the limits on the monarch were validated by a constitutional contract.[9]

The obvious contradiction in terms between constitutional government and the monarchical claim for undivided power manifest in the *Charte* was overcome by the distinction of *ius* and *exercitium*, that is the idea that political power is monopolized by the crown, but its execution in part left to other subordinate constitutional institutions.

While the provisions of the new constitution were nothing short of a full concession to the existing political and legal realities, at least in argumentative terms the monarch was able to keep up the appearances of constitutionalism as an act of voluntary grace and as an uncontested variation of monarchical rule. In line with this logic it was, therefore, natural that the constitution's founding fathers avoided using the term *Constitution*, with its revolutionary connotations. Instead, they sought an alternative and finally agreed upon *Charte*,[10] rooted in the language of the *Ancien Régime* and thus stressing both awareness of tradition and the fact that the new order was not a mere continuation of existing constitutional documents, but was in fact a phenomenon *sui generis*.

While the term 'constitutional monarchism' seems to squeeze two seemingly contradictory concepts together at first glance, a closer examination reveals that it is exactly this seeming contradiction which is the soul of the *système Charte*. The Constitutional Charter was created out of a necessary compromise between 'old' and 'new' France, and for that reason it ultimately served as a potential means to overcome the political fragmentation of post-Napoleonic France. Its characterization as 'a considerable regression'[11] when compared to former constitutions is therefore not quite appropriate. What is true is that the *Charte* does mark a clear backward step when considered from the point of view of democratization – especially regarding the actual number of those who received the franchise – when compared with the constitutions drawn up during the Revolution and also with the Senatorial draft of the *Charte*. But taken as a whole and given the contemporary political challenges, the *Charte* was in some aspects more 'balanced' and 'viable' than its predecessors. There can be no doubt that the crown was not only the sole holder of executive power, but also had a dominant position in the legislative process, disposing of a set of constitutional tools to exert influence on the composition and activity of the parliament as well as the judiciary.

Nevertheless, monarchical power was far from unrestricted, and despite the king's leading role, he could no longer rule devoid of parliament without violating the provisions of the constitution. Many of the royal prerogatives such as the right of initiative in the legislation and the right to dissolve the second chamber were certainly powerful, but they could not obscure the fact that every bill and every budget proposal required the approval of both chambers. Moreover, the catalogue of fundamental rights set down in the *Charte* codified a sacrosanct legal space, which could, at least in theory, not be violated by the executive power. Critics might still object that the new constitutional system was unable entirely to satisfy any particular political group in France, but it is exactly this impartiality which could also be considered to be its very advantage.

In summary, it can be argued that constitutional monarchism as put into practice by the French *Charte* was a genuine innovation, representing a fragile but appropriate response to the demands of the post-Napoleonic age. However, this is with the important proviso that 'innovation' should not and must not be seen as an 'unprecedented novelty', but a sagacious re-shuffling of existing doctrines and institutions: natural and positive law, 'revolutionary' and 'classical' constitutionalism, liberalism and conservatism, parliamentarianism and monarchism, representative government and monarchical sovereignty, civil rights and royal prerogatives.

With the proclamation of the *Charte constitutionnelle*, an archetypal constitutional model undoubtedly saw the light of day. But which role would *Charte*-constitutionalism, shaped by and developed under its own unique 'French' conditions, be likely to play beyond the borders of France? This leads us to the question of the impact of the *Charte* on nineteenth-century constitutionalism in Europe compared to other potential models, and the challenges of actual constitutional reception and transfer.

Reception and transfer: constitutional monarchism as a European model?

The potential appeal of constitutional monarchism was the way in which it provided a viable alternative to revolutionary constitutionalism, offering a somewhat fragile, but functional compromise capable of mastering the political challenges of the post-Napoleonic age. In particular, the crown – while defending claims to being the sovereign and the institutional power hub – could position itself in a tradition of 'royal adaptability' and 'modernity', thus making 'Restoration' a dynamic adjustment concept rather than a synonym for outward repudiation of the revolutionary and Napoleonic legacy.[12] And indeed, a large number of European nineteenth- and early twentieth-century constitutions can be classified as following the model of 'constitutional monarchism' as represented by the French *Charte*. Among them are those of the United Netherlands (1815), the Kingdom of Poland ('Congress Poland'; 1815), the Southern German states of Bavaria, Baden and Württemberg (1818 and 1819 respectively), Spain (1834), Greece (1844), Denmark (1849), Austria (1861/1867), the German Empire (1871) or Russia (1906), to name but a few.

Yet it would be misleading to infer that there was no alternative to constitutional monarchism, or even that there was an immediate and linear 'transfer' of the French *Charte* to those countries eventually opting for a monarchical-constitutional legal framework. Rather, evidence shows that throughout the entire nineteenth century constitutional monarchism remained but one – although certainly prominent – option among others. Besides (state) absolutism and autocracy as the most obvious counterpoints to constitutionalism, a number of constitutional options existed for nations with monarchical forms of government (leaving aside the radical path of republicanism): parliamentary-monarchical constitutionalism, represented by constitutions such as the Norwegian of 1814, that of Naples 1820/21, but also the revised French *Charte constitutionnelle* of 1830 in the wake of the July Revolution,[13] the Belgian Constitution of 1831, and the Spanish of 1837; British parliamentary constitutionalism; or specific national variants of constitutional government such as parliamentary-corporatist constitutionalism (Swedish Constitution of 1809).

At the same time, it is evident that even within states opting for constitutional monarchism there was hardly ever a simple imitation of already existing constitutions and of the *Charte* in particular. In fact, attitudes towards any constitution were nuanced, as were motivations for constitutional takeovers. All in all, perception and transfer of constitutional ideas and texts was an intricate process – and often much less 'informed' than one might expect. Germany, a keen implementer of constitutional monarchism and later one of the most consistent defenders of this system until the First World War, is a case in point, and at the same time characteristic of the often diverging dynamics of public discourse and governmental politics.

When considering public constitutional discourse in Germany around 1814, one can observe that among the middle class(es) an interest in constitutional matters had been gradually growing since the second half of the eighteenth century. The *Befreiungskriege* in particular had served as a catalyst, and after the victory over Napoleon *Verfassung* was on everyone's lips. Conflict over 'constitution' and 'non-constitution' became *the* distinguishing hallmark of *Vormärz* Germany. Most contemporaries were aware that constitutionalism was not an issue specific to Germany. Instead, across Europe the *zeitgeist* of the period begged for some kind of 'harmony' between monarchical power and the widespread desire for freedom and liberty:

> Since ... the social order in all realms and states of Western Europe is, with minor variations, basically the same, they are all facing the same task. One might certainly argue as to the nature of this task; but what always really matters is to harmonize princely power and liberty in such a way that they are no longer in conflict.[14]

However, one would be wrong in presuming that awareness of the 'international' nature of the constitutional question resulted in some kind of 'pan-European' discourse, or an unbiased approach to foreign constitutional alternatives. Despite the intensity of intellectual debate in Germany, the perception of foreign political and constitutional 'models' – the number of which had sharply increased since the late eighteenth century – was characterized by a lack of information, selectivity and widespread scepticism. Many non-German constitutional documents available at the time were more or less disregarded in public debate. This holds true for the constitutions of the Nordic countries (the Swedish Constitution of 1809, the Norwegian Constitution of 1814), the United Netherlands (1814) and Congress Poland (1815), but also, with certain reservation, for the Spanish Cádiz Constitution of 1812 and the United States Constitution of 1787. Rather, the German *Bürgertum*'s interest in foreign constitutional systems was predominantly focused on two countries: France and Great Britain.

Public interest in these two nations was considerable, but knowledge of them could not by any means be regarded as comprehensive, and the way these two systems were perceived was anything but unanimously positive. French revolutionary constitutionalism based on popular sovereignty was met with open hostility and regarded as a negative counterpoint to the understanding of a 'good' and 'balanced' constitution. In matter of fact, the Constitution of 1791 and even more so the constitutional documents of 1793 and 1795 as well as the Napoleonic Constitutions of 1799, 1802 and 1804 could be taken as classic examples of 'negative reception'. French revolutionary constitutionalism was a handy enemy concept not only because Germany lacked the experience of revolutionary turning-points and sudden new beginnings of regime change, but also since antipathy against the Revolution could be conveniently combined with general anti-French resentments nurtured by the experience of the Napoleonic wars: 'If one asks ... what general opinion agrees upon unconditionally and unanimously: it is hate and contempt of France.'[15] Rejection was common among both conservatives and liberals. Many of the latter certainly accepted a number of the fundamental principles of the (French) Revolution, such as the limited monarchy, a written constitution, the abolition of feudal privileges, and guarantees of civil rights. However, more often than not, liberals disclaimed any association whatsoever with the Revolution and rarely would they come out wholly in favour of revolutionary constitutionalism. In contrast, the English constitution enjoyed a good reputation amongst most political camps in Germany. However, while some liberals deemed Britain's constitutional system a worthy model for the constitutionalization of Germany, most contemporaries, especially conservatives, argued that its 'home-grown' nature made it non-transferable. Not least, the British parliamentary system was considered to be incompatible with German historical traditions, particularly that of strong executive power.

Against this background, the *Charte* seemed to present a more favourable model, since it actually incorporated many worthwhile elements of the English constitution, for example bicameralism, yet preserved monarchical sovereignty. Still, enthusiasm for the French Charter among the German intelligentsia remained subdued. There were favourable comments on the constitutional text and recognition that the *Charte* was a useful means for pacifying the country under the restored Bourbon monarchy and was probably the best constitution France had manufactured so far. But any unreserved acknowledgement of the Charter as a model for Germany was foredoomed to failure simply on account of its French origin and widespread Francophobia.

Biased reception and only fragmentary knowledge of foreign constitutions and political systems – characterized moreover by a frequent confusion of constitutional ideal and existing practice – made foreign constitutions mainly serve the purpose of a stockroom of arguments for political debate, not legal models for lasting institutional solutions. At the same time, the language of *landständische Verfassung*, which swamped the press around 1814/15, embodied the emerging trend of self-referential political discourse. The term *landständische Verfassung* itself was very vague, but even without much agreement as to what it actually meant, without even a clear understanding of the distinction between 'representative' and *landständische* constitutions, it did suggest German genuineness and originality, thus satisfying growing demands for 'national constitutions'.[16] These demands went hand in hand with doubts about the transferability of constitutions in general. There was suspicion as to whether constitutions generated in one country could be implemented in another. The historico-genetic argument was that differing political, social, economic and cultural contexts would hinder any such implementation. Such arguments were often put forward regarding the English constitution given its common-law character, but could also be generalized:

> The actual wording of a constitution and legislation may be the same in different nations; but they never produce the same results, which are more the outcome of the spirit and character of the people. Words can be transferred but not the spirit, which only develops and evolves in and through life.[17]

The idea that a constitution was the product of specific national conditions was to remain a – if not *the* most – crucial element in public constitutional discourse over the next few decades, both in Germany and beyond.

Public constitutional discourse, however, was just one side of the coin; practical politics was the other. Despite the fact that most German intellectuals were themselves closely involved in state administration or worked for politicians, the ideas and objectives of intellectuals and state authorities were by no means the same. The former tended towards the legalization of state power and the extension of political rights. The latter, however, wanted consolidation of rule, which had to be accomplished with a minimum of political concessions.

For the ruling class, the need to transform politics and polity had become clear during the Napoleonic age, resulting in a range of reform processes throughout Europe including Germany. Demands for reform, however, had not been fully met, and at the end of the Napoleonic era, German rulers could no longer turn a blind eye to the 'constitutional problem'. During the Congress of Vienna, the promise to set up constitutions in all German states was finally put down in writing in the German Federal Act. This promise, however, was so vaguely expressed – 'All Confederal states will be given a *landständische* constitution' (Art. 13) – that it was neither clear nor certain when, how or if it would be fulfilled at all.[18] Nonetheless, prospects for constitutionalization were better than ever before, especially in those German states confronted with burning domestic and foreign policy challenges like the Southern German *Mittelstaaten* ('medium-sized states') of Bavaria, Baden and Württemberg. The question which remained was what these new constitutions should actually look like. While it was certain that 'revolutionary constitutionalism' would attract the ruling classes even less than the intelligentsia, monarchs were presumably more open to foreign models in general and French-style constitutional monarchism in particular. This was due to the fact that for them the constitutional question was above all a pragmatic one, and '(monarchical) class consciousness' after all more important than 'national consciousness'. With pragmatic considerations of securing and stabilizing political power prevailing, the appeal of the *Charte* is not particularly surprising. Given that the English constitution could be regarded as being either too 'home-grown' or conceding too much competence to Parliament, and *landständische Verfassung* more of a slogan than a feasible model, constitutional monarchism as exemplified by the *Charte* was simply 'constitutional common sense' – and hence the only real alternative, if a formal written constitution maintaining the principle of monarchical sovereignty and granting continued political preponderance of the crown was the ultimate goal.

Prospects of constitutional monarchism and its role for European constitutionalism

This observation leads us to the final question concerning the long-term 'potential' of constitutional monarchism and its role within the context of European constitutional history. Constitutional monarchism can be argued to have been a universal constitutional model. It found implementation in many different national contexts throughout Europe, representing a broad range of social, political and cultural traditions. At the same time, not only were the motives for setting up monarchical-constitutional systems most diverse – securing the restoration of the monarchy (France 1814), consolidating rule in newly formed states and demonstrating foreign-political sovereignty (Southern Germany in 1818/19), or making concessions to revolutionary movements (Prussia 1848 or Russia 1906), but the various monarchical-constitutional systems also kept their distinctive features. They thus differed not only regarding the setup of the political institutions, civic rights granted or franchise, but even regarding the definition and interpretation of the monarchical principle itself: the very nucleus of constitutional monarchism, which could be formulated more or less rigidly. In terms of performance, constitutional monarchism has encountered criticism both from contemporaries and in later scholarly research. This is not least because of a structural antagonism – and thus a potential source of fundamental conflict – between monarchical power on the one hand, and parliament on the other, considered immanent to such political systems. Nevertheless, their legislative output in the nineteenth and early twentieth century was not necessarily bad, and in many cases constitutional practice actually proved that such systems were able to tackle political, social and economic reforms effectively. What is true, however, is that perhaps more than is the case with most other forms of constitutional government, it was the model of constitutional monarchism that was challenged by the ongoing radical shifts in the way political power was legitimized and exercised.

Since the late seventeenth century, the general trend had been towards democratizing, legalizing, functionalizing and mediatizing political rule, a process which intensified and accelerated in the course of the nineteenth century. The democratic principle gained in importance, which was manifest in growing demands for political participation, for civil rights to be granted, and the franchise to be introduced or extended. It became progressively more difficult to argue for and justify the unrestricted political powers of the princes, whose role gradually changed from 'ruler' into responsible 'regent'.[19] This was all the more so since the political field was increasingly subjected to laws and left fewer and fewer legal 'black holes'. Accordingly, it became all the more problematic, particularly for monarchs, to solve constitutional conflicts without recourse to juridical arguments. During the Revolutionary age, political confrontation had become radicalized in style and approach, and a number of constitutional conflicts were solved by overt coups (France, Italy, the Netherlands, Switzerland). But after 1814, even in monarchical-constitutional systems any assaults on existing constitutional regimes had to be strengthened with legal arguments, as demonstrated by the attempts of Charles X to justify the July Ordinances of 1830 and hence the de facto repeal of crucial constitutional provisions by referring to Article 14 of the *Charte*.[20] In the second half of the century, constitutional conflicts were rarely solved by unilateral action on the part of the monarch. Long drawn-out political and juridical struggles between monarch and parliament as in Prussia (1862–6) and Denmark (1884–94) became the rule.

Parallel to the process of 'juridification' of the political realm was a drastic downgrading of established concepts of legitimacy. 'Tradition', the idea of an 'authority of the past', had been characteristic of the pre-modern age and served as a regulator for political life. In the modern age, however, tradition was to be replaced by functionality[21] and originality as main categories, thus fundamentally changing the nature of politics. It was no longer possible to base political rule exclusively upon conviction about what had previously existed. Political institutions were forced to reassert their legitimacy through continuous activity and innovation. The concept of the 'divine right of kings' was no longer a solid basis for monarchical legitimacy. Favoured by their legal abstraction into 'constitutional bodies', the monarchs – no matter how powerful they might be – were increasingly seen and judged rationally, and former awe for the office holder was now replaced by respect which first had to be earned:

> [N]o one any longer believes in the divine origin of the regent, no one any longer fears his physical power – thus there remains only the regard for him, the belief in the excellence of his intentions and the allegiance to institutions whose guardian he is and of which he is a part.[22]

But the more rational the understanding of political institutions was, the clearer it became that monarchs too were replaceable, especially if they did not live up to public expectations. In former times, monarchs might nobly and convincingly write about freedom or constitutional government, and yet continue to govern like despots. In the nineteenth century, 'the royal amateurs would now be taken at their word, and their pleasant speculations turned into anxious realities'.[23] In fact, Louis XVIII's Restoration project was essentially based on the promise that the Bourbon monarchy was a better guarantee for the future development of the country than any other political alternative: one crucial, if not the only, foundation stone on which Louis could confidently base his rule. All the more disastrous, then, if this promise was not kept.

A no less demanding challenge for monarchical rule was the burgeoning 'mediatization' of Western society. The increasing importance of the press as (mass) medium from the eighteenth century onwards ran parallel with the politicization process among broader parts of the population and helped make politics an accessible 'mass market'. During the nineteenth century, political rule became more public – though not automatically more transparent – than ever before and increasingly dependent on popular opinion created under the influence and within the framework set down by the press. Its capacity to set the 'political agenda' was clearly demonstrated during the French Restoration, when the press became one of the central players on the political stage. In such an environment, it became increasingly important for political actors to win over the press or suppress it, to consider the impact their political decisions would have on the media, and to develop strategies on how to 'sell' and 'market' themselves and their political programmes. In this respect the legitimacy of monarchical rule underwent crucial changes, too. Whether they liked it or not, the princes were now forced to live up to the expectations of the public. They were no longer free agents, and were controlled rather than independent in their decisions and actions. By the end of the nineteenth century, the ideal of an autonomous monarch had lost most of the foundations it may once have had.

Faced with such obstacles, the long-term prospects of constitutional monarchism were limited, even if the monarchical power maintained the ability and will to reform. It is certainly true that the monarchical-constitutional systems established in France, Germany and other parts of Europe were not doomed to failure a priori, but had some potential for development. In spite of this, however, the adaptability and capacity for reform of these systems had clear limits. The more politics developed into a mass phenomenon and the more omnipresent was the public desire and need to be actively involved in the political process, the more anachronistic the concept of unrestricted monarchical sovereignty and authority became. As tradition lost its role as a cohesive element of monarchical rule, the more unstable the legitimacy of that rule became and the more exposed the monarch was likely to be to public discontent and criticism.

The dilemma was, basically, that in order to equip monarchical-constitutional systems to stand up to and surmount the challenges of the time through reform and evolution, the only reasonable way to go about it was by allowing uncompromising democratization and parliamentarianism, and by withdrawing the monarch from the political frontline. Indeed, the need for such parliamentarianism and de-politicization was recognized in contemporary political thought by writers such as Benjamin Constant, François-René de Chateaubriand or Robert von Mohl.[24] If consistently applied, however, this meant that monarchs had to forgo their dominant political position, the typical feature of constitutional monarchism. Or to put it in another way: the only way to reform constitutional monarchism in the long term was by means of a change of regime, which would inevitably deprive the system of its very soul.

In this respect, constitutional monarchism – while giving the notion and practice of monarchy new vigour and perspective after 1814 – was more or less forced to be a transitional phenomenon: an 'independent' constitutional type distinct from both absolutist and parliamentary monarchy, but one with a clear expiry date. This role was actually corroborated by historical reality. Monarchical-constitutional systems remained episodes of the nineteenth century that had not existed before, and only lasted until the First World War. As such, they represented neither a 'zero hour' nor 'the end' of European constitutionalism.

Notes

1 For a detailed assessment of 'constitutional monarchism' in post-Napoleonic Europe see Markus J. Prutsch, *Making Sense of Constitutional Monarchism in Post-Napoleonic France and Germany* (Basingstoke, 2013). See also Markus J. Prutsch, '"Monarchical Constitutionalism" in Post-Napoleonic Europe', in Kelly L. Grotke and Markus J. Prutsch (eds), *Constitutionalism, Legitimacy, and Power: Nineteenth-Century Experiences* (Oxford, 2014), 69–83.

2 In his final report on the Congress of Vienna, Talleyrand described the unanimous disappointment felt by the European powers at the neo-absolutist way in which Ferdinand VII had returned to the Spanish throne in 1814. See 'Rapport fait au Roi pendant son voyage de Gand à Paris' (June 1815), in Georges Pallain (ed.), *Correspondance inédite du Prince de Talleyrand et du Roi Louis XVIII pendant le Congrès de Vienne, publiée sur les manuscrits conservés au dépôt des Affaires étrangères avec préface éclaircissements et notes* (Paris, 1881), 474.

3 'Charte constitutionnelle' (4 June 1814), in *Bulletin des lois du Royaume de France*, Vol. 1 No. 133, 197–207.

4 Eugene N. Anderson and Pauline R. Anderson, *Political Institutions and Social Change in Continental Europe in the Nineteenth Century* (Berkeley, CA, 1967) 39f. and 78f.

5   'State and Prospects of Europe', in *The Edinburgh Review*, Vol. 23 No. 45 (April 1814), 1–40, citation p. 14f.
6   The 'monarchical principle' found its clearest expression in the preamble of the Constitutional Charter. See 'Charte constitutionnelle' (4 June 1814), in *Bulletin des lois du Royaume de France*, Vol. 1 No. 133, 197–207, preamble 197–9.
7   See Samuel Freiherr von Pufendorf, *Samuelis Pufendorfii de jure naturæ et gentium libri octo* (Lund [= Londini Scanorum]: Junghans, 1692), Book 7 Ch. 5, para. 13, and Book 7 Ch. 6, para. 6–12.
8   See Hugo Grotius, *De jure belli ac pacis libri tres. In quibus jus naturae et gentium: item juris publici praecipua explicantur* (Paris, 1625), especially Book 1 Ch. 3. The term *monarchia limitata*, however, is not yet explicitly used by Grotius.
9   See Pufendorf, *De jure naturæ et gentium*, Book 7 Ch. 6. Para 10.
10 Jacques-Claude comte de Beugnot (1761–1835), who had been a leading figure in the royal commission entrusted with drafting the actual text of the new constitution, took the credit for having urged for the term *Charte*. See Jacques-Claude comte de Beugnot, *Mémoires du comte Beugnot, ancien ministre (1783–1815)* [ed. by Albert comte de Beugnot], 2 Vols. (Paris, 1866), Vol. 2, 218f.
11 Wolfgang Schmale, 'La France, l'Allemagne et la constitution (1789–1815)', in *Annales Historiques de la Révolution Française* 286 (1991), 459–81, here 476.
12 For such an interpretation of Restoration see, e.g. Volker Sellin, *Die geraubte Revolution. Der Sturz Napoleons und die Restauration in Europa*. (Göttingen, 2001) and Volker Sellin, *Das Jahrhundert der Restaurationen: 1814 bis 1906*, (München, 2014).
13 On the revision of the *Charte constitutionnelle* in the crisis of 1830, shifting constitutional powers from the crown to parliament, see Markus J. Prutsch, *Die Charte constitutionnelle Ludwigs XVIII. in der Krise von 1830. Verfassungsentwicklung und Verfassungsrevision in Frankreich 1814 bis 1830* (Marburg, 2006).
14 'Ueber den historischen Standpunkt bei dem Verfassungs-Werke', in *Journal für Deutschland, historisch-politischen Inhalts*, Vol. 8 (1817), 231–55, citation p. 252.
15 Joseph Görres, *Gesammelte Schriften* [ed. by Marie Görres], 9 Vols (München, 1854–74), Vol. 2, 13.
16 The German noun *Landstände* or *Landtag* – the corresponding adjective being *landständisch* – had traditionally signified the assembly of (feudalistic) representatives of the estates of the realm, called together to advise and pass legislation. The return to an estates-based political order proper (now becoming constitutionalized), however, was rarely envisaged in nineteenth-century Germany.
17 Friedrich Murhard in *Allgemeine politische Annalen*, Vol. 10 (1823), 71.
18 'Deutsche Bundesakte vom 8. Juni 1815'. Art. 13. Printed in Ernst Rudolf Huber (ed.), *Dokumente zur deutschen Verfassungsgeschichte. 1. Deutsche Verfassungsdokumente 1803–1850* (Stuttgart, 1978 [1961]), 84–90, citation p. 88.
19 On legitimization – and indeed survival – strategies of European monarchies in the nineteenth century see Volker Sellin, *Gewalt und Legitimität. Die europäische Monarchie im Zeitalter der Revolutionen* (München, 2011).
20 Article 14 specified that 'Le Roi est le chef suprême de l'Etat, il commande les forces de terre et de mer, déclare la guerre, fait les traités de paix, d'alliance et de commerce, nomme à tous les emplois d'administration publique, et fait les règlements et ordonnances nécessaires pour l'exécution des lois et la sûreté de l'Etat'.
21 On the functional character of the monarchy, particularly in the nineteenth century, see e.g.: Martin Kirsch, 'Die Funktionalisierung des Monarchen im 19. Jahrhundert im

europäischen Vergleich', in Stefan Fisch, Florence Gauzy and Chantal Metzger (eds), *Machtstrukturen im Staat in Deutschland und Frankreich/Les structures de pouvoir dans l'État en France et en Allemagne* (Stuttgart, 2007), 81–97.
22 Viktor Franz Freiherr von Andrian-Werburg, *Oesterreich und dessen Zukunft* (Hamburg, 1843 [1841]), 178.
23 'Political State of Prussia', in *The Edinburgh Review*, Vol. 83 No. 167 (January 1846), 224–39, citation p. 229.
24 See, e.g. *Réflexions sur les constitutions, la distribution des pouvoirs et les garanties, dans une monarchie constitutionnelle* (Paris: Nicolle; Gide, 1814); Benjamin Constant, *Principes de politique, applicables à tous les gouvernements représentatifs et particulièrement à la constitution actuelle de la France* (Paris, 1815); François René Auguste vicomte de Chateaubriand, *Réflexions politiques sur quelques écrits du jour et sur les intérêts de tous les français* (Paris, 1814); François René Auguste vicomte de Chateaubriand, *De la monarchie selon la Charte* (Paris, 1816); Robert von Mohl, 'Constitutionelle Erfahrungen. Ein Beitrag zur Verfassungs-Politik', in *Zeitschrift für die gesamte Staats-Wissenschaft*
2 (2) (1845), 191–233; Robert von Mohl, 'Das Repräsentativsystem, seine Mängel und die Heilmittel. Politische Briefe', in *Politische Schriften. Eine Auswahl* [ed. by Klaus von Beyme] (Köln and Opladen, 1966 [1852]), 118–224.

9

The Practical Politics of Restoration Constitutionalism: The Cases of Scandinavia and South Germany

Morten Nordhagen Ottosen

Introduction

In the eleven years from 1808 to 1819 the Scandinavian states of Sweden and Norway and the states of southern Germany (Bavaria, Baden and Württemberg) all introduced constitutions that would remain in effect throughout the nineteenth century and beyond. Denmark followed suit, albeit only in 1849. At first glance, the constitutions in Scandinavia and South Germany might appear so different as not to warrant much in the way of comparison. The differences between the historical experiences and political cultures of these two regions were even acknowledged by contemporaries, and probably contributed to the minimal transfer of constitutional ideas between the two regions. Indeed, the constitutions introduced in these two regions were based on different constitutional models and principles of sovereignty.[1] These differences notwithstanding, the contexts in which the constitutions were introduced had several similarities insofar as they reflect how constitutionalism in the early nineteenth century was also a very pragmatic matter of confronting the challenges of the post-Napoleonic world. This helps explain why, and when, the Scandinavian and South German states adopted constitutions, why they introduced the kind of constitutions they did, and also the sometimes similar concerns that guided their introduction.

Constitutionalism and the Restoration

Several recent syntheses have established that Restoration politics was anything but a matter of undoing the legacies of the French Revolution and Napoleonic Empire to replicate a lost pre-revolutionary world.[2] Rather, it was a period of transition, although the ideal end point of this process was contested. Yet, even if this contest was in many ways a struggle between the forces of reaction and progress, it was not merely a deadlock between opposite extremes. Reactionaries and radicals were largely kept on the margins of post-Napoleonic political life, leaving conservatives and liberals as the major political groups. Although their struggles could sometimes lead conservatives and liberals to opt for cooperation with the reactionary and radical extremes, under certain circumstances compromise was also possible, as the power-brokers of Europe were striving to resolve the pressing post-revolutionary questions of sovereignty, legitimacy and boundaries.[3] This is crucial to understanding Restoration constitutionalism.

After the French Revolution, constitutionalism was largely associated with popular sovereignty, division of power and equal rights for all citizens. Constitutions were consequently perceived as representing a 'democratized' creed, as it were, and juxtaposed to any type of government based on monarchic sovereignty. This has also affected constitutional history, as historians and legal scholars have long been inclined to regard the French 'revolutionary' constitutions and their offspring as a benchmark for subsequent constitutional development in narratives that, if sometimes inadvertently, have resembled a 'Whig interpretation'. The monarchical constitutions of the Restoration have thus been equated with the death throes of monarchies on history's path to modern democracy.[4] German scholars have even labelled the constitutions of the Napoleonic and Restoration eras as *Scheinkonstitutionalismus* ('fake constitutionalism').[5]

Yet constitutionalism was not the exclusive preserve of liberals and radicals on their path to an inevitable triumph of modern democracy. In the international political climate after 1815 the prevailing attitude among the major powers was that if constitutional reform was sanctioned by rulers at the request of their subjects, it was a legitimate, and hence acceptable, expression of how their states were best ruled. In an international order created to restore peace and stability, stable governments were paramount and generally mattered more than how states were governed.[6] Conservatives and reactionaries were thus not necessarily opposed to constitutions per se, but they preferred corporate constitutions that preserved the social hierarchy as well as monarchic sovereignty. Some conservative states, such as Prussia and Austria, rejected constitutional government, but not even absolutism was necessarily incompatible with a constitution. Absolutist Denmark did in fact have one until 1848 – unique though it was – vesting absolute powers in the king, though he was not free to wield them as he pleased.

Thus, as Markus Prutsch puts it, by the early nineteenth century '[t]he spectrum of constitutional concepts that had evolved or even been put into practice ranged from "ultra-revolutionary" to "ultra-reactionary" and from "radical-democratic" to "radical-autocratic", and a crucial question was whether these contradictory standpoints could be united in some way or other'.[7] This was a highly contemporary concern, underlining the importance of treating the Restoration era on its own merits. As Michael Broers aptly remarks, 'the men of Restoration Europe forged their own, unique political culture, to confront the problems of their own times'.[8] This lay at the heart of the constitutional projects of the era, reflecting the obvious, but often forgotten, fact that constitutions were as much means to concrete ends as the realization of grand philosophies and universal truths. As Loyd Lee notes, '[t]he idea of a constitution is perhaps an abstract one, but any given constitution is devised to deal with a concrete political society. Constitutions must be read not only for their content, but also for what they do not contain, and in relationship to the problems they were designed to solve.'[9] The different constitutional models at hand and the pragmatic concerns which guided their application gave constitutionalism during the Restoration many faces, as the cases of Scandinavia and South Germany show.

Constitutions as bulwarks against foreign influence

A key element in modern constitutionalism is the idea of the inviolability of constitutions. While this may be seen as applying primarily to domestic affairs, it is also a principle to be reckoned with in foreign relations, especially in the context of federal structures and unions. The Bavarian first minister from 1799 to 1817, Maximilian von Montgelas, was acutely aware of this as he steered Bavaria in the stormy waters of Napoleonic Europe.[10] Montgelas was the mastermind behind the Bavarian constitution of 1808, which was hastily drafted and promulgated to forestall a Napoleonic *Diktat* and with it an avenue for external influence through a future constitution over the newly established Confederation of the Rhine. A major concern was thus to safeguard Bavaria's newly acquired full sovereignty and territorial gains by introducing a constitution that was intended not only to frame and consolidate the administrative reforms of recent years, but also to serve as a bulwark against external infringements upon the country's domestic affairs.[11] Similar concerns lay behind simultaneous efforts to introduce a constitution in Baden, though they stalled under the burdens of economic crisis and war. The consolidation and legitimization of territorial gains and sweeping reforms made during the Napoleonic wars was a major impetus for South German constitutionalism. This was different from the Scandinavian kingdoms, which had been consolidated territorial states for centuries. It was testament to the intricate legal and political conflicts in the German lands after the demise of the Holy Roman Empire that these contributed significantly to preventing king Christian VII of Denmark (1839–48) from introducing a modern constitution, as a consequence of the complications caused by Denmark's ties to Holstein.[12]

The immediacy of the question of the sovereignty of the individual German states was revived after the Napoleonic wars. The German Federal Act of 1815 stipulated rather vaguely that all German states were to adopt *landständische* constitutions. This raised all sorts of questions as to what exactly this article meant and its precise implications for the German Confederation, which seemed destined to be dominated by Austria and Prussia.[13] In fear that federal legislation and integration would undermine their sovereignty and also serve as a back entrance for direct Austro-Prussian meddling in their domestic affairs, several German states embarked on constitutional paths, either introducing a constitution even before the Congress of Vienna was convened, as in Nassau, or began drafting new constitutions, as in Bavaria, Württemberg and Baden.

It was no coincidence that a constitutional committee in Bavaria was set up on 17 September 1814, the day before the proceedings at Vienna were to commence, initially to revise the 1808 constitution. Various disagreements, resistance from Montgelas until his dismissal in early 1817, and the apparent fading of the immediate prospect of federal integration brought the process to a momentary halt, but Metternich's submission in late 1817 of a draft constitution for Bavaria reminded the Bavarian government of the threat of foreign incursions into its domestic affairs, and of Austrian ambitions to bring the German states closer together under Vienna's auspices.[14] Alongside fears of Russian intervention, territorial conflicts with Baden and the personal intervention of the liberal-minded Crown Prince Ludwig, this revived the process of constitutional remodelling. A new constitution was rather quickly drafted in the spring of 1818 and was promulgated by the king in late May.[15] Meanwhile in Baden, fears of being subjected to Austrian and Prussian constitutional dictates and of federal infringement upon its sovereign powers had also contributed to speeding up a constitutional process that had ground to a halt, leading to the promulgation of a constitution in August 1818.[16]

In a related turn of events, in Württemberg a constitution, having long been negotiated between the king and the estates, was eventually introduced on 25 September 1819, just as the Frankfurt Diet was rubber stamping the Carlsbad Decrees as federal law. The timing was no coincidence. The Württemberg constitution explicitly asserted its primacy over federal legislation, thereby holding the Carlsbad Decrees largely at a distance until the government was eventually browbeaten into submission in 1824.[17] Likewise, the Bavarian government made determined efforts to safeguard its sovereignty and limit the scope of federal legislation.[18] This was not without irony as King Max Joseph, disgusted by the stormy parliamentary sessions of 1819, had considered revoking the constitution. However, the crown prince maintained that 'retaining one's constitution is not as humiliating as having one's laws dictated by other powers' and warned that abolishing the constitution, or raising doubts as to its integrity, could seriously compromise Bavarian sovereignty.[19]

A foreign policy incentive for constitutionalism was also apparent in Norway, for many of the same reasons as in the South German states. Already in 1809, at the height of the Napoleonic wars, dissatisfaction with the nature of Danish rule made some Norwegians begin to think in terms of a constitution in the context of the union with Denmark, before escalating conflicts with the government in Copenhagen set most Norwegian constitutionalists on a path to full national independence. After the cession of Norway from the king of Denmark to the king of Sweden in January 1814, the country's political élite and the prince regent Christian Frederick (the later Christian VIII of Denmark) agreed on a course of action whereupon a constitutional assembly was hastily convened and a constitution drafted over an intense six weeks in April and May. Time was indeed of the essence, as Swedish troops were still fighting Napoleon and unable to claim their prize just yet. The overriding purpose of the assembly was to assert Norwegian sovereignty, preferably as an independent state, but if need be by erecting a powerful obstacle to integration in the event of a union with Sweden. This also goes some way in explaining why the distribution of power was tilted heavily in favour of the legislature. In this sense, the constitution was a foreign policy tool, both as a legal argument in hopes of swaying the major powers and as an obstacle to Sweden. A union of Sweden and Norway was nevertheless the outcome of the events of the year 1814, but the Norwegians retained their constitution with only minor amendments. To some extent, this reflected foreign policy concerns on the part of the Swedes, who wanted the Norwegian matter settled before the Congress of Vienna could intervene.[20] As far as the Swedes were concerned the constitutional grounds of the union were not written in stone and could be subject to later alteration under more favourable circumstances.

In the next few decades the Norwegians vigorously defended their constitution against any attempt at change or reform that could potentially enhance integration of Norway and Sweden. This contributed to turning the Norwegian constitution into a veritable national and political symbol. For this reason, the appeal of the Pan-Scandinavian ideology and movement was negligible in Norway as compared to in Sweden and especially Denmark, where Pan-Scandinavianism to a certain extent served as a cloak for liberal constitutional demands. As such it had several ideological similarities with German nationalism before 1848, although the Pan-Scandinavian and German national movements clashed bitterly over Schleswig and Holstein.

In South Germany the individual states' constitutions became increasingly associated with the conservative turns of several monarchs and consequently lost much of their liberal appeal. Instead liberals turned to the idea of a constitutional German nation-state. This contributed to undermining the efforts of South German governments to utilize constitutions as a means of forging identity and patriotism within the individual states.[21] For example, official Bavarian constitution days were hijacked by the liberal opposition, as it were, culminating with the Hambach Festival in May 1832, a Bavarian constitution day that turned into a veritable manifestation of liberal German nationalism.[22] In Norway, efforts on the part of King Charles XV John to install 4 November, the day of the revised Norwegian 1814 constitution and, hence, the union of Sweden and Norway, as the official constitution day also failed, showing how difficult it was for established regimes, whether in Scandinavia or South Germany, to channel constitutional culture and loyalties in particular directions.[23]

Sovereignty and division of power

The Scandinavian constitutions were based on the principle of popular sovereignty. In Norway this owed much to genuine ideological belief, but did not mean that anything but a 'revolutionary' constitution was unthinkable or that Norwegians were primordial modern democrats, nor that the choice of sovereignty, as it were, was devoid of practical considerations. Popular sovereignty was not only the preferred ideal, but was also a very convenient legal option against the background of the Norwegians' rejection of the right of the king of Denmark to cede them to the king of Sweden 'like a herd of cattle'. This stance rendered any adherence to the principle of monarchic sovereignty impossible, as it would undermine their claim to legal justification in defying the lawful international treaty by which Norway had been ceded. This argument also appears to have swayed the prince regent, who otherwise appears to have preferred a monarchic constitution or even absolutism.[24]

After the Napoleonic wars the Norwegian constitution remained the only one still in effect in Europe mirroring the 'revolutionary' model established with the French constitution of 1791. Had the Congress of Vienna and its aftermath marked a restoration in the fullest sense of the term, the major powers would have rejected it, but even Metternich could live with such a constitutional order as long as it was contained and posed no threat to the international order. The same logic applied to the South German constitutions. Metternich may not have liked them, but the main point was that they ensured order and stability. Even though translations of the Norwegian constitution occasionally cropped up in several parts of Europe, and became a model for Scandinavian liberals, few saw Norway as a revolutionary threat. Instead this fate befell Naples when the revolution there in 1820 spread to Piedmont-Sardinia, and then to the Iberian Peninsula. This prompted the major powers to intervene, seeing in these events something of a repetition of the early 1790s when the French Revolution had led to major war.[25] The sense that revolutions were bound to follow a certain script, with participants playing out the parts allotted to them before everything culminated in major war, also did much to determine anticipations and actions in 1848.[26]

Yet in the minds of those who sought to retain the Norwegian constitution as it was, the greatest threat to it was not external, but domestic. Among them was Christian Magnus Falsen, one of the authors of the original constitutional draft, who soon had a change of mind and wanted a more equal distribution of sovereign powers between king and parliament. Hinting at the French revolutionary experiences under the National Convention, he warned in 1824 that 'as soon as a portion of the executive power comes into the hands of the legislature, the liberty of the people is over with and despotism is at the doorstep; all the more dangerously so because there are many to exercise it ... What would then become of the liberty of the people and the constitution?'[27] Falsen's change of mind was motivated by King Charles XIV John's efforts to revise the constitution to provide for a stronger executive. Whether King Charles John – the former marshal Jean Baptiste Bernadotte, who had been elected crown prince of Sweden in 1810 and ascended the throne in 1818 – merely wanted a slight revision of the existing Norwegian constitution or a new constitution altogether, based on the principle of monarchic sovereignty, is not clear, but he did express his admiration for the Bavarian constitution of 1818.[28] In any event, his efforts at constitutional change failed and in later years the increasingly frustrated and conservative former revolutionary general even came, in principle, to praise absolutism as superior to constitutional rule.[29]

Sweden's constitution of 1809, introduced to replace a near-absolutist order with a constitutional monarchy after a *coup d'état* and defeat in war, was a reflection of the country's historical experience. After almost a century of political instability caused by deep-running conflicts between monarchs and a powerful nobility (costing at least one Swedish king his life), and political strife in the diet of the estates, the Swedish constitution of 1809 was a pragmatic solution that incorporated many of the main principles of the French Revolution, popular sovereignty chief among them, but retained corporate representation and a powerful monarchy, thereby also protecting the interests of traditional and new élites. In a peculiar way the monarch and the diet of the estates even shared legislative powers. This flexible solution proved to be durable, which allowed for subsequent parliamentary and constitutional reforms to absorb many of the conflicts of the day.[30] Much the same can be said of Württemberg, whose political culture and experiences in the eighteenth century bore a very strong resemblance to those of Sweden. Both countries' subsequent constitutional orders also had certain similarities. While Württemberg's constitution adhered to the principle of monarchic sovereignty it was a product of negotiation between the king and representatives of the estates and, much like the Swedish constitution, struck a carefully crafted balance of interests and power between the monarch and old as well as new élites.[31] This offered something for everyone and proved to be a durable compromise. It provided the nobility with influence and guarantees of certain privileges, while for the new bureaucratic élites that had emerged during the Napoleonic era its provisions for civil equality and freedoms were considered as bulwarks against the forces of reaction both within and outside the state.[32]

Similar historical experiences were also the cause of a striking similarity between Norway and Baden. It was no coincidence that both states adopted fully representative constitutions and also had the most extensive suffrage in post-Napoleonic Europe – at about 70 and 40 per cent of males over 25 years of age, respectively. Both states had a weak or virtually non-existent nobility, which elsewhere often constituted a major corporate obstacle to fully representative constitutions. Moreover, a majority of the peasantry in the two states were freeholders and not under seigneurial obligations, and therefore more likely to comply with the qualification criteria of the liberal 'political culture of limited suffrage', as Alan Kahan has labelled it.[33] For liberals, property, income and/or education implied a stake in society and, hence, the ability to cast qualified votes. Modern democracy was not on the minds of liberals of the time and, moreover, Norwegian constitution-makers were not necessarily any more liberal than their Badenese peers. In any event, what ultimately mattered in terms of representation were the eligibility of parliamentarians and the actual powers of the parliaments, which were far more restricted in Baden than Norway.[34]

In theory the two concepts of popular and monarchic sovereignty were fundamentally different, if not incompatible. Yet the difference between the principles of popular and monarchic sovereignty under a constitutional monarchy was more one of degree than of kind, which in practical terms left the Scandinavian and South German constitutional orders more as two sides of the same coin than polar opposites.[35] On the one hand, indivisible popular sovereignty was incompatible with a constitutional monarchy in which the monarch held actual power. When the Norwegian constitutional assembly, which went very far in asserting the principle of popular sovereignty, offered prince regent Christian Frederick the crown in May 1814, it did so with the words that it had striven to 'divide the sovereign powers so that legislation is left in the hands of the people, and the executive in those of the king'.[36] The Swedish and Danish constitutions went even further in vesting sovereign powers in the monarch; the Danish constitution of 1849, though to some extent modelled on its Norwegian predecessor, was even technically a *constitution octroyée* (a 'sanctioned' constitution).[37]

On the other hand, 'the constitutionalism of the nineteenth century was characterized by the incompatibility of the undivided monarchical prerogative and the Chambers' legislative or budget rights', as the legal historian Ulrike Müssig argues.[38] Whenever the monarch shared sovereignty with the people by contractual obligation, this was theoretically a royal concession that could at any time be repealed or altered at the discretion of the monarch. In practice, however, this was not so easy – neither politically nor in legal terms. The grand duke of Baden and the king of Bavaria found out as much when they wanted to repeal their constitutions shortly after their introduction in 1818, only to be strongly advised against it by the Austrian and Prussian governments.[39] Vienna and Berlin warned that such arbitrariness could unleash revolution, which is exactly what they wanted to avoid. Repealing the constitutions thus became a political impossibility, and arguably even a legal impossibility.[40] Nor could the monarchs revise the constitutions as they pleased. The Vienna Final Act of 1820 stipulated that the individual constitutions of the German Confederation could only be revised by constitutional means. According to the South German constitutions revisions could only take place by parliamentary procedure. As such, the otherwise rather reactionary Vienna Final Act came, somewhat ironically, to offer protection for these constitutions and helped perpetuate the sharing of sovereignty between monarch and people.

Still, Metternich knew where to strike to make sure that the South German constitutions and the representative institutions established under them would not become the focus of liberal or radical agitation. The Carlsbad Decrees and subsequent federal legislation all but curtailed the political public sphere in the German states, thereby ensuring that whatever potential the individual constitutions and parliaments held for the emergence of a vibrant liberal political culture was effectively cancelled out.[41] Even though the South German states would from time to time challenge federal censorship legislation, it was a testament to Metternich's overall success that the Badenese liberal Theodor Welcker despaired in 1831 that, 'A representative constitution without freedom of the press is a lie!'[42] This stood in marked difference to the Scandinavian countries, where a rather free and open public sphere gradually emerged, eventually even in absolutist Denmark. This was not an inevitable development, however, as the battles fought between Swedish liberals and King Charles XIV John over freedom of the press show.[43] Yet it helped establish a constitutional and political culture that was largely able to absorb conflicts, as seen by the relative quietness of the events of 1848 in Scandinavia, at least compared to continental Europe, save for a national civil war in Denmark over Schleswig and Holstein in 1848–51.

Conclusion

The Scandinavian and South German constitutions introduced in the early nineteenth century were not worlds apart, even if they appear quite different. Above all they reflected the overall progressive nature of constitutionalism in both regions. This involved more than a mere choice between incompatible constitutional models and principles of sovereignty, of which the longevity and success of the Scandinavian constitutions as the more 'democratic' option have long seemed predetermined to historians. At the heart of Scandinavian and South German constitutionalism lay a number of practical and pragmatic concerns, rooted in the historical experiences and contemporary challenges confronted by each individual state, which were crucial to the content and timing of their constitutions. The pragmatic considerations that shaped their constitutional endeavours are especially evident in how foreign policy concerns guided the timing of Norwegian and South German constitution-making and how constitutions in this respect were also considered as foreign policy tools to ward off foreign influence on domestic affairs. What is more, the practical realities of the constitutional orders in Scandinavia and South Germany ensured that the differences between them were of degree rather than kind, as the practical overlaps between monarchic and popular sovereignty show. As such, Scandinavian and South German constitutionalism during the Restoration cannot be regarded merely as part of a deadlocked ideological clash between the extreme ends of progress and reaction. Rather, it was a matter of working out workable compromises to serve concrete and ultimately progressive ends.

Notes

1   Markus J. Prutsch, *Making Sense of Constitutional Monarchism in Post-Napoleonic France and Germany* (Basingstoke, 2013), 52–3. See also Eirik Holmøyvik, *Maktfordeling og 1814* (Bergen, 2012), 113–14 and 538–41.
2   Paul W. Schroeder, *The Transformation of European Politics, 1763–1848* (Oxford, 1994); Michael Broers, *Europe after Napoleon. Revolution, Reaction and Romanticism, 1814–1848* (Manchester, 1996); Jonathan Sperber, *Revolutionary Europe, 1780–1850* (Harlow, 2000); Dieter Langewiesche, *Europa zwischen Restauration und Revolution 1815–1849* (Munich, 2004 [1985]); Martyn Lyons, *Post-Revolutionary Europe, 1815–1866* (Basingstoke, 2006).
3   See the essays in Michael Broers, Peter Hicks and Augustun Guimerá (eds), *The Napoleonic Empire and the New European Political Culture* (Basingstoke, 2012) as well as David Laven and Lucy Riall (eds), *Napoleon's Legacy. Problems of Government in Restoration Europe* (Oxford and New York, 2000).
4   See for example C. A. Bayly, *The Birth of the Modern World 1780–1914* (Oxford, 2004), 427. For similar views, see also Robert Tombs, *France 1814–1914* (London, 1996), 329–353; Jacques Droz, *Europe Between Revolutions, 1815–1848* (Glasgow, 1967); Eric Hobsbawm, *The Age of Revolution 1789–1848* (London, 1962), 99–131, 234–52.
5   Ernst Rudolf Huber, *Deutsche Verfassungsgeschichte zeit 1789*, vol. 1: *Reform und Restauration bis 1830* (Stuttgart, 1967), 88 and 91, cf. Manfred Botzenhart, *Deutsche Verfassungsgeschichte 1806–1849* (Stuttgart, 1993), 13.
6   Schroeder, *Transformation*, 477–636.
7   Prutsch, *Making Sense*, 2.
8   Broers, *Europe after Napoleon*, 3.
9   Loyd E. Lee, *The Politics of Harmony. Civil Service, Liberalism, and Social Reform in Baden, 1800–1850* (Newark, NJ, 1980), 41.
10 For this reason, his biographer, Eberhard Weis, argues that Montgelas' primary concern was in fact foreign policy, cf. Eberhard Weis, *Montgelas 1759–1799. Zwischen Revolution und Reform*, 2nd edn (Munich, 1988), x.
11 Michael Doeberl, *Rheinbundverfassung und bayerischen Konstitution* (Munich, 1924), 73–9; Eberhard Weis, Napoleon und der Rheinbund', in Eberhard Weis [edited by Walter Demel and Bernd Roeck], *Deutschland und Frankreich um 1800. Aufklärung – Revolution – Reform* (Munich, 1990), 195–6 and 200–5.
12 Rasmus Glenthøj, *1864 – Sønner af de slagne* (Copenhagen, 2014), 118–47, cf. William Carr, *Schleswig-Holstein 1815–48. A Study in National Conflict* (Manchester, 1963).

13 Wolfgang Mager, 'Das Problem der landständischen Verfassungen auf dem Wiener Kongress 1814/15', in *Historische Zeitschrift*, 217 (1974), 296–346; Bernd Wunder, 'Landstände und Rechtsstaat. Zur Entstehung und Verwirklichung des Art. 13 DBA', in *Zeitschrift für historische Forschung*, 5 (1978), 139–85.
14 Karl Otmar von Aretin, 'Metternichs Verfassungspläne 1817/1818. Dargestellt an Hand des Briefwechsels des bayerischen Gesandten in Wien Frhr. v. Steinlein mit dem bayerischen Aussenminister Graf Aloys Rechberg', in *Historisches Jahrbuch*, 74 (1955).
15 Michael Doeberl, *Ein Jahrhundert bayerischen Verfassungslebens* (Munich, 1918), 40–8; Heinz Gollwitzer, *Ludwig I. von Bayern. Königtum im Vormärz. Eine politische Biographie* (Munich, 1986), 213–28; Friedrich Dobmann, *Georg Friedrich Freiherr von Zentner als bayerischer Staatsmann in den Jahren 1799-1821* (Kallmünz, 1962), 141–51.
16 Lee, *Politics of Harmony*, 40–87; Elizabeth Fehrenbach, 'Bürokratische Reform und gesellschaftlicher Wandel. Die badischer Verfassung von 1818', in Ernst Otto Bräunche and Thomas Schnabel (eds), *Die badische Verfassung von 1818. Südwestdeutschland auf dem Weg zur Demokratie* (Ubstadt-Weiher, 1996).
17 Eberhard Büssem, *Die Karlsbader Beschlüsse von 1819. Die endgültige Stabilisierung der restaurativen Politik im Deutschen Bund nach dem Wiener Kongress von 1814/15* (Hildesheim, 1974), 425–54. See also Robert D. Billinger, Jr, *Metternich and the German Question. States' Rights and Federal Duties, 1820-1834* (Newark, NJ, 1991), 26–30.
18 Büssem, *Karlsbader Beschlüsse*, 437–46.
19 Quoted from Prutsch, *Making Sense*, 134.
20 Rasmus Glenthøj and Morten Nordhagen Ottosen, *Experiences of War and Nationality in Denmark and Norway, 1807-1815* (Basingstoke, 2014), 141–4 and 208–56.
21 Elizabeth Fehrenbach, *Verfassungsstaat und Nationsbildung 1815-1871* (Munich, 1992), 1–38.
22 Paul Nolte, 'Verfassungsfeste im Vormärz. Liberalismus, Verfassungskultur und soziale Ordnung in den Gemeinden', in Manfred Hettling and Paul Nolte (eds), *Bürgerliche Feste. Symbolischen Formen politischen Handelns im 19. Jahrhundert* (Göttingen, 1993); Barbara Stollberg-Rillinger, 'Verfassung und Fest. Überlegungen zur festlichen Inszenierung vormoderner und moderner Verfassungen', in Hans-Jürgen Becker (ed.), *Interdependenzen zwischen Verfassung und Kultur. Tagung der Vereinigung für Verfassungsgeschichte in Hofgeismar vom 22.3-24.3.1999* (Berlin, 2003); Cecilia Foerster, 'Das Hambacher Fest 1832. Volksfest und Nationalfest einer oppositionellen Massenbewegung', in Dieter Düding, Peter Friedemann and Paul Münch (eds), *Öffentliche Festkultur. Politische Feste in Deutschland von der Aufklärung bis zum Ersten Weltkrieg* (Reinbek bei Hamburg, 1988).
23 Rolf Laache, *Torvslaget den 17de mai 1829. Et hundreårs minne* (Oslo, 1929); Yngvar Nielsen, *Grev Platens Statholderskab 1827-1829* (Kristiania, 1875), 67–74; Henrik Edgren, *Publicitet för medborgsmannavett. Det nationellt svenska i Stockholmstidningar 1810-1831* (Uppsala, 2005), 220–3, 297–301.
24 Jes Fabricius Møller, 'Det indskrænkede monarki og teorien om statsmagtens ligevægt', in *Historisk tidsskrift*, 93/4 (2014), 547; Lars-Roar Langslet, *Christian Frederik. En biografi* (Oslo 2014), 95–105. See also Morten Nordhagen Ottosen, 'Konstitusjoner som politiske og nasjonale realiteter og symboler i Norge og Sør-Tyskland, ca. 1800-1848', in Odd Arvid Storsveen, Amund Pedersen and Bård Frydenlund (eds), *Smak av frihet. 1814-grunnloven. Historisk virkning og sosial forankring* (Oslo, 2015), 338–44. See also the introductory essay and documents in Ruth Hemstad (ed.), *'Like a*

Herd of Cattle'. Parliamentary and Public Debates Regarding the Cession of Norway, 1813-1814 (Oslo, 2014).
25 Schroeder, *Transformation*, 606-14.
26 John Breuilly, 'The Revolutions of 1848', in David Parker (ed.), *Revolutions and the Revolutionary Tradition in the West 1560-1991* (London, 2000), 114; cf. idem., '1848: Connected or Comparable Revolutions?', in Axel Körner (ed.), *1848 – A European Revolution? International Ideas and National Memories of 1848* (Basingstoke, 2000), 34-6.
27 Christian Magnus Falsen, *Bemærkninger i Anledning af Constitutions-Forslaget om Kongens Veto* (Christiania, 1824), 4, 8 and 12.
28 Ottosen, 'Konstitusjoner', 352-8.
29 Torvald T: son Höjer, *Carl XIV Johan*, vol. 3: *Konungatiden* (Stockholm, 1960), 125, 233, 331.
30 Fredrik Lagerroth, *1809 års regeringsform: Dess ursprung och tolkning* (Stockholm, 1942); Rolf Karlbom, *Bakgrunden till 1809 års regeringsform. Studier i svensk konstitutionell opinionsbildning* (Gothenburg, 1964).
31 For concise overviews of constitutionalism in Württemberg, which has been extensively researched, see for example Hartwig Brandt, 'Früher Liberalismus im konstitutionellen Gehäuse. Die Württembergische Verfassung 1819', in Otto Borst (ed.), *Südwestdeutschland. Die Wiege der deutschen Demokratie* (Tübingen, 1997) and Rolf Grawert, 'Der württembergische Verfassungsstreit 1815-1819', in Christoph Jamme and Otto Pöggeler (eds), *'O Fürstin der Heimat! Glückliches Stutgard!': Politik, Kultur und Gesellschaft im deutschen Südwesten um 1800* (Stuttgart, 1988).
32 Volker Press, 'Der württembergische Landtag im Zeitalter des Umbruchs 1770-1830', in *Zeitschrift für Württembergische Landesgeschichte*, 42, (1983), 259-266; Franz Mögle-Hofacker, *Zur Entwicklung des Parlamentarismus in Württemberg. Der 'Parlamentarismus der Krone' unter König Wilhelm I* (Stuttgart, 1981), 10-24.
33 Alan Kahan, *Liberalism in Nineteenth-Century Europe. The Political Culture of Limited Suffrage* (Basingstoke, 2003), 1-17.
34 Ottosen, 'Konstitusjoner', 344-8, cf. Fehrenbach, *Verfassungsstaat*, 6-7.
35 Møller, 'Det indskrænkede monarki', 545-47.
36 Quoted from Møller, 'Det indskrænkede monarki', 547.
37 Glenthøj, *1864*, 182-201; Møller, 'Det indskrænkede monarki', 539-64. See also Rasmus Glenthøj, 'Eidsvold! De danske liberales forbillede', in Storsveen, Pedersen and Frydenlund (eds), *Frihet*.
38 Cf. Ulrike Müssig, 'Reconsidering Constitutional Formation. Research Challenges of Comparative Constitutional History', in *Giornale di storia costituzionale/Journal of Constitutional History*, 27/1 (2014), 124.
39 Büssem, *Karlsbader Beschlüsse*, 174-81.
40 Cf. Helmut Quaritsch, *Staat und Souveränität*, vol. 1: *Die Grundlagen* (Frankfurt am Main, 1970), 489-53. See also Ludwig Doeberl, *Maximilian von Montgelas und das Prinzip der Staatssouveränität* (Munich, 1925).
41 On South German constitutionalism as background to the Carlsbad Decrees, see Büssem, *Karlsbader Beschlüsse*, 156-200 and 311-34.
42 Quoted from Fehrenbach, *Verfassungsstaat*, 20.
43 Stig Boberg, *Carl XIV Johan och tryckfriheten 1810-1844* (Gothenburg, 1989), cf. Höjer, *Carl XIV Johan*, 327-61.

10

Royal Opposition against the *Ancien Régime*: The Case of Württemberg[1]

Georg Eckert

From 1815 to 1819, the kingdom of Württemberg seemed deeply divided by conflict over its constitution. Both in 1815 and again in 1817, kings Friedrich I and Wilhelm I respectively failed to get their estates to assent to the constitutions they had proclaimed unilaterally. In the end, the revised constitution of 1819 sealed the compromise King Wilhelm I and his parliament had reached.[2]

Prior to this, foreign observers were monitoring closely the growing struggle in the small state of Württemberg. In 1818, the *Edinburgh Review* gave Württemberg some space in its pages by observing: 'Wirtemberg [sic] weighs lightly in the balance of power; but its history is singularly interesting.'[3] Following Charles James Fox's witticism, it stated that there are 'only two constitutions in Europe, the British constitution, and that of Wirtemberg'.[4] However, the history of this *Mittelstaat* was neither singularly interesting nor that singular. It was quite a common story, among the German states at least: its protagonist was a prince who demanded further reform, while his estates, on the contrary, demanded restoration. The king of Württemberg pleaded for innovation. His estates, in contrast, embraced tradition. This apparent inversion of roles questions traditional understandings of 'restoration' which have tended to place representative institutions in opposition to reactionary monarchs. However, as other, more modern contexts have shown: 'no restoration is *just* a return to the past'.[5]

Remarkably, the king of Württemberg was seeking almost a return to the future. A ruler seeking innovation makes 'restoration' an awkward label for the period between 1815 and 1848. With regard to Württemberg, neither 1815 nor 1848 mark vital turning points that distinguish this era from others. After all, the conflict over the constitution had already begun in the late eighteenth century during an age of reform, which in some respects did not end until the 1860s. This argument requires further elaboration to judge whether the concept of 'restoration' and its periodization can be applied to Württemberg. Such debates have already been given space in some impressive studies that have altered our view of the Napoleonic era by focusing on long-term processes rather than simply on events.[6]

Therefore, if historians cannot find distinctive events to mark an era, they need to search for other heuristic devices. One could identify certain groups of individuals whose agency determined the political culture of an era, for example: in the case of Württemberg, civil servants deserve more scholarly interest. Equally, one may examine crucial ideas that epitomize an era in which they originated or became dominant. In Württemberg, the notion of rule by experts emerged at this time, that is the vision of an overarching 'technocracy' in charge of the state. This development seems to define the entire era, from the late eighteenth century right up to the late nineteenth century (some might say arguably to the late twentieth century). The peculiarities of Württemberg consist in an almost 'topsy turvy restoration'. This happened mainly through the ascendancy of a group of technocrats within the administration, who made a vital contribution in the creation of the constitution of 1819. As will become clear later, this was something of a scientific achievement, so to speak.

Restoration upside down: The reversal of arguments during the constitutional conflict

The struggle over the constitution dominated the politics of Württemberg from 1815 to 1819. Two royal constitutions were rejected, before the estates consented to a third proposal. Surprisingly, the estates at first preferred not to have a constitution, not least to escape heavy taxation after the expensive Napoleonic wars.[7] The motives behind rejection also had an international dimension. Many subjects of the king of Württemberg felt like foreigners in their own land. This was something King Friedrich recognized, especially during the opening 'moves' at the Vienna Congress. He could only view any settlement approaching a real 'restoration' in Germany as a nightmare. Indeed, several other kings and dukes in Germany experienced similar forebodings and abhorred restoration. A complete return to the past would have entailed the resurrection of the baronial and even ecclesiastic territories these very rulers had seized thanks to Napoleon's dissolution of the Holy Roman Empire. At Vienna, this danger had seemed imminent. Former territorial rulers within the old Reich had tried to take advantage of the deliberations at the congress to seek a return of their lands,[8] even employing press campaigns.[9] After all, Metternich, who was effectively the chairman of the congress, was hardly a friend to this *Mittelstaat*. King Friedrich of Württemberg had subordinated his *Standesherren* in a quite humiliating manner;[10] this had included Franz Georg von Metternich (the father of the Habsburg chancellor). The Metternich family had been granted the landed estate of Ochsenhausen to compensate them for the loss of their ancient territories in the Rhineland. The former abbey of Ochsenhausen sat precariously within the enlarged kingdom of Württemberg, whose king was quite determined to discipline and control his new aristocratic subjects.[11]

There were also other traditional clients of the Habsburg dynasty who could be suspected with some justification of seeking a substantial restoration of their former territories. The state of Württemberg had incorporated much more *Reichsunmittelbare* (imperial immediacy that is, imperial cities, prince-bishoprics, secular principalities, and free imperial knights) than any other state. This set of circumstances made it much more vulnerable during the proceedings at Vienna. A considerable number of former imperial cities had lost their sovereignty by being subsumed within Württemberg. To these were also added lands formerly part of Vorderösterreich, which had lived throughout the *ancien régime* in a state of benign neglect. There were also a large number of former aristocratic rulers, the *Patriziat* of the imperial cities and the estates of other territories who had been annexed to the duke (from 1806, the king) of Württemberg.

There was a further threat to monarchical power that hid in the very bosom of the state's bureaucracy.[12] Encouraged by Napoleon, Friedrich had usurped power successfully in 1805. Until then, the estates of Württemberg had controlled their rulers tightly – in particular, by consenting to taxes (or, to be more accurate, by rejecting them).[13] Compared with other territories of the Holy Roman Empire, the estates of Württemberg had reached a unique preponderance, abruptly brought to an end in 1805. To reverse this, the *Ehrbarkeit* (or worthies), as the civic elite of Württemberg had been called, tried to reclaim their ancient prerogatives in 1815; even loyal counsellors to the king complained about the consequences of the radical breach of 1805.[14]

Surrounded by so many enemies, King Friedrich felt compelled to proclaim a constitution, unexpectedly casting himself in the role of a supporter of legal and political progress. Before his council, Friedrich denounced the ancient constitution as outworn and as contrary to the spirit of the time.[15] The constitution was meant as a coup, or pre-emptive strike, against the old intermediate powers of the *ancien régime*. His draft thus came as a surprise not only to his determined enemies, but also to many of his supporters. This constitution promised certain rights to which the future estates could scarcely object. Indeed, it was quite a liberal project, and the first post-Napoleonic constitution in Germany, not to mention the second to be adopted through parliamentary consent in Europe (the French *Charte constitutionnelle* having been the first).[16]

However, the king's expectations were to be thoroughly disappointed. The estates assembled in the *Landtag* dismissed the proposed constitution unanimously: its delegates (both those who were co-opted and those who were elected) insisted on the restoration of what they described as their *altes, gutes Recht* (the old, good laws).[17] A flood of publications inundated the public sphere and attacked what the king had considered a safe harbour for his own power. The 'ancient constitution' became the foam on the waves of discontent or, as Hegel put it, 'the shibboleth of former petty despots,' as he ridiculed the opponents to the constitution.[18]

This does seem to make the case of Württemberg a 'singularly interesting' one, as the *Edinburgh Review* put it. The *Landtag*, the estates, praised the ancient constitution, whereas the king strove to enhance his power by modernization. In the unique circumstances of Württemberg, 'restoration' served as a constitutional weapon against the ruler. Perhaps no other contemporary ruler so openly rejected tradition as a source of legitimation; tradition simply did not meet his ambition of reforming the country under his uncontested supervision.

In Württemberg and its newly integrated territories, tradition weakened the monarch. This united such diverse factions as the *Ehrbarkeit* of the ancient Duchy of Württemberg with people they had detested for hundreds of years, namely the mediatized princes of the former Holy Roman Empire. If they wanted to reclaim their former prerogatives, they had to rely exclusively on the power of tradition. Restoration would have meant the reconstitution of the powerful estates and of former sovereign imperial entities, to the disadvantage of the king and of those not represented in the old estates. Restoration, in the case of Württemberg, thus was turned upside down. The monarch was in fundamental opposition to the very *ancien régime* his estates adored (somewhat ironic given that the king had corresponded enthusiastically with Edmund Burke during the 1790s).[19]

Reform of career and careers of reform: Technocrats in the administration

This process was a familiar one and was not limited to the post-1815 era. To some extent, it was the reiteration of the constant opposition which the estates of Württemberg had manifested towards reform proposals from 1797 to 1806, a tradition that to some extent went back to the mid-eighteenth century, when Duke Karl Eugen had initiated a policy of modernization which was to exert a powerful influence on Württemberg well into the next century. The dukes had tried to strengthen their power by introducing new practices, whereas the estates insisted upon a long chain of precedents, dating from the Treaty of Tübingen in 1514 to the *Erbvergleich* of 1770 (which was the triumph of the *Ehrbarkeit*).[20] Every innovation proposed by the government was dismissed with the reply that tradition made such alterations impossible.

Duke Karl Eugen thus sought to bring about change through education and founded the *Karls-Schule* in 1770, and a *Hohe Schule*, from 1781 onwards (a university supervised by the duke himself). The *Karls-Schule* qualified its pupils in philosophy and in arts, medicine, natural sciences, jurisprudence and cameralism. This was how both the duke and many families in Württemberg intended to foster a new elite of technocrats[21] – even families traditionally opposed to ducal ambitions started to send their scions into the *Karls-Schule* (for example the Kerner dynasty).[22]

The effects of the *Karls-Schule* featured in the poetry of Friedrich Schiller, in many ways its model student, who was tutored amongst others by Jakob Friedrich Abel, one of the earliest and firmest adherents of Kantian philosophy.[23] Above all, they entered the bureaucracy, during the last two decades of the eighteenth century. They were admitted to it at the top, as was the norm under enlightened despotism. As long as the despot seemed skilled and benign, he could draw on the loyalty of his highly qualified servants. Indeed, those public servants who had been trained during the reign of Karl Eugen joined their colleagues in the higher ranks of the administration after only a few years.

If one were to fix a time when Württemberg moved beyond the *ancien régime*, one could argue it had already done so before the French Revolution – without radical reforms or disastrous disturbances. This transformation was a quiet and peaceful one, much less conspicuous and noticeable than the noisy *Reformlandtag*, that is, the diet which had sought to alter the political structures of Württemberg from 1797 to 1799 within existing constitutional frameworks.[24] This diet both failed and succeeded to some extent in its goals. Major debates emerged over such fundamental issues as suffrage, free or imperative mandate, the relationship between the diet and its committees, qualifications for the public service and the conditions of promotion for civil servants. But, to cut a long story short, the outcome proved relatively insignificant. Not a single one of the many reform proposals, some of them recorded in real or fictional *Cahiers,* such as the Nagold *Cahier* that critiqued an ignorant oligarchy, was accepted, and thus the political system of Württemberg remained impervious to change.[25]

What did change, however, was political thinking within Württemberg. The way in which people thought and acted politically evolved in the 1790s and 1800s as a slow but steady reshuffle transformed both public debate and administration. Young authors who started their careers in these years, among them Georg Wilhelm Friedrich Hegel, lamented the lack of skilled men within the ruling elite.[26] Fledgling civil servants climbed fast into the higher ranks, such as Friedrich List, who rose from subaltern clerk to professor of political economy (*Staatswirtschaft*) within an astonishing twelve years.[27] Liberalism had been fostered to a certain extent by the king of Württemberg. Although the *Karls-Schule* was dissolved in 1794, by then its effects had trickled down to the bureaucracy. Its former students entered its offices, ready to modernize the administration according to the precepts learned from their professors of cameralism. This development had benefited from the introduction of compulsory examinations prior to employment, and from the creation of performance standards in office that determined promotion.

Further measures sought to establish some sort of technocratic bureaucracy, even though they turned out to be far less effective than their proponents had hoped. Moreover, many of the professors of the *Karls-Schule* had taught part-time: their main occupations lay within the administration itself. Notable examples of this trend include Philipp Christian Friedrich von Normann-Ehrenfels, who later became first minister of King Friedrich,[28] Benjamin Ferdinand von Mohl, the father of Robert von Mohl, and many others. They combined theory and practice. Other professors also joined the administration, August Friedrich Batz, Karl Friedrich Elsässer, Johann August Reuß amongst them (who all rose to substantial positions in the next two decades and became involved in the quarrel over the constitution). Many more public servants who had been trained in the *Karls-Schule* pursued careers, both in the expanding head offices (for example in the *Staatsrat* and at the top of the new ministries) and in the local administration. In particular, the higher appointments within the administration were occupied by former students of the *Karls-Schule*, whose heyday came in the 1810s.[29]

Until then, many of these former students had excelled in the expanding state of Württemberg, especially in Neu-Württemberg (those territories acquired under Napoleon), in a way the 'nursery school of reorganisation'.[30] It was Neu-Württemberg that provided their most formative experiences. In order to integrate the territorial expansion that had followed the *Reichsdeputationshauptschluß* and subsequent treaties (roughly doubling both the territory of Württemberg and the number of inhabitants),[31] several commissions were established, consisting of young experts that had proved loyal both to the ruler and the new sciences of administration.

In fact, these men put into practice in these new territories those lessons which they would later apply to the entire state of Württemberg. From 1803 to 1806, Neu-Württemberg was exempted from the estates' jurisdiction. Following the *coup d'état* of

1805, these principles were applied to the entire state of Württemberg.[32] Around 1810, the former students of the *Karls-Schule* had reached senior positions within the newly formed ministries, within the *Kreise* (intermediate authorities) and within the *Oberämter* (districts). It was also the task of some former students of the *Karls-Schule* to sketch the constitution that King Friedrich eventually proclaimed in 1815.

For this reason, one can scarcely define this as an era of 'restoration' in the history of Württemberg. On the contrary the period is marked by continuity: the protagonists within the administration carried on much of the reform programme from the last decades of the eighteenth century into the first decades of the nineteenth. Moreover, the *Karls-Schule* was reborn to a certain extent, in 1817, with the foundation of a pioneering faculty of political economy (*Staatswirtschaft*) at the University of Tübingen. Indeed, many of its professorships were occupied by fervent critics of the *Schreiber* (scribes) within the administration.[33] King Wilhelm I sought to solve a fundamental problem: that is, the reality that some sections of his own administration frequently had frustrated modern reformist ideals of scientific administration. It was not coincidental that the son of a former professor of the *Karls-Schule* was to exert the deepest influence on the training of future public servants within and beyond the frontiers of Württemberg: namely Robert von Mohl.[34] This was all the more significant given that, though Württemberg still remained a small state, it was a vital hub within wider networks of intellectuals. Members of its elite knew each other personally and even celebrated the centenary of the birth of Karl Eugen in 1828.[35] These technocratic networks need further research, and their persistence may lead to a reassessment of how one should periodize the 'restoration.'

Conflict into consent: Mediation by science

The quarrel about the constitution soon led to a dilemma. Those who opposed the constitution had only one argument on which to rely: *das alte, gute Recht* ('the old, good laws'),[36] which was the only cause capable of uniting the divergent interests of an unstable coalition.

This coalition crumbled well before the constitutional quarrel itself was resolved. Some weeks after the rejection of the constitution in 1815, the gaps that separated the *Standesherren* from the *Ehrbarkeit* widened. The inhabitants of the old duchy distanced themselves from the inhabitants of the newly integrated territories, as did the deputies of the cities from the deputies of the rural population. The quarrel, as is so often the case, was caught in the narrow gulf that divides idealism from self-interest: some initially sought publicity (which no one knew better than Johann Friedrich Cotta, deputy and publisher, who with careful timing changed sides to favour the royal constitution)[37] only to eventually succumb to the need for career-building. A significant political compromise took place between spring 1815 and autumn 1819 (it was accelerated by a petitioning campaign).

The negotiations (some of them public, some of them secret, some of them commissioned, some of them rather ill-intentioned) revolved around the very nature of the state of Württemberg. Added to this were some very specific issues (such as forest management or hunting), the reform of institutions, practices and not least some government offices. For example, Ludwig Uhland cared little about the *altes, gutes Recht*. He coveted one of the attractive posts within the bureaucracy. He only opportunistically became a staunch proponent of the restoration of the ancient rights, once his ambitions were definitively frustrated.[38] On the contrary, Hegel might well have hoped to gain a well-paid position within the administration by publishing a witty article that condemned the ancient constitution as a malign fiction. In these pages, he attacked dull pretences of the estates as despotism, while at the same time praising the royal government (which unsurprisingly commissioned a partial reprint of his essay).[39]

In numerous cases, the government offered lucrative offices to former opponents of the royal constitution amongst myriad political concessions. These arrangements helped to cool the violent quarrel over the constitution in 1819. Yet the real interest lies elsewhere: even the most fervent adherents of the *altes, gutes Recht* did not actually wish to return power to the former estates. Rather, the *altes, gutes Recht* served as a rhetorical device to compel the king to make concessions. In the end, it became an instrument through which the government made excessive use in its quest to denounce the proponents of the 'ancient constitution', in order to present itself as the promoter of modernization.

In particular, the foundation of the *Staatswirtschaftliche Fakultät* at the University of Tübingen was intended to undermine the ostensibly backward-looking opposition to the new constitution. Its first professor, Friedrich List, had shown himself to be an eager, even esteemed reformer within the administration and an active propagandist in favour of the rational organization of the state as set out in the royal constitution.[40] This proved a risky move for List, who did not stop at just supporting the constitution, but pleaded for further reorganization of the state of Württemberg. This ultimately led to his dismissal from office.

This new university faculty redeemed a pledge from the 1790s; during the *Reformlandtag*, many publications had called for government by technocrats.[41] In 1817, the deputies of the *Landtag* did not resent the foundation of the new faculty at all, indeed they could not have resented it – simply because they made clear that they wanted to play a major role in modernizing the state. Accordingly, the former opposing parties found common ground in the idea that historical change had made some alterations of the 'ancient constitution' necessary. Even in the hectic rejection of the first constitution, the estates embraced the idea that some 'modifications' to the old statutes were necessary.[42]

The government swiftly followed these recommendations, especially Karl August von Wangenheim who was the closest adviser to King Friedrich.[43] He opined, in a conciliatory fashion, in his 1815 treatise, 'that the ancient constitution of Württemberg indeed contains some outdated features that have to be eradicated by a common resolution of ruler and people'.[44] Such was the basis of compromise, one that had its roots in the reforms of the 1790s. Administration was understood to rest upon science; the notion of an expert bureaucracy or, to be more accurate, 'technocracy',[45] had many supporters in Württemberg and scarcely any enemies. Such continuity challenges the concept of the 'restoration' as a completely distinct period – there were powerful ideas and trends that linked the years after 1815 to reform initiatives from the late eighteenth century: namely the promotion of the science of administration.

Conclusion: The hour of 'technocracy'

From 1815 to 1819, Württemberg seemed deeply divided by the conflict over its constitution. As a matter of fact, this division was more apparent than real. The quarrel about the *alte Verfassung* (ancient constitution) was more akin to a 'mock battle' than a genuine struggle. The royal opposition to the *ancien régime* found adherents even among those who at first had opposed the constitution. The scramble to resurrect old estates-based prerogatives resulted from an equally intense scramble for new offices. Instead of a romantic commitment to the medieval origins of the state of Württemberg, there was not much real support for the *alte Verfassung* other than some tactical opportunistic references to these old defunct statutes. The adherents of the *altes, gutes Recht* disappeared in 1819, as suddenly as they had appeared in 1815.

The estates' brief clamour for restoration was more a request for a specific form of modernization; indeed, the rule of skilled experts prepared the common ground on which the constitution of Württemberg could be established safely. There was firm continuity with the constitutional debates from the 1790s. Equally, there was firm continuity in the higher personnel of the administration (at least in their own self-perception as technocrats). And there was firm continuity in the vision that the state of Württemberg should be managed by highly skilled civil servants. This was a vision whose effects were felt well beyond Württemberg, and included the unruly professors of the 1830s, right up to the *Professorenparlament* of the *Paulskirche* in 1848, and the subsequent *Kathedersozialisten* (that is, those professors who used their chairs for socialist purposes from the 1870s onwards).

This leads into another 'long' nineteenth century, that of the professors. It makes Württemberg appear much less singular than the *Edinburgh Review* might have supposed. Such a diagnosis applies to other German states such as Bavaria, Baden, Hesse-Darmstadt, probably to Prussia, and perhaps even to Austria (from Joseph von Sonnenfels to Lorenz von Stein). These findings make the term 'restoration' questionable in many respects. In truth, there was scarcely any 'restoration' in Württemberg. One questions the value of the very term 'restoration' itself, and whether the years from 1815 to 1848 possess any form of unity, whether heuristic or otherwise. In the case of Württemberg, there was a continuous and consistent process of state reform from the 1790s to at least the 1860s – this was the era of technocrats. Most joined the king's opposition to the *ancien régime* and rejected 'restoration'.

Notes

1 This chapter is drawn from the author's Habilitationsschrift. For further details see Georg Eckert, *Zeitgeist auf Ordnungssuche. Die Begründung des Königreiches Württemberg 1797–1819* (Göttingen, 2016).

2   For the quarrel over the constitution see Joachim Gerner, *Vorgeschichte und Entstehung der württembergischen Verfassung im Spiegel der Quellen (1815–1819)* (Stuttgart, 1989).
3   In the words of a review of the proceedings within the Assembly of the States – 'Verhandlungen in der Versammlung der Landstände des Königreichs Württemberg. Stuttgart, 1816–17' (Proceedings in the Assembly of the States of the Kingdom of Wirtemberg), *The Edinburgh Review*, no. 58, February 1818, 337–63, 338.
4   Ibid., 340.
5   Fritz René Allemann, *Bonn ist nicht Weimar* (Köln/Berlin, 1956), 110.
6   Ina Ulrike Paul, *Württemberg 1797–1816/19. Quellen und Studien zur Entstehung des modernen württembergischen Staates*, 2 vols (München, 2005); and for the continuity of some sort of civic liberalism throughout the nineteenth century is highlighted in Bernhard Mann, 'Württemberg 1800 bis 1866', in H. Schwarzmaier (ed.), *Handbuch der Baden-Württembergischen Geschichte*, vol. 3: *Vom Ende der Alten Reiches bis zum Ende der Monarchien* (Stuttgart, 1992), 235–331, 330.
7   Friedrich Wintterlin, 'Die württembergische Verfassung 1815–1819', *Württembergische Jahrbücher für Statistik und Landeskunde* (1912), 47–83, 49.
8   Georg Grupp, 'Die Verfassungskämpfe 1815–17 und der hohe Adel, insbesondere Fürst Ludwig v. Öttingen-Wallerstein', *Württembergische Vierteljahrshefte für Landesgeschichte* 27 (1918), 177–214, 203.
9   Rudolf Vierhaus, 'Eigentumsrecht und Mediatisierung. Der Kampf um die Rechte der Reichsritterschaft 1803–1815', in R. Vierhaus (ed.), *Eigentum und Verfassung. Zur Eigentumsdiskussion im ausgehenden 18. Jahrhundert* (Göttingen, 1972), 229–57, 253sq.
10 Heinz Gollwitzer, *Die Standesherren. Die politische und gesellschaftliche Stellung der Mediatisierten 1815–1918. Ein Beitrag zur deutschen Sozialgeschichte*, 2nd edn (Göttingen, 1964), 54.
11 Wolfram Siemann, *Metternich. Stratege und Visionär* (München, 2016), 246–50.
12 Albert Friedrich von Lempp and Eberhard Friedrich Georgii composed expert opinions against the royal constitution: Gerner, *Vorgeschichte und Entstehung der württembergischen Verfassung*, 61.
13 Sabine Koch, *Kontinuität im Zeichen des Wandels. Verfassung und Finanzen in Württemberg um 1800* (Stuttgart, 2015), 34.
14 Auszug aus der Darstellung der Beschwerden der Lands, 07. September 1815, Hauptstaatsarchiv Stuttgart E 31 Büschel 190.
15 Rede Seiner Königlichen Majestät, gehalten im versammelten StaatsRath den 11t. Jan. 1815, Hauptstaatsarchiv Stuttgart E 7 Büschel 116.
16 Hartwig Brandt, 'Die deutschen Staaten der ersten Konstitutionalisierungswelle', in W. Daum et al. (eds), *Handbuch der europäischen Verfassungsgeschichte im 19. Jahrhundert. Institutionen und Rechtspraxis im gesellschaftlichen Wandel*, vol. 2: *1815–1847* (Bonn, 2012), 823–77, 829.
17 Eckert, *Zeitgeist auf Ordnungssuche*, 357.
18 The 'ancient constitution' of Württemberg served the purpose of countering the royal prerogative in a very similar way as the English 'ancient constitution' in the seventeenth century had done: John G. A. Pocock, *The Ancient Constitution and the Feudal Law: A Study of English Historical Thought in the Seventeenth Century* (Cambridge, 1987). Georg Wilhelm Friedrich Hegel, '[Beurteilung der] Verhandlungen in der Versammlung der Landstände des Königreichs Württemberg im Jahr 1815 und 1816. XXXIII Abteilungen', in: E. Moldenauer and K. M. Michel (eds), Georg Wilhelm

Friedrich Hegel, *Werke*, vol. 4: *Nürnberger und Heidelberger Schriften 1808–1817*, 4th edn (Frankfurt am Main, 2003), 462–597, 533.

19 Erwin Hölzle, *Das Alte Recht und die Revolution. Eine politische Geschichte Württembergs in der Revolutionszeit 1789–1805* (München/Berlin, 1931), 144.

20 Matthias Stickler, 'Von der Landschaft zur Verfassung von 1819. Württembergs Weg zum monarchischen Konstitutionalismus (1514–1819)', in R. Gehrke (ed.), *Aufbrüche in die Moderne. Frühparlamentarismus zwischen altständischer Ordnung und monarchischem Konstitutionalismus 1750–1850: Schlesien – Deutschland – Mitteleuropa* (Köln, 2005), 74–102, 83.

21 Isa Schikorsky, 'Hohe Schulen', in N. Hammerstein and U. Herrmann (eds), *Handbuch der deutschen Bildungsgeschichte*, vol. 2: *18. Jahrhundert. Vom späten 17. Jahrhundert bis zur Neuordnung Deutschlands um 1800* (München, 2005), 355–68, 361.

22 Justinus Kerner, 'Bilderbuch aus meiner Knabenzeit', in G. Grimm (ed.), Justinus Kerner, *Ausgewählte Werke* (Stuttgart, 1981), 111–363, 358.

23 Peter-André Alt, *Schiller: Leben – Werk – Zeit, vol. 1* (München, 2000), 113–35.

24 Ewald Grothe, 'Der württembergische Reformlandtag 1797–1799', *Zeitschrift für Württembergische Landesgeschichte* 48 (1989), 161–200, 163.

25 Barbara Vopelius-Holtzendorff, 'Das Nagolder Cahier und seine Zeit. Beschwerdeschrift mit Instruktionen für den Abgeordneten zum württembergischen Landtag von 1797 (Edition)', *Zeitschrift für Württembergische Landesgeschichte* 37 (1978), 122–78, 162.

26 Georg Wilhelm Friedrich Hegel, 'Daß die Magistrate von den Bürgern gewählt werden müssen [Über die neuesten inneren Verhältnisse Württembergs, besonders über die Gebrechen der Magistratsverfassung] (1798)', in E. Moldenauer and K. M. Michel (eds), Georg Wilhelm Friedrich Hegel, *Werke*, vol. 1: *Frühe Schriften*, 4th edn (Frankfurt am Main, 1999), 268–73, 272sq.

27 Paul Gehring, *Friedrich List. Jugend- und Reifejahre 1789–1825* (Tübingen, 1964).

28 Ina-Ulrike Paul, 'Diplomatie und Reformen "für Württembergs bleibende Größe." Philipp Christian Friedrich Graf von Normann-Ehrenfels und die Entstehung des modernen württembergischen Staates', *Zeitschrift für Württembergische Landesgeschichte* 78 (2009), 321–43.

29 Eckert, *Zeitgeist auf Ordnungssuche*, 340–6.

30 Max Miller, *Die Organisation und Verwaltung von Neuwürttemberg unter Herzog und Kurfürst Friedrich* (Stuttgart/Berlin, 1934), 50.

31 Karl Göz, *Das Staatsrecht des Königreiches Württemberg* (Tübingen, 1908), 7sq.

32 Ernst Rudolf Huber, *Deutsche Verfassungsgeschichte seit 1789*, vol. 1: *Reform und Restauration 1789 bis 1830*, 2nd edn (Stuttgart, 1967), 329.

33 Karl Erich Born, *Geschichte der Wirtschaftswissenschaften an der Universität Tübingen 1817–1967. Staatswirtschaftliche Fakultät – Staatswissenschaftliche Fakultät – Wirtschaftswissenschaftliche Abteilung der Rechts- und Wirtschaftswissenschaftlichen Fakultät* (Tübingen, 1967), 18.

34 Wilhelm Bleek, 'Die Tübinger Schule der gesamten Staatswissenschaft', in W. Bleek and H. J. Lietzmann (eds), *Schulen in der deutschen Politikwissenschaft* (Opladen, 1999), 105–29.

35 Werner Gebhardt, *Die Schüler der Hohen Karlsschule. Ein biographisches Lexikon* (Stuttgart, 2011), 19sq.

36 This was indeed a 'magic formula': Volker Press, 'Der württembergische Landtag im Zeitalter des Umbruchs 1770–1830', *Zeitschrift für Württembergische Landesgeschichte* 42 (1983), 256–81, 273.

37 Bernhard Fischer, *Johann Friedrich Cotta. Verleger – Entrepreneur – Politiker* (Göttingen, 2014), 464–8.
38 See his correspondence with his father: Ludwig Uhland to Johann Friedrich Uhland, Stuttgart, 4 October 1818, in Julius Hartmann (ed.), *Uhlands Briefwechsel*, vol. 2 (Stuttgart 1912), 74sq.
39 Walter Jaeschke, *Hegel-Handbuch. Leben – Werk – Schule*, 2nd edn (Stuttgart, 2010), 257–9.
40 Eugen Wendler, *Friedrich List (1789–1846). Ein Ökonom mit Weitblick und sozialer Verantwortung* (Wiesbaden, 2013), 27sq.
41 For example: *Wirtembergische Blätter. Eine Beilage zu der Zeitschrift: Die Verhandlungen auf dem Wirtembergischen Landtage im Jahre 1797, Erstes bis Zehendes Stük* (Stuttgart, 1797), 27; [Johann Gottfried Pahl,] *Wohlgemeyntes, in Vernunft und Schrift bestgegründetes, jedoch unmaaßgebliches Gutachten, über die Wahlfähigkeit eines Landtagsdeputirten in Wirtemberg; auf ausdrükliches Verlangen der ehrsamen Amtsversammlung zu Ypsilon, salvo meliori, gestellt, aus Liebe zur Wahrheit an den Tag gegeben, und den sämtlichen wirtembergischen Ortsmagistraten devotest dedicirt von Sebastian Käsbohrer, t. Schulmeister in Ganslosen. Gedrukt am ersten April 1797*, 40sq.
42 *Verhandlungen in der Versammlung der Landstände des Königreichs Württemberg, im Jahr 1815, Zweite Abtheilung, März/April 1815*, 8.
43 Friedrich Wintterlin, 'Wangenheim, Karl August Frhr. v.', *Allgemeine Deutsche Biographie* 41 (1896), 153–5.
44 [Karl August von Wangenheim,] *Die Idee der Staatsverfassung. In ihrer Anwendung auf Wirtembergs alte Landesverfassung und den Entwurf zu deren Erneuerung* (Frankfurt am Main, 1815), 279.
45 For the modern idea of technocracy see Helmut Schelsky, *Auf der Suche nach Wirklichkeit. Gesammelte Aufsätze* (Düsseldorf/Köln, 1965), 439–80.

Part Three

Composite Monarchy Restored

11

The Austrian Empire as a Composite Monarchy after 1815[1]

Karin Schneider

The concept of the 'composite monarchy' dates back to H. G. Koenigsberger and was elaborated by J. H. Elliott in 1992.[2] The concept refers to early modern territories consisting of several nations with differing constitutional structures, but ruled by one monarch. Classical examples of this category of historical statehood are Spain and the Ottoman Empire.[3] Elliott refers to the seventeenth-century Spanish lawyer Juan de Solórzano Pereira, who differentiated two ways in which rulers could unite recently acquired territories with their traditional dominions. On the one hand, there was the possibility of collective national integration, in which the newly acquired region was regarded as a legal component of the existing territory. But there was also the possibility of an *aeque principaliter* link, in which the different territories were considered different constitutional entities. In this formulation, the traditional privileges, laws and customs remained valid, and the connecting element between the different regions consisted in the person of the monarch.[4]

Despite the many administrative reforms of the eighteenth century, the Austrian Empire, created in 1804, still ranked as a composite state. However, in the light of the challenges posed by the Napoleonic wars, the traditional relations between a collective overall government and the regions became open for discussion.

This process is reflected in the recent historiography of the Habsburg Monarchy. In 2018 William D. Godsey published a monograph exploring the functionality of the Habsburg Monarchy and the efficiency of its internal structure through the prism of the relationship between the Lower Austrian Estates and the central government during the revolutionary and Napoleonic periods. Applying the concepts of 'composite monarchy' and the 'fiscal-military state' he stresses the central importance of the resilience of the power of the Habsburg state over time. Composite states, he argues, were not an abnormality in the early modern period or even in the nineteenth century, but under certain circumstances were a successful and dynamic model for adapting to internal and external challenges.[5]

John Deak, on the other hand, follows a more traditional approach in stressing the importance of a strong central authority for a 'modern' state. In his study, *Forging a Multinational State*, Deak focuses on the process of 'state building' in the Habsburg Monarchy in the period between the reforms of Maria Theresa in the mid-eighteenth century and the First World War. Central to his discussion are the theories of the central authorities on how an 'ideal' state should be structured, the development of the bureaucracy, and its resultant impact on society.[6]

Finally, Pieter Judson explores in his *The Habsburg Empire: A New History* the integrative powers of bureaucracy, administration, science, culture and – not least – of the imperial court in Vienna. Judson challenges some prevailing historiographical perceptions, particularly the traditional understanding of nation and empire as opposites, and Judson qualifies the national conflicts by comparing the Habsburg Monarchy with other European states in the nineteenth century, where similar developments can be observed.[7]

Based on two reform projects from the first decades of the nineteenth century, this chapter addresses various perspectives on the composite statehood of the Austrian Empire and analyses their possible consequences for the structure of the Habsburg Monarchy. This will be placed against the backdrop of the dynamic developments initiated in the Monarchy by the Napoleonic wars.

Internal structures of the Austrian Empire

Around 1800, the constitutional character of the Austrian Empire was a recurring topic in publications about the Habsburg Monarchy. The geographer and statistician Joseph Constantin Bisinger, for instance, observed in 1809 'that there was not one state in Europe whose constitution was composed of so many anomalies as that of the Austrian Empire'.[8] And in 1807, the expert in constitutional law, Wenzel Gustav Kopetz, referred to the 'peculiar nature of the Austrian Monarchy', that is 'its composition of so many states that are more or less different from one another in terms of constitution'.[9]

Since the thirteenth century, the Habsburgs had united many territories through marriage, inheritance and war. Following the Congress of Vienna in 1814–15, the empire was divided into twelve provinces,[10] each constitutionally linked to the dynasty by a specific relationship. The cohesion between the individual components was primarily provided by the ruler, who reigned over the different regions as an emperor, king or prince, although numerous reforms in the course of the eighteenth century had effected greater integration within the western portion of the Monarchy. A territorial and nominally binding link had been created in 1804 with the assumption of the title of Emperor of Austria by Francis II/I. Yet, at the same time the monarch also confirmed the rights and the independence of the individual regions. In addition, according to the decree on the assumption of the imperial dignity, the concept of 'Austria' did not relate to a territory, but to the name of the Habsburg dynasty.[11] There is no mention of an Austrian Empire in the text.[12] This assumption of the title of emperor *ad personam* continues to reflect the composite nature of the Monarchy, and this was deliberate: Emperor Francis meant to maintain his equal status with the other rulers in Europe, particularly with Tsar Alexander I of Russia and Napoleon, who had crowned himself Emperor of the French.

Two years later, in 1806, Francis bowed to Napoleon's pressure and relinquished the crown of the Holy Roman Empire and simultaneously abolished the old Reich. Then, in the autumn of 1806, Francis decided that 'the words Austrian Empire or Austrian Imperial State were to be employed in all official writings or documents'.[13] Thus, the name of the dynasty was removed from official parlance and now referred to a dominion. On the symbolic level, the newly established empire legitimized itself through a kind of *Translatio Imperii*, and transfer of empire. The history of the Habsburg dynasty had been linked to the tradition of the Holy Roman Empire for centuries; this tradition was now transferred to the Austrian Empire and adapted accordingly. Henceforth, the Austrian Emperor took over not only buildings, such as the Imperial Court Chancellery in the Hofburg, as well as symbols, like the colours black/gold and the imperial insignia, but also continued to exercise the rights of the Holy Roman Emperor. They included, for instance, the *Jus exclusivae*, conceding the emperor a veto right in the election of the Pope or the presentation of the so-called *fasciae*, swaddling clothes blessed by the Pope, on the birth of a child to the Emperor.

Many European governments acknowledged this: Pope Pius VII expressed his desire in 1806 that Emperor Francis, like the Holy Roman Emperor, 'should continue to view himself as the protector of the Holy See'.[14] Nevertheless, integrative language usage did not create an empire, as the Prussian envoy to Vienna, Karl Friedrich von dem Knesebeck, reported to King Friedrich Wilhelm III: 'The alien parts of which [the Austrian Monarchy] is composed still do not form an entity living in union and over which the emperor is the lord. [The individual regions have such] different interests..., over which the emperor is only more or less master, to the extent that the constitutions of the individual states permit such. But it can be said brazenly that he [is] not at all the ruler in Hungary'.[15] In Hungary, as early as 1802, the Estates had exacted from Francis the promise to convene them every three years.[16] The heterogeneous character of the territory could not be achieved simply by the acceptance of the title of Emperor or an amendment of linguistic conventions, especially as Francis had expressly confirmed the rights of the individual regions of the Monarchy in a decree of 1804.

The Austrian Empire after the Congress of Vienna

The Congress of Vienna in 1814–15 undertook the political and territorial realignment of Europe after the fall of Napoleon.[17] For the Habsburg Monarchy, the Congress of Vienna afforded the prospect of territorial expansion. Regions and provinces that had had to be relinquished during the Napoleonic wars could be reclaimed, together with former territories of the Holy Roman Empire, such as the erstwhile Prince-Archbishopric of Salzburg. Amongst other areas, Bavaria had to cede Tyrol and Vorarlberg, which had been granted to it by Napoleon by the Peace of Pressburg in 1805. In a secret protocol to the First Peace of Paris, it had been stipulated that Lombardy and Venetia were to return to the Habsburgs. Tyrol, Vorarlberg, Lombardy and Venetia had all seen fundamental reforms during the Napoleonic era, and traditional structures of domination and privileges had been eliminated. Francis appointed the Central Organizational Court Commission to integrate these reacquired territories. Given the establishment of the new Austrian Empire, it must be asked how the integration of these areas into Habsburg dominion proceeded. Did the idea of a unified state come into effect by refraining from restoring federal institutions, or were the territories endowed with a high degree of self-administration in terms of a composite state?

The princely county of Tyrol had been part of the Habsburg dominions since 1363. The relationship between the territorial prince and the representatives of the county was regulated by a charter of liberties of 1342, confirming its traditional rights and customs, and stipulating that no exceptional taxes might be collected without the consent of the Estates. In 1406, the Habsburgs issued a new charter of liberties, by which they confirmed the traditional rights once more and restricted military service by the aristocracy to a month per year, and only within the territory of the province.[18] In the course of the late Middle Ages and the early modern era, Habsburg policy in Vorarlberg developed from a group of small demesnes into a consolidated territory. After Napoleon transferred it to Bavaria in 1806, the traditional ruling structures were abolished in Tyrol and Vorarlberg. The Bavarian government sought to create a centralized, unitary state on the French pattern. Comprehensive constitutional and administrative reform put an end to self-administration at the level of communities and courts.[19]

Article 93 of the final act of the Congress of Vienna stated that, among other things, Tyrol and Vorarlberg were to be placed under the sovereignty of the Austrian monarch. Following the historic provincial constitution, on 24 March 1816 Emperor Francis proclaimed the 're-introduction of the estates-based constitution in Tyrol'. Simultaneously, the government took the opportunity to consolidate the rights intervention of the administration in Vienna, by not restoring the rights of the Estates to their original extent. Compared to the pre-Napoleonic situation, Francis introduced various 'improvements . . . required by changed conditions and the needs of the time'. The monarch reserved the right of taxation 'in its entire extent', as well as inclusion in the provincial registers. Among other things, the Estates retained the rights to send petitions to the Emperor, to collect property tax in keeping with imperial stipulations and for its officials to wear a uniform.[20]

In Vorarlberg, the Austrian government did not revoke the Bavarian reforms, but rather supplemented them. Thus they ensured Vorarlberg became more modernized in comparison with most other crownlands, creating the prerequisites for the economic boom the region experienced in the second half of the nineteenth century.[21] When Vorarlberg returned to the Habsburg crown in 1816, the Estates abolished by the Bavarian government in 1808 were restored. However, this was merely a formality, as no authority was assigned to the Estates in the relevant patent, which was never published. By contrast, the restoration took place under the aegis of the Provincial Homage of 1816, to which Vorarlberg could now despatch a legitimized deputation.[22]

The historical and political conditions were fundamentally different in the Kingdom of Lombardy-Venetia, established in 1815. Lombardy had belonged to the Monarchy since the eighteenth century and became part of the Transpadanian Republic, under French influence, in 1796 and of the Cisalpine Republic in 1797. Venice and its hinterland were granted to the Habsburg Monarchy by the Peace of Campo Formio in 1797. By the Peace of Pressburg in 1805, Venice became part of the Napoleonic Kingdom of Italy.[23] After 1814, Austria retained some of the Napoleonic reforms and created an efficient administration in the Kingdom, following the example of the other provinces.[24] In administrative terms, the rivalries between La Serenissima and Lombardy were balanced by the equal treatment of both regions by Vienna. Central congregations were established in Milan and Venice, and subordinate provincial congregations in the provinces, whose members were appointed by the emperor from three candidates proposed after a complicated selection procedure. The central congregations had competence over tax administration, the distribution of military obligations, the maintenance of infrastructure and public welfare, and acted as advisory bodies. Unlike the Estates, their activities were not subject to convocation by the monarch.[25] Hence, the recently acquired regions took their bearings from Vienna, whilst the Viceroy installed in Milan, Archduke Rainer, merely had a representative function.[26]

These examples – which could be multiplied – show the different ways in which the Viennese government dealt with the territories acquired during the Congress of Vienna. Depending on historical conditions and whether the region had been seized or awarded in a peace treaty, the constitutional relationships of the individual regions and their links to the Austrian Empire were modernized. The recently enacted provincial constitutions evince a tendency towards weakening autonomous rights, replacing them with a closer alignment towards Vienna. Yet, after the Congress of Vienna, the provinces still had individual constitutional relationships with the monarch which determined their assertiveness towards the government. Whereas in 1816 the rights of the Tyrolean Estates were not fully restored, those of Hungary continued to possess extensive rights over tax collection and military recruitment. With the congregations, the Kingdom of Lombardy-Venetia, for its part, obtained bodies with far-reaching advisory competencies, yet directly subordinate to the emperor in Vienna.

Reform projects

After 1804, the heterogeneous nature of the Austrian Empire repeatedly gave cause for further plans for reform. According to the foreign minister at the time, Count Johann Philipp Stadion, apart from retaining equality in status, the assumption of the title of Emperor of Austria entailed achieving '*en passant* ... a new constitutional relationship common to the hereditary states, a point of unity, and of erecting a symbol of liberty that had been lacking up to then'.[27] The first decades of the nineteenth century witnessed repeated deliberations as to how this objective was to be achieved. Constitutional integration is closely linked to increased administrative activity and an intensive penetration of the provinces by central authority. With the foundation of a state council and a consistent state administration, Maria Theresa and Joseph II had taken decisive steps in this direction in the eighteenth century, but the Hungarian provinces were not affected by these measures.[28]

Around 1800, various reform ideas emerged about the constitutional structure of the Habsburg Monarchy, often focusing on the relationship with Hungary. They originated within the government and the imperial family, exemplified by a memorandum by Archduke Rainer in 1809 entitled: 'Ideas about reforms and improvements to be initiated in the Austrian Monarchy'. At first sight, it is striking that the traditional term 'Austrian Monarchy' should still be employed by a member of the imperial family five years after the assumption of the title of Austrian Emperor and contrary to the imperial decree mentioned above. However, the archduke argued that this gave the Monarchy a grave problem, as its economic, political and military progress was inhibited by its composite nature. This structural problem could only be met by removing all the divisive elements between the two sides of the Monarchy.[29] The goal had to be the creation of a nation that could be ruled according to a uniform constitution.[30] Archduke Rainer regarded the moment after the defeat by France in the Fifth Coalition War in 1809 as the perfect juncture for a reform of this nature, since reforms would have to be undertaken in any case, because of the territorial changes brought about by the Peace of Schönbrunn; he surmised the public would welcome them after suffering such an ignominious military defeat.[31]

The archduke considered Hungary and Transylvania as the main obstacles to constitutional reforms. Thus Hungary – not the German-speaking provinces – was to be placed at the core of the intended homogeneous state entity. The other regions were to be modelled on the Hungarian pattern for the time being. In this way, he hoped to gain the support of the Hungarian Estates for his proposal. In the medium term, however, a commission of experts from all the parts of the Monarchy was to elaborate a constitution, to govern the whole the Austrian Empire. The constitution was then to be implemented equally in all the provinces.[32]

In particular, Archuke Rainer recommended removing the remaining rights of the Hungarian and Transylvanian Estates, which exercised powerful political influence. In his view, the Estates were to act merely as advisors to and recipients of orders from the monarch. He planned to reform the composition of the Estates by having the representatives of all the social classes replaced by proxies.[33]

In his memorandum, Archduke Rainer presented a concept aimed at creating centralizing structures in the Austrian Empire. The traditional constitutions of the individual provinces of the Monarchy were to be abolished in favour of a uniform state law, and the status of the Estates was to be marginalized as a result. This was meant to weld the population together into a homogeneous nation. He hoped to subvert the expected Hungarian opposition to these measures by ostensibly extending the Hungarian constitution to the whole territory of the Monarchy. Ultimately, Rainer sought to consolidate the government and Vienna, and especially the position of the monarch, who was to reign independent in his decisions and free from interference by the Estates. The model for these deliberations was probably France, efficiently ruled by Napoleon, which had impressively proved its military superiority in recent years, or the Kingdom of Bavaria, which was implementing an extensive reform project on Napoleonic lines.[34]

A completely different approach was taken by a reform proposal of 1817, elaborated by the foreign minister of the Austrian Empire at the time, Prince Clemens Wenzel Metternich,[35] dealing with the administrative structure of the Monarchy and the representation of the different provinces in Vienna. The goal of the changes proposed was to strengthen the Monarchy against future challenges such as social turmoil and revolutions. This was to take place by systematically restructuring internal administration, which was to respect the wishes of local elites, thus creating a balanced equilibrium between the government in Vienna and the representatives of the crownlands. An important point in Metternich's reform proposals concerned the treatment of the different nations united under the Habsburg crown. In his view, they were to be treated equally and their traditions, language and customary rights respected. Metternich rejected any idea of Germanizing or enforcing uniformity on different peoples.

Metternich criticized past and current practice, especially the prevailing imbalance between the administrations in the western and the eastern provinces of the Monarchy. Hungary, for instance, was present in Vienna through two Court Chancelleries – a Hungarian one and a Transylvanian one – whereas only the Joint Bohemian-Austrian and Galician Court Chancellery was responsible for the remaining provinces.[36] Metternich's plan envisaged a restructuring of internal administration on two levels: he recommended creating a Supreme Chancellor and Minister of the Interior, presiding over a relevant authority, to act as the guardian and representative of the unity of the government. On a lower level, Metternich assigned the Supreme Chancellor four more chancelleries: a Bohemian-Moravian-Galician Chancellery, an Italian Chancellery, an Austrian Chancellery and an Illyrian Chancellery. In addition, the Hungarian and Transylvanian Chancelleries were to continue to exist. In Metternich's project, the chancelleries were to represent the interests of their respective provinces in Vienna. Through this dialectic system, combining federalist and centralist approaches, Metternich hoped to achieve a 'unity in diversity' that would provide the Austrian Empire with more internal coherence.[37]

The proposal was received favourably by Emperor Francis, but its implementation took place in a form and manner that ran contrary to Metternich's intentions. The Austrian and Illyrian Chancelleries were amalgamated into a single body, the creation of a unifying control authority did not take place and the position of a Supreme Chancellor and Minister of the Interior was not filled. Moreover, only the Italian and the Bohemian-Moravian-Galician Chancelleries received their own chancellors.[38]

Unlike Archduke Rainer, Metternich had a critical view of a uniform, centralized constitution for the entire Monarchy. It would, he reasoned, involve the 'idea of a central representation of the nation'.[39] Whereas Archduke Rainer wished to constitute this central body from the representatives of the estates, assigning it an advisory role, Metternich discerned the fundamental problem in the large number of different nations living in the Austrian Empire and the associated diversity of languages. Therefore, he advocated retaining the composite state structure and respecting regional and national interests and identities.[40]

Conclusion

As this chapter has shown, the Austrian Empire was categorized as a composite state by constitutional experts in the nineteenth century. They spoke of 'states' within the Monarchy, ruled according to their own constitutions. The reforms of the eighteenth century had brought no fundamental changes, especially in Hungary and Transylvania.

Yet in the western half of the Monarchy, around 1800 the traditional provincial constitutions were still in force, as the example of Tyrol shows, determining the relationship between the government in Vienna and the representatives of the provinces. The assumption of the title of a hereditary Emperor of Austria in 1804 changed nothing in the internal structures of the Monarchy; quite the opposite for they were confirmed in 1804.[41] For the time being, this new title related exclusively to the person of the monarch. It was only after the end of the Holy Roman Empire in 1806 that the title acquired an empire to go with it, covering all the lands ruled by the Habsburgs. The Austrian court compensated for the absence of a historical legitimation for this elevation in status by a form of *Translatio Imperii* whereby the symbols and rights pertaining to the Emperor of the Holy Roman Empire were transferred to the Emperor of Austria. An 'invention of tradition'[42] came about, in which the Austrian Empire was set in the tradition of the German Reich – in the genealogical form of the Habsburg dynasty.

The aftermath of the Napoleonic wars provided the Austrian Empire with territorial gains. Not only did many areas that had been ceded to France and its allies revert to the Habsburgs, but new territories were acquired. Their integration in the empire did not occur in a uniform manner but, rather, according to historical conditions. Nevertheless, we can observe a tendency towards curtailing historical provincial rights, as in the provincial constitutions enacted after 1816, or in the character of the government in the Kingdom of Lombardy-Venetia. In all these cases, the person of the monarch remained the linking element between the different provinces of the Habsburg Monarchy.

For some Habsburg statesmen, the composite nature of the Austrian Empire posed multiple obstacles. In the opinion of contemporaries, the Napoleonic wars demonstrated military and financial deficiencies in the confrontation not only with a militarily powerful France, but also in comparison to Bavaria, which was implementing an extensive and centralized reform programme under von Montgelas.[43] Despite these constraints, however, that the Austrian Empire offered tenacious resistance to French aggression. The Monarchy was the only continental power to participate in nearly all the coalition wars and was able to raise enormous armies repeatedly. Its subjects, still in temporarily occupied areas, proved resistant to Napoleon's promises. Even after 1809, the Austrian Empire remained a great power and a player in international politics.[44]

The reform projects developed in the Austrian Empire in the first decades of the nineteenth century covered a broad spectrum, extending from radical centralism on the pattern of the ill-fated Josephinian reforms to federal approaches. On the one hand, they fed the idea that, in the short run, a composite monarchy was hardly equal to a centrally organized state in many respects. Here, ruling implied to a certain extent negotiating, as is shown by the provincial diets in Hungary in the first decade of the nineteenth century.[45] Whether these ideas were justified may, however, be doubted in light of the resilience of the Austrian Empire to French expansionism.

Conversely, many diverse nations lived within the borders of the Habsburg Monarchy who saw themselves represented in this composite character and hence the federal structures associated with it. These thoughts guided Metternich, who wanted to secure the existence of the Monarchy in the medium and long term. None of the reform projects presented here were ever realized. It was only during the first years of Emperor Francis Joseph's reign that the introduction of neo-absolutism in 1851 led to a centralized state which, however, only represented the beginning of the constitutional era and the dualism between Austria and Hungary after 1867.

Notes

1. Following contemporary usage, the terms 'Austrian Empire' and 'Austrian Monarchy' or 'Habsburg Monarchy' are used with equal value here. This article was written with financial support from the Jubilee Fund of the Austrian National Bank (project number 16866) and translated by Ian Mansfield.
2. J. H. Elliott, 'A Europe of Composite Monarchies', *Past & Present* 137: *The Cultural and Political Construction of Europe* (1992), 48–71, on Koenigsberger 50–1.
3. Regarding the Ottoman Empire see Daniel Goffman and Christopher Stroop, 'Empire as Composite: The Ottoman Polity and the Typology of Dominion', in B. Rajan and E. Sauer (eds), *Imperialisms. Historical and Literary Investigations, 1500–1900* (New York, 2004), 129–45.
4. Elliott, 'A Europe of Composite Monarchies', 52–3.
5. William D. Godsey, *The Sinews of Habsburg Power. Lower Austria in a Fiscal-Military State 1650–1820* (Oxford, 2018).
6. John Deak, *Forging a Multinational State. State Making in Imperial Austria from the Enlightenment to the First World War* (Stanford, 2015).
7. Pieter Judson, *The Habsburg Empire. A New History* (Cambridge, MA, London, 2016). In his review essay, 'Visions and Revisions of Empire: Reflections on a New History of the Habsburg Monarchy' (published in *Austrian History Yearbook* 49 (2018), 261–80) Laurence Cole places Judson's new interpretation of the Habsburg Monarchy in the context of the scholarly literature published since 1989 on this topic. The author analyses several histories of the Habsburg Monarchy, highlights the innovative aspects of the texts and provides a good survey of the recent scholarly literature on the Habsburg Monarchy. See Alan Sked, *The Decline and Fall of the Habsburg Empire 1815–1918* (Harlow, 2001). Idem, *Metternich and Austria. An Evaluation* (Basingstoke, New York, 2008). Charles Ingrao, *The Habsburg Monarchy 1618–1815* (Cambridge, 2000). Robin Okey, *The Habsburg Monarchy c. 1765–1918. From Enlightenment to Eclipse* (Basingstoke, 2001). Paula Sutter Fichtner, *The Habsburg Monarchy 1490–1848* (Basingstoke, New York, 2003). Helmut Rumpler, *Österreichische Geschichte 1804–1914. Eine Chance für Mitteleuropa: bürgerliche Emanzipation und Staatsverfall in der Habsburgermonarchie* (Vienna, 1997). R. J. W. Evans, *Austria, Hungary, and the Habsburgs. Essays on Central Europe, c. 1683–1867* (Oxford, 2006). Marco Bellabarba, *L'impero asburgico* (Bologna, 2014). Jean Bérenger, *L'Autriche-Hongrie 1815–1918* (Paris, 1994). Steven Beller, *The Habsburg Monarchy 1815–1918* (Cambridge, New York, 2018).
8. Joseph Constantin Bisinger, *Staatsverfassung des österreichischen Kaiserthumes* (Vienna, Trieste, 1809), V–VI.
9. Wenzel Gustav Kopetz, *Österreichische politische Gesetzkunde, oder systematische Darstellung der politischen Verwaltung in den deutschen, böhmischen und galizischen Provinzen des österreichischen Kaiserthumes*, Vol. 1 (Vienna, 1807), n. p. (Vorerinnerung).

10 Cf. the table of contents in Joseph Marx von Liechtenstern, *Kleine Geographie des Österreichischen Kaiserstaates* (Vienna, 1819).
11 Otto Posse (ed.), *Die Siegel der deutschen Kaiser und Könige*, Vol. 5 (Dresden, 1913), 249–60.
12 Grete Klingenstein, 'Was bedeuten "Österreich" und "österreichisch" im 18. Jahrhundert? Eine begriffsgeschichtliche Studie', in R. G. Plaschka, G. Stourzh and J. P. Niederkorn (eds), *Was heißt Österreich? Inhalt und Umfang des Österreichbegriffs vom 10. Jahrhundert bis heute* (Vienna, 1995), 150–220, here 204–7.
13 Friedrich Tezner, *Der österreichische Kaisertitel, das ungarische Staatsrecht und die ungarische Publicistik* (Vienna, 1899), 136.
14 *Vortrag* by Johann Philipp count Stadion, Vienna 23 September 1806, ÖStA, HHStA, St.K. Vorträge, Kart. 174, fol. 217r–v.
15 Report by Karl Friedrich von dem Knesebeck in 1809, quoted after Eduard Wertheimer, *Geschichte Österreichs und Ungarns im ersten Jahrzehnt des 19. Jahrhunderts*, 2 Vols (Leipzig, 1884 and 1890), here Vol. 2, 102–3.
16 Ibid., Vol. 1, 333.
17 Reinhard Stauber, *Der Wiener Kongress* (Vienna, Coloyne, Weimar, 2014). Brian E. Vick, *The Congress of Vienna. Power and Politics after Napoleon* (Cambridge, MA, London, 2014). Mark Jarrett, *The Congress of Vienna and its Legacy. War and Great Power Diplomacy after Napoleon* (London, New York, 2013).
18 Astrid von Schlachta, 'Konfrontation oder Konsens? Landständische Argumentationen gegenüber territorialen Obrigkeiten – Ostfriesland und Tirol im 18. Jahrhundert', in S. Wendehorst (ed.), *Die Anatomie frühneuzeitlicher Imperien. Herrschaftsmanagement jenseits von Staat und Nation* (Berlin, Munich, Boston, 2015), 143–66, here 161.
19 Alois Niederstätter, *Vorarlberg 1523 bis 1861. Auf dem Weg zum Land* (Innsbruck, 2014), particularly 105–41.
20 'Act on the re-introduction of the corporate constitution in Tyrol', 24 March 1816, in *Sr. k.k. Majestät Franz des Ersten politische Gesetze und Verordnungen für die Oesterreichischen, Böhmischen und Gallizischen Erbländer*, Vol. 44 (Vienna, 1818), 127–34.
21 Niederstätter, *Vorarlberg 1523–1861*, 140.
22 Karl Heinz Burmeister, 'Die Vorarlberger Landesverfassungen bis 1919', in *75 Jahre selbständiges Land Vorarlberg, 1918–1993* (Bregenz, 1993), 107–34, here 111–17. Hermann Gsteu, 'Ein Beitrag zur Geschichte der Vorarlberger Ständeverfassung. Die ständische Verfassung Vorarlbergs von 1816 bis 1848', *Vierteljahresschrift für Geschichte und Landeskunde Vorarlbergs* 9 (1925), 1–12.
23 Cf. Michael Erbe, *Revolutionäre Erschütterung und Erneuertes Gleichgewicht. Internationale Beziehungen 1785–1830* (Paderborn, Munich, Vienna, Zurich, 2004), 206, 306–7.
24 Franz Pesendorfer, *Eiserne Krone und Doppeladler. Lombardo-Venetien 1814–1866* (Vienna, 1992), 187–99. Giorgo Candeloro, *Storia dell'Italia moderna*, Vol. 2: *Dalla Restaurazione alla Rivoluzione nazionale 1815–1846* (Milan, 1977), 21–31. Brigitte Mazohl-Wallnig, *Österreichischer Verwaltungsstaat und administrative Eliten im Königreich Lombardo-Venetien 1815–1859* (Mainz, 1993).
25 David Laven, *Venice and Venetia under the Habsburgs, 1815–1835* (Oxford, 2002), 53–90. Marco Merrigi, *Amministrazione e classi sociali nel Lombardo-Veneto (1814–1849)* (Bologna, 1983), 17–42. Andreas Gottsmann, Stefan Malfèr, 'Die Vertretungskörperschaften und die Verwaltung in Lombardo-Venetien', in H. Rumpler and P. Urbanitsch (eds), *Die Habsburgermonarchie 1848–1918*, Vol. V II: *Verfassung*

und Parlamentarismus, Teilband 2: *Die regionalen Repräsentativkörperschaften* (Vienna, 2000), 1593-1632, here 1593-7. [Josef Alexander] von Helfert, *Kaiser Franz von Österreich und die Stiftung des Lombardo-Venetianischen Königreichs* (Innsbruck, 1901).

26 Cf. Ellinor Forster, Brigitte Mazohl, 'Vom "aktiven" Reformer der Monarchie zum "passiven" Vizekönig von Lombardo-Venetien? Erzherzog Rainer (1783-1853)', in A. Ableitinger and M. Raffler (eds), *"Johann und seine Brüder". Neun Brüder und vier Schwestern – Habsburger zwischen Aufklärung und Romantik, Konservativismus, Liberalismus und Revolution* (Graz, 2012), 165-86, here 176-7.
27 *Vortrag* by Johann Philipp count Stadion on 6 September 1806, quoted after Wertheimer, *Geschichte Österreichs*, Vol. 2, 58.
28 There is a good overview in Judson, *The Habsburg Empire*, 28-36.
29 For the diverse concepts of nation cf. ibid., 85-8.
30 Eduard Wertheimer, 'Zwei Denkschriften Erzherzog Rainers aus den Jahren 1808 und 1809', *Archiv für österreichische Geschichte* 78 (1892), 299-375, here 348-9.
31 Ibid., 338.
32 Ibid., 349-50.
33 Ibid., 351.
34 However, financing of French expansion policy was effected mainly by payments from the occupied areas or by contributions. Cf. Jean Tulard, 'Der "Domaine extraordinaire" als Finanzierunginstrument napoleonischer Expansion', *Geschichte und Gesellschaft. Zeitschrift für Historische Sozialwissenschaft* 6 (1980), 490-9.
35 Cf. Wolfram Siemann, *Metternich. Stratege und Visionär* (Munich, 2016),
36 Cf. *Hof- und Staatsschematismus des österreichischen Kaiserthums*, Teil 1 (Vienna, 1817), Register p. 3.
37 Cf. Siemann, *Metternich*, 623-7.
38 Arthur G. Haas, *Metternich, Reorganization and Nationality 1813-1818. A Story of Foresight and Frustration in the Rebuilding of the Austrian Empire* (Wiesbaden, 1963), 118-32, 147-8, 179 (*Vortrag* by Metternich of 27 October 1817 [excerpt]).
39 *Vortrag* by Metternich of 27 August 1817, ÖStA, HHStA Wien, St.K., Vorträge, Kart. 209, fol. 72-84, quoted after Siemann, *Metternich*, 624.
40 Ibid., 624.
41 Posse, *Die Siegel*, 249.
42 Cf. a basic overview by Eric Hobsbawm, 'Introduction', in Hobsbawm and T. Ranger (ed.), *The Invention of Tradition* (New York, 1983), 1-14.
43 Cf. Eberhard Weis, *Montgelas. Der Architekt des modernen bayerischen Staates 1799-1838* (Munich, 2005).
44 William D. Godsey, 'Das Habsburgerreich während der Napoleonischen Kriege und des Wiener Kongresses', in A. Husslein-Arco, S. Grabner and W. Telesko (eds), *Europa in Wien. Der Wiener Kongress 1814/15* (Vienna, Munich, 2015), 29-35.
45 Cf. Ignaz Aurelus Fessler, *Die Geschichte der Ungarn und ihrer Landsassen*, Vol. 10: *Die Ungarn aus der Linie der Oesterreichisch-Ernestinischen Linie* (Leipzig, 1825), 659-734.

12

A Monarchical Regime based on Republican Antecedents: The Constitution of the United Kingdom of the Netherlands

Ido de Haan

Between November 2013 and September 2015, the Netherlands celebrated the two-hundredth birthday of the Kingdom of the Netherlands. The very fact that these celebrations were spread out over two years, starting with the re-enactment of the landing of William Frederick, son of the last stadholder, at the beach at Scheveningen on 30 November 1813, and ending on 26 September 2015, celebrating two hundred years of 'unity in diversity' but no historical event in particular, indicates that the new-founded Dutch state had no specific founding moment. Not only is it difficult to pinpoint constitutional turning-points with precision, but the constitutional monarchy that came into being shared many aspects of previous regimes.

The unitary Dutch state had been long in the making. Already from the middle of the eighteenth century onwards, Enlightened commentators were ascribing the apparent decline of the Dutch Republic to the political fragmentation of its overlapping sovereign powers, and calling for greater national unity. The Patriot movement between 1780 and 1787 rejected the regime of the stadholder and local regents in the name of a unified nation, but it was the French invasion of 1795 which finally created the conditions for the establishment of a unitary Batavian state, and a constitution based on equal citizenship and popular sovereignty. Also the monarchical aspect of the state established around 1814 was not completely new. Militarily and in its foreign relations, the republican *ancien régime* in the Netherlands had been represented by a stadholderate, which in the eighteenth century had developed monarchical traits. More importantly, the first Dutch monarchy had been established in 1806 by Napoleon's brother Louis, who made a decisive contribution to the development of a strong and centralized bureaucratic state in the Netherlands.

In addition, the Dutch monarchy established after its constitutional ratification on 29 March 1814 was not very resilient. Within a year, it had its second constitutional turning-point, when the incorporation of the southern Netherlands (modern Belgium) was ratified on 24 August 1815. The new state collapsed after fifteen years, even if Belgian independence was only acknowledged eight years later by the Dutch king William, who in 1840 abdicated as king of a much-reduced Kingdom of the Netherlands.

According to most historians, the first decades of the Kingdom of the Netherlands are therefore to be considered a 'failed experiment'. In most historical accounts of the Dutch nineteenth century, it is the constitutional revision of 1848 that is considered to be the actual foundational moment of the modern Dutch state.[1]

In this contribution, I will assess the weight of the various legacies that composed the early Kingdom of the Netherlands, and evaluate the strength and weaknesses of the institutional amalgam that came about. Rather than a failure, the Dutch experiment with a constitutional monarchy is perhaps better perceived as a process of trial and error, in which various constitutional legacies of previous decades, and even centuries, were consolidated. In this respect, the Kingdom resembles other Restoration monarchies in Europe. In contrast to earlier scholars, who have generally emphasized the reactionary nature of Restoration regimes, in this paper I follow the more recent trend by emphasizing the innovative and experimental nature of the period, presenting it as a quest for an adequate form of the state and public life, and for the consolidation of a revolutionary heritage.[2]

1813: revolution in the Netherlands

The experiment of the Kingdom of the Netherlands came about in a fluid political context. Both internally and internationally, the years 1813–15 were yet another revolutionary period, once again leading to a major reconfiguration of political institutions, cultural patterns and social relations. It is important to keep this is mind, not only because this political fluidity created plenty of opportunities for radical institutional transformations, but also because there was a large measure of historical contingency and unpredictability, which is in general characteristic of such transitional political moments. Even if there were long-term institutional path-dependencies at the basis of the new state, bold actions, tactical coalitions and imaginative reinventions had major institutional consequences.

These moments of political contingency were first of all the result of the collapse of French authority. After the Low Countries had been incorporated into the French Empire in 1810, the Napoleonic regime had imposed a despotic rule of exploitative taxation, massive conscription and harsh repression, which increasingly met with violent resistance. After Napoleon's defeat at the Battle of the Nations at Leipzig, French troops and administrators were chased by Cossacks through northern Germany into the northern Netherlands, creating a scare in Holland, which in its turn undermined the authority of local French rule. On 15 November 1813, the French general Molitor unexpectedly retreated from Amsterdam, leaving the city and its local National Guard in a state of confusion. A provisional city government by local notables declared itself ready to follow a 'systema van onzijdigheid' – impartiality between the French authorities and citizens who had started rioting, waving orange colours or the 'prinsenvlag'.[3]

In The Hague, the French prefect of the Department of Bouche-de-la-Meuse, Goswin de Stassart, handed over his authority to the commander of the National Guard, yet here three Orangist notables, Gijsbert Karel van Hogendorp, Leopold van

Limburg Stirum and Frans Adam van der Duyn van Maasdam, seized the moment by issuing a declaration, stating 'Oranje boven. Holland is vrij' (Up with Orange. Holland is free), calling for an end to all past hostilities, the resumption of trade and a government of notables, headed by the Prince of Orange. The declaration ended by assuring the public 'The old times will return, Up with Orange'. As with the notables of Amsterdam, most of the notables of The Hague were afraid to declare sides, after which the triumvirate presented itself as a provisional government, legitimized by what they claimed as 'the call from all sides for a government for the rescue of the fatherland'.[4]

The provisional government sent two envoys to London, to call for a return of Prince William Frederick, son of the last stadholder, Willem V. William Frederick's father had died in 1806, acquiescing in his loss of power, yet William Frederick had courted the Prussians, the British and finally Napoleon to receive new territory. For a short while, the latter had allowed him to govern the tiny German principality of Fulda, but after he was ousted by Napoleon, William Frederick had lost all support and respect for his opportunist attitude and retreated to his estate in East Prussia, only to return to England in early 1813 to launch another bid for power, this time with more success.[5] Like the Dutch notables, William Frederick initially hesitated to accept the offer of the triumvirate, but their letter assuring the prince that 'the nation has risen, it wears your colours, it proclaims your name' convinced him to cross the North Sea and to accept sovereignty, 'by acclamation, so to speak'. Three days after his landing on the Dutch shore, he issued a declaration that the Dutch people 'through its trust and love' had conferred sovereignty on him, which he accepted if it could be guaranteed by a 'wise constitution'.[6]

The constitution of the United Kingdom of the Netherlands was largely the result of the international balance of power created in the context of the Congress of Vienna. Even before the Congress met, a decisive step had been taken with the help of the British, who since Pitt's 'Memorandum for security and deliverance of Europe' of 1805 had advocated a strong unified state in the Low Countries as a bulwark against France. The unification of the Low Countries was further facilitated by the Austrians, who were more interested in strengthening their influence in the Italian peninsula than in regaining the former Austrian Netherlands. The principle of an 'intimate and complete union' of the northern and southern Netherlands was formally acknowledged in the London Protocol of 21 June 1814, and within a month confirmed on the ground after King William, as he was called since his inauguration on 31 March 1814, invaded the southern Netherlands, asserting his power over the Low Countries at his entry into Brussels on 31 July 1814. The new state received international recognition in the final declaration of the Congress of Vienna, and within a week asserted its practical relevance by contributing to the Allied victory over Napoleon at Quatre-Bras and Waterloo.[7]

The constitution of sovereignty

The first constitution of the new state was drafted by a committee William Frederick had established in December 1813, three weeks after his acceptance of the position of sovereign of the Netherlands. The starting point of the discussion within the committee was a 'sketch for a constitution of the united Netherlands', which its chair Van Hogendorp had drafted as early as 1812. The basic principle of Van Hogendorp's draft was that the constitution should follow national historical traditions.[8] Even if he incorporated many of the elements which had emerged in the revolutionary era, Van Hogendorp insisted on an archaic conceptualization of essentially modern notions like national unity, popular sovereignty and centralized sovereign power. This historical foundation of Dutch society was 'the Constitution of the Provinces, Knighthoods and Cities'. Van Hogendorp claimed this 'ancient constitution' was confirmed in his sketch for a new 'Grondwet', which left everything 'as it was before, except for those things that are manifestly improved'. At the same time, Van Hogendorp rejected a return to the constitution of the Republic and presented his sketch as 'a return to the ancient Constitution as it was before the times of the Republic, which had been a great innovation. The ancient freedom, so dear to our ancestors, is completely transferred to this Constitution.'[9]

The most urgent question the constitutional committee had to address was the location of sovereignty: was it in the people, the king or maybe somewhere else? In the Dutch Republic, this had been a very problematic issue – *de jure* and de facto, sovereignty was dispersed among several institutions. It had been the miracle of the Dutch Republic in its Golden Age that this fragmented sovereignty had not hindered its flourishing but, after 1750, a consensus had grown that the Republic's decline was the result of structural institutional shortcomings. Van Hogendorp acknowledged these considerations, but at the same time, wanted to maintain a link with the past. As a result, his sketch contained a complicated mixture of historical elements.

On the one hand, he proposed a historicized conception of popular sovereignty by depicting an imaginary freedom in the Burgundian Netherlands, when the citizens still exerted their sovereignty by the right to elect their rulers which, during the republican era, had been taken away by city governments and stadholders. This popular sovereignty had to be restored. However, Van Hogendorp rejected the revolutionary republican conception, which located popular sovereignty in the nation as a whole, and had provided the basis of the first Dutch constitution, the Staatsregeling of 1798.[10] Discussing the actual exercise of popular sovereignty, Van Hogendorp introduced a second source of sovereignty, namely the provincial estates, which according to eighteenth-century theorists were the core institutions of the Republic.[11] The exercise of popular sovereignty had to be conferred on the Estates-General, or *Staten-Generaal*, which even today is the name of the two chambers of the Dutch parliament combined, and which also according to article 50 of the current Dutch constitution 'represents the whole people of the Netherlands'. Representatives of the people in the Estates-General were elected indirectly, through the provincial estates, which in turn were divided into representatives of the cities, knighthoods and the countryside. Until 1848, this remained the basis of the electoral system; and even today, the Dutch Senate is elected indirectly through the Provincial Estates.[12]

However, Van Hogendorp was aware of the critique that the dispersion of sovereignty among estates at the provincial and general level had to be avoided. He therefore indicated that a king was a third and final locus of sovereignty. While the cities and provinces were good at governing at the local level, they should abstain from ruling in general. Except for nominating the representatives to the Estates-General, their authority was limited. At the general level of the nation, the 'Constitution restores a sovereign king, just as of old, with all the conventions, rights and privileges he appealed to before his inauguration. This is the Constitution for which our highly esteemed ancestors have taken up arms, and for which instead a consecutive generation has exchanged the Republic ... with its perfidious partisanship and divisions, that weakened and destroyed us.'[13]

A major issue in the debates of the constitutional committee was whether Van Hogendorp's sketch had not left too much power to the ancient provincial estates. Proponents of the preservation of local self-rule followed the arguments presented by the classical republican Johan Hendrik Swildens, who in 1795 had published Gelykheid-Vryheid-Broederschap. 1795. Politiek Belang-Boek voor dit Provisionele Tydperk. Gewigt tans, Gedenkwaardig hierna (Equality-Liberty-Fraternity. 1795. Political interest-book for this provisional period. Important today, memorable thereafter), in which he defended the rights of local authorities against an overpowering central state.[14] They were opposed by the members of the committee who had made a career during the Napoleonic regime, such as the Minister of Justice Cornelis Felix van Maanen and Cornelis Theodorus Elout, who had drafted the Napoleonic Criminal Code for the Netherlands. They advocated an even greater strengthening of the sovereign executive power. In particular, they objected to Van Hogendorp's suggestion that the provincial estates had to be seen as a continuation of the ancient constitution before 1795 that granted them an independent authority, and not as a product of the new constitution as the sole source of provincial powers. Even though much of the older terminology, such as *Staten-Generaal* and *Provinciale Staten*, was maintained, Van Hogendorp accepted the reduction of the powers of the ancient republican institutions in favour of monarchical centralization.[15]

At the same time, modern republican or democratic aspects, such as popular sovereignty and political accountability of government, remained underdeveloped. Even if steps were taken towards a parliamentary regime, granting the Estates-General the power to consent to laws and to the budget (every ten years, with the exclusion of military and colonial aspects) as well as the right to initiate legislation, there was little concern for political opposition. Only at one point in the proceedings of the constitutional committee did Van Maanen raise the possibility that members of parliament might disagree with the king's decisions, to which Van Hogendorp responded, 'that is not to be feared, according to the stated principles of love and mutual trust'. 'Pia vota', was the only response of Van Maanen (the conversation of the members of the committee was lusciously interspersed with Latin phrases).[16] Also, the Constitution was not submitted to a popular vote, but ratified by an ad-hoc council of six-hundred notables, of whom on 2 March 1814 only 448 supported the constitution – 26 voted against it, while another 126 did not show up for the occasion.

The lack of democratic inspiration of the Constitution of 1814 became manifest a year later, when the integration of the southern Netherlands had to be made constitutional. Another committee was set up, with equal representation of notables from north and south, with the Jewish lawyer Jonas Daniel Meijer as its secretary, who was supposed to be able to balance impartially the interests of Protestants and Catholics.[17] The southern representatives were strongly influenced by French liberal ideas, which after the flight of many of the French radicals and Bonapartists to Brussels had become even more dominant. As a result of southern pressure, a Senate was introduced, which, despite the fact that it consisted of notables appointed by the king, strengthened the idea that a stable government was a mixed regime of a monarchy, an aristocratic Senate and a democratic representation of the people.[18] Moreover, a series of basic rights were better secured, including religious liberty, protection of property, the right to petition and freedom of the press. However, parliamentary powers were not expanded, and the government did not become more accountable.

Furthermore, the ratification of the constitution of 1815 was even less democratic than the one of the year before. Again a council of notables had to vote, but in this case only 527 of 1,604 notables voted in favour. The rejection of the constitution was avoided by 'Dutch arithmetic': those who had voted against for religious motives were not counted, and all those who had not showed up for the meeting were counted among the votes in favour of the constitution. At the same time, the fact that the constitution was ratified by a representation of the nation, and not as the French *Charte*, *octroyée* (sanctioned) by the king, was seen as a confirmation of a deep-seated republican tradition in the Netherlands. Yet there was at least one man who held a different opinion on these issues. As King William declared: 'I existed before the constitution; the estates-general only exist because of it.'[19]

A new monarchy

According to Van Hogendorp, the creation of a Kingdom of the Netherlands was a return to an ancient constitution. This was a problematic claim, not only because he had little to say about the nature of the late-medieval monarchy, but more importantly because the Dutch Restoration monarchy had at least four more recent sources of inspiration: the court of the hereditary stadholder, the Kingdom of Fulda, the autocratic rule of the grand pensionary Schimmelpenninck and the Kingdom of Holland under Louis Napoleon.[20] While William Frederick had initially hesitated to assume the title of king, he soon came to favour the more autocratic option among these various monarchical alternatives.

A first example was the increasingly monarchical Dutch stadholderate. In 1747, the title of stadholder had become hereditary. In the course of the eighteenth century, the practices of the stadholderate became modelled after the European court culture, notably that of Vienna. The court of the stadholder was divided in three parts, with the actual court headed by an *opperhofmeester* (chief steward), the stables under the *opperstalmeester* (master of the horse) and a *chambre* headed by the chief chamberlain. Moreover, the stadholder increasingly became the spider at the centre of a web of clientelist relations with the regents in the cities, creating a network of political co-optation that was one of the major sources of discontent in the final decades of the Republic.

The short-lived position of William Frederick as king of Fulda, which he received from Napoleon in 1803 together with some other Streubesitz in Germany as compensation for the loss of his family's position in the Netherlands, was a second source of inspiration. In Fulda, William Frederick hoped to emulate the enlightened absolutist rule of his great-uncle, the Prussian Frederick the Great, by presenting himself as an authoritarian Landsvater who took personal care of each of his 90,000 subjects. In this daunting task he was assisted by a Geheime Conferenz Commission without any say in matters great or small, with the result that William Frederick soon drowned in all the paperwork he failed to delegate.[21]

A third model for the new Dutch monarchy was provided by Napoleon's introduction of autocratic rule in the Netherlands under the leadership of raadpensionaris Rutger Jan Schimmelpenninck in 1805. At this point in the development of the Batavian Commonwealth (as it came to be called by 1801), all democratic aspects were suppressed. In an attempt to cloak autocratic rule in the robe of ancient Dutch republicanism, the French had insisted on the title of Grand Pensionary, but more apt was the term 'president' Schimmelpenninck had preferred. He was aided by a *Staatssecretarie*, which had a similar subordinate position as the Geheime Conferenz Commission.[22]

The final monarchical model was provided by the Kingdom of Holland of Louis Napoleon. At its establishment in 1806, this had met with some resistance from the Batavian political elite, who deemed a monarchy unfit for a nation with a republican legacy, yet under pressure from the French minister Talleyrand, they hesitantly accepted Louis as king.[23] Louis was also discreet about the nature of his rule, claiming to represent *majesté nationale* above political conflict and institutional form:

> What matter if the form of government is monarchical, republican or oligarchic, as long as it is real government and fit to govern men? Their conservation, their well-being, their improvement, are equally the point of all of them.[24]

Louis created yet another model of monarchical rule, with a new Etiquette Royale, and an ambitious programme of political centralization and administrative rationalization, yet he gave the ministers of the *Staatssecretarie* much more independence to develop their own policies. He also sought the cooperation of the members of the previous regimes as well as of *homines novi*. As such, his rule was characterized by an attempt to overcome the divisions of the past and to strengthen national unity.[25]

As before in Fulda, William presented himself as the father of the nation, united under his wise rule. Like Louis Napoleon, he included several members of previous regimes in his government, while he also forged the commitment of *homines novi* by creating new aristocratic titles, establishing a network of patronage similar to that of the stadholders of the previous century. But as he told his son as part of his training as his successor, 'The king alone decides.' He reinstated the *Staatssecretarie* in the autocratic form in which Schimmelpenninck had used it, and avoided parliament by issuing Royal Decisions which required no parliamentary consent. In 1818 he convinced the Estates-General to accept the Blanketwet, which gave these decisions the power and sanctions of regular laws, and in 1822 enforced a decision which gave him a final say in conflicts between different organs of the state. He worked every day of the week, on an endless numbers of dossiers, all of which he read, and signed, from early morning till late at night, ruling on finances, infrastructure, colonies, poor relief, education, religion and many other issues.[26]

Constitution of the polity as a limit to monarchy

Despite his amazing energy, William I soon lost control over his Kingdom. As had happened before in Fulda, he became overwhelmed by all the plans and paperwork, leading to a political mess, the fragmentation of his Kingdom, and the bankruptcy of the remaining northern part. His main challenge was the geographical, social and cultural constitution of the new state. The new country was small, but not at all unified. Since the end of the sixteenth century, north and south had followed different paths, but were also internally divided, each in their own way. Economically, the north was oriented towards trade and supported *laissez-faire*, while the south participated in an early industrial take-off and sought protection of its home market. There was also no monetary union. Until 1825, the south used the French franc, and after that southern banks issued guilders, which were not accepted in the north. William I tried to alleviate these economic tensions with all kinds of (personal) investment plans and infrastructural projects, but as a result of distrust, these generally failed in the south and succeeded in the north, adding to the rift between the two.[27]

Culturally, the north was religiously pluralistic, yet linguistically uniform; in the south this was the reverse. William pursued policies aimed at the development of national unity through propaganda for the new state, but these were generally modelled after the patriotic feelings that in the eighteenth century had emerged in the north, while a similar national movement had been lacking in the south. This national programme was therefore as divisive as his language policy, which installed Dutch as an administrative language in 1819. Religiously, William I aimed at reunification of all churches under the kings of Europe in an ambitious attempt to end the conflict of the Reformation. This required a tight control of the churches, which was generally accepted by the Dutch Reformed elite, yet rejected by common people, and by the Catholic Church, which suspected a return of the policies of the Austrian Joseph II, who had ruled the southern Netherlands before 1792, and had provoked the abortive Belgian Revolution of 1789. There was equally strong resistance to William's attempt to control the training of priests, and this opposition became a crucial element of Belgian mobilization at the end of the 1820s.[28]

The Belgian uprising of 1830–1 was therefore not so much the result of a strong Belgian nationalism, but mainly a consequence of structural tensions within the social and cultural constitution of the United Kingdom of the Netherlands.[29] The political constitution, as codified in the Grondwet of 1815, had the potential of redress: there were elements of the rule of law, a measure of parliamentary control on the basis of limited suffrage, indirect election by social rank, and an appointed Senate. Yet William resisted and circumvented parliamentary control. This was most problematic in the field of financial policy: to a large extent the finances of the state were not public. Publicity in the Kingdom of the Netherlands consisted mainly of the public audience

William held each Wednesday, in which the king as *pater familias* forged the domestication of public debate.[30]

As a last element of tension, these autocratic tendencies were more accepted in the north than in the south. After the Vonckist revolution of 1789 there had been a continuing French and liberal influence, and a significant revolutionary potential, which eventually created an unlikely coalition of Liberals and Catholics against a Protestant king, inspiring the revolt of 1830 and leading to the most liberal constitutional monarchy of Europe under Leopold I von Saxen-Coburg. In the north, this had a reverse effect. The loss of Belgium resulted in an even more strained and repressive nationalist climate, in support of William's refusal to acknowledge defeat.[31] His persistent mobilization of an enormous army added to the financial disaster, the size of which only became clear after he had abdicated in 1840. He then made room for his more liberal-minded son, who in 1848 accepted a fundamental constitutional revision which is generally perceived as the second founding of the Dutch state.

A failed experiment?

Considering the territorial disintegration, the financial bankruptcy, the dishonourable abdication of the king and the complete constitutional overhaul of 1848, the United Kingdom of the Netherlands was a complete failure. In this respect, it did not differ fundamentally from most other Restoration monarchies in Europe, first of all France. Yet as in France, the period can also be perceived as a time of political experimentation. From that perspective, at least four innovations can be distinguished.

First of all, in this period the first steps towards parliamentary democracy were taken. There were regular elections and an orderly parliamentary debate, which even if it was little acknowledged by the king, still provided a training ground for a parliamentary culture. Secondly, both royal propaganda and the opposition developed new notions of national integration, in part inspired by attempts to create national unity, but partly also in contrast with one-sided official images of the nation. As a third element, the period brought the consolidation of the administrative state, first of all in terms of the integration of civil servants from previous regimes, who as weathervanes had to emphasize professional skills over ideological commitment, thus contributing to the development of an apolitical civil service. But William's projects also contributed to the strengthening of the capacities of the bureaucratic state, foreshadowing the interventionist state emerging at the end of the century.

Finally, a lasting legacy of this period is the bad press it has received, not just with hindsight, but even during the period itself, notably with regard to the monarchy. This is to be taken literally: all monarchs after King William were critically discussed in the press, and had in the end little means of countering this. It was the same elsewhere: in France, Italy and even in the United Kingdom during this period, the monarchy had a dismal reputation. This only changed at the end of the century, during the emergence of a mass society, when the monarchy was rebranded as the embodiment of the nation. But until that, the monarchy had to carry the burden of the Restoration, and reconstruct a past that was in many ways completely new.

Notes

1. Ido de Haan, 'Een nieuwe staat', in Ido de Haan, Paul den Hoed and Henk te Velde (eds), *Een nieuwe staat. Het begin van het Koninkrijk der Nederlanden* (Amsterdam, 2013), 9–33; Remieg Aerts, 'Een staat in verbouwing. Van republiek naar constitutioneel koninkrijk 1780-1848', in Remieg Aerts et al., *Land van kleine gebaren. Een politieke geschiedenis van Nederland 1780-1990* (Nijmegen, 1999), 9–95: 61; A. Peper, 'Woord vooraf', in N. C. F. van Sas and H. te Velde (ed.), *De eeuw van de Grondwet. Grondwet en politiek in Nederland, 1798-1917* (Deventer, 1998), 7.
2. Michael Broers, *Europe After Napoleon: Revolution, Reaction, and Romanticism, 1814-1848* (Manchester/New York, 1996); Emmanuel de Waresquiel and Benoît Yvert, *Histoire de la Restauration 1814-1830. Naissance de la France moderne* (Paris, 1996); David Laven and Lucy Riall (eds), *Napoleon's Legacy. Problems of Government in Restoration Europe* (Oxford/New York, 2000).
3. George W. Chad, *A Narrative of the Late Revolution in Holland* (London, 1814), 43–52; Herman Th. Colenbrander, *Gedenkschriften van Anton Reinhard Falck* ('s-Gravenhage, 1913), 74–6; Johanna W. A. Naber, *Overheersching en Vrijwording. Geschiedenis van Nederland tijdens de inlijving bij Frankrijk juli 1810-november 1813* (Haarlem, 1913), 262–70; see also E. J. Vles, *Twee weken in november. De omwenteling van 1813* (Amsterdam, 2006), 55–65; Johan Joor, *De adelaar en het lam. Onrust, opruiing en onwilligheid in Nederland ten tijde van het Koninkrijk Holland en de Inlijving bij het Franse Keizerrijk (1806-1813)* (Amsterdam, 2000) 335–9, 666–74.
4. Gijsbert Karel van Hogendorp, 'November 1813', in Mr. H. Graaf van Hogendorp (ed.), *Brieven en Gedenkschriften van Gijsbert Karel van Hogendorp IV* ('s-Gravenhage, 1887), 179–422: 236; see also Dick H. Couvée and Guus Pikkemaat, *1813-15. Ons koninkrijk geboren* (Alphen aan den Rijn, 1963), 17–54.
5. Jeroen Koch, *Koning Willem I. 1772-1843* (Amsterdam, 2013), passim.
6. Herman Th. Colenbrander (ed.), *Ontstaan der Grondwet* I ('s-Gravenhage, 1908), 15–16.
7. Niek C. F. van Sas, *Onze Natuurlijkste Bondgenoot. Nederland, Engeland en Europa* (Groningen 1985), 40–79.
8. See Niek C. F. van Sas, 'De representatieve fictie. Politieke vertegenwoordiging tussen oude orde en moderniteit', *BMGN /Low Countries Historical Review* 120 (2005) 3, 397–407: 398.
9. Gijsbert Karel van Hogendorp, 'Aanmerkingen op de Grondwet', in H. T. Colenbrander (ed.), *Ontstaan der Grondwet* I ('s-Gravenhage, 1908), 56–64: 58.
10. Wyger R. E. Velema, 'Revolutie, Republiek en Constitutie. De ideologische context van de eerste Nederlandse Grondwet', in Niek C. F. van Sas and Henk te Velde (eds), *De eeuw van de Grondwet. Grondwet en politiek in Nederland, 1798-1917* (Deventer, 1998), 20–44.
11. Theo Veen, 'De legitimatie van de souvereiniteit der Staten bij Huber en Kluit', *BMGN/ Low Countries Historical Review* 97 (1982), 2, 185–215.
12. Lodewijk Blok, *Stemmen en kiezen: het kiesstelsel in Nederland in de periode 1814-1850* (Groningen, 1987).
13. Van Hogendorp, 'Aanmerkingen op de Grondwet', 57.
14. See Wyger R. Velema, 'Conversations with the Classics: Ancient Political Virtue and Two Modern Revolutions', *Early American Studies: An Interdisciplinary Journal* 10 (2012) 2, 415–38: 430.

15 Bernard D. H. Tellegen Azn, *Overzicht van het tot stand komen der Grondwet van 1814* (Groningen, 1912), 63-74.
16 'Vergadering van woensdag 29 December 1813', in Colenbrander (ed.), *Ontstaan der Grondwet,* 94; cf. Tellegen Azn, *Overzicht,* 40.
17 Nochem de Beneditty, *Leven en werken van Mr. Jonas Daniel Meyer (1780-1834)* (Haarlem, 1925), 54.
18 Stefaan Marteel, 'Constitutional thought under the Union of the Netherlands: The "Fundamental Law" of 1814-15 in the political and intellectual context of the Restoration', *Parliaments, Estates and Representation* 27 (2007) 1, 77-94: 85.
19 'Gesprek tusschen den koning en den prins van Oranje, 20 februari 1820', in Herman Th. Colenbrander (ed.), *Gedenkstukken der Algemeene Geschiedenis van Nederland van 1795 tot 1840* V I.3 (Den Haag 1912), 235; Ids J. H. Worst, 'Koning Willem I. Het begin van "ons grondwettig volksbestaan"', in Coen A Tamse and Els Witte (eds), *Staats- en natievorming in Willem I's Koninkrijk (1815-1830)* (Brussels, 1992), 56-75.
20 Coen A. Tamse, 'Plaats en functie van de Nederlandse monarchie in de negentiende eeuw', in Tamse, *Het huis van Oranje en andere politieke mythen* (Amsterdam, 2002), 178-222: 178; see also Koch, *Koning Willem I.*
21 J. A. Bornewasser, 'Koning Willem I', in Coen A. Tamse (ed.), *Nassau en Oranje in de Nederlandse geschiedenis* (Alphen aan den Rijn, 1979), 229-72: 236-40.
22 Martijn van der Burg, 'Transforming the Dutch Republic into the Kingdom of Holland: the Netherlands between Republicanism and Monarchy (1795-1815)', *European Review of History: Revue européenne d'histoire* 17 (2010) 2, 151-70: 156; Ido de Haan, *Het beginsel van leven en wasdom. De constitutie van de Nederlandse politiek* (Amsterdam, 2003), 190-1.
23 Van der Burg 'Transforming the Dutch Republic', 158.
24 Louis Bonaparte, *Documents historiques et réflexions sur le gouvernement de la Hollande I* (Bruxelles, 1820), 141-2, as quoted by Van der Burg 'Transforming the Dutch Republic', 160.
25 Ido de Haan and Jeroen van Zanten, 'Le roi Louis, un modèle pour Guillaume?', in Annie Jourdan (ed.), *Louis Bonaparte, Roi de Hollande* (Paris, 2010), 213-31; Matthijs Lok, *Windvanen, Napoleontische bestuurders in de Nederlandse en Franse Restauratie (1813-1820)* (Amsterdam, 2009).
26 Niek C. F. van Sas, 'Het politiek bestel onder Willem I', in Van Sas, *De metamorfose van Nederland. Van oude orde naar moderniteit 1750-1900* (Amsterdam, 2004), 413-35.
27 Eric Buyst, 'De onmogelijke integratie. Economische ontwikkelingen in Nederland en België', in De Haan et al. (eds), *Een nieuwe staat,* 189-210.
28 Joep Leerssen, 'De Nederlandse natie', in De Haan et al. (eds), *Een nieuwe staat,* 285-308; Joris van Eijnatten, 'Religie en het koninkrijk: een dwars verband', in De Haan et al. (eds), *Een nieuwe staat,* 285-308; De Haan, *Het beginsel van leven en wasdom,* 36-47, 131-8.
29 Cf. Els Witte, *Het verloren koninkrijk. Het harde verzet van de Belgische orangisten tegen de revolutie 1828-1850* (Antwerpen, 2014).
30 See the contributions to Remieg Aerts and Gita Deneckere (eds), *Het (on)verenigd Koninkrijk 1815-1830-2015. Een politiek experiment in de Lage Landen* (Rekkem, 2015); Koch, *Koning Willem I,* passim.
31 Jeroen van Zanten, *Schielijk, Zwaarhoofd, Winzucht en Bedaard. Politieke discussie en oppositievorming in Noord-Nederland 1813-1840* (Amsterdam, 2004).

13

Ruling over the Ruling Class: Doctrine and Practice of Government in the Kingdom of Sardinia

Enrico Genta Ternavasio

The *ancien régime* was severely shaken by the Napoleonic Empire. Despite the French attempt to wipe the slate clean, the Piedmontese monarchy preserved and incorporated some traditional institutions after 1815.[1] The *Restaurazione* was a very complex historical period and it is pointless to label it with rigid and short-sighted characterizations that are thoroughly sterile. On the one hand, *Restaurazione* meant a return to the pre-revolutionary world, on the other hand it was evident that, as far as the principal institutions of the European monarchies were concerned, there was a growing tendency to take full advantage of Napoleon's legal and administrative heritage.[2] This hybridization of administrative and governmental structures across Europe could be described as 'legal eclecticism.' Its contours can be perceived in the practices of the governments of this period. This 'model' sought to deal with numerous issues, whose multiformity could not be solved by simply going back to the eighteenth-century precedents. It was necessary, where possible, to adapt and adopt Napoleonic reforms. The most remarkable example of this process can be found in the restructuring of mortgages in the Kingdom of Sardinia. Inspired by the French example, Piedmontese creditors were protected through the creation of public registers (*Bureaux des Hypothèques*). In this context, the allure of French experiences, precedents and models could lead to their imitation, which often seemed the best means of escaping the dilemmas of the post-1815 world. Moreover, it is interesting to remark that this pragmatic behaviour was often accompanied by a sense of nostalgia for even older political patterns, which traced their ancestry to medieval times, long before the rise of what we call the modern state.

In the Congress of Vienna, the Kingdom of Sardinia-Piedmont – the House of Savoy – obtained the Mediterranean region of Liguria, which was not restored as the ancient aristocratic Republic of Genoa.[3] During the *Restaurazione* this 'Composite State' was ruled by two sovereigns: the 'meek and mild' Victor-Emmanuel I, and his tougher brother, Charles-Felix, who came to the throne after a stormy, but ephemeral, revolution known as the Moti of 1821. Having experienced such turmoil in 1822, Charles-Felix summoned the members of the nobility of his States to swear allegiance to him. He cast himself as a feudal *suzerain* by demanding an oath of allegiance, which was guaranteed by Almighty God. At first sight this practice might seem archaic, yet, in the ideological context of the *Restaurazione*, it held a precise significance and displayed important values. The purpose of this ritual, from the king's point of view, was to confirm the nobility's duty and loyalty, by reminding them of the *absoluta potestas* of the sovereign.[4]

Prior to the Restoration, some Piedmontese and Savoyard aristocrats had been reluctantly willing to cooperate with Napoleon. These gentlemen were not blamed for their collaboration with the French (with the exception of a few cases like Count Botton of Castellamonte, or Count Villa of Villastellone). As a matter of fact, it was often the case that such patricians had been authorized to join Napoleon's imperial machinery of government by the king himself. Victor-Emmanuel I, when in exile on Sardinia, protected by the Royal Navy, was sincerely concerned about the maintenance and continuity of traditional Sabaudian institutions. When some nobles submitted to the French Imperium, he manifested, tacitly, his consent to such collaboration. Indeed, the king gave his secret blessing for nobles to take charge of justice, administration, finances, international relations, in the passionate hope that Napoleon's usurpation would soon come to an end. In the event of the Empire's fall, the king hoped to regain quickly control of his possessions, which were managed largely by his former subjects.

This explains why after the Moti of 1821, and the abdication of Victor-Emmanuel, a major cause of resentment for the new king, Charles-Felix, was that the nobility formed the most substantial social group accused of plotting against the government. If one examines carefully the positions of these revolutionaries, it was clear that hardly any of them were republicans. The majority continued to pledge allegiance to the House of Savoy. However, for the king, noble subjects, who had instigated an ominous push towards a constitutional monarchy and tried with all their might to subvert the status quo, were simply traitors to their country.

The relationship between the Head of the House of Savoy and his nobilities (that is, feudal magnates, courtiers, holders of venal offices, urban patricians, 'gentry' etc.) had evolved significantly during the eighteenth century. The foundations of the system had largely been established by the energetic and authoritarian reforms of Victor-Amedeus II, who acquired in 1713, in the Treaty of Utrecht, the Kingdom of Sicily (which was swapped for Sardinia in 1720). He was to force successfully the feudal aristocracy to disclose their possessions and justify their legal entitlement to their estates, privileges and prerogatives. The king was thus able to seize and reintegrate hundreds of feudal possessions, held by ancient aristocratic clans, into the Crown Estates. Later he auctioned this large number of estates and lands that had been seized through this dramatic policy. This process had two important consequences. On the one hand, it improved the State's finances, and, on the other hand, it favoured a rising bourgeoisie. The most pre-eminent members of this ambitious new social group were able to change their social, and legal, status by purchasing lands which led to their ennoblement.[5] It goes without saying that this new nobility showed itself more loyal and faithful to the king (who had created it) than its predecessor whose feudal origins made it less pliant towards the royal will.

The government of Restoration Piedmont when it returned to power needed to decide whether to retain or overhaul its old system of nobility. In the first years of the *Restaurazione,* the Kingdom of Sardinia behaved towards its elites in rather new and unexpected ways. As with so many other issues it had to balance political imperatives with ethical and moral considerations. The political culture of the age of Romanticism compelled contemporaries to construct a narrative about how things stood before the French Revolution; a new emphasis was given to the very idea of sovereignty. This strengthening of royal power (one would hesitate to describe it as the rebirth of absolutism) was more apparent than real, as the ceremony of the oath of allegiance in 1822 had highlighted. Besides, it was certainly the case that, during the first years following the Congress of Vienna, many issues were solved through a re-evaluation of many of Napoleon's innovations in governance, administration and legal process. Just as 'modern' reforms were being implemented, King Victor-Emmanuel promulgated the royal edict of 18 November 1817 which established inheritance through male primogeniture, one of the cornerstones of *ancien régime* noble privilege. This struck at the very heart of revolutionary and Napoelonic reforms which had created a system of paritable inheritance. This edict had the potential to cause great offence and resentment amongst the Piedmontese bourgeoisie.[6]

In fact, according to the law, the members of the middle classes were not allowed to create entails or leave their estates according to rules of primogeniture; this was a privilege reserved for the nobility. As everybody knows, the aristocracy's material and economic prosperity had been preserved for centuries by allowing, in most cases, the eldest son to inherit the fortune of a noble house. Thus, families were able to secure multigenerational prosperity and continuity through this unequal system. Many felt that this system was akin to a spiritual communion between the dead and the living. This custom was particularly apparent in the highest nobility.[7]

From this perspective, we can conclude that in the first years of the *Restaurazione* in Piedmont the traditional values of the aristocracy remained virtually unchallenged. Among the many factors that influenced the granting of titles of nobility, visions of chivalry and military endeavour were of great importance. Gentlemanly values of honour, bravery, *politesse,* the ancientness of one's house, one's roots in the region and, above all, proven loyalty to the reigning House remained paramount in noble identity. It would be an exaggeration to argue that the previous Napoleonic social structure, based on the centrality of non-noble *notables* (substantial men of property, especially the bourgeoisie), had been eradicated.[8] Indeed, the lines between *ancien régime* precedents and Napoleonic practices were far more blurred.

The State Archives of Turin contain the papers relating to the creation of new nobles for this period.[9] These registers cover thirty years beginning in 1814 right up to the *Statuto Albertino* (that is the Constitution that was *octroyée* (bestowed) by King Charles-Albert on his kingdom in 1848) and record nearly 360 sovereign acts. Some 8 per cent of these elevations to noble status can be ascribed to the reign of Victor-Emmanuel I. Another 30 per cent (approximately a hundred) were ennobled by Charles-Felix, whose reign lasted ten years. The lion's share, that is 62 per cent, from 1831 to 1848, were the result of Charles-Albert's policies. This chapter shall attempt to analyse the importance of these ennoblements in Piedmont's history. If one takes into account that Victor-Emmanuel reigned for seven years, Charles-Felix for ten, Charles-Albert for eighteen, a small rise in the number of ennoblements can be observed. Yet, it would be wrong to argue that the monarchy of Charles-Albert, to some extent liberal, was responsible for a substantial increase in the rate of ennoblement. This chapter fundamentally disagrees with some historians, who have argued that Charles-Albert was far more generous and socially liberal than his predecessors.[10]

During the eighteenth century the princes of Savoy were mostly concerned with the economic benefits of the whole process of *anoblissement*. They have often been characterized by historians as borderline Enlightened absolutists.[11] Yet, they were able to rule, administer and organize effectively, without any prejudice to their States. This was especially evident in the the creation of new nobles. In eighteenth-century Piedmont, it was possible to rise high in society, and there had been plenty of social mobility. Often the self-made man had little difficulty in joining the ranks of the lesser country gentry; afterwards, if he became rich, he could try to buy a feudal estate and obtain a real title of nobility. This is precisely what happened in a very large number of cases. Such transactions may be considered as a very practical, if somewhat cynical, expedient, through which the Sabaudian kings raised much-needed cash quickly. By the early nineteenth century, chivalry, and its myths, were distant memories and the nobility had lost much of this older mystique.[12]

A high proportion of families raised to the nobility owed their position not only to territorial possessions, but also fortunes made in trade, banking or other professions. However, if one compares them to the oldest and wealthiest clans of traditional aristocratic stock, few of these newcomers had estates large enough to elevate them into the 'real' nobility. Yet such was the government's wish to widen the State's social structures and hierarchies that the monarchy conferred hereditary titles upon them. It is easy to find examples of successful men who, from more or less obscure beginnings, rocketed up the social ladder to obtain important titles (even though the great majority of new nobles rose through the ranks more gradually). Antonio Manno provides an interesting series of examples of such sharp social ascents.[13] For instance there was the case of the newly elevated marquis of Sant'Albano, previously a tailor, who decided to spend his substantial savings to buy an important fief. This allowed him take revenge on an arrogant nobleman who had offended him prior to his ennoblement. That had been the eighteenth-century way.

As hinted, such social mobility – which mixed pragmatism and ruthlessness in equal measure – was replaced during the first years of the *Restaurazione* by a new attention towards the personal or moral characteristics of an applicant seeking elevation. On the surface, nobility as a concept acquired new religious and social significance. It transformed from being simply a legal rank to becoming an honour, conferred for bravery, military prowess or simple loyalty, and was bestowed to anyone deemed worthy. Having said this, one should note that once these criteria had been met by an application, new qualities (or perhaps old qualities) were required. Indeed, the personal or moral characteristics of the recipient were in practice taken for granted. The real issue that needed to be ascertained was the exact level of income and property that belonged to the applicant. By the end of the reigns of the first two kings of this period, the honour of nobility was no longer exclusively 'moral', and leaned again towards wealth and economic status.[14]

Naturally applicants should not be devoid of all moral character; but wealth and position counted far more than knightly virtues in determining who was able to obtain a title. In the first half of the nineteenth century, much legal advice was provided by the office of the *Procuratore Generale di Sua Maestà* (His Majesty's chief prosecutor/ attorney). He was charged with providing a legal opinion on every dossier and certificate relevant to the ennobling process. These dossiers contained all the necessary information and were collected in every town and village in the kingdom. These opinions – *Pareri* – give useful insights into the process of granting nobility or refusing it. One *Parere* from 1826 reads that 'normally persons who humbly request the title of count' must have an estate worth at least 150,000 Piedmontese lire; in 1833, the figure had soared to 300,000 lire. To obtain the lowest rank of nobility (a position that carried no honorific title) an estate worth 60,000 lire was insufficient, and up to 100,000 lire needed to be raised to attain this qualification. Simple nobility without an honorific title was always a controversial issue. Indeed, being raised to the simple rank of 'noble' meant little in practice. After all, the recipient could not display any real mark of distinction or make his status publicly known. In everyday usage, he could not receive any special treatment or social deference, whereas barons, counts and marquesses were referred to and addressed as *signor barone, signor conte, signor marchese*. On the contrary, a simple nobleman did not enjoy any similar distinction. This is why the lowest rank of nobility was scarcely attractive to most postulants. Having said this, some untitled noblemen were not averse to styling themselves illicitly counts or other such, which was obviously totally spurious, and the source of some confusion.

In 1834, the grant of a barony, the lowest rank of *nobiltà titolata* (titled nobility), necessitated an estate worth at least 200,000 lire. Consequently, an accurate valuation of one's family wealth became essential in order to secure a title. Equally, a charge was payable by aspirants for the bestowal of Letters Patent conferring titles of nobility. This normally amounted to a few thousand lire and in some cases the stamp duty was near to zero. It could be argued broadly that the old eighteenth-century practice of the crown explicitly selling titles and estates as a means of raising money was over. Yet, one cannot stress enough that the importance of wealth, in the process of ennoblement, must be understood in its correct perspective. Neither land nor other properties, nor money alone were sufficient to obtain a title. Nobody dared to ask for a title on the bare grounds of wealth; the essential requirement consisted in one's proximity to the king, in being able to find some supporter, or broker, in His Majesty's entourage at court, or in having a close, or even distant, relative who belonged to the titled nobility. Essentially the fusion of economic capital with social capital was the fast track to nobility. During the *Restaurazione* the process of ennoblement lost, to some extent, its 'public' dimension and became something of a private matter, to be conducted with some modesty.

Since the vast majority of titles conferred in the nineteenth century could pass only to the eldest son, the legal instrument of the primogeniture became closely connected with nobility. The relationship between primogeniture and noble status was exceedingly complex throughout nineteenth-century history. This was to become a complex chapter in the history of Piedmontese and later Italian *diritto nobiliare* (laws of nobility). There was a lot of debate, among jurists of the *jus commune* school, about entails, primogenitures and *maggioraschi*. Many felt that this custom might appear inhuman toward younger children who were excluded from inheriting. The principal and stated aim of this legal instrument was to keep family estates intact for future generations.

The king himself, Charles-Albert, had in 1837 prepared and promulgated a new Civil Code (similar to the *Code Napoléon*). He discussed the issue of noble inheritance with Count Barbaroux, his loyal and competent Minister of Justice.[15] The debate over primogeniture caused a strong disagreement between the king's conservative and progressive ministers. Repeated divisions and sub-divisions of land were not encouraged, and the king's concern for the poor nobles could not be ignored, but Barbaroux insisted firmly on cancelling for good any form of *maggiorasco*, entail or primogeniture.[16] For his part, the king declared that the monarchy would foster the status, power and role of the aristocracy by protecting its wealth and economic prosperity. Eighteenth-century political thought, culminating with the French Revolution, had destroyed many ancient institutions, privileges and practices associated with nobility.[17] In the context of the Restoration it seemed sensible to resurrect older programmes of reform for strengthening social and aristocratic elites. At the same time, it was typical of Charles-Albert to check any reactionary measures that would impede the forward march of what liberals defined as 'modernity' or 'civilization'.

It is true that the king's government was formally absolute until 1848 (especially during the last decade of his reign). In practice however, Charles-Albert summoned to his Council different personalities who were the expression of two existing political forces (it would be improper to qualify them as 'parties'): the conservatives and the liberals. The king was extremely careful in balancing these two opposing factions. He constantly sought to steer a middle course without supporting or promoting either the conservative group or the liberal one. This policy of political equilibrium was apparent when in 1847 the king dismissed the staunchly conservative minister Clemente Solaro della Margarita, while at the same time ordering Emanuele Pes di Villamarina, a well-known progressive minister, to quit his cabinet. So, though lacking any constitutional framework or parliamentary rule, the king's Council was finely balanced between these two proto-political parties.[18] The debate surrounding nobility, strictly speaking, could not be openly discussed, as it pertained to the sacred sphere of royal prerogative and sovereignty. Yet, the law of primogeniture was, on balance, a legal issue and controversy that had been gathering momentum since Enlightenment thinkers had questioned it during the previous century. Consequently, liberals knew it could not be abrogated overnight.

Charles-Albert had a complex personality: he sincerely wanted the 'ammodernamento della monarchia' (the modernization of the monarchy), as he was so fond of saying. However, from time to time he had 'medieval' dreams, filled with nostalgia for ancient forms that had promoted a harmonious relationship between the king and his subjects. Or, more simply, he knew that, despite eighteenth-century critics of aristocracy many European countries continued successfully to find different ways of keeping noble family estates safe and intact.[19] In other words, he doubted whether it was a good idea to abolish primogeniture for good. For all his uncertainty, in a formal meeting of the

Plate 1 Jean-Baptiste Isabey, *Costume of an Inspector General of Artillery*. Watercolour, 31.7 × 24 cm. Musée du Louvre, Paris. Photo: Thierry Le Mage. © RMN-Grand Palais/Art Resource, NY.

Plate 2 Jean-Baptiste Isabey, *Isabey and His First Wife, His Brother Louis and His Wife, Their Four Children*. Pen, ink and watercolour, 27.6 × 33 cm. Musée du Louvre, Paris. Photo: Michèle Bellot. © RMN-Grand Palais/Art Resource, NY.

Plate 3 Jean-Baptiste Isabey, *Frederick William III of Prussia*, 1815. Watercolour, 13.4 × 9.8 cm. Musée du Louvre, Paris. Photo: Gérard Blot. © RMN-Grand Palais/Art Resource, NY.

Plate 4 Gerard ter Borch, *The Swearing of the Oath of Ratification of the Treaty of Münster*, 1648. Oil on copper, 45.4 × 58.5 cm. National Gallery, London. Photo: © National Gallery, London/Art Resource, NY.

Plate 5 Jean-Baptiste Isabey, *The Congress of Vienna*, 1815. Pen and brown ink, 46 × 66 cm. Musée du Louvre, Paris. Photo: Christian Jean. © RMN-Grand Palais/Art Resource, NY.

Plate 6 Detail of Jean-Baptiste Isabey, *The Congress of Vienna*, 1815. Pen and brown ink, 46 × 66 cm. Musée du Louvre, Paris. Photo: Christian Jean. © RMN-Grand Palais/Art Resource, NY.

Plate 7 Louis-Léopold Boilly, *Gathering of Artists in the Studio of Isabey*, Salon of 1798. Oil on canvas, 72 × 111 cm. Musée du Louvre, Paris. Photo: Scala/Art Resource, NY.

Plate 8 Jean-Baptiste Isabey, *The Congress of Vienna*, 1815. Pen and ink with wash, 61 × 83 cm. The Royal Collection, Windsor. Photo: Royal Collection Trust. © Her Majesty Queen Elizabeth II 2017.

Plate 9 Jean-Baptiste Isabey, *Costume Study for Count Rasoumoffsky*. Pencil, pen and brown ink with wash, 11.8 × 8.5 cm. Musée du Louvre, Paris. Photo: Thierry Le Mage. © RMN-Grand Palais/Art Resource, NY.

Plate 10 Detail of Jean-Baptiste Isabey, *The Congress of Vienna*, 1815. Pen and ink with wash, 61 × 83 cm. The Royal Collection, Windsor. Photo: Royal Collection Trust. © Her Majesty Queen Elizabeth II 2017.

Plate 11 Jacques-Louis David, drawing for *Oath of the Tennis Court*, 1791. Pen and ink with wash and white highlights, 66 × 101 cm. Musée du Louvre, Paris. Photo: Gérard Blot. © RMN-Grand Palais/Art Resource, NY.

Plate 12 Jacques-Louis David, painted sketch for *Oath of the Tennis Court*, 1791. Pencil, charcoal, and oil on canvas, 400 × 660 cm. Musée National du Château de Versailles. Photo: © RMN-Grand Palais/Art Resource, NY.

Council of State on 26 July 1836, the king announced his decision to admit 'perpetual primogenitures'.

Napoleon had established that the titles he had granted his Piedmontese subjects (Piedmont had been part of the *départements réunis* of the Napoleonic Empire)[20] became hereditary only when the recipient established an entail or *maggiorasco* that tied primogeniture to an income that would sustain the dignity of the title (*Statut du* 1er Mars 1808).[21] On the contrary, Charles-Albert decided that when an aspirant noble created a *maggiorasco,* authorized by the king, he could become noble and obtain the grant of a title. That is, if his income and wealth exceeded the criteria already mentioned in this chapter.[22] This decision seemed particularly favourable to the high bourgeoisie, which was notoriously rich. The most ambitious members of the prosperous middle class could be easily attracted by the allure of golden coats of arms and solemn certificates which bestowed the ultimate accoldate of social superiority.

Naturally, the king reserved for his supreme sovereignty the freedom to create, without any recourse to legal formalities, new nobles. He was always free to decide and choose which persons he judged fit for elevation into the highest ranks of society. In Charles-Albert's reform of civil law, the *maggiorasco* appeared as an ambiguous legal institution. At first glance it seemed to pertain to private law, but quickly transformed itself into a pillar of those laws regulating access to nobility. Moreover, it seemed to contradict the very basis of the Civil Code which declared the legal equality of all subjects before the law.[23] Paradoxically the law appeared to reject noble privilege in principle whilst simultaneously instituting it in practice. It is worth noting that the Code stated that both nobles and non-nobles' rights, as far as the inheritance was concerned, could not be violated and must be protected by the law. Therefore, nobody could make a will without adhering to provisions on the paritable division of an estate, which, according to the Code, belonged to the legitimate offspring of a testator and thence descending by degrees of family affiliation.

Consequently, whatever the law of primogeniture might have been, nobody could create a *maggiorasco* damaging the prospects of younger sons, whose property rights were safeguarded by the Civil Code. For example, according to this same Code, when a father had three sons, a half of his estate was reserved to his two younger sons. The freely disposable (or alienable) portion of property was limited to a half. If this hypothetical father desired to become a baron, he had to manage his estate within these civil restrictions and limitations. Considering that the minimum amount of wealth to be promoted to the rank of baron was 200,000 lire, the size of the actual estate necessary to endow this title rose vertiginously to 400,000 lire. Only by respecting these complex legal arrangements, which effectively established two competing legal systems, could a gentleman achieve his intention of creating primogeniture backed by an inheritance entail or *maggiorasco*.

There were several reasons why during the nineteenth century this apparent rebirth of primogeniture proved unsuccessful in the long run. The Piedmontese and Savoyard nobility, though wealthy, rarely reached the property levels of some other European elites. In addition to this comparative poverty, the notion of concentrating on the eldest heir the entire estate was on the whole alien to Piedmontese mentalities and traditions. The Marquis La Tour, president of the Council of State, said to the French ambassador:

In Piedmont, there is still a nobility, that is rich enough, to fill the principal offices of the court and army. Yet, it is not a true aristocracy, there are hardly any entails or maggioraschi left here and most family estates have become divided due to the abolition of primogeniture. Thus, the foundations on which the landed aristocracy has rested have been destroyed.[24]

One can conclude that during the *Restaurazione* the kings of the House of Savoy considered that modernizing the social and economic structures of their elites was of the utmost importance. The kings' principal objective was to strengthen the ties that bound the nobility to the throne, imitating the experiences of other courts in Europe. To achieve this result, they debated the extent to which a law of primogeniture was necessary. The traditional tendency to dominate, and to a certain extent distrust, their nobility prevented the Savoy dynasty from giving their magnates an autonomous political role. The Marquis La Tour himself, in 1847, a year before the granting of the *Statuto Albertino*, suggested that the king should create a parliament, whose upper chamber would imitate the British House of Lords. Consequently, the nobility would have held the lion's share of power as hereditary legislators and become an independent *contre-poids* to the Crown's authority. It goes without saying that Charles-Albert was very disappointed and threw into the waste-paper basket this imprudent proposal of his Anglophile adviser. As a result, the Piedmontese Constitution, the *Statuto Albertino*, which eventually became the Constitution of the united Kingdom of Italy in 1861, proclaimed the equality of all the king's subjects, rejected the French and English model of an upper chamber reserved for the titled nobility. It ultimately reduced titles of nobility purely to marks of distinction. Thus, the Piedmontese kingdom, though aware and familiar with the *Restaurazione's chartes* and constitutions, steered well clear of these foreign models.

Notes

1 For a comprehensive account of French domination see the volumes published by the Archivi di Stato of Turin, entitled *All'ombra dell'Aquila Imperiale. Trasformazioni e Continuità Istituzionali nei Territori Sabaudi in Età Napoleonica (1802–1814), Atti del Convegno, Torino 18 ottobre 1990* (Rome, 1994); Michael Broers, *Napoleonic Imperialism and the Savoyard Monarchy 1773–1821. State Building in Piedmont* (Lewiston, 1997), 275–311.

2 Luigi Bulferetti, *La Restaurazione 1815–1830* (Turin, 1965). Rosario Romeo, in his otherwise excellent essay, *Dal Piemonte sabaudo all'Italia liberale* (Bari, 1974, 6–113) persisted in describing the Piedmontese *Restaurazione* using the usual rigid model of reaction and repression. Given the state of recent research, the reigns of Victor-Emmanuel I and Charles-Felix cannot simply be dismissed as oppressive exercises of narrow-minded government. Strong opposition to 'traditional' historiography is expressed in my essay, *Eclettismo giuridico della Restaurazione, Studi in memoria di M.E. Viora* (Rome, 1989), 351–75, recently reprinted in Enrico Genta Ternavasio, *Dalla Restaurazione al Risorgimento. Diritto, diplomazia, personaggi* (Turin, 2012). For an example of a stimulating revisionist interpretation of the

Piedmontese *Restaurazione*, see Giulio Stolfi, *Dall'Amministrare all'Amministrazione. Le aziende nell'organizzazione statuale del Regno di Sardegna 1717-1853* (Firenze, 2014), 83-93.

3   Nello Rosselli, *Inghilterra e Regno di Sardegna dal 1815 al 1847* (Turin, 1954), see especially 5-29; Mark Jarrett, *The Congress of Vienna and its Legacy. War and Great Power Diplomacy after Napoleon* (London, 2014), 40-1.

4   For a well informed and stimulating overview of the Piedmontese nobility see the work (ex multis) of Gustavo Mola di Nomaglio, *Feudi e Nobiltà negli Stati dei Savoia, materiali, spunti, spigolature bibliografiche per una storia. Con la Cronologia Feudale delle Valli di Lanzo* (Lanzo Torinese, 2006), *passim*; Andrea Merlotti, *L'Enigma delle Nobiltà. Stato e Ceti dirigenti nel Piemonte del Settecento* (Florence, 2000), chap.VIII; Enrico Genta Ternavasio, 'Territorio, Nobiltà e Sovrano Sabaudo in Età Moderna', in M. Ortolani, O. Vernier, M. Bottin (eds), *Pouvoir et Territoires dans les Etats de Savoie* (Nice, 2010), 241-9.

5   Enrico Genta Ternavasio, *Le Abilitazioni a possedere Feudi negli Stati Sabaudi nel secolo XVIII, Studi in onore di Ugo Gualazzini*, II (Milan, 1982), 187-222.

6   *Raccolta di Regi Editti, Manifesti ed altre Provvidenze*, VIII (Turin, 1817), 164; Isidoro Soffietti, 'La Nuova Società e il Diritto: il Caso delle Successioni in Piemonte', in *All'Ombra dell'Aquila Imperiale*, I (Rome, 1994), 300-10; Elisa Mongiano, *Ricerche sulla Successione intestata nei secoli XVI-XVIII. Il Caso degli Stati Sabaudi* (Turin, 1998), *passim*; Caterina Bonzo, *L'inevitabile Superamento della Tradizione. Il Destino del Fedecommesso nel XIX secolo* (Naples, 2014), see especially 97-126.

7   The difference between English and Continental practices of primogeniture is this: in England, depending on a peer's rank, a younger son could be a plain 'Mr', and often had to earn his living, in Europe younger sons belong invariably to the nobility and were seldom ready, let alone willing, to make their own way in the world. In Piedmont, the feudal system was not restored to its *ancien régime* basis: it is often forgotten that seigneurialism had been abolished, not by the French, but by the legitimate king, Charles Emmanuel IV, in 1797. See Courtney S. Kenny, *The History of the Law of Primogeniture in England and its Effect upon Landed Property* (Cambridge, 1878) *passim*; Mark Bence-Jones and Hugh Montgomery-Massingberd, *The British Aristocracy* (London, 1979), 20-42; Mola di Nomaglio, *Feudi e Nobiltà*, 30-1; in the first years of the *Restaurazione*, a few members of the ancient Piedmontese aristocracy attempted to obtain indemnification for feudal rights they had lost, but in general the *Camera dei Conti* (the supreme Financial Court) refused their request.

8   Of particolar interest see Marco Violardo, *Il Notabilato Piemontese da Napoleone a Carlo Alberto* (Turin, 1995).

9   Archivio di Stato di Torino, Sezioni Riunite, Art. 688, par.1: Elenco dei Titoli di Concessione di Nobiltà. Dall'Indice generale Patenti dal 1814 a tutto il 1849.

10 See Nicolò Rodolico, *Carlo Alberto negli anni di Regno 1831-1843* (Florence, 1936), 83 ff.; Narciso Nada, 'La politica interna del governo sabaudo durante la Restaurazione', in *Ombre e luci della Restaurazione* (Rome, 1997), 776 ss.

11 Giuseppe Ricuperati, *Lo Stato sabaudo nel Settecento. Dal trionfo delle burocrazie alla crisi d'Antico regime* (Turin, 2001).

12 Enrico Genta Ternavasio, 'Ordres et classes dans les reformes des Rois de Sardaigne, Ducs de Savoie', *Bibliotheque de l'Archivum Augustanum*, XXIV (1989), 83-9.

13 Antonio Manno, *Sulla riunione dei feudi ordinata da Vittorio Amedeo II* (Turin, 1876), 8 ff.

14 Bertrand Goujon, 'Distinguer et intégrer? Anoblissement et élites en France 1814–1830,' in J-C. Caron and J-P. Luis (eds), *Rien appris, rien oublié? Les Restaurations dans l'Europe postnapoléonienne 1814–1830* (Rennes, 2015), 75–89.
15 Gian Savino Pene Vidari, 'La Codificazione e i Codici: Cenni', in E. Genta and G. S. Pene Vidari (eds), *Storia del Diritto Contemporaneo* (Turin, 2005), 3–60; Paola Casana, *Tra Rivoluzione Francese e Stato Costituzionale. Il Giurista Giovanni Ignazio Pansoya (Torino 1784–1851)* (Naples, 2005) 88–97.
16 Bonzo, *L'Inevitabile Superamento*, 216–370; Enrico Genta Ternavasio, 'Codici della (piccola?) Borghesia. Note su Proprietà, Successione e Maggioraschi dal Codice Napoleone al Codice Albertino', in O. Vernier (ed.), *Etudes d'Histoire du Droit Privé en Souvenir de Maryse Carlin* (Nice, 2008), 385–402.
17 Michael P. Fitzsimmons, *The Night the Old Regime Ended: August 4, 1789 and the French Revolution* (Pennsylvania, 1998), *passim*.
18 Romano Ferrari Zumbini, *Tra Norma e Vita. Il Mosaico Costituzionale a Torino. 1846–1849* (Roma, 2016), 17–57; Adriano Viarengo, 'Tendenze radicali nel liberalismo subalpino prequarantottesco', in *Ombre e luci della Restaurazione*, 570–611.
19 Arno Mayer, *The Persistence of the Old Regime. Europe to the Great War* (New York, 1981), *passim* and esp. 17–78.
20 Broers, *Napoleonic Imperialism*, 275–311.
21 Jean Tulard, *Napoleon et la Noblesse d'Empire. Avec la liste des members de la Noblesse Imperiale 1808–1815* (Paris, 2001), *passim*.
22 Bonzo, 'L'Inevitabile Superamento', 421–34.
23 An echo of the comparative poverty of the Piedmontese nobility can be found in Costanza d'Azeglio, *Lettere al Figlio (1829–1862)*, D. Maldoni Chiarito (ed.), II (Rome, 1996), 306.
24 Giancarlo Sallier de La Tour, *The Italian Levy of 1812–1816 and its Legacy on the Kingdom of Sardinia during the Restoration* (Exeter, 2014): esp. 65–7.

Part Four

Dynasty Re-Invented

14

Heroic Heirs: Monarchical Succession and the Role of the Military in Restoration Spain and France

Heidi Mehrkens and Richard Meyer Forsting

After the tumultuous years of the French Revolution and the Napoleonic wars, the Bourbons in France and Spain were looking for a hero: someone from their own ranks, with the potential to reconnect the armed forces to the monarchy and restore the dynasty's claim to military glory. The power of the early modern monarchy traditionally had been forged, expanded or destroyed by means of war. Yet from the late seventeenth century the Bourbon monarchs had put more emphasis on courtly representation than on physical presence at the head of their armies, with the result that Spain and France had not been ruled by a *roi de guerre* for a very long time.[1] This chapter will discuss how, after 1815, two Bourbon princes, the Duc d'Angoulême in France and Don Carlos in Spain, sought to restore their dynasty's severely damaged military image.

The French Revolution and the Napoleonic wars fundamentally changed the character of the armed forces across Europe. In Spain and France the expansion of the officer corps and a more meritocratic promotions system created a people's army, which was no longer dominated exclusively by noble officers. In addition, the armed forces in Spain came to be seen as liberators from foreign subjugation, which is why the Peninsular War (1808–14) is also known in Spain as the 'War of Independence'. Yet the Spanish monarchy failed to defend the national territory, and the Bourbons in France were unable to stem the revolutionary tide. In 1814, after years in exile, both dynasties had to find new sources of legitimacy, one of which was the army. The monarchy aimed to contain its revolutionary potential, especially in Spain where officers carried out various military rebellions, known as *pronunciamientos*, to re-establish a constitutional system.[2]

In both constitutional and neo-absolutist systems after 1815, the monarch remained in nominal command of the army. This position allowed the ruler to influence the relationship between the dynasty and the army and to address the changing demands and challenges that came with the post-Revolutionary period. The military became a tool to preserve the political and social status quo, quell internal unrest and thus defend the monarchy against its enemies within the national borders as well as outside. The monarchy was forced to accept that the army's loyalty did not rest on feudal aristocratic bonds. Regaining the armed forces' allegiance meant developing more direct links with the military and at least nominally subscribing to its meritocratic spirit.

One way to strengthen the dynasty's control over the military was to enhance the dynasty's standing with officers. The Spanish and French Bourbons sought to achieve this closer union through financial, political and symbolic support for the armed forces. They also emphasized the dedication of members of the dynasty to the army. Angoulême participated in the Spanish expedition (1823) and Don Carlos in the First Carlist War (1833–9), and both were involved in military administration. Their position within the dynasty, close to the throne, yet not in the limelight and occupied with matters of ruling, placed them in an ideal position to foster, as royal intermediaries, links between the army and the monarchy. As heirs to the throne they had few specific tasks and duties to fulfil within the state, despite their importance to the dynasty as representations of the monarchy's future. This allowed them to engage in military service, which showcased their virtue, preparedness and ability to rule.[3] Contributions of royal princes in the European Restorations to strengthening the monarchy politically, socially or indeed as soldiers deserve further attention. In the Spanish case, Don Carlos ultimately employed his soldierly image to destabilize his niece Isabel II's reign, convinced that he was the legitimate heir to the Spanish crown. Despite this challenge to the ruling monarch, the projection of a soldierly image was always meant to enhance monarchical power.

This chapter will assess the two princes' military education and career in the army. It will then discuss practical and symbolical aspects of their leadership and ask to what extent both princes were in a position to establish, improve or stabilize the relationship between the monarchy and the armed forces at a time of rapid political and social change. To conclude, it will briefly analyse examples of the public reception of both princes as soldiers. Visibility was key for this renewed partnership of the military and the monarchy. In order for this to be widely accepted and believable, royal princes had to be seen as military leaders in public. This image was influenced not only by ancient heroes of the dynasty, but also by the immediate past: Napoleon Bonaparte's successes and skills as a military commander who shared the hardships of his soldiers had a strong impact on the representation of Restoration period princes. Mimicking Bonaparte's style, Angoulême and Don Carlos appeared as closely involved generals in battered uniform, endearing themselves to their troops, while carefully avoiding the image of the detached royal visitor to the battlefield.

The pacifying hero? Louis Antoine Duc d'Angoulême

Born on 6 August 1775 into the glittering world of the Palace of Versailles, Louis Antoine d'Artois, Duc d'Angoulême was the eldest son of Charles Comte d'Artois and a nephew of King Louis XVI of France. During the Bourbon Restoration, Angoulême became second in line to his uncle Louis XVIII and, upon the king's death in 1824, heir to his father Charles X. Crown prince in a constitutional monarchy, he swore to respect the Charter of 1814. When the July Revolution of 1830 ended the reign of the Bourbons in France, Angoulême renounced his right to the throne. He died on 3 June 1844, after another long and trying period in exile.[4]

Angoulême's education, from the tender age of five, was placed in the hands of Armand Louis de Sérent, a distinguished hero of the Seven Years' War. As military governor, de Sérent educated the prince and his younger brother, Charles Ferdinand Duc de Berry (1778–1820), at the Château de Beauregard, deliberately removed from the fashionable world of the royal court.[5] Here the boys received their basic military education which included lessons in geometry, military history and tactics. The princes were never meant to become professional soldiers, though. They were given a firm grounding in the essential subjects of the day to form rounded personalities rather than to become specialists in a single field: divinity was part of this education programme, as were the Classics. What is more, younger princes of the French Bourbon dynasty – this included Charles d'Artois and his sons – were not supposed to receive full-scale military training and pursue a career as professional military officers who could potentially threaten the position of the king or his successor.[6]

The Revolution of 1789 abruptly ended the sheltered childhood at Beauregard and threw the fourteen-year-old Angoulême into the vicissitudes of long years of exile. It also opened up the unusual path of a professional military career for the two princes. Angoulême and Berry underwent practical and theoretical military training at the renowned artillery school in Turin, where they had been invited to stay with their uncle, the King of Sardinia. The *Regie Scuole teoriche e pratiche di Artiglieria e Fortificazione*, founded in 1739, taught mathematics at a high level, blended with other scientific disciplines in order to develop the field of military technology. According to the 1755 school regulations, the students learned arithmetic, geometry, surveying, algebra, the theory of conic sections, physics, mechanics, differential and integral calculus, artillery and fortifications.[7]

Between 1789 and 1792, Angoulême and Berry served in the ranks and earned their captain's epaulettes. 'Ils chargeoient, pontoient et tiroient leurs pièces avec rapidité et précision', Chateaubriand noted in his *Mélanges historiques*. During the years of the war with France (1792–6), the princes were eager to follow in the footsteps of their father and lead an *émigré* army into battle.[8] According to Beach, both sons of Charles d'Artois would enjoy the company of soldiers and be 'far more at home on the battlefield than their father'.[9]

In April 1800, Angoulême took command of a Bavarian cavalry regiment and fought at the Battle of Hohenlinden.[10] His position as a French refugee prince prevented further military engagements. Angoulême spent more than ten years in England, where he waited impatiently for an opportunity to join the fight against Napoleon. The Revolutionary and Napoleonic wars had opened up a welcome opportunity for the prince to prove himself, to earn recognition on the battlefield rather than at the Bourbon exile courts, where others constantly outshone him. The young Angoulême is described as a decent and very shy lad, always thoughtful. He certainly lacked the easy manners of his charismatic father Artois and the carefree attitude of his younger brother Berry. A contemporary even considered the prince 'less than a man, nothing, a human envelope, voilà tout'.[11]

Intermediary between monarchy and army

After the downfall of the Napoleonic Empire this human envelope assisted the reinstallation of the Bourbons rather successfully. In 1814, Angoulême was finally allowed to join the British invasion of France. His entry into the city of Bordeaux on 12 March, on the heels of a small corps of British and Portuguese soldiers, marked the beginning of the Bourbon restoration. The population acclaimed the prince, who presented himself in uniform and on horseback to win local support for his uncle's reign.[12] A year later, in March 1815, Angoulême was again in Bordeaux when he learned that Bonaparte had escaped his exile on the island of Elba. Following orders from the king, Angoulême commanded the royalist army in the southern Rhône river valley but was unable to prevent Napoleon's return to Paris.[13]

Louis XVIII had granted a Charter in 1814, the centrepiece of the new monarchical system, but the monarch did not rely on a constitution alone.[14] In 1823 the king embraced the idea of a military expedition into Spain to help reinstall the hapless Ferdinand VII on the throne. It provided the Bourbon dynasty with an opportunity to put France back on the diplomatic map of Europe and to secure domestic support for the constitutional monarchy.[15] The Spanish campaign of 1823 was probably Angoulême's finest hour as a military leader. The king put his nephew in command of a French corps, the Hundred Thousand Sons of Saint Louis (in Spanish the *Cien Mil Hijos de San Luis*).[16] This popular name illustrates how the monarchy had in fact been restored 'on the basis of the historic and divine legitimacy of the Bourbons'.[17] It invoked the name of the crusader Louis IX of France (r. 1226–70), the only canonized French monarch.[18]

The Spanish campaign was rapidly (and for many surprisingly) successful in ending the Liberal Triennium (1820–3) and restoring the rule of Ferdinand VII. Angoulême's troops fought victoriously in the decisive Battle of Trocadero. The duke was awarded the title Prince of Trocadero for his achievements, but Angoulême was less successful in preventing Ferdinand's return from turning into a cruel and bloody reaction. Disillusioned, he left Spain and 'refused the honors and titles which Ferdinand VII wished to shower upon him'.[19]

This reaction reveals aspects of the prince's style of leadership as a military officer, but also of his style as a prospective future ruler. Like Don Carlos, Angoulême was a devout Catholic. He was also serious about representing a constitutional monarchical system in times of war. As a commander he did his best to tread very carefully on foreign soil, reassuring the Spanish population that France was not their enemy. He issued orders to his soldiers 'to respect religion, laws and property' and to keep up discipline under all circumstances.[20] The French army command's strict surveillance of the troops, to ensure that Angoulême's pacifying orders were respected, was an important factor for the success of a campaign in which French soldiers experienced few hostile encounters with the local population.[21]

What exactly was Angoulême's position in this campaign? The prince had been given an important command, and his performance in Spain mattered on more than just the military level. For all contemporaries, it was highly symbolic. Napoleon Bonaparte had experienced severe difficulties in defeating Spanish and British resistance during the Peninsular War. If the Bourbon dynasty now was to conquer

Spain and succeed where Bonaparte had failed, this could help consolidate the French Restoration monarchy.[22]

The French army of the early 1820s was a heterogeneous body. The soldiers fighting for the king represented diverse political sympathies: there were royalists, Bonapartists, republicans. The former Imperial military had been sidelined and persecuted in the early years of the Bourbon regime, which still caused distrust and bitterness among Napoleon's veterans.[23] The challenge for Louis XVIII, on his path to national reconciliation, was to manage this structure and make it work. In order to win this campaign, he needed officers with fighting experience (ideally Spanish fighting experience) in charge. As a consequence, pro-Bourbon commanders were given the secondary commands; senior commands went to the former generals of the Revolution and Empire.[24]

As opposed to Spain, where army officers often intervened politically in *pronunciamientos*, the French army of the Restoration period can be seen as a loyal body, serving a government that would promote the armed forces' interest and keep order at home. The army, in other words, was an asset for the Bourbon monarchy.[25] The prince went to Spain as commander-in-chief of the Army of the Pyrenees. In this highly professional environment, Angoulême was probably the least experienced officer. And as the future ruler of France, he needed special protection. He agreed to consider this appointment as a merely honorary role. Angoulême oversaw the political direction of the expedition and left the military command to Major-General Armand Charles Guilleminot (1774–1840), a tried-and-tested general of the First Empire.[26] Playing a less dominant role turned out to be a wise decision in the end – Angoulême was celebrated for his level-headedness, always de-escalating disputes in the field.

However unprofessional or inexperienced he was in comparison to others, military service created a niche and an occupation for a prince who otherwise had no say in dynastic or political decisions and was held at arm's length from power. It seems fair to argue that Angoulême's minor position within the dynasty – where he was dominated by his father, his uncle and to some extent by his wife – increased his passivity in politics as well as his love for the military.[27]

Angoulême became heir to the throne (Dauphin) in 1824, upon the succession of Charles X. Despite the severe damage to the dynasty caused by his father's constant meddling with government affairs, he refused to engage in political opposition against the king and respected both monarchical and paternal authority. Since he was also a stout defender of the Charter of 1814, his political opinion was not much sought after during his father's reign. Baron d'Haussez described the prince's participation in the council in 1829 as follows: 'The Dauphin would leaf through the military almanack on which he would note in pencil the transfer of [military] assignments … Otherwise, the Dauphin took very little part in the discussions, hardly spoke except to make some brief remarks, and too often introducing them with some such apologetic phrase as: "Perhaps what I'm going to say is crazy, but you won't pay any attention to it anyway."'[28]

Notwithstanding his reserve in the field of politics, the prince remained a dedicated military leader right until the final day of the Bourbon regime. On 29 July 1830, Angoulême was appointed supreme commander of the royal troops and sent to face the July revolutionaries in Paris. Charles X relied on his son's example of loyalty and bravery to refresh the soldiers' commitment to defending the king and his dynasty. Angoulême was all in favour of mobilizing the army and crushing the uprising in Paris, exclaiming in the session of the council: 'Let's accept our destiny proudly and perish with arms in our hands.'[29] He wanted to mount a horse (*monter à cheval*) and make a difference on the territory he was most familiar with – military engagement and personal leadership. All hope of conquering Paris was lost, when large parts of the remaining royal troops refused to fight and abandoned the prince.[30] On his way to England, facing renewed exile, Angoulême is reported to have said: 'I have only one regret: it is that I did not die in Paris at the head of the guard.'[31]

The military formed a decisive element of the prince's career in these fifteen years of Bourbon reign, and especially after the death of the Duc de Berry in 1820. We can assume it seemed safe for Louis XVIII and Charles X to accept, even promote Angoulême's particular role as the only professionally trained soldier in the immediate family. It was unlikely that the prince could build a dangerous power base within the army, and Angoulême's dedication to the troops offered soldiers of all ranks potential for identification with the royal family. In a sense his military engagement complemented the public presence of the two Bourbon monarchs. While Charles X cut a dashing figure on horseback he was pretty much an amateur in all things military and notorious for not taking the rank and file seriously. Louis XVIII was intelligent and benign, but hampered by gout and had not been seen riding a horse in a very long time. The king was nicknamed *roi fauteuil* for a reason. Hence both kings relied on Angoulême to help shape a new, modernized image of the Restoration 'military monarchy', with the potential of gathering a reconciled French nation behind the constitutional Bourbon regime. What is more, a glorious monarchy might help exorcize the spirit of the most formidable soldier and military leader of the time, the still widely revered Napoleon Bonaparte.

Angoulême's visibility as a soldier

Bonaparte's legacy haunted the Bourbon dynasty. At the beginning of the Restoration, Bonapartist cartoons circulated en masse in France. These affordable and widely read prints poked fun at Angoulême's military career – they showed the prince in uniform but denied him the qualities of a military leader. One example is the print *L'Enjambée Impériale* from 1815: It shows a dwarfish royal family idly standing by and watching in awe as Napoleon takes a giant step from Elba to invade France.[32] The Bourbons seem too afraid to stop Napoleon from seizing power again. Angoulême wears a terrified expression and a candle-snuffer on his hat, which mocks his military uniform and symbolizes the Bourbons' rule being terminated. Clearly, the cartoon suggests, this tiny soldier was no match for the mighty Napoleon.

The official military portraiture reveals a different agenda. In 1827 the painter Paul Delaroche was commissioned to commemorate the capture of the Trocadero in 1823.[33] At the centre of Delaroche's work is Angoulême, on foot, at the head of his commanding officers marching in uneven terrain. His boots are not polished, he is neither fighting nor striking a heroic pose, and yet this image radiates both competence and manliness. The prince's face is not beautiful in a classic sense, but handsome, inviting trust. His gaze seems to be focused on action and soldiers we do not see. Delaroche's Angoulême is a military leader all over, in the company of his men, almost painfully aware of the people relying on him.

The calm, plain beauty of the official portraiture was clearly idealized, but it also captured aspects of the prince's personality. Unlike his Spanish counterpart Don Carlos, Angoulême lacked handsome features and a dashing appearance. He was not known for a winning personality or charm. Since the prince had no children, there were rumours that he was impotent.[34] Delaroche's interpretation underlined Angoulême's military prowess, but also other qualities expected of a leader: a sense of responsibility, altruism, simplicity and approachability. The portrait shows an officer in plain uniform, not immediately recognizable at first sight as a royal prince. Delaroche's painting suggests that Angoulême's authority stemmed not only from his royal descent but from his natural gifts and professional ability as a soldier.

The Christian soldier-king? Carlos María Isidro de Bórbon

Carlos María Isidro de Bórbon, most commonly referred to as Don Carlos, was born on 29 March 1788 at the Aranjuez palace outside Madrid, into the splendour of the Bourbon court. He was the second eldest son of Charles IV and María Luisa of Parma and younger brother of Ferdinand VII. Don Carlos spent a significant part of his life as one of his brother's closest confidants and heir presumptive to the Spanish throne (1814–30). His biography and political life are intimately linked to that of Ferdinand VII: Don Carlos accompanied his brother into exile to France during the Peninsular War (1808–14), returned with him to Spain in 1814 and, like the king, grudgingly swore an oath on the constitution during the Liberal Triennium.[35] As heir, he became an icon of the reactionary Catholic right, often referred to as *ultras*, who were disappointed with Ferdinand VII. They looked to Don Carlos as the future king, who would restore the Church's and nobility's privileges and powers.[36] While Don Carlos never openly defied his brother, his unsuccessful six-year rebellion against his niece Isabel II's claim to the throne (1833–9) meant that he died in exile as an outcast. Whereas his life, thought and his religious and political convictions have been studied, insufficient attention has been paid to his relationship with the armed forces and his symbolic representation as a heroic military figure.[37]

The relative scarcity of male heirs among the Spanish Bourbon family and the precarious health of Charles IV's firstborn – the future Ferdinand VII – meant that Don Carlos received a similar education to that of his older sibling.[38] Unlike in France, Spanish princes were still exclusively educated at court. Don Carlos's most famous teachers were the priests Fernando and Felipe Scio of the *Escuelas Pías*, which demonstrated the importance that was placed on religious education and Christian virtues as a source of morality. Juan Ardazun's assertion that Ferdinand's and Carlos's upbringing was purely 'a regime of the seminar' should nonetheless be taken with at least a pinch of salt.[39]

Interpretations that focus excessively on religious education ignore the fact that other areas of study, such as military instruction and sciences, were by no means neglected. When Don Carlos was thirteen, the highly regarded veteran officer Don Vincente Maturana was appointed to teach Don Carlos military history, strategy and tactics. Besides, Charles IV's children were accustomed to wearing military dress from an early age. Antonio Moral Roncal has estimated that a large part of the Spanish *Infante*'s allowance was spent on expensive army uniforms.[40] Ferdinand and Don Carlos were made to *look like* officers and acquired knowledge of military matters. Appearance and a symbolic connection with the troops were important elements in a Bourbon prince's life even prior to the Napoleonic wars.

While the effects of the 1789 Revolution were not as immediately felt at the Spanish court as they were at the French one, they still had significant consequences for the development of Ferdinand's and his brother's political beliefs. The excesses of the Revolution, its rampant anti-clericalism and disregard for tradition played an important role in reinforcing Don Carlos's ultra-conservative, Catholic worldview.[41] Charles IV's sons were both, in their differing ways, ardent counter-revolutionaries and hardened absolutists. Ferdinand VII was a strong proponent of a powerful, rationalized central state apparatus controlled by the king, while Don Carlos favoured the re-institution of local aristocratic and Church privileges and a 'medieval coordinating role' for the monarchy, ostensibly harking back to a pre-eighteenth-century conception of absolutist rule.[42] Eventually, the upheavals of the Napoleonic era also engulfed Spain and like Angoulême, Don Carlos and the royal family were forced into exile in 1808. Constitutions sought to regulate and circumscribe royal power, including its prerogatives over the armed forces. The absence of the king, the fight against French occupation and the 1812 Cadiz Constitution's proclamation of national sovereignty altered the self-conception of many officers. The army's allegiance was no longer solely to the monarch, but to the nation. This complicated the crown's relationship to the army, even after the abolition of the constitution in 1814.[43]

Under Napoleon's surveillance at the Bourbons' guarded residence at Valençay, the *Infante* – unlike Angoulême – found few opportunities to make a name for himself. The king and his brother were isolated from the men fighting in their name and Ferdinand VII was busy keeping his options open with Napoleon. Don Carlos's chance to get involved with military matters and government only arose once Ferdinand VII was restored to the throne in 1814. Shortly after returning to Spain, the king reinstated an absolutist regime.[44] Yet the changes Spain had experienced meant the monarch had to find ways to adapt to a fundamentally different environment. The army not only became the main defence against the threat of revolution, but harboured revolutionary potential itself, as demonstrated by rebellions led by senior officers against the regime. It was in this context that Don Carlos was gradually introduced to military service. In July 1814, he was appointed colonel of the *Brigada Real de Carabineros*, conferring a position of military authority on the *Infante*. A special royal secretary, Captain Manuel Moxo, was appointed to exercise Don Carlos's command in his name.[45] Don Carlos's role was therefore largely a symbolic one, intended to strengthen the bonds between the monarchy and the army, rather than turning the heir presumptive into a man of the military. For the time being, Don Carlos remained more interested in spiritual, rather than military matters. For one of his few public appearances he demonstratively took part in the opening of a Jesuit college in Madrid in 1816.[46] As the liberal nineteenth-century historian and contemporary of the Carlist War Antonio Pirala put it, Don Carlos 'confided more in his *generalísima*, the Lady of Sorrows, than in his soldiers' weapons'.[47] He thus continued the association between the monarch and the Catholic Church, which were both linked to conceptions of Spain as a political and cultural entity.

In 1820 Don Carlos only accepted the restoration of the constitutional settlement half-heartedly and it was apparent that this was not an act of conviction but of pragmatism. The radical paper *La Tercerola* openly attacked the heir's reactionary attitudes and mocked him for 'that uniform that you use without ever having commanded a company'.[48] While liberals saw in Don Carlos's ultra-conservative views a threat to the constitution, among conservative elements, including some high-ranking officers, he became the hope for a return to a traditionalist, Catholic absolutism. The orientation of the most reactionary forces toward a monarchical solution linked to the heir presumptive rather than the king laid the foundation for the growth of Carlist agitation during the second half of the decade.[49] Like Angoulême, the *Infante* was not a schemer. He constantly kept his brother informed about his opinions, solicited his advice on major decisions and was never implicated in any rebellions. Only shortly before Ferdinand VII's death would Don Carlos openly defy his older brother. This old-fashioned loyalty and a strong belief in absolute royal authority, what Mark Lawrence has called 'legitimist propriety', was one of the factors that undermined his fight for the right to the succession.[50]

Intermediary between monarchy and army

Unlike his father Charles IV, Ferdinand VII did not keep the next-in-line to the throne out of government and military affairs.[51] The correspondence between Ferdinand VII and Don Carlos reveals that the king was happy for his sibling to play an active role in politics, the military and administration, at least prior to the birth of his daughter Isabel in 1830. The heir presumptive attended the Council of State, the de facto cabinet during the periods of absolutist rule, and in Ferdinand VII's absence presided over its sessions. Don Carlos was involved extensively in government affairs and was actively encouraged to do so by his brother.[52] The delegation of such far-reaching responsibilities to the heir to the throne was new at the Spanish court, reflecting the wider role heirs to the throne were now expected to play.

One pressing military issue for the restored Bourbon monarchy was Spain's effort to restore control over its American empire. The Napoleonic occupation of Spain had gravely undermined the Spanish monarchy's authority overseas and strengthened independence movements across the continent. By 1824 the Crown was left with Cuba and the Philippines as the main remnants of its sizeable imperial possessions.[53] The Bourbons had been clinging on to hopes of re-establishing control over their former colonies. The *Infante* was a strong proponent of building a powerful fleet and sending troops overseas to restore Spanish rule. Ferdinand VII, Don Carlos and their advisors seriously considered the option of dispatching the heir presumptive overseas to lead the troops in a reassertion of the Spanish monarchy's dominion over the Americas.[54]

Ultimately, though, Ferdinand VII proved unwilling to send a Bourbon prince on such a risky mission.

While a *Reconquista* of the Americas remained an imperial pipedream, more concrete steps had been taken to introduce the heir to the armed forces and thus rekindle the bond between monarchy and army. On 18 August 1814, the *Infante* was given the title of *Generalísimo* of Ferdinand VII's armies and the following month he was appointed Vice President of the War Council, which allowed him to attend all its sessions.[55] These measures gave Don Carlos direct access to the military apparatus, allowed him to make connections with other officers and enabled him to gain experience in army administration. It also meant that he was involved and associated with attempts to modernize the armed forces after their overseas defeats.

After a brief period of exclusion from military matters during the Liberal Triennium, Don Carlos returned to his political and military duties. When the *Junta de Caballería* was created in 1829, with a similar pre-eminence in military matters as the earlier War Council, Don Carlos was appointed its president. This meant that he was in contact with the military establishment on daily basis, gave audiences to officers and assisted military inspections and parades in full uniform. These contacts and the recognition the post gave Don Carlos would prove significant when he challenged Isabel II's claim to the throne. Don Carlos's contacts and network within the armed forces 'favoured the prestige of the Infante among the high command of the army, many of whom put their swords to his service during the Carlist War'.[56] Don Carlos was not only depicted as a soldier but was directly involved with military affairs and officers. This points toward the development of a more functional role for the heir to the throne as an intermediary between the monarchy and the armed forces.

Don Carlos did not lack self-confidence – his belief in the righteousness of his cause gave him 'a valour that bordered on imprudence'[57] – but he was not a great schemer. Don Carlos's loyalty and deep respect for the hierarchical organization of the royal family meant he did not actively seek to establish a network to rival his brother and sister-in-law. This allowed his enemies to carry out a purge of his followers in the administration, government and most importantly the army.[58] Don Carlos and his supporters became a threat to Isabel's claim to the throne, and later on to the reorientation of the Spanish state in a more modern, liberal and ultimately constitutional direction. Nonetheless, despite Don Carlos's private rejection of the Pragmatic Sanction, which replaced Salic Law and legitimized the female succession, the *Infante* did not publicly oppose his brother, as this would have constituted a rebellion against the legitimate king: an act contrary to his strongly held royalist and legitimist principles.[59]

There is also no indication that Don Carlos initially tried to enhance his personal prestige or cement his position as the legitimate heir by cultivating a strong military image or taking advantage of the public acclamations sporadically made in his favour. One reason his uprising initially failed was exactly this lack of preparation.[60] It left the Carlists reliant on the 'foral' regions in the Basque country, Navarre and Cataluña, who saw him as a defender of their regional privileges, the *fueros*.[61] In the rest of the country, uprisings were relatively quickly suppressed by Cristino forces, who were not beyond using violent repression to achieve their aims.[62] Furthermore, the pretender was initially unable to join his fighters in the Carlist strongholds in the Basque country, which undermined his efforts at establishing a parallel government, gaining a stronger personal following and motivating his troops.

Don Carlos's troubles were not entirely of his own making. Ferdinand VII had sent his brother to Portugal and even urged him to leave the Peninsula for the Vatican after he had refused to swear an oath to Isabel as Princess of Asturias in 1833. The reinforcement of the Spanish-Portuguese border did not allow Don Carlos to cross into Spain without risking capture by the Cristino general Rodil, who viciously pursued the pretender. After leaving Portugal for Britain, Don Carlos crossed the Pyrenees via France, reaching Carlist-held territory on 6 July 1834. As Jordi Canal has argued, the 'incorporation of the figure of the king gave wings to a fight in danger of short-term stagnation'.[63] This underlines the importance of Don Carlos's personal presence, in particular for his soldiers. They wanted to see their king, the man they had been fighting and risking their lives for. The increasing importance of charisma and personal leadership is further highlighted by the role played by the brilliant Carlist general Zumalacárregui. The Basque general's strategic acumen and forceful command sustained the Carlists' war effort in the face of their numerical inferiority. As a reward, and perhaps as a way personally to associate himself with Zumalacárregui, Don Carlos appointed him field marshal and conferred wide-ranging military powers on him in March 1834.[64] The pretender quickly sought to link his image to that of his most successful officer.

While 'Don Carlos came to be regarded by his supporters as one of the most complete princes of Christianity',[65] it took longer for him to construct a believable heroic image of himself on the battlefield. As strong as his appeal to extreme royalists and Catholics was, he did not reach out to larger sections of the military leadership, which had become more meritocratic, less aristocratic and, all in all, more liberal. Don Carlos's conception of kingship did not fit with an army that increasingly saw itself as the ultimate representation of the nation, rather than the monarch's personal fighting force. He was unable to appeal to the less reactionary sections of the population and the armed forces, especially in larger urban areas. The post-1808 Spanish army was much less likely to rally behind a call to arms for a return to an imagined, feudalist and absolutist past. Outside of the foral regions – the Basque country, Navarre and Cataluña – and the reactionary Catholic milieu, Don Carlos's appeal was severely limited.

Don Carlos's visibility as a soldier

Representations of Don Carlos can broadly be divided into two phases. The first is his period as the heir presumptive, prior to his brother's death, when he would frequently be portrayed in military uniform in official portraits of the highest quality. After he was banished and had openly revolted against Ferdinand VII's wife and daughter, he lost access to court painters and official channels to disseminate images of himself as a military leader. This meant that Don Carlos had to rely on propaganda in the form of more modest prints and written reports to showcase his martial qualities.[66] In some ways, Don Carlos was forced to mount a media campaign against his sister-in-law and her daughter to strengthen his claim to the throne.

As soon as Ferdinand VII returned to Spain, efforts were made to reinforce the royal family's dignity using ostentatious paintings that harked back to the court's pre-Napoleonic splendour. At the same time as creating the impression of continuity, some of these images aimed to appropriate the image of the military leader so successfully popularized by Napoleon. Portraits of Don Carlos frequently depict him in uniform and exhibiting military insignia. The court painter Vicente López's *Retrato del Infante Carlos María Isidro Bórbon* (c. 1814) is a good example of this. The heir apparent is shown in the full gala uniform of a Spanish captain general, holding the standard issue rifle of his regiment, the *Reales Carabiñeros*. The uniform and weapon create a visual link between the heir apparent and the troops under his command. This and other portraits present the heir apparent as a dignified, stern and manly ruler-in-waiting. Don Carlos wears a prominent moustache, a stern expression and the Order of the Golden Fleece, which serve to reinforce his masculinity and his commitment to the traditions of the Spanish monarchy. What tipped the scales further in Don Carlos's favour was that Ferdinand VII – corpulent, sickly and unattractive – cut a less than impressive figure even in official portraits.[67] As has been shown above, the Bourbon monarchy had not been a fighting but a court dynasty. Don Carlos's military representation was meant to re-establish the credibility the Spanish crown had lost as a defender of national integrity after the foreign invasion.

After his de facto exclusion from the succession and his subsequent rebellion against the Queen Regent and her supporters, Don Carlos neither enjoyed access to court painters nor did he have the economic resources to commission grand portraits after the confiscation of his and his family's properties.[68] Simpler, more basic, but also new, less traditional and somewhat modern means were employed to enhance the pretender's visibility as a soldier. These often took the form of sketches, lower-quality, easily reproducible paintings and written propaganda published in the emergent Carlist press. There were plenty of images that depicted Don Carlos on horseback, surrounded by officers in Basque uniforms. An example of this is Francisco Sainz's sketch *Don Carlos y su acompañamiento*, which shows the pretender – easily identifiable due to his prominent moustache and location at the centre of the image – conferring with his generals. Most remarkably perhaps, Don Carlos is not portrayed as a courtly king, but in an almost bourgeois fashion, as a man of the people. Other images such as *Don Carlos, Zumalakarregi y el Estado Mayor* sought to explicitly link the pretender's representation with that of his most successful and admired general. Don Carlos is seen deliberating with Zumalacárregui on the siege of Bilbao, surrounded by soldiers in their distinctive red berets; the allusions to his direct involvement in military actions and regional identity are unmistakable. Even though he in many ways cut the figure of an anti-Napoleon, as a Christian soldier, this image's composition is almost reminiscent of the portraits of Napoleon strategizing with his officers.

The allusion to his military credentials, valour and manliness formed an important part of Don Carlos's representation. This is evident in some of the sexist anti-Cristino propaganda intended to discredit Isabel II's claim to the throne and a woman's capacity to rule Spain. One such leaflet read, 'Philip V [who introduced Salic Law in Spain] knew how nature demands that a man should command and women obey, and that there is barely one out of a million of the fairer sex fit for something greater than home spinnning.'[69] It is evident that Don Carlos was the masculine, strong commander the pamphlet had in mind. Despite his traditionalism, Don Carlos was forced to engage in a media campaign against his niece and use relatively modern means to undermine his rival and gain support.

The image of Don Carlos as a brave leader endured and served as a Carlist propaganda tool even beyond his lifetime. According to Bolaños, writing in *El Correo Español* in 1894, the pretender in 1833 presented himself in front of General Rodil's troops, who were preparing to engage Don Carlos's men in battle. The – somewhat naïve – idea was that the troops would refuse to fight and join the pretender as they came face to face with the 'legitimate' king. The sight of the *Infante* with only 58 of his officers apparently caused perplexity, admiration and indecision in equal measure. Rodil eventually ordered his squadrons to march against the Carlist forces; suffice to say they obeyed. To Bolaños, however, the feat demonstrated that the pretender had 'the heart of a lion, a soul of extraordinary fortitude, and a serenity up to all challenges in the face of danger'.[70] Moreover, the episode demonstrates Don Carlos's and the author's striking conviction in the power of personality and presence as a tool for winning over supporters among the armed forces. Furthermore, it demonstrates the value of heroic martial behaviour as a weapon in the increasingly meaningful battle for the hearts and minds of Spaniards.

It is difficult to gauge the effectiveness of Don Carlos's projection of the image of a valorous, virtuous and competent officer. Some observers were not convinced by Don Carlos's adoption of the image of a common soldier. Despite writing a sympathetic account of the campaign, Adolf Loning, a German who travelled to Spain to join the Carlists, accused Don Carlos of not sharing the hardships of his troops. Loning wrote that while his army was engaged in combat, Don Carlos was 'an hour away from the battlefield, holding court while many of his soldiers suffered from hunger'.[71] The pretender also found out that his early modern conception of military leadership was increasingly ineffective in the context of nineteenth-century warfare when Rodil's troops refused to switch their allegiance.

All in all, his followers, as well as some of his detractors, found the pretender to be a man of extraordinary bravery and strong principles, if not necessarily of military genius. Fernando Fernández de Córdoba, a famous Cristino general, describes the qualities of his enemy at length in his memoirs. In his opinion, Don Carlos displayed 'truly impeccable integrity and honour of character' and 'the most serene valour in the face of the responsibilities of history and the great danger in combat'.[72] For Pirala, it was Don Carlos's 'superstitious fanaticism' that 'made him appear like a hero on the battlefield', who 'remained serene, fearless, motionless [while] covered in the dust lifted by the bullets landing at his feet'.[73] The pretender's valour made a highly favourable impression even on his adversaries. One of his own officers, Florencio Sanz Baeza, described the pretender as 'a king who presents himself without fear in the danger of many battles'. It impressed him that Don Carlos would 'like the simple soldier submit himself to the rigour of the season and fatigue', while 'asking of his friends for what he needs only for the army'.[74] Even the famous nineteenth-century republican novelist Pérez Galdos concluded that 'Don Carlos maintained his dignity in ostracism and bad fortune, and ended his days loved by those that served him'.[75]

Conclusion

Both Angoulême and Don Carlos were deeply affected by the 1789 French Revolution and the Napoleonic wars. However, their experiences of exile differed markedly. Don Carlos did not have any opportunities to prove himself on the battlefield and acquire military experience. Angoulême, on the other hand, gained at least limited military experience and was able to enhance his reputation further by successfully commanding the *Cien Mil Hijos de San Luis*. In the light of the convulsions of the Revolution and the constant threat of renewed popular unrest, both princes were expected to reinforce the legitimacy of the monarchy and the bond between a transformed army and the Crown.

Presenting a martial image, being visible as men in uniform and able commanders became significant qualities again for a Bourbon prince. It also provided a natural outlet for heirs, whose position in the state was not well defined. Widely marginalized at court, Angoulême was particularly apt at playing the role of the capable commander. The French heir's heroic image also aimed to replace and imitate Napoleon's glorious victories for the Bourbon dynasty. Don Carlos was closely engaged in the armed forces' administration and governance. He forged significant connections with military leaders and was able to portray himself credibly as a man of the military. The emergence of the armed forces as an important political actor was more of a factor in Spain than in France, where the army sought to guard its professional neutrality.

Angoulême and Don Carlos both functioned as intermediaries between the army and the Crown. It mattered to them and to their supporters that they were regarded as military leaders and associated with masculine and martial virtues such as valour, strength and honour. These desirable qualities were exhibited publicly in pamphlets and paintings, serving as a tool to enhance the heirs' prestige and thus tying the armed forces more closely to the monarchy. This became all the more necessary because the thoroughly aristocratic character of the officer corps had been replaced by a more diverse intake during the Napoleonic wars. This new army's allegiance was primarily to the nation, not the monarchy. This, together with the armed forces' potential as an instrument for revolution, added to the need to identify members of the royal family with the military and its values. The function and representation of the heir as a capable military leader was therefore also part of Restoration monarchies' efforts to find new sources of legitimacy and to adapt their appeal to a more meritocratic society.

Heirs to the throne were central actors in the early nineteenth-century French and Spanish restorations. They deserve to be studied in depth and from new perspectives of public perception and functionality within the monarchical systems that emerged after 1814. Heirs played important roles as heroic leaders and as intermediaries between the Crown and other state institutions such as the military. An analysis of monarchs-in-waiting significantly broadens our understanding of the monarchy's place in nineteenth-century politics, culture and society.

Notes

1   Joël Cornette, *Le roi de guerre. Essai sur la souveraineté dans la France du Grand Siècle* (Paris, 2010), 213–50, here: 246.

2   José Cepeda Gómez, *Los pronunciamientos en la España del siglo XIX* (Madrid, 1999).
3   For the importance of military virtues and masculinity to kingship see Richard Meyer Forsting, 'The Importance of Looking the Part: Heirs and Male Aesthetics in Nineteenth-Century Spain', in Frank Lorenz Müller and Heidi Mehrkens (eds), *Royal Heirs and the Uses of Soft Power in Nineteenth-Century Europe* (Basingstoke, 2016), 181–200.
4   *Charles X et Louis XIX en exil. Mémoires inédits du Marquis de Villeneuve, publiés par son arrière-petit-fils* (Paris, 1889).
5   Michel Bernard Cartron, *Louis XIX celui qui fut roi 20 minutes. Mémoires de Louis Antoine d'Artois duc d'Angoulême* (Versailles, 2010), 16–17 (a biography in the form of fictitious memoirs); *Œuvres de M. Le Vicomte de Chateaubriand. Tome VI. Mélanges historiques et politiques* (Paris, 1838): *Mémoires sur S.A.R. Monseigneur le duc de Berry. Première partie. Vie de Mgr le duc de Berry hors de France. Livre premier. Education et émigration du Prince: sa vie militaire jusqu'à la retraite de l'armée de Condé en Pologne*, ch. IV, 6.
6   Jean Lucas-Dubreton, *Le Comte d'Artois, Charles X: le prince, l'émigré, le roi* (Paris, 1927), 11.
7   Roberto Scoth, 'Higher Education, Dissemination and Spread of the Mathematical Sciences in Sardinia (1720–1848)', *Historia Mathematica* 43 (2016), 172–93, here: 181–2; V. Leschi, *Gli istituti di educazione e di formazione degli ufficiali negli stati preunitari, vol. II. Stabilimento grafico militare* (Rome, 1994), 179.
8   Vicomte de Guichen, *Le Duc d'Angoulême (1775–1844)*, 2nd edn (Paris, 1909), 11–14; Chateaubriand, *Mélanges*, ch. VII, 9.
9   Vincent Beach, *Charles X of France: His Life and Times* (Boulder, CO, 1971), 92.
10 Chateaubriand, *Mélanges: Livre Second. Vie militaire du Prince jusqu'au licenciement de l'armée de Condé*, ch. VII, 29.
11 José Cabanis, *Charles X. Roi Ultra* (Paris, 1972), 442.
12 Guillaume de Bertier de Sauvigny, *The Bourbon Restoration*. Translated from the French by Lynn M. Case (Philadelphia, PA, 1967), 26–8.
13 Michel-Bernard Cartron, *Seul contre Napoléon. Les Cent Jours du Duc d'Angoulême* (Paris, 2008); Bertier de Sauvigny, *Restoration*, 94.
14 Bettina Frederking, '"Il ne faut pas être le roi de deux peuples": Strategies of National Reconciliation in Restoration France', *French History* 22/4 (2008), 446–68; Sheryl Kroen, *Politics and Theater: The Crisis of Legitimacy in Restoration France, 1815–1830* (Berkeley, CA, 2000); Robert Alexander, *Re-Writing the French Revolutionary Tradition: Liberal Opposition and the Fall of the Bourbon Monarchy* (Cambridge, 2003); Munro Price, *The Perilous Crown: Ruling France 1814–1848* (Basingstoke, 2007); Volker Sellin, 'Restauration et légitimité en 1814', *Francia* 26 (1999), 115–29.
15 François-René de Chateaubriand, *The Congress of Verona*, Vol. II (London, 1838), 397; Emmanuel de Waresquiel and Benoît Yvert, *Histoire de la Restauration 1814–1830. Naissance de la France moderne*, 2nd edn (Paris, 2002), 358.
16 See for the campaign Emmanuel Larroche, *L'expédition d'Espagne. 1823: de la guerre selon la Charte* (Rennes, 2013).
17 Frederking, 'Il ne faut pas', 467–8.
18 Jacques Le Goff, *Saint Louis* (Paris, 2009); Jennifer R. Davis, 'The Problem of King Louis IX of France: Biography, Sanctity, and Kingship', *Journal of Interdisciplinary History* 41/2 (2010), 209–25.
19 Bertier de Sauvigny, *Restoration*, 192–3; Cabanis, *Roi Ultra*, 444; Waresquiel and Yvert, *Histoire*, 355–8.

20 Larroche, L'expédition, 175.
21 Larroche, L'expédition, 176; Jean Baptiste Honoré Raymond Capefigue, Récit des opérations de l'armée française en Espagne sous les ordres de S.A.E. Mgr Duc d'Angoulême (1823).
22 Waresquiel and Yvert, Histoire, 358.
23 Beach, Charles X, 142–3.
24 Larroche, L'expédition, 36.
25 Which is underlined by the smooth financing of the expedition: Larroche, L'expédition, 91–7.
26 Guichen, Le Duc d'Angoulême, 288.
27 Angoulême was married to his cousin Marie-Thérèse-Charlotte de France (1778–1851). Michel Bernard Cartron, Madame Royale. L'énigme résolue (Versailles, 2014).
28 Bertier de Sauvigny, Restoration, 272–3.
29 Bertier de Sauvigny, Restoration, 380–2; quoting Souvenirs du Comte de Montbel, 246; Cabanis, Roi Ultra, 434.
30 Cabanis, Roi Ultra, 453; Castelot, Charles X, 490–1.
31 Bertier de Sauvigny, Restoration, 406; quoting d'Urville's diary, 19 August 1830, 470.
32 Souvenirs de 1815. L'Enjambée Impériale (1815): Bibliothèque Nationale de France, Gallica: http://gallica.bnf.fr/ark:/12148/btv1b6954531r?rk=21459;2 (accessed 6 April 2017).
33 Hippolyte (Paul) Delaroche, Duke of Angoulême at the capture of Trocadero, 31st August 1823 (1828): Stephen Bann and Linda Whiteley (eds), Painting History: Delaroche and Lady Jane Grey (London, 2010), 72–3.
34 Bertier de Sauvigny, Restoration, 56.
35 Jordi Canal, El Carlismo (Madrid, 2000), 53.
36 Mark Lawrence, The First Carlist Wars (Basingstoke, 2014), 37–9.
37 The most comprehensive study of his life and thought is Antonio Moral Roncal, Carlos V de Borbón (Madrid, 1999). For a recent collection on Carlist ideology see IV Jornadas de Estudio del Carlismo (ed.), Por Dios, por la patria y el Rey: las ideas del carlismo: actas de las IV Jornadas de Estudio del Carlismo, 22-24 septiembre 2010, Estella (Pamplona, 2011).
38 Roncal, Carlos V, 64–5.
39 Juan Ardazun, Fernando VII y su tiempo (1942), 30.
40 Roncal, Carlos V, 33.
41 Carlos Seco Serrano, 'Don Carlos y el carlismo', in Tríptico Carlista (Barcelona, 1973), 14–20.
42 Lawrence, First Carlist War, 37.
43 Eric Christiansen, The Origins of Military Power in Spain, 1800–1854 (London, 1967), 18.
44 José Cepeda Gómez, Los pronunciamientos en la España del siglo XIX (Madrid, 1999), 19.
45 Roncal, Carlos V, 95.
46 Archivo General de Palacio-Reinados-FernandoVII-Caj.27, Don Carlos to Ferdinand VII, 27 July 1816.
47 Antonio Pirala, Historia de la guerra civil, y de los partidos liberal y Carlista: escrita con presencia de memorias y documentos inèditos (Madrid, 1855), vol.1, 16.
48 'Consejo que da al Infante Don Carlos Un Patriota', La Tercerola, no.19, c. 1821–2.
49 Antonio Manuel Moral Roncal, 'Don Carlos Y El Carlismo Durante El Trienio Liberal (1820–1823)', Trienio: Ilustración Y Liberalismo 36 (2000), 141–60.

50　Lawrence, *First Carlist Wars*, 4.
51　See Pedro Voltes Bou, *Fernando VII: vida y reinado* (Barcelona, 1985), 29–36.
52　Roncal, *Carlos V*, 96–7.
53　See Michael P. Costeloe, *Response to Revolution: Imperial Spain and the Spanish American Revolutions, 1810–1840* (Cambridge, 1986).
54　Roncal, *Carlos V*, 111
55　*Gaceta de Madrid*, 18 August 1814.
56　Roncal, *Carlos V*, 119.
57　Roncal, 'La Impronta Religiosa En La Vida Del Infante Don Carlos María Isidro de Borbón', *Hispania Sacra* 53 (2001), 126.
58　Lawrence, *First Carlist Wars*, 45–6.
59　Seco Serrano, 'Don Carlos y el Carlismo', 24.
60　Roncal, *Carlos V*, 267.
61　Alexandra Wilhelmsen, *La formación del pensamiento del Carlismo (1810–1875)* (Madrid, 1995), 189.
62　For a regional study that does not focus on the traditional strongholds of Carlism see Manuela Asensio Rubi, *El Carlismo en Castilla-La Mancha (1833–1875)* (Ciudad Real, 2011), 251–81.
63　Canal, *El Carlismo*, 73.
64　Don Carlos to Zumalacárregui, 18 March 1834 mentioned in José María Azcona and Tomás Zumalacárregui, *Zumalacárregui. Estudio crítico de las fuentes históricas de su tiempo* (Madrid, 1946), 491.
65　Pirala, *Historia de la guerra civil*, 17.
66　On the Carlist press during the First Carlist War see Urquijo Goitia and José Ramón, 'Prensa carlista durante la primera guerra (1833–1840)', in Alberto Gil Novales (ed.), *La Prensa en la revolución liberal* (Madrid, 1983), 319–36.
67　Both portraits can be found in the *Real Academia de Bellas Artes de San Fernando*.
68　Roncal, *El enemigo en Palacio! Afrancesados, liberales y carlistas en la Real Casa y Patrimonio (1814–1843)* (Alcalá de Henares, 2005), 161–2.
69　Lawrence, *The First Carlist War*, 4.
70　B. Bolaños, 'Un episodio de la vida de Carlos V', *El Correo Español*, Madrid, 6 January 1894.
71　Adolf Loning, *Das spanische Volk in seinen Ständen, Sitten und Gebräuchen mit Episoden aus dem Karlistischen Erbfolgkriege* (1844), 267.
72　Fernando Fernández de Córdoba, *Mis memorias íntimas* (Madrid, 1966), vol.1, 79.
73　Pirala, *Historia de la Guerra civil*, vol. 1, 16
74　Florencio Sanz Baesza, cited in J. del Burgo, *Para la historia de la Primera Guerra Carlista. Comentarios y anotaciones de un manuscrito de la época, 1834–39* (Pamplona, 1981), 329.
75　Benito Pérez Galdos, *De Oñate a la Granja* (Alicante, 2001), online publication, 207.

15

Southern Influences on Nordic Political Culture: Bernadotte as King of Norway and Sweden

Bård Frydenlund

The life of Jean Baptiste Bernadotte is a unique story of steep social climbing during significant political transitions. Bernadotte entered Scandinavian politics at a time when Northern Europe was in transition, and even in turmoil. At the end of his reign as king of Sweden and Norway, Scandinavia was at peace; it was an area where states formerly at odds with each other had been reconciled. No individual in Scandinavia could match Bernadotte for influence of the political situation in the first half of the nineteenth century. His background as a soldier of revolutionary France and a marshal of Napoleon gave him an extraordinary basis to become the founder of a royal dynasty.

In this chapter I will discuss Bernadotte's politics in Scandinavia, and certain characteristics of his rule as Charles John which shaped political culture in the Nordic states. More specifically I concentrate on Charles John's political relationship with Norway and his use of the Norwegian parliamentary session in 1821, to analyse how a former revolutionary and Napoleonic marshal adapted his political methods to a new political culture at the other end of Europe.

Political culture is a contested term in historiography as well as other social sciences. Broadly defined, political culture consists of all those accepted ideas, institutions, commonly shared values and normal practices which are relevant to the exercise of power and the maintenance of order in society.[1] In other words, political culture comprises the norms, values, concepts, discourses and practices that surrounded and structured political thought and action.[2] If or how one individual could influence these structures by himself is a central question, but even acknowledging the fact reveals its potential significance.

Bernadotte before 1810

'No one has made a career like mine.' These were his famous last words on his deathbed in February 1844. Although not as spectacular as Napoleon Bonaparte's career, his curriculum vitae was extraordinary, nevertheless.[3] Jean Baptiste Jules Bernadotte was born in the southern French town of Pau in 1763. His father was a local prosecutor and Jean Baptiste entered the royal army in 1780. He became a revolutionary officer in 1791 and advanced through the ranks during the 1790s. From 1799 onwards, his career advanced apace. He became first Minister of War and then a member of Bonaparte's *Conseil d'état* and Commander of the Western Army the year after. His first real administrative office was as governor of Hannover in 1804, the same year he became a marshal of France. He got his first taste of nobility in 1806 when he was made Prince of Pontecorvo, and became governor of the Hanseatic cities in northern Germany the following year. In 1808 he was appointed Commander of the Combined French-Spanish forces in the operations in Scandinavia, and the year after he took charge of the XI Imperial Army Corps. This amounted to a distinguished career, holding important civil and military offices, in which he wielded authority independently.

Often described as an armchair general whose main ambition was to keep his troops supplied, his personality as a leader has been characterized quite differently. The French historian Patrice Gueniffey describes Bernadotte in the service of France and Napoleon thus:

> His charm, his way with words, his cordial, open manner ... even his cheek, gave him the appearance of a leader of men ... Rare were those who did not succumb to his charm. Yet, this man who so seemed to ... possess the ability to slake the thirst for the power he so craved, was also the most irresolute of men, hiding this defect behind a lot of bluff and diversion.[4]

This image does not correspond to that of Bernadotte as a Scandinavian ruler and statesman, and Scandinavian historians disagree whether he brought these traits with him, as king of Sweden and Norway.

Scandinavia before 1810

Scandinavia in the late eighteenth century was a divided region. Two longstanding arch-enemies dominated its policies: Sweden (including the duchy of Finland), ruled from Stockholm, and Denmark-Norway, ruled from Copenhagen, had often been at war in the seventeenth century but had relatively peaceful relations in the following century. Denmark-Norway was one of the most uniform and centralized autocracies in eighteenth-century Europe, while Sweden in contrast had experienced more liberal rule in some decades. From the early 1770s onwards, Sweden became more absolutist, while the Danish state became more liberalized during the 1780s in terms of freedom of speech and in its economic policies.[5]

The last years of the Napoleonic wars changed the power structure of the whole region. Peaceful foreign relations between the Scandinavian states during the eighteenth century permitted profitable trade, because of Denmark and Sweden's neutral status during the wars of the period. This ended in 1807, when Great Britain bombarded Copenhagen and forced Denmark-Norway into an alliance with Napoleonic France. Obliged to join Napoleon's continental system, Norway became the most injured party as its vital trade with Great Britain was choked. Sweden also entered the Napoleonic wars in 1808, as part of an anti-French coalition, and became the pivot in a war on two fronts against Denmark-Norway to the west and Russia to the east. When the coalition was defeated, Sweden lost Finland to Russia, causing discontent among the powerful Swedish elites.

In April 1809, a palace coup in Stockholm deposed king Gustavus Adolfus IV and established a new constitution. The ruling elite, a landed military and administrative nobility, sought out a successful military commander who would also be a more reliable and predictable head of state than the deposed monarch. The situation in Denmark-Norway was perilous. Although a patriotic wave created optimism in the first months of 1807–8, Norway suffered from famine, economic chaos, unrest and increasing instability in the rest of the period. As Napoleon's power collapsed, the Danish monarchy was left in a difficult position, as one of France's last remaining allies.[6]

Bernadotte becoming Charles John

After the deposition of Gustavus Adolfus IV, the Danish-born, German-speaking commander of the forces in Norway, Prince Christian August was elected Crown Prince of Sweden and adopted by the new king, Charles XIII, as his heir, in the summer of 1809. His sudden death in May 1810 created another crisis in Sweden as the search for a new head of state and heir to the throne had to begin anew. These were the circumstances in which Swedish diplomats contacted Bernadotte, and convinced him to allow the Swedish authorities to propose him as the new Crown Prince and head of state. Charles XIII, an old uncle of the deposed Gustavus Adolfus, had been elected king, but was neither capable nor ambitious enough to rule Sweden.

The greatest legacy of Bernadotte as Charles John was what Swedish historians term the 'policy of 1812'. Essentially, this entailed Charles John forming an alliance with the Russian Tsar Alexander and then gaining the support of Prussia, Austria Hungary and Great Britain to receive Norway as compensation for the loss of Finland. On 14 January 1814, the four great powers, Sweden and Denmark made a treaty at Kiel in northern Germany, which transferred Norway from the king of Denmark to the king of Sweden.[7]

A substantial problem for Charles John was that the Norwegian elites opposed this and rallied around the Crown Prince of Denmark, Christian Frederik, as their regent for the new independent state of Norway. A constitutional assembly was called for in February and representatives were elected for the whole country, to gather at the Eidsvoll Iron Works in April. Their task was to create a constitution and elect a king of Norway. Prince Christian Frederik was then officially elected king on 17 May 1814. At this time Charles John was still fighting Napoleon in Germany during these months, but after futile attempts at great power negotiations in Norway in the summer, Charles John decided to act, and attacked Norway with experienced veteran troops, superior weaponry and supply systems. The war was over in a fortnight and a peace convention was held at the Norwegian town of Moss in August. Another constitutional assembly, now called the parliament of Norway or *Stortinget*, was called for to ratify the union with Sweden, and to amend the constitution to permit a political union of Norway and

Sweden, and finally, to elect the king of Sweden as the king of Norway. This made Charles John head of two nations and two countries with their respective capitals, Stockholm and Christiania (contemporary Oslo). The new state comprised two distinct political systems with separate institutions, separate economies and separate political cultures.[8]

The two constitutions diverged on several points, most significantly on the relative places of the national assemblies in political life. Although the Norwegian constitution was written only five years after that of Sweden and both emerged from Scandinavian political environments, the Swedish parliament, the *Riksdagen*, was organized according to the estates of the realm, and so was more aristocratic in character than its Norwegian counterpart. The Norwegian parliament, the *Stortinget*, was technically a two-chamber system, which in reality functioned as a much more egalitarian one-chamber assembly. Informally, both nations had a growing public sphere in the largest towns, with a wide range of associations, societies, newspapers, clubs, Masonic lodges and other organizations with a shifting degree of direct links to the state and the monarchy. Swedish associative life was more refined and extended than the public sphere in Norwegian towns, due to the politically very liberal decades during the Swedish Age of Liberty (1719–72), and the sheer size of cities like Stockholm and Gothenburg. These were the conditions Charles John had to cope with, but he wanted a more uniform political system for the dual monarchy. This policy of *amalgamation*, as it was known, proved unpopular, especially in Norway, and the Norwegian constitution was intended from the outset to be the natural bulwark against any attempts to merge the systems.

Charles John after 1814: two kingdoms, two constitutions, two political cultures

Bernadotte's formative years were dominated by the violence, paranoia and the unbounded political, deeply competitive ambition which characterized the age of the French Revolution. As such, it seems surprising that an individual like Bernadotte did not enforce a more ruthless *Realpolitik* on Scandinavian geopolitics in his early years as ruler of Sweden. The chaotic years of 1813–14 demanded swift decisions, and this lack of time affected Charles John's actions.

The uniqueness of Scandinavian political culture rested on two pillars: religious uniformity and widespread literacy.[9] Lutheranism had always been characterized by an emphasis on widespread literacy. Reading skills in the Nordic countryside were well developed; although highly concentrated on religious texts, reading interests gradually extended to a broader variety of texts, including natural philosophy, agriculture, history and fiction. Despite these similarities in literacy and faith, internal differences existed in Scandinavia, and the Nordic societies developed different political cultures. The small population of hilly and rural Norway differed greatly from the more continental Denmark (at least in Zealand, Fyn and parts of Southern Jutland). Norway had no city like Copenhagen or Stockholm, only coastal towns that were county seats or bishoprics as well as hubs of trade. Norway, unlike Sweden or Denmark, had only a small landed nobility, with merchants and public officials becoming the foundation of a very different kind of aristocracy than those of Denmark and Sweden.[10]

The dual monarchy of Sweden and Norway consisted of two internally different political systems, with the development of two corresponding political cultures. Although Norway was the politically underdeveloped part of the monarchy, its status as a separate kingdom under the Swedish royal house was a negotiated agreement, sanctioned by the Convention of Moss, and finally accepted by the *Stortinget* in November 1814, and confirmed by the joint Act of Union (*Riksakten*) in the summer of 1815. Charles John had been a guarantor of it all, but knew that political asymmetries existed. Norway's position as the smaller partner made it part of an older problem of centre–periphery relations. Charles John's centre of government was in Stockholm, and he visited Norway only occasionally. The Norwegian national assembly had substantially more power than its Swedish counterpart, and the unclear division of power between the different parts of the dual monarchy created uncertainties and possible internal conflicts.

The organization of Charles John's ministerial council of the dual monarchy was not a consistent model of government. Apart from a superior council of three prime ministers (the Swedish, the Norwegian and the Foreign Minister), the government was divided into a Swedish and a Norwegian council of ministers. The Norwegian branch was then subdivided into two other branches, six ministers in Christiania and three in Stockholm (including the Norwegian prime minister). Charles John wanted the Norwegian ministerial positions in Stockholm to be switched every second year, but the Norwegian prime minister was to reside permanently in Stockholm (Peder Anker from 1814–22). Another complicating factor was that Charles John commissioned a Swedish Governor General (*stattholder*) to be the ex officio head of the Christiania branch of the Norwegian government.[11] Apart from widespread discontent about the Swedish Governor General's mandate and position, and an increasing distrust of the Norwegian ministers' loyalty to the king and other Norwegian authorities, the confusion inherent in this method of government engendered displeasure in the *Stortinget* and with the Norwegian public in general.

Even if he disliked many of the principles of the Norwegian constitution, Charles John accepted its liberal terms as a compromise to achieve more peaceful relations domestically and abroad. This did not mean he did not try to modify the terms of the Norwegian constitution, but it was defended to the letter of the law by the Norwegian parliament. Known in Norwegian historiography as 'constitutional conservatism', this principle rallied to its defence rural and urban representatives alike, occasionally with the support of some Norwegian ministers in both Christiania and Stockholm.[12]

In addition to the official channels he used to amend the Norwegian constitution and politics, Charles John had to resort to other means. Generally, he sought out individual allies among Norwegian ministers, representatives and other politicians to further his political ends. In the early phase of the union it was natural to contact the former opposition in the Eidsvoll assembly of 1814 which supported a liberal union with Sweden. Charles John appointed Peder Anker as the Norwegian prime minister and Count Wedel Jarlsberg as the Norwegian minister of finance in Christiania. They had been the most significant leaders of the opposition to full independence at the constitutional assembly at Eidsvoll (the 'Union Party') and spoke French well. They acted as mediators between the king, the *Stortinget* and the Norwegian public. As men of integrity, the two Norwegian aristocrats broke with Charles John in 1821.

Charles John also made use of the public sphere in both countries. Central to this was his own information bureau in Stockholm, the so-called *Enskilda Byrån*.[13] Its purpose was to seek information about public opinion and to find ways of influencing popular opinion, which was modelled on Napoleon's surveillance system. Translation was a key objective for the bureau. Charles John never learned either Swedish or Norwegian sufficiently to use the languages publicly. This meant that he was very dependent on French-speaking mediators. The staff consisted of individuals Charles John trusted implicitly, like his childhood friend from Pau, Louis Marie de Camp, and the Swedish publicist Pehr Adam Wallmark. Even in Norway, journalists and writers were on Charles John's payroll, translating texts from Norwegian to French to be sent to the king, or writing optimistic bulletins about the king's policies in the foreign press. Even editors, clergy and state officials gained extra income for surveillance work in the king's service. Charles John used Wallmark to introduce him to Norwegian writers, and the king placed regime-friendly publicists in significant posts, such as the editor Niels Wulfsberg, founder of the Norwegian journal *Morgenbladet*: he was appointed archivist in the Stockholm branch of the Norwegian government against the will of the Norwegian ministers. Wulfsberg became even closer to Charles John and *Enskilda Byrån* as a translator and tutor to Charles John's son, Oscar, in the Norwegian language.[14]

The financial settlement for the loss of the principality of Pontecorvo gave Charles John a substantial capital foundation, which he spent effectively to establish the new dynasty in Scandinavia. Not only did he sponsor public buildings, or the refurbishment of royal buildings formerly used by the royal families of the Vasa and Augustenborg dynasties, he also generously sponsored and granted individual pensions.[15] This was used to create informal networks and ties on a personal level, and he formed friendships with several Norwegians to obtain information and promote his own views on current political issues. Contact was often made through a royal visit or by issuing a royal gift, like a brooch set with gems or a golden snuff-box (usually with the image of the king himself painted on). More controversial was the issuing of royal Swedish honours to Norwegians and the granting of pensions. These actions became known publicly, and the individuals receiving pensions were openly looked on with suspicion as 'being on the king's pay-roll'.[16] Another means of influencing the Norwegian public, and the members of the *Stortinget* specifically, was to finance a social club, a Norwegian salon, where members of parliament could get their free drinks and mingle with Swedish officials and Charles John's loyal men.[17] But this salon was not the only place where the representatives gathered informally. During the parliament session of 1821 at least four other places in Christiania were used as venues for open deliberations among the members of the *Stortinget*, and even the members most loyal to Charles John's policies preferred other inns or clubs rather than the club sponsored by the king, to avoid suspicions.[18]

In a modern perspective, the corrupt elements in Charles John's politics were not something totally new. Even as Napoleon's governor of the Hanseatic cities he had been known as the most susceptible of the French general-governors.[19] The German coastline was very exposed to smuggling, much of it going through the island of Heligoland and by several other illegal routes undermining Napoleon's continental system.[20] Flexible measures were needed to keep trade flowing.

Charles John's political repertoire was plentiful, but he still did not achieve his main ambition – to amalgamate the two political systems. In 1821 he came close to this, but the Norwegian constitution, parliament and ministers thwarted him.

Interaction between king and parliament: Charles John in Norway during the parliament session of 1821

The year 1821 presented the hardest test for the new union and might be seen as the lowest moment in relations between Charles John and the Norwegian parliament in the early nineteenth century. The session opened on 1 February, but lasted until 21 August, including an extension of the session Charles John very reluctantly admitted, a very prolonged period.

The political atmosphere was deeply affected by four factors which heightened the political temperature that year. First, the financial settlement between Denmark and Norway after the Treaty of Kiel in 1814 was a recurring issue. It involved more or less annual negotiations between 1814 and 1821, with frequent changes of negotiators on each side. Norwegian authorities thought it unfair to pay a war debt to Denmark for something initiated by the king of Sweden, while Charles John thought the *Stortinget* postponed the whole issue deliberately. Second, a proposal was made by the Norwegian parliament to abolish nobility in Norway, an issue with which Charles John disagreed. Third, an initially straightforward case of smuggling had become an international incident, the 'Bodø Affair'. A British smuggler was caught in the act in 1818, but he resisted arrest and the case developed into an international crisis as the smuggler's family used their network to influence the British foreign ministry to side with the smuggler. British authorities made formal complaints directly to Charles John, who decided in 1821 that the Norwegian authorities should compensate the British company employing the smuggler. Although it was a smaller sum than the Kiel treaty compensation, it still had an effect on Norwegian national budgets and thereby angered both Norwegian parliamentarians and the press alike. Lastly, the conditions of the freedom of speech were debated intensely, as Charles John wanted to limit the freedoms of the press.[21]

Another issue was the political institution of the royal veto. The king had only a suspensive veto over the proposals made by the *Stortinget*, but he wanted to strengthen the grip on the liberal Norwegian constitution by the introduction of an absolute veto. He saw this as the only way to avoid ill-conceived and damaging reform projects.[22] The *Stortinget* debated the issue and ultimately decided to oppose the royal claim. This led to increased tensions during the winter and spring 1821 and angered the king still more.

Charles John's scope for action was limited, as his former supporters in the Norwegian government (who had been consistent supporters of a union between

Norway and Sweden even before 1814) now became his enemies. The Norwegian minister of finance, Count Herman Wedel Jarlsberg, felt forsaken after getting no support from the king when he was charged with impeachment by the *Stortinget*. Worse still, the Norwegian prime minister, Peder Anker (the father-in-law of Wedel Jarlsberg), was personally slapped in the face by Charles John in a government meeting, in May 1821.[23] Both Wedel Jarlsberg and Anker offered their resignations, which were accepted the following year. Charles John's temper flared ever more frequently with Norwegian ministers and created rumours of his increasing hotheadedness. The parish priest of the Akershus Palace church in Christiania reported that another minister, Jonas Collett, was '... daily exposed to the King's outbursts of temper'.[24]

With no other means of action, Charles John issued a 'circular note' in June 1821 to the great powers of Europe, making it clear internationally that he was determined to make changes in the government of Norway. His 'circular' merits close reading. It opens with a description of the situation in Norway, especially what the king thought wrong. It explains how the proposal to abolish nobility in Norway would be driven through parliament against his will; it then asserts that the *Stortinget* was not prepared to sanction payments to Denmark and other financial settlements under the Treaty of Kiel. The use of force had to be an option as a final solution, according to Charles John. He then put forward his plan for a new political order in Norway, and his right to do so. He would force through a radical expansion of the king's prerogatives, establish an absolute royal veto over decisions made by parliament, and give himself the right to dissolve parliament, dismiss Norwegian officials without court proceedings (except for judges), appoint ministers in the Norwegian government by himself and appoint the head of parliament for every session. In addition, he would establish a new hereditary nobility and he argued for heavy restrictions on the freedom of speech in Norway, especially potential restraints of the Norwegian press.[25]

He made further arrangements for Norway. He ordered the creation of a temporary army camp just outside the Norwegian capital in July 1821. In response, 6,000 soldiers met at the field of Etterstad, 3,000 Norwegians and 3,000 Swedes. Bullets were issued only to Swedish soldiers.[26] Simultaneously, he commissioned a naval squadron of eighteen ships and 2,000 Swedish able seamen for the Christiania-fjord in close proximity to the *Stortinget*. This provoked anger among Norwegian politicians, and what appeared as outright threats and preparations for something more serious, intensified tensions. Norwegian politicians had high hopes of the king's liberal opinions, hoping he would be influenced favourably by the Neapolitans' insurrections against the Austrians that year, and so would support the Norwegian parliament.[27] But the realities were different. When he arrived in Norway in late July, Charles John used all his meetings with the Norwegian ministers to reprimand them. On his last day in Norway, 26 August, he told them that he intended to rule more by himself henceforth. The king claimed that the people was dissatisfied, and the reason for this, he argued, was that he had given the Norwegians too much power and put too much trust in them. Every minister got two kisses on the cheek and he abruptly returned to Sweden.[28]

The entire political situation bore witness to the fact that the king lacked constitutional means to influence parliament to do his bidding. Although Charles John threatened a *coup d'état*, it did not happen. American-Swedish historian Arnold

Barton argues that the paradoxical effect was that the 'policy of 1812' protected Norwegian parliamentary interests against Charles John's periodic efforts to strengthen the crown's authority there. Russia had no desire to see a strong Scandinavia across the Baltic. Alexander I (and later Nicholas I) repeatedly reminded Charles John of his commitment to the Norwegian constitution and cautioned him against any change in Norway's status.[29]

The 1821 session was not the only moment when Charles John deployed a wide range of strategies to influence Norwegian politics. In 1824, 1828 and 1836 he claimed that the *Stortinget* had endangered the whole constitution, threatening to dissolve parliament or resort to other controversial methods. However, the 1821 session was the closest Charles John came to using a coup to sanction his own wishes and policies through unconstitutional means.[30]

The legacy of Bernadotte in Nordic political culture

The reign of Bernadotte as Charles John of Sweden and Norway made him the single most influential individual in the Nordic states in the first half of the nineteenth century. It was not as the 'hotheaded Gascon', but as a statesman establishing a new political order rejecting absolutist rule for constitutional government. The use of mediators and a surveillance system, and the occasional emotional outburst and open threat, might have caused unease in Norwegian society, but not to such an extent that it jeopardized the system, nor anything like the scale seen in the neighbouring states of post-Napoleonic, reactionary Europe. Risking a contradiction in terms, it is possible to argue that Charles John saw his own version of monarchic rule as a kind of meritocracy – something different from other European monarchies. The Swedish historian Jørgen Weibull describes Charles John as 'a cat among ermines',[31] and he was certainly a parvenu among the other royal houses in Europe. Russian Empress Elizabeth considered him merely a 'bad stain on the restored ... order.'[32]

Charles John's new approach to monarchy is underlined in a recent study by Swedish historian, Per Sandin. He argues that Charles John maintained the legitimacy of the royal house of Bernadotte through a transition from an older form of society – elite-ruled society – to a new civic society. This was done by three measures: the modernizing of the court (new ceremonies and more public receptions); the direct involvement in and support of voluntary associations in both countries; and a more civic-minded royal education for the Bernadotte princes.[33] Whether this implied a drastically altered political culture in both nations is another issue.

Although the king tried to influence political life by informal measures, this had its limits. To say that Charles John XIV had an extensive personal network in Norway is an overstatement, but his use of mediators was effective. The early alliances with the Norwegian elite secured his information flow and some political support. With the exception of the tensions of the 1820s, there was no real destabilization of society. Discontent existed, but no dangerous revolts occurred during Bernadotte's reign. Increasingly, until his death in 1844, he remained remote from the Norwegians, secluded in his inner sanctum in the royal palace in Stockholm. The flexible rule of the first decade as head of state changed in the more consolidated period from the late 1820s until 1844. Although exaggerating, Jørgen Weibull makes a fair point on Charles John's change of governance: 'The revolutionary general was by then transformed into a royal autocratic ruler of the old regime.'[34]

Bernadotte was still a ruler, but neither revolutionary nor autocratic. Charles John had a political philosophy for Norway, but the outcome and effects of the political processes were not quite what he had intended. He laid the foundation of, and subsequently guaranteed, one of Europe's most liberal constitutions in 1814. The unicameral parliament and the egalitarian electoral system were among the most radical systems of their time. He might have regretted granting this freedom, but he was very conscious of the promises he had made to the Norwegian people and to the neighbour states. His regrets may have influenced the slow pace of democratic development for Norway after 1814, but the political culture that developed during his reign was not characterized by the political actions of an ambitious, pretentious, opportunistic and hotheaded ruler. Those days were over. The social climber had met his 'dead end', and accepted his situation, securing peace in Scandinavia and consolidating his own royal dynasty. Although he was partially reluctant about it, the modernization process of monarchic rule in the northern outskirts of Europe was undoubtedly part of his legacy.

Notes

1 Thomas Munck, 'Preface', in Pasi Ihalainen, Michael Bregnsbo, Karin Sennefelt and Patrik Winton (eds), *Scandinavia in the Age of Revolution. Nordic Political Cultures, 1740–1820* (Surrey, 2011), xviii.
2 Pasi Ihalainen and Karen Sennefelt, 'General Introduction', *Scandinavia in the Age of Revolution*, 3.
3 The information on Bernadotte's offices is taken from several books, but mostly from the anthology *Jean Baptiste Bernadotte. Fra menig soldat til konge av Sverige og Norge. Carl XIV Johan* (Oslo, 1998).
4 Patrice Gueniffey, *Le Dix-huit Brumaire. L'Epilogue de la Révolution francaise* (Paris, 2008), 229. Translation by Michael Broers, in *Napoleon. Soldier of Destiny* (London, 2014), 207.
5 Ihalainen and Sennefelt, 'Introduction', 1–13.
6 Bård Frydenlund, 'The Case of Norway. Domestic Developments and External Influences on the Periphery of Napoleonic Europe', in Ute Planert (ed.), *Napoleon's Empire. European Politics in Global Perspective* (Basingstoke, 2016), 200–4.
7 Jørgen Weibull, 'Katt blant hermeliner', in *Carl XIV Johan. Jean Baptiste Bernadotte. Fra menig soldat til konge av Norge og Sverige* (Oslo, 1998), 90–1.
8 Frydenlund, 'The Case of Norway', 204–8. Bård Frydenlund, *Spillet om Norge. Det politiske året 1814* (Oslo, 2014).
9 Ihalainen and Sennefelt, 'General Introduction', 3.
10 Bård Frydenlund, 'Political Practices among Merchants in Denmark and Norway in the Period of Absolutism', *Scandinavia in the Age of Revolution*, 243.
11 Bård Frydenlund, *Stormannen Peder Anker. En biografi* (Oslo, 2009), 258–9.
12 Alf Kaartvedt, 'Carl Johan i Norge. Forfatningskamp og utenrikspolitikk', in *Jean Baptiste Bernadotte. Fra menig soldat til konge av Norge og Sverige. Carl XIV Johan* (Oslo, 1998), 124–5.

13 Cecilie Rosengren, 'Journalism on Royal Duty. Pehr Adam Wallmark in Defense of Charles XIV John', in Mikael Alm and Britt-Inger Johansson (eds), *Scripts of Kingship. Essays on Bernadotte and Dynastic Formation in an Age of Revolution* (Uppsala, 2008), 149.
14 Frydenlund, *Stormannen Peder Anker*, 269–72.
15 Britt-Inger Johansson, 'Housing a Dynasty. Tradition and Innovation within the Walls of the Stockholm Royal Palace', in *Scripts of Kingship*, 49–50.
16 Yngvar Nielsen, *Breve fra grev H.H. von Essen til H.K.H. kronprins Carl Johan. Indeholdende Bidrag til Norges og Sveriges Historie 1814–1816* (Christiania, 1867), 104.
17 Thorvald T. Höjer, *Carl XIV Johan. Band III Konungatiden* (Stockholm, 1960), 199.
18 Bård Frydenlund, 'Opposisjon eller samfunnsstøtte. Borgerskap og kjøpmannstand som politiske aktørgrupper etter 1814', in Odd Arvid Storsveen, Amund Pedersen and Bård Frydenlund (eds), *Smak av frihet. 1814-grunnloven. Historisk virkning og sosial forankring* (Oslo, 2015), 82–3.
19 Michael Broers, *Europe under Napoleon 1799–1815* (London, 1996), 145. Michael Broers, *Napoleon. Soldier of Destiny* (London, 2014), 410.
20 Katherine Aaslestad, 'Introduction', in Katherine Aaslestad and Johan Joor, *Revisiting Napoleon's Continental System. Local, Regional and European Experiences* (Basingstoke, 2015), 6–12.
21 Frydenlund, 'Opposisjon eller samfunnsstøtte', 80–1.
22 Höjer, *Konungatiden*, 201.
23 Frydenlund, *Stormannen Peder Anker*, 324–6.
24 Claus Pavels' diary, 11 July 1821. Dokumentasjonsprosjektet, University of Oslo (1997). http://www.dokpro.uio.no/litteratur/pavels/frames.htm (accessed 21 April 2017).
25 Kaartvedt, 'Carl Johan i Norge', 119–20.
26 Peter Motzfeldt, 'Dagbog under Storthingets Samvær 1821, 25de Juli', in Ketil Mottzfeldt, *Breve og Optegnelser af Peter Motzfeldt* (Copenhagen, 1888), pp. 361–2.
27 Ibid., 269–70.
28 Ibid., 398.
29 Arnold Barton, *Essays on Scandinavian history* (Carbondale, IL, 2009), 211.
30 Kaartvedt, 'Carl Johan i Norge', 120–4.
31 Weibull, 'Katt blant hermeliner', 79.
32 Höjer, *Konungatiden*, 11.
33 Per Sandin, *Ett kungahus i tiden. Den bernadotteska dynastins möte med medborgarsamhället ca. 1810–1860* (Uppsala, 2011), 291–301.
34 Weibull, 'Katt blant hermeliner', 103–4.

16

Madame Adélaïde, Female Political Power and the July Monarchy

Munro Price

The July monarchy was a crucial period in the history of modern France – her longest experiment with constitutional monarchy, and her most substantial attempt to reconcile this principle with the legacy of the French Revolution. Compared to other nineteenth-century French régimes – the third republic, the first and second empires, even the Bourbon restoration – it is also the most neglected. Some aspects of the July monarchy – its political thought and its contribution to the history of liberalism – have received scholarly attention over the last few decades. There are, however, far fewer recent works on the actual political history of the era. A substantial biography of Louis-Philippe, by Guy Antonetti, did appear in 1994, but less than half of it is devoted to the period after 1830, and its tone towards its subject is hostile throughout. The standard reference work for the July monarchy remains one written less than half a century after its fall, Paul Thureau-Dangin's seven-volume *Histoire de la monarchie de juillet*.[1]

Reappraising the entire July monarchy would be a huge task, and is certainly not the purpose of this chapter. Instead, the focus here will be on one particular aspect of it, though it is a central one – the political partnership at its apex, between Louis-Philippe and his devoted, unmarried sister Adélaïde, from the July revolution through to Adélaïde's death on 31 December 1847. This involves a significant reassessment of how politics at the centre of the Orléanist régime was conducted. Because Louis-Philippe was such an active and visible king, he has always been seen as the dominant figure of the July monarchy. Highly intelligent and terrifyingly loquacious, with an iron constitution, throughout his reign he exploited his prerogatives to the full, and especially the most important – those of choosing his ministers and directing foreign policy. Under these circumstances, it is hardly surprising that Louis-Philippe has consistently appeared as the principal player in his own reign.[2]

In one important area, however, this picture is incomplete. It ignores the critical policymaking role played by Adélaïde from 1830 to her death. Born in 1777 and four years younger than Louis-Philippe, Adélaïde was his companion throughout much of the emigration, and after 1808 rarely left his side. She is almost completely forgotten today – there are only two biographies of her, both popular.[3] Yet in three areas she made a crucial contribution to the July monarchy. On 30 July 1830 it was she who accepted the crown from the representatives of revolutionary Paris on behalf of

Louis-Philippe, who had gone into hiding. This was the single act that did most to found the Orléanist régime. During the reign itself, she exercised a constant influence on policy through daily private meetings with her brother. Finally, in the area of responsibility he guarded most jealously, foreign policy, Louis-Philippe delegated to Adélaïde the day-to-day handling of France's most important diplomatic relationship, that with Britain. Though Adélaïde wielded her power discreetly, well-informed contemporaries realized how much Louis-Philippe relied on her. Writing in his diary a few years after her death, Victor Hugo commented: 'She had shared his exile; to an extent she shared his throne.'[4]

Adélaïde's life was defined by four things: her father, her brother, her education and the French Revolution. Her father was Louis-Philippe-Joseph, duc d'Orléans, notorious after 1792 as Philippe-Egalité. Although Philippe-Egalité's public reputation has never recovered from the dubious role he played during the Revolution, in private he was a devoted father, much loved by all his children, and especially Adélaïde, his only surviving daughter. In particular, he equipped them with a rigorous and avant-garde education supervised by his own mistress, the educationalist and disciple of Rousseau, Mme de Genlis. By the age of seventeen, when she left Mme de Genlis' care, Adélaïde was far better educated than most women of her age and status.[5]

By November 1793, the Revolution had guillotined Adélaïde's father and forced her into exile. Most cruelly, the fact that Philippe-Egalité had sided with the Revolution made her an object of hatred to those who would otherwise have been her companions in misfortune, the royalist émigrés. This was crucial in shaping Adélaïde's political views, and her actions after 1814. Her father's regicide also ruined any hope of a suitable marriage after 1793. The Revolution thus made Adélaïde what she remained: a spinster whose emotional energies were concentrated on her elder brother Louis-Philippe, after 1808 her sole surviving sibling, who had provided her only security during these perilous years.

The remarkable closeness between brother and sister was only marginally diminished by Louis-Philippe's marriage in 1809 to Maria Amalia of the Two Sicilies, the future Queen Marie-Amélie. Indeed, Louis-Philippe once joked to Adélaïde that he had only started looking for a wife because he could not marry her: 'Various people have got it into their heads that ... they should marry me off ... but I've replied ... that before thinking of getting married, I needed to find a woman I could marry and who wanted to be married to me, that *unfortunately* you were my sister ... but that if I wasn't your brother, I'd get on with it straight away.'[6] Adélaïde and Marie-Amélie soon became close, united by their mutual devotion to Louis-Philippe. A crucial, and insufficiently recognized, ingredient in Louis-Philippe's successes both before and after 1830 was the unfailing support of these two remarkable women.

The origin of Adélaïde's fascination with politics is unclear, but this was certainly well developed by the time of the Bourbon restoration in 1814. As her friend, the great memoirist Mme de Boigne, put it: 'Nobody in the world, I think, has a more complete grasp of politics than [Madame Adélaïde].' Ideologically, Adélaïde was significantly more left wing than her brother; fiercely loyal to the memory of their father, she consistently defended the French Revolution, even, according to one source, 'going so far as to excuse even some of its excesses'.[7] In particular, no doubt as a result of their hostility to her in the 1790s, Adélaïde hated the émigrés and their political offspring, the ultra-royalists of the restoration, and this dislike extended to her cousins of the elder Bourbon branch.[8]

The question of when, if at all, Louis-Philippe began conspiring to replace his cousins of the elder Bourbon branch after the restoration of 1814 remains controversial. In general, his strategy seems to have been to refrain from any overt acts of disloyalty to Louis XVIII and then Charles X, but to present himself with great care as a moderate and patriotic alternative should the rightward drift of government after 1820 lead once again to revolution. He certainly received advice from political allies, such as Talleyrand in June 1830, to hold himself in readiness for this possibility. It is, however, very unlikely that he actively plotted after 1815, simply because he did not need to. In Chateaubriand's elegant formulation: 'Le duc d'Orléans conspired, not in fact but by consent.'[9]

All the eyewitness accounts agree that Louis-Philippe and his household were taken by surprise by Charles X's four ordinances, which sparked off the 1830 revolution, when the news reached them at their château at Neuilly, then a country village just west of Paris. Significantly, while Louis-Philippe kept his own counsel, Adélaïde immediately espoused the revolutionary cause, even apparently exclaiming: 'Ah! If only I had a sword!' In the meantime, it was decided that Louis-Philippe should go into hiding at a nearby Orléans property at Villiers, in case either side should try to take him hostage.[10]

It was in these circumstances that, on 30 July, the thirty-three-year-old journalist and future prime minister Adolphe Thiers arrived at Neuilly as the representative of several leading politicians to offer Louis-Philippe the crown. The government forces had been driven out of Paris, but the situation was extremely fluid. Charles X still had a viable army at St Cloud, and if he used it energetically or fell back on the royalist western provinces the outcome would be civil war. In the capital, on the other hand, the mood on the streets was increasingly for a republic, which alarmed those moderate politicians who had opposed Charles X yet were also haunted by the spectre of 1793 and 1794. It was on behalf of this group that Thiers came to seek out Louis-Philippe.

In Louis-Philippe's absence, Thiers was received by Marie-Amélie and Adélaïde. However, in the detailed account of what followed that Thiers left in his papers, he presents the ensuing conversation as entirely between himself and Adélaïde. Thiers began by stressing that the political situation was now wide open, and that Louis-Philippe needed immediately to come forward. Finally, he appealed to Adélaïde's own courage: 'I cannot hide from you that you will have to overcome great perils. But you need perils. They are titles to the crown.'[11]

Whether deliberately or not, Thiers struck the right note. 'Touched above all by this last consideration', he later wrote, '[Mme Adélaïde] rose and said: "If you think that the adhesion of our family can be of use to the revolution, we give it gladly. A woman is nothing in a family. She can be compromised. I am ready to go to Paris. What happens to me there is in God's hands. I will share the fate of the Parisians . . ."'[12]

It will never be entirely clear whether this response was spontaneous, or had been concerted beforehand with Louis-Philippe. It is possible that Louis-Philippe anticipated that an appeal to take power might come, but that not wishing to compromise himself too soon, he arranged for Adélaïde to give a message of support instead. It is also entirely possible, perhaps even likely, that Adélaïde's response to Thiers was spontaneous; she had committed herself to the revolution days before, whereas her brother, often indecisive in moments of crisis, had not. In particular, she triumphantly turned to her advantage the restrictions her sex placed on her by giving assurances on her brother's behalf that, coming from a woman, were entirely deniable. This was shrewd, but also required some courage; had Charles X emerged victorious in July 1830, she would surely have faced some sort of vengeance.

However it came about, Adélaïde's intervention was crucial, and Thiers immediately recognized it as such. As he put it in his famous reply to her: 'Today, Madame, you have gained the crown for your house.'[13] It was on the basis of Adélaïde's promise, which Thiers and all his colleagues accepted as a sufficient guarantee, that the plan was set on foot to launch Louis-Philippe's candidature for the throne, culminating on 9 August 1830 with his proclamation as King of the French. By her actions on 30 July, Adélaïde played a decisive part in the foundation of the July monarchy.

After 1830, Adélaïde took pains to project herself to the public in the conventional aristocratic female roles of patroness of charities and devoted aunt to her brother's children. In reality, however, her key function was political, as her brother's closest adviser, particularly on foreign affairs. She did not attend the council of ministers; instead, Louis-Philippe reserved for her two hours of the evening in his study, between 10 pm and midnight, where he would discuss past and plan future policy with her. As a rule, nobody else was present at these meetings. One of the few who sometimes was, the Intendant of the Civil List Montalivet, has left a remarkable description of them, which implies strongly that Louis-Philippe's policymaking role during the July monarchy was not his alone, but a joint enterprise with his sister. After the king's dinner, Montalivet recalled:

> Madame Adélaïde's hour had arrived at last; she hurried to join her brother, with some needlework in her hand, and took a seat beside him; silent when a piece of work absorbed all her brother's attention, she was always happy when the king broke off to think out loud both before her and with her. Then she was no longer the silent witness and passive confidante ... at this hour of the evening, when the king belonged wholly to her, she took her turn to speak, generally addressing questions in the order the king assigned, but sometimes bringing up subjects of her own. In this way, through this intimate communication, mingled two streams of thought drawn from the same source, retaining, through all the events of their diverse and agitated lives, a remarkable common basis ...[14]

Given her closeness to her brother and the fact that apart from this passage no record has survived of her late-night conversation with him, it is difficult to recreate Adélaïde's political role after 1830 precisely or to determine when her views differed from the king's. Her main task, which she accomplished successfully at least until 1840, was to second her brother's extremely wide-ranging interpretation of the royal prerogative, and to ensure that he, and not the deputies or ministers, played the leading part in politics. To her, the ministers were simply auxiliaries to the king, supplementing rather than replacing his efforts. As she lamented to a confidant during a ministerial crisis in 1836: '[The king] can't do everything, he needs instruments, and alas that's what he lacks.'[15] Yet she never committed the error of thinking, as had Charles X, that the king could change these instruments at will, or go on using them once they had lost the confidence of the Chambers. As she put it in 1839, when Louis-Philippe's trusted prime minister Molé lost an election, making his resignation inevitable: 'In the spirit of his loyalty and constitutional principles, our beloved king will submit and conform to the country's will.'[16] If she drew the demarcation line between the king's powers and those of the ministers and Chambers distinctly in favour of the former, she wholeheartedly accepted the basic rules of the parliamentary game.

It is easier to reconstruct Adélaïde's influence on foreign than on domestic policy, because here substantial written evidence has survived. From the beginning of his reign Louis-Philippe delegated to her the day-to-day management of France's most important diplomatic relationship, that with England. Adélaïde handled this through an almost daily correspondence with two successive French ambassadors to London who, almost certainly not coincidentally, were her personal friends – Talleyrand from 1830 to 1834, and from 1834 to 1840 Talleyrand's protégé, the former Napoleonic soldier and diplomat General Horace Sébastiani. Some of her letters to Talleyrand were published in 1890; those to Sébastiani – 235 in all – have until now remained unused in the Orléans papers in the Archives Nationales.[17] It is clear that Adélaïde wrote in the king's name, and that this was understood by all concerned. She made this explicit in a moment of anger to Sébastiani, when he failed to reply to one of her letters: 'I confess, your silence towards me, at such an important juncture ... and especially after my letter which gave you the king's positive opinion and decision, is painful and incomprehensible.'[18]

If it is difficult to distinguish between Adélaïde's foreign policy views and those of Louis-Philippe in these letters, it is hardly surprising, since the instructions she gave had by definition been agreed beforehand in evening meetings with the king. To all intents and purposes, she was expressing a joint policy. This was based firmly on the premise that England was France's natural ally, both on ideological and geopolitical grounds. As she put it to Sébastiani in December 1835: 'I am convinced like you that England is our sincere friend, and desire everything that can consolidate and strengthen our union with her, because I feel it's as much in our interest as hers.'[19]

This so-called 'first Entente Cordiale' was vehemently attacked in France at the time, and has often been so since, as a complete diplomatic surrender to Britain, and a policy of peace at any price. Yet on many major issues, such as the question of intervention in the civil war in Spain, the July monarchy – and Adélaïde – steered a very different course from their ally. For example, writing to Sébastiani in June 1836 Adélaïde made it clear that her loyalty to the Entente was not unconditional: 'Certainly we want alliance and union with England, frankly and decidedly, but on her part she must also consult us and concert her actions with us, and march in step with us.'[20]

If Louis-Philippe and Adélaïde were at one over foreign policy, their differences over domestic affairs, while small, were significant. Here, Louis-Philippe was appreciably more conservative than his sister, and inclined towards a policy of order – or, as contemporaries termed it, of *résistance*. Adélaïde, on the other hand, found the methods of the *résistance* divisive, and was concerned about their effect on her brother's popularity. She disliked Casimir Périer, the leading early exponent of *résistance*, and was only reconciled to Guizot at the end of her life. It is no coincidence that in the intermittent diary she kept, the passages expressing fears that Louis-Philippe had lost confidence in her occur during Périer's and Guizot's ministries.[21]

The politicians Adélaïde did support were essentially of the centre-left – Molé, Pasquier, Dupin, Marshal Gérard and her friend Sébastiani. While just as determined to preserve the political and social order as Périer and Guizot, this grouping believed in using more flexible methods. As Sébastiani elegantly put it, they were practitioners of 'resistance without rigidity'.[22] The high point of their influence came during Molé's ministry of 1836–9, with its policy of national reconciliation symbolized by the amnesty for political detainees of May 1837. Adélaïde strongly supported Molé, and his ministry marked the high-water mark of her power. His fall marked the beginning of her eclipse; although she continued to advise her brother regularly, after 1840 she increasingly lost ground to Guizot, particularly in foreign affairs. Growing ill-health played a part in her grudging acceptance of this. When Sébastiani and Pasquier, alarmed by the growing immobilism of the régime, begged her in 1847 to persuade Louis-Philippe to dismiss Guizot, she replied that she was simply too exhausted to do so.[23] Adélaïde died on 31 January 1847; had she lived, one can only speculate what her advice to Louis-Philippe would have been in February 1848.

There is one further important aspect to Adélaïde's political role. This is how it was perceived by public opinion, and in particular how this was affected by her being a woman. From the early 1830s she began to be attacked, in newspapers and cartoons, both for interfering unjustifiably in public life, and for her allegedly debauched private life. This campaign reached its height in 1838 and 1839, as a reaction to Adélaïde's supposed influence over the Molé ministry. It was led by the legitimist journal *La Mode*, which in the spring of 1838 published an article dramatically entitled 'The Hidden Power Visible to the Naked Eye':

> Open all the newspapers that have not sold themselves to the ministry; for some time they have written about nothing else but a hidden force, an elusive influence, a mysterious power that hampers all government business and throws a multitude of unconstitutional spokes in the wheels of the machinery of the state. Nobody dares call this secret power by its real name, and we know very well the reason why; because it is generally supposed to be where it has never been. But we ... know exactly where it lies, and see it not on the throne, but next to it ... Yes, Madame Adélaïde, that is the name of the mysterious influence which holds sway above the head of M. Molé ... Nothing is decided, nothing is done, without taking Madame Adélaïde's advice: she is the nymph Egeria of the Tuileries, she gives on anything and everything ... In a word, Madame Adélaïde does not reign, but she governs.[24]

La Mode did not limit its attacks to Adélaïde's political role. It consistently dropped hints that she was having an affair with – or was even secretly married to – one of Louis-Philippe's aides-de-camp, General Atthalin.[25] No reliable evidence has ever surfaced to support this contention. Since Adélaïde's rough skin and reddish complexion, in fact an inheritance from her father, was assumed to be the product of a fondness for drink, she was regularly pilloried as an alcoholic. In May 1833, the author of a slanderous pamphlet about Adélaïde's private life was brought to trial, in closed session to protect her honour. As a result, it is unclear what the allegations against her were.[26]

All these themes were taken up in cartoons as well as words. Before the September laws imposed preliminary censorship on them, Adélaïde was a regular target of caricaturists. In several, she was portrayed as swigging from a bottle or clutching it to her bosom. In others, she was shown surrounded by a brood of illegitimate children, including, in a broad hint at incest, some with Louis-Philippe's features. The most remarkable cartoon of Adélaïde, although circulated in France, was published in Brussels in 1833. This portrayed her literally as the power behind the throne. The seated king is represented addressing a crowd of deputies while Adélaïde, crouching behind, manipulates him by a system of hidden pulleys. Out of the side of his mouth, Louis-Philippe whispers to her: 'Don't pull the wrong string, Madame!'[27] The image is striking, and further evidence that, to the better-informed newspapers and caricaturists, Adélaïde's extensive role in policymaking was an open secret.

Adélaïde's gender clearly played an essential role in these attacks. At first sight, the campaign against her seems further proof of the argument that hostility to powerful women in this era was driven by a perception that they had transgressed the limits of the domestic 'private sphere' reserved for women into the 'public sphere' of politics, an exclusively male preserve. For their detractors, it was natural that this perversion of the traditions of their sex should be mirrored in a debauched private life – hence, in Adélaïde's case, their insistence on her alcoholism, incest and illicit progeny.[28]

This approach, however, needs qualification. As the pioneering collections of essays edited by Clarissa Campbell Orr, *Queenship in Britain, 1660–1837* and *Queenship in Europe, 1660–1815* argue, in reality the dividing line, at least for well-born women, between the 'public' and 'private' spheres was more porous than has up until now been supposed. At the highest level, a queen consort had an important say in public appointments, often extending beyond her household or the court. In countries where a reigning queen was permitted, of course, she had all the normal powers of a head of state.[29]

Problems arose, however, when a woman who was not actually a reigning queen became heavily involved in policymaking. This clearly was the case with Adélaïde. Trespassing on this masculine domain, particularly in the open and direct way she did, made her highly vulnerable to public attack. The contrast with Marie Amélie, who kept well out of politics and was rarely lampooned either in cartoons or in print, is striking.[30]

Adélaïde was pilloried partly, but not solely, because she was a woman. The opposition press preyed on her because, regardless of her sex, they disliked her political views. Sometimes, they attacked them openly. At others, they used a method that, then as now, has always proved effective in discrediting a foe – sexual slander. It is significant that the most sustained assault on Adélaïde came from the legitimist *La Mode*, which clearly knew of her profound hatred for the elder Bourbons, as well as her specific role in July 1830. For the republican press, which did not have this particular political reason to detest her, she was generally far less of a target.

Comparison between Adélaïde and her near-contemporary, Marie-Antoinette, reveals a similar picture. As a particularly high-profile and powerful queen, Marie-Antoinette became the object of an exceptionally violent campaign of pornographic pamphlets and cartoons, accusing her of rampant sexual promiscuity, especially incest and lesbianism. The most common conclusion is that she was vilified because the increasing influence she acquired went well beyond traditional gender boundaries.[31] Yet as Vivian Gruder has recently and convincingly argued, the scurrilous attacks on Marie Antoinette only became a flood after 1789, when she took up an unpopular political position against the Revolution. In the struggle that ensued, the queen's opponents turned on her with every weapon they could, including the stock repertory of sexual smears. As Gruder comments, pornography was merely 'a handmaiden to politics, following in its path, an instrument in a preceding and larger political combat'.[32] Adélaïde was attacked in the same way, less because she was a woman per se, than because her political choices made her enemies.

To conclude, Adélaïde d'Orléans clearly played a crucial political role in the July monarchy, and all the more remarkable because she was a woman. Was this role constructive, or destabilizing? On the one hand, her interpretation of the royal prerogative, like her brother's, gave significantly more power to the crown than many politicians were prepared to accept. Her forceful, and above all unaccountable, presence next to the throne often exacerbated deep-seated suspicions of royal power in a political nation whose memories of Charles X were still fresh. On the other hand, there is no evidence that Adélaïde ever urged Louis-Philippe to appoint or sustain a ministry in defiance of a clear majority of deputies, as Charles X had done. Of the July monarchy's two most successful prime ministers, Molé and Guizot, she enthusiastically supported the former, and was reconciled to the latter once he had made it clear that he did not see the throne, in his own words, as 'an empty chair'.[33] To her credit, more than many other leading figures of her day she saw the need for national reconciliation as well as order. Adélaïde d'Orléans played an important part in the development of constitutional monarchy in France. Fortunately for her, she did not live to see its ultimate failure.

Notes

1 H. A. C. Collingham with R. S. Alexander, *The July Monarchy: A Political History, 1830–1848* (London, 1988); D. H. Pinkney, *The French Revolution of 1830* (Princeton, NJ, 1972) and *Decisive Years in France, 1840–1847* (Princeton, NJ, 1986); M. Price, *The Perilous Crown: France 1815–1848* (London, 2007); G. Antonetti, *Louis-Philippe* (Paris, 1994); P. Thureau-Dangin, *Histoire de la Monarchie de Juillet* (7 vols, Paris, 1884–92).
2 See, for example, Collingham and Alexander, *The July Monarchy*, 95–8.
3 R. Arnaud, *Adélaïde d'Orléans (1777–1847)* (Paris, 1908); D. Paoli, *Madame Adélaïde: soeur et égérie de Louis-Philippe* (Paris, 2016).
4 Victor Hugo, *Journal 1830–1848* [ed. H. Guillemin] (Paris, 1954), 312.
5 On Philippe-Egalité and Mme de Genlis, the best recent biographies are E. Lever, *Philippe-Egalité* (Paris, 1996), and G. de Broglie, *Madame de Genlis* (Paris, 1985).
6 Louis-Philippe to Adélaïde d'Orléans, 31 January 1806, Archives Nationales, 300 AP(IV) 8, pièce 62.
7 *Mémoires de la comtesse de Boigne, née d'Osmond: récits d'une tante* (2 vols, Paris, 1999), vol. 2, 328; Comte de Montalivet, *Fragments et Souvenirs* (2 vols, Paris, 1899–1900), vol. 1, 15–16.

8   See, for example, Louise d'Orléans to Adélaïde d'Orléans, s.d., AN 300 AP(IV) 18, 'Madame Adélaïde. Lettres recues de Marie-Amélie et de ses enfants, 1815–1829', dossier 19, 167.
9   AN 300 AP(III) 73, Journal de Vatout, 1830, pièce 63, 31, 'Juin 1830'; Vicomte de Chateaubriand, *Mémoires d'outre-tombe* (3 vols, Paris, 1973), vol. 2, 346.
10 AN 300 AP(III) 73, Journal de Vatout, 1830, pièce 63, p. 29, '28 juillet 1830'.
11 BN Nouvelles acquisitions françaises 20601, Papiers Adolphe Thiers, vol. 1, Correspondance 1830–1834. 'Notes sur les événements de 1830. Visite de M Thiers à Neuilly pour offrir la couronne au duc d'Orléans. Note dictée par lui.' Fos 88–89.
12 Ibid., fos. 89–90.
13 Ibid.
14 Montalivet, *Fragments et Souvenirs*, vol. 1, 16–18.
15 Adélaïde d'Orléans to General Sébastiani, 6 February 1836, AN 300 AP(III) 959, pièce 234.
16 Adélaïde d'Orléans to Sébastiani, 8 March 1839, ibid., pièce 372.
17 The correspondence between Mme Adélaïde and Talleyrand is published in Comtesse de Mirabeau, *Le prince de Talleyrand et la maison d'Orléans* (Paris, 1890), and by F. Masson, 'Lettres du prince de Talleyrand et de Mme de Dino à Mme Adélaïde', *Nouvelle Revue Rétrospective* (1901), vol. 15, 145–68, 217–40, 337–60, 385–408 and vol. 16 (1902) 49–65. Mme Adélaïde's letters to Sébastiani are in AN 300 AP(III) 959.
18 Adélaïde d'Orléans to Sébastiani, 2 June 1835. AN 300 AP(III) 959, pièce 206.
19 Adélaïde d'Orléans to Sébastiani, 11 December 1835, ibid., pièce 225.
20 Adélaïde d'Orléans to Sébastiani, 26 June 1836, ibid., pièce 261.
21 See, for example, AN 300 AP(III) 6, Mme Adélaïde (1777–1847). Dossiers 37, 38 (25 February 1832).
22 Sébastiani to Thiers, 5 March 1836, BN, nouvelles acquisitions françaises 20606, vol. 6, Correspondence 1836, M-S, fo.191.
23 Montalivet, *Fragments et Souvenirs*, vol. 2, 86–7.
24 *La Mode*, 34–5, janvier–juin 1838, 9ème livraison, 237–8.
25 See, for example, *La Mode*, 34–5, janvier–juin 1838, 9ème livraison, 213–16.
26 *Le Charivari*, le 31 janvier 1839, 8ème année, no. 31; *La Mode*, le 29 février 1840, 38–9, janvier–juin 1840, 261; Arnaud, *Adélaïde d'Orléans*, 295–96.
27 BN, Cabinet des Estampes, Qb-1 (1833)-FOL, M112331.
28 See L. Hunt (ed), *Eroticism and the Body Politic* (Baltimore, MD, 1991), 5; J. Landes, *Women and the Public Sphere in the Age of the French Revolution* (Ithaca, NY 1988). For a detailed analysis containing many examples, see A. Corbin, J. Lalouette and M. Riot-Sarcey (eds), *La femme dans la cite, 1815–1871* (Grane, 1997). For the July monarchy in particular see J. Burr Margadant, 'Gender, vice and the political imaginary: reinterpreting the failure of the July Monarchy, 1830–1848', *American Historical Review* vol. 104, no. 5 (December 1999), 1461–96.
29 C. Campbell-Orr (ed.), *Queenship in Britain, 1660–1837: Royal Patronage, Court Culture and Dynastic Politics* (Manchester and New York, 2002), 34–6, and *Queenship in Europe, 1660–1815: The Role of the Consort* (Cambridge, 2004).
30 For this aspect of Marie-Amélie, see J. Burr Margadant, 'Representing Queen Marie-Amélie in a "bourgeois" monarchy', *Historical Reflections* (summer 2006), vol. 32, no. 2, 421–51.
31 See L. Hunt, 'The many bodies of Marie Antoinette: political pornography and the problem of the feminine in the French Revolution', in L. Hunt (ed.), *Eroticism and the*

Body Politic, 108–30; S. Maza, *Private Lives and Public Affairs: The Causes Célèbres of Prerevolutionary France* (Berkeley and Los Angeles, CA, and London, 1993) 207–10; C. Thomas, *La reine scélérate: Marie Antoinette dans les Pamphlets* (Paris, 1989).

32 V. Gruder, 'The question of Marie Antoinette: the queen and public opinion before the Revolution', *French History* vol. 16, no. 3 (September 2002), 298.

33 F. Guizot, *Mémoires pour servir à l'histoire de mon temps* (8 vols, Paris, 1858–67), vol. 8, 84.

Part Five

New States, New Borders

17

'... to be Norwegians, not Swedish': Identity Adaptations in the Norwegian Officers Corps, 1814–45

Roald Berg

Introduction

The Treaty of Kiel, signed in January 1814, witnessed the birth of a new Scandinavian order, when the Danish king was forced to cede Norway to the king of Sweden. When the message of this handover reached Christiania, the ruling elite, led by the governor, Prince Christian Frederik, rebelled. A national assembly was organized. On 17 May, this assembly adopted a constitution for a sovereign Norway and elected Christian Frederik to become its king. Christian Frederik noted during these turbulent times that the Norwegians 'unanimously want to be Norwegians and not Swedish'.[1] He realized that the Swedish Crown Prince, Charles John, as soon as Napoleon had been defeated on the continent, would invade Norway to enforce the terms of the Kiel treaty.

Although the Swedish takeover was backed with overwhelming force, many members of the elite supported resistance. Bishop Johan Nordahl Brun in Bergen urged his clerical colleague in Christiania, Claus Pavels, to 'grab his rifle'.[2] He inflamed his congregation never to surrender, and declared to Pavels that Norway could not give in until at least 20,000 Norwegian lives had been sacrificed.[3] The war came, but it did not end in a clear-cut Swedish victory. Charles John accepted a ceasefire, recognized the May Constitution after christian Frederik had abdicated, and negotiated with the Parliament for an amended constitution that would allow for a union between Norway and Sweden to be established. On 4 November, the Norwegian Parliament voted for this constitution, and elected the Swedish king to their throne.

Promptly, bishop Brun and his colleagues appealed for loyalty to the new king and the union.[4] So did the rest of the clergy, as well as the legal profession, and certainly the military's officer corps. Some military men noted that the eagerness for bellicose heroism had been 'as usual greatest with the gentlemen sitting comfortably in their living rooms by the fire in the winter'.[5] The theme for this chapter is *not* the shifting of loyalty from one to another and then to a third head of state. Such shifting allegiances were as unavoidable in the early nineteenth century as they had been during the Napoleonic wars and indeed under the ancien régime. Heads of states had ruled and continued to do so within the Vienna system, as constitutional rulers.

Much more fundamental was the psychological transformation that people experienced when Danish sovereignty over Norway was replaced with Swedish. The change in collective identity, from Danish, to Norwegian and then to Swedish,[6] was both a complicated and a vital process. It mirrored similar developments throughout Europe, during the first half of the nineteenth century. Many composite dynastic states/empires slowly metamorphosed into agglomerations of national 'imagined communities', so memorably described in the work of Benedict Anderson.[7] The sociologist Amitai Etzioni has argued compellingly that there is nowhere in Europe where culture, language and religion 'are as similar as they are in the Nordic region.'[8] Even the Swedish and Norwegian languages might seem as close to each other as the English spoken by an American or an Australian.[9] Nevertheless, Rasmus Glenthøj has discovered that from the very beginning of 1814, distinguishing between purportedly 'genuine Norwegians' and allegedly 'un-Norwegian or spurious Norwegians' became a key issue in Norway.[10] The test case for proper 'Norwegianness' revolved around the issue of whether one should be 'called a Norwegian rather than a Swede', as Claus Pavels remarked.[11] This identity, based on labelling, became a symbol around which the ruling elites of Norway rallied to resist the perceived 'Swedification' that the forced union with powerful Sweden had, to their minds, unleashed.

This chapter will explore the essential question of how the officer corps participated in the resistance against 'Swedification', and made an essential contribution to building a shared sense of 'Norwegianness' during the period 1814–45. The ruling elite in Norway consisted mainly of 'civil servants': the rulers who had administered Norway for the absolutist Danish king until 1814, and who continued to do so after having shifted their allegiance from him to Christian Frederik in May 1814, and ultimately, in November, to Charles John.[12] As administrators, the civil servants and military officers[13] ruled Norway, which was only superficially controlled by the new Swedish governor.[14] Such was the case also in France, for instance, before, during and after the Napoleonic era. While Napoleon was occupied on his Russian expedition in 1812, rumours of his death led to an attempted coup by General Malet, which the Parisian authorities stopped 'as the Empire could "fly on auto pilot."'[15] Correspondingly, Norwegian civil servants and military officers were leaders of a self-propelled and self-managing state apparatus, generally unperturbed by Charles John who usually stayed in Stockholm. The officers and their civil colleagues were of course loyal to him. But they were also *Norwegian* servants of His (Norwegian) Majesty as they referred to him in Norway. They participated on a routine basis in ruling Norway as a natural administrative unit. Thereby, they developed, almost imperceptibly, an identity as Norwegian rulers, politically and culturally. The culmination of this process was reached in 1845 when military bands and honour guards led the burial procession of Henrik Wergeland, the most distinguished national poet of the nineteenth century. This ritual event symbolized the breakthrough achieved by Norwegian identity within its military ruling elite.

The officers' transferral of identities

The officers constituted a minor part of the ruling elite, not more than 500 persons or about 25 per cent of the total numbers of judges, clergymen and military men that governed the kingdom from its centre in Christiania (modern Oslo) to the peripheries to the west and north.[16] One-third of them were born outside Norway.[17] As Norway did not have her own naval defence before 1814, all naval officers had been cadets at the Naval Academy in Copenhagen and, thereafter, served in different parts of the Danish empire before 1814. Most land officers had been trained in Copenhagen or served outside Norway. As the Danish composite state was a multi-ethnic empire, ranging from Jutland, and German-speaking Altona, to Greenland and the Sami land in the northernmost provinces of Norway, as well as to the West Indian colonies and the Danish colonies in India,[18] the officers were true internationalists, used to service under a host of different commanders and in distant parts of the world.

The commander of the Norwegian Military College in 1814, Diderik Hegermann, was born in German-speaking Altona, and educated as an officer in Copenhagen. He was dispatched to Norway in 1790 at the age of twenty-seven.[19] The minister for the army from 1815 until his retirement in 1837, Peter Motzfeldt was born in Norway, but educated to become an artillery officer in Copenhagen. He had served at a variety of stations in the multi-ethnic Danish empire. Starting in 1802 he was posted to St Thomas, where he was captured by the British in 1807 and finally, two years later, at the age of thirty-two, the king transferred him to Norway.[20]

A third example is the commander of Fredriksten fortress in 1814, the greatest symbol of centuries-long Swedish-Norwegian enmity and the death place of the Swedish warrior king, Charles XII, in 1718. In 1814, the commander of this legendary national symbol, General Johan Andreas Cornelius Ohme, refused to participate in the official Swedish takeover of Fredriksten out of his love for his Norwegian fatherland. This great expression of national resistance was rewarded on 17 May 1905 when a memorial was erected over his grave. Each 17 May since then, flowers have been placed there to honour his refusal to surrender to the foreign intruder.[21] However, his Norwegian identity in 1814 was of recent origin, as he was born in the Danish duchy of Holstein, dispatched to Norway for the first time in 1805, at the age of fifty-nine, and only from 1810, at the age of sixty-four, had he been commander at Fredriksten and simultaneously removed from the Danish Army's register.[22] When overwhelming Swedish forces conquered his fortress four years later, his heroic refusal to capitulate established Fredriksten fortress as the ultimate bedrock of 'Norwegianness' as synonymous for 'non-Swedishness.' He did so, however, after less than five years as a 'Norwegian.' His Norwegian identity was fresh for a man in his sixties. Even Baron Ferdinand Carl Maria Wedel Jarlsberg, a renowned Norwegian officer, who was to make the most splendid carrier for himself, was a newcomer in 1814. His brother was Baron Wedel Jarlsberg who was to become a strong leader in the government after 1814. The baron's career had nothing to do with nepotism. It was the result of his ability to combine loyalty to the king with public and conspicuous Norwegianness.[23]

The baron was born in Naples, the son of a Norwegian nobleman who served as a Danish diplomat. He became an officer in the Norwegian cavalry from 1814, when he was thirty-one years old. In 1829, he served as commander of the Akershus fortress in Christiania at the time when a group of students, led by the national poet Henrik Wergeland, celebrated the 17 May Constitution and thus challenged the official Constitution Day of 4 November and so, implicitly, the king. The Norwegian authorities, as well as the Swedish governor, feared all kinds of popular disturbances just as much as their opposite numbers everywhere in Europe. Therefore, the demonstrators were dispersed by cavalry. The supreme responsibility for authorizing this use of arms against civilians fell to the Swedish governor. The local commander, Wedel Jarlsberg, who used his cavalry to repress demonstrators, therefore escaped the risk of desecrating his Norwegianness and, ultimately, blame for this harsh form of crowd control. The office of governor, which was detested from its establishment in 1814, became terminally unpopular for its use of force against the students, and was never again held by any Swede.

A few years later, Wedel Jarlsberg was appointed commander-in-chief of the Norwegian army.[24] As such, he was responsible for the military guard of honour and band accompanying the poet Wergeland's funeral in 1845.[25] To associate the military forces, under his command, with the funeral of a national icon such as Wergeland was a master stroke. Norway's local defence forces gained a reputation as the defenders and custodians of Norwegianness and the Norwegian state – against any kind of Swedish encroachment or intrusion into Norway.[26]

One lasting political legacy of these events was that any temptation by Sweden to use force against Norway henceforth became unthinkable. Norwegian officers had proven, once and for all, that they were defenders not just of Wergeland, but of the 17 May Constitution, and the nation he had so loving elegized. Thus, Norway's sovereignty in the union with Sweden was consolidated by Baron Wedel Jarlsberg's exoneration from ultimate responsibility for the cavalry charge of 1829 as well as by sending his military musicians to escort the national poet to his grave, in 1845.[27] In both of these highly symbolic events, the baron consolidated the symbolic barriers erected to protect Norwegian identity against Swedification. Through such symbolic policies of indirect loyalty to the 17 May Constitution, especially its most prominent ideological representative, Henrik Wergeland, the officer corps contributed to safeguarding the sovereignty and distinctiveness of Norway.

The culture elite, the road builders and the map makers

As members of the civil servant elite, the officer corps participated actively in the process of cultural Norwegianization after 1814. There was no professional or academic music in the country at this time, apart from military bands and music.[28] Officers, like Wedel Jarlsberg, even participated in the establishment of theatres and art museums, and indeed he was chairman of the theatre in Christiania during the 1840s.[29] Others participated in the establishment of art schools.[30] The teachers at the Military College in Christiania, together with the few professors at the Norwegian university, established in 1811, and other leading civil servants, formed an intellectual elite with broad competence in architecture, engineering, science, statistics and history.[31] Norway's first historical journal, *Samlinger til det norske Folks Sprog og Historie* (1833-9), was published from 1833 by Gerhard Munthe, a captain and a teacher at the Military College, who is famous for introducing modern orcharding within the parishes of the country's western valleys.[32] The officer corps were pioneers in the creation of Norway as a cultural entity. Thus, they became Norwegians, whether they originated from Naples, Altona or Norway.

Like anywhere in Europe, officers in Norway constructed roads, canals, railways and drew maps that surveyed the natural obstacles – the deep fjords and the huge mountains – that isolated the parishes. This topography, and its concomitant system of infrastructure, distinguished Norway quite radically from Sweden. As road constructors, officers were desperately needed, as the country had been more or less without any infrastructure at all. When bishop Brun died in 1816, Claus Pavels' coach had to be carried 'beyond the precipices' while travelling to Bergen to become his successor.[33] In contrast, the Secretary of the Constitutional Assembly of 1814, Wilhelm F. K. Christie, noted, during a voyage northwards from Bergen, in 1846, how steamships, ironworks and timber mills had transformed the country from a backwater into an emerging industrialized nation.[34] As late as 1863 – when the first civil engineers returned home from Germany – two out of three engineers involved in public works remained military officers.[35] The Military College in Christiania was for Norway what the Army Corps of Engineers was for the United States:[36] that is, the only institution in the country that provided personnel for the 'practical nationalism' that reshaped Norway from a conglomerate of isolated settlements into an integrated state.[37]

The Military College in Christiania also turned out competent surveyors. That was a job for pioneers, as the interior of the country was more or less *terra incognita* until British mountain hikers and fishermen penetrated into the Norwegian wilderness from the 1830s onwards.[38] Together with the census and the museum, mapping has been defined as the key factor behind the creation of nation states.[39] Consequently mapping was 'loaded with political significance', according to the geographer John Short.[40]

Norway and Sweden offer excellent case studies for the development of politicized cartography. Charles John, in 1814, ordered his cartographers to map his new 'peninsula state', as he called the union.[41] The result was disappointing. The Norwegian half of the map, published in 1826, by captains Christian Collins and Gerhard Munthe,[42] was not harmonized with the Swedish equivalent because the Swedish officers had placed the map meridian in the geographical centre of the union, namely in the city of Karlstad, while their Norwegian colleagues claimed that the Norwegian 'national meridian', as they called it, must be located in the old fortress city Kongsvinger.[43] The 'national meridian' became the first symbol of a 'Norwegianness' that was incompatible with any shared identity based on dynastic union.

The meridian dispute was by no means a specifically Scandinavian sport in the age of the global commercial revolution. Similar international conflicts emerged elsewhere: for instance, the struggle on the Prime Meridian of Greenwich or Philadelphia (among other candidates). Eventually Greenwich won in 1884.[44] After all, Britannia ruled the waves. It is remarkable that Norway, the weak partner in the union, managed to veto the meridian, and that this struggle ended with strengthening and increasing the importance of the frontier with, or rather against, Sweden. The border remained a dividing line behind which Norway developed from being a state to becoming a nation, and not the hub of the 'peninsula state'. Even if the union meant the end of the traditional military threat from Sweden in the west,[45] the border never lost its role as a military buffer zone – and even a cultural *cordon sanitaire* – that was vital for Norway's security and for Norwegianization. In the 1820s the leading military intellectual, Colonel Nicolai Tidemand, noted that the fear of, and hatred against, real and imagined Swedish plans for amalgamation, became more deeply rooted year by year.[46] In this perspective, the 'national meridian' was nothing less than a long-term national expression of Norwegian identity.

The map maker's delimitation of Norway and insistence on a 'national meridian' increasingly separated Norwegians from their Swedish partners in the dynastic union. This had the opposite consequence to the celebrated survey carried out by Lewis and Clark, two American officers, who, between 1804 and 1806, charted vast territories located up the Missouri river and westwards towards the Pacific. Their expedition opened up the 'wild west' and the American empire's 'manifest destiny' to reach from the Atlantic to the Pacific Ocean.[47] In contrast, the Norwegian mapping officers, by insisting on their meridian, strengthened the concept of Norway as a natural and distinct geographical unit. This weakened rather than strengthened the union with a predominant Sweden.

The Norwegian officers supplemented their map, drawn according to national borders, with topographical surveys that highlighted 'a separate water system', as the main rivers in Norway run from the north and into the sea. Thus, according to Norwegian map makers, Norway's natural defence system possessed quite different military and natural features than those which characterized the Swedish equivalent.[48] In other words, Norway was not Sweden and the Norwegian officers were Norwegians who participated in the construction of Norway. But first and foremost, they were Norwegian *officers* who wanted to be soldiers.

The professionalization agents

Samuel Huntington dates the 'the beginning of the military profession in the West' to the reforms in the Prussian army after Jena and Austerlitz in 1806.[49] Many of the reforms were copied in Norway in 1815–16. But the most interesting forms of professionalization followed in the wake of the officers' daily struggle to release themselves from civilian duties. In 1825, for example, the army leadership refused to supply soldiers to stop flooding in the river Nøra in Hedmark, as this would detract from 'the general rule that military troops should not be used as working brigades' which were 'irrelevant for the defence of the realm'.[50] Through such expressions, the officer corps became the true defenders of their fatherland.

In 1825, some officers founded the Christiania Military Society, which quickly became the centre for military intellectuals. Five years later, they established the Norwegian Military Journal.[51] In its very first volume, in January 1831, the editor, Captain Jacob Gerhard Meydell, launched a specific Norwegian strategic threat analysis. Instead of the official threat analysis against the union – a Russian invasion towards

Stockholm – Meydell focused on a scenario in which Russian forces invaded the Finnmark region in Norway with forces from Archangel. To meet that threat, the official union war strategy would 'not be adequate'.[52] A few years later, Meydell supplemented the theory of the Russian menace to Norway by reiterating a geostrategic analysis, made in the early 1820s by the military analyst, Colonel Tidemand, that Russia needed ice-free Atlantic harbours to continue its expansion westwards.[53] Thus Norway, not Sweden or the union, needed her own war establishment to meet this perceived threat.

Jens Petter Nielsen and Bruno Naarden have – respectively on the Norwegian and the general European levels – showed that the genesis of the confrontation between east and west emerged during Napoleon's invasion of Russia in 1812, which France represented as a clash between 'civilization' and 'barbarism'. The outcome was French retreat and the Russian invasion of France, culminating in the capture of Paris in the spring of 1814, which convinced the European bourgeoisie that civilization was, indeed, threatened by Russia.[54] That was the general background for European Russophobia. The specific background for the corresponding Norwegian Russophobia was more complex. First, the new state's elite wanted to stay in the western camp. Secondly, they wanted to safeguard their identity against Swedification. Third, the theory of the Russian menace to Norway seemed to further both of these objectives. Indeed, it provided the foundations for the Norwegian officers' own sense of identity. Ultimately, it could be used for the legitimization of the military branch of the Norwegian nation as the Russian scare became the 'national threat', just as the Kongsvinger fortress was the 'national meridian'.

Conclusion

In 1817 Charles John expressed his satisfaction in the 'devoted affection from the brave Norwegian people'.[55] During the early 1820s he compared 'the tranquillity that prevails in Norway' with 'the troubles in many of the other European countries'.[56] The peace and tranquillity in Norway is striking in a century that was both internally turbulent and riven by wars and interventions by the great powers. Such internal peace was, however, not the same as acceptance of the union. The officers participated actively in raising fences against Swedification, such as the 'national meridian' and the 'Russian threat'. They participated in, and even led, the engineering projects that resulted in a road network which lowered mountainous and fjord barriers between isolated rural districts and major cities. Gradually, Norway became a country bound together by roads, maps and art galleries, and the ruling class became Norwegian, whatever their background in 1814, cemented all the more by a shared sense of Norwegian-centred Russophobia.

However, that does not mean that either officers or their civilian colleagues were nationalists. As Richard Evans has emphasized, ideas of nationhood and national identities were, during the first generation after Napoleon, not as disruptive and divisive in nature as the waves of nationalism that characterized the second half of the nineteenth century. Neither the Czechs nor the Hungarians struggled for the dissolution of the Habsburg monarchy but, rather, to enhance home rule in this period.[57] The Norwegian elite, essentially, did the same. As the military committee in

Parliament wrote to promote the budget for the military forces in 1836: 'The Norwegian people wants to preserve its rank as a state that ranks equally to Sweden, and must therefore not neglect the necessary care for its own defence and trust that Sweden will defend it.'[58]

That encapsulates the meaning of Norwegianness during the first half of the nineteenth century in the officer corps. It was not a question of national independence, nor of nation building in order to reach the status of one people, speaking one language and sharing one territory. It was merely a question of being a decent military professional in a country in which the officers lived and had their loved ones. Therefore – according to one military historian – they wished to 'conjure up' threats that suited the national need for raising a professional defence complex. Unfortunately, this conjuring 'made the Norwegian Defence chronically irrelevant' in the political tool box.[59] But as the constructors of civilian infrastructure, military officers were the pre-eminent builders of the state's *and* nation's frontiers. At Wergeland's funeral in 1845 they became the nation's finest emblem.

Notes

1. Mona Ringvej, *Christian Frederiks tapte rike* (Oslo, 2016), 189.
2. Knut Mykland, *Kampen om Norge 1784–1814*, vol. 9 in *Norges historie* (Oslo, 1978), 450.
3. Ruth Hemstad, *Propagandakrig. Kampen om Norge i Norden og Europa 1812–1814* (Oslo, 2014), 368; Bård Frydenlund, *Spillet om Norge. Det politiske året 1814* (Oslo, 2014), 226.
4. Runar Jordåen, *Wilhelm F. K. Christie. Presidenten* (Bergen, 2014), 258; Rasmus Glenthøj, *Skilsmissen. Dansk og norsk identitet før og efter 1814* (Odense, 2012), 348.
5. Quoted from Rasmus Glenthøj and Morten Nordhagen Ottosen, *Experiences of War and Nationality in Denmark and Norway, 1807–1815* (London, 2014), 246.
6. Frydenlund, *Spillet om Norge*, 226–33.
7. Benedict Anderson, *Imagined Communities. Reflections on the Origin and Spread of Nationalism* (London, 1991 [1983]).
8. Amitai Etzioni, *Political Unification. A Comparative Study of Leaders and Forces* (New York, Chicago, San Francisco, Toronto and London, 1965), 220f.
9. Ibid., 217. H. Arnold Barton has on the other hand claimed that the changes were more significant in Scandinavia than in the rest of Europe after 1815, cf. H. Arnold Barton, *Scandinavia in the Revolutionary Era, 1760–1815* (Minneapolis, 1986), 361; for a detailed analysis of geopolitical change in Scandinavia post-1815, see Roald Berg, 'Denmark, Norway and Sweden in 1814. A geopolitical and contemporary perspective,' *Scandinavian Journal of History*, vol. 39, no. 3 (2014), 265–86.
10. Glenthøj, *Skilsmissen*, 237–9.
11. Quoted from Barton, *Scandinavia*, 353. On 'norwegianness' and 'norwegianization', see Roald Berg, 'From "Spitsbergen" to "Svalbard". Norwegianization in Norway and in the "Norwegian Sea", 1820–1925,' *Acta Borealia*, vol. 30, no. 2 (2012), 154–73.
12. Jens Arup Seip, *Fra embedsmannsstat til ettpartistat og andre essays*, (Oslo, 1974 [1963]), 12f; Øystein Rian, *Embetsstanden i dansketida* (Oslo, 2003); Øystein Rian, 'Det norske embetsaristokratiet', in Marthe Hommerstad and Morten Nordhagen

Ottosen (eds), *Ideal og realitet. 1814 i politisk praksis for folk og elite* (Oslo, 2014), 111–25.
13 Norwegian historians have traditionally neglected the role officers played in shaping national identity in Norway after 1814; see Roald Berg, *Profesjon-union-nasjon 1814–1905*, vol. 2 in *Norsk forsvarshistorie* (Bergen, 2001), 86; see also Rune Slagstad, *(Sporten). En idéhistorisk studie* (Oslo, 2008), 23 and *passim*.
14 On the rise and fall of the Swedish governors in Norway, see Berg, *Profesjon*, 82f; Roald Berg, 'Embetsmannsstat, rettsstat eller generalguvernement 1814–1829', *Nytt Norsk Tidsskrift* 1 (2003), 73–84; Bo Stråth, *Union og demokrati. Dei sameinte rika Noreg-Sverige 1814–1905* (Oslo, 2005), 107f.
15 Michael Broers, *Europe under Napoleon, 1799–1815* (London, New York, Sydney and Auckland, 1996), 270f.
16 Berg, *Profesjon*, 86.
17 Ståle Dyrvik, *Norges historie*, vol. 8 in *Den lange fredstiden 1720–1784* (Oslo, 1978), 332.
18 On the Danish empire, see Michael Bregnsbo and Kurt Villads Jensen, *Det danske imperium. Storhed og fald* (Copenhagen, 2004); Berg, 'Denmark, Norway and Sweden'.
19 J. B. Halvorsen, *Norsk Forfatter-Lexicon 1814–1880*, vol. 2 (Oslo 1888), 589–91.
20 *Norsk Biografisk Leksikon*, vol. 6 (Oslo, 2003), 374f.
21 Roald Berg, 'Symbolpolitikkes seier. Stortinget og Fredriksten festning 1814–1905', *Nordisk Tidskrift*, 1 (2005), 43–9.
22 J. C. W. and K. Hirch, *Fortegnelse over danske og norske officerer m. fl. 1648–1815*, vol. VII, 5 (Copenhagen, 1888); Olav Risøen Nagell, *Fredriksten Festning, kommandanter og historiske høydepunkter* (Halden, 1997), 64–8.
23 Of course, the concept of conspicuous norwegianness is inspired by the sociologist Torstein Veblen.
24 Berg, *Profesjon*, 74.
25 Ibid., 139.
26 Ibid.; *Norsk Biografisk Leksikon*, vol. 9 (Oslo, 2005), 424f.
27 In 1821 Charles John did threaten the Parliament with armed force. That was the last time in the history of the union where the king tried to force Norwegians to bend to his will, though several times during the nineteenth century he considered doing so again; see Berg, *Profesjon*, passim.
28 Hans Fredrik Dahl and Tore Helseth, *To knurrende løver. Kulturpolitikkens historie, 1814–2014* (Oslo, 2006), 23 and 39.
29 *Norsk Biografisk Leksikon*, vol. 9, 424f; Berg, *Profesjon*, 34f for another example.
30 Dahl and Helseth, *To knurrende løver*, 22f; Hans Hosar, *Kunnskap, dannelse og krigens krav. Krigsskolen 1750–2000* (Oslo, 2000), 116f.
31 Dahl and Helseth, *To knurrende løver*, 23.
32 Ibid., 29f; Hosar, *Kunnskap*, 116–20. See also Jordåen, *Wilhelm F. K. Christie*, 423, 432 and passim.
33 Wilhelm Keilhau, *Tidsrummet 1814 til omkring 1840*, vol. 8 in *Det norske folks liv og historie* (Oslo, 1929), 98.
34 Jordåen, *Wilhelm F. K. Christie*, 445–7.
35 Hosar, *Kunnskap*, 113.
36 Tod A. Shallat, *Structures in the Stream. Water, Science, and the Rise of the US Army Corps of Engineers* (Austin, TX, 1994).
37 Hosar, *Kunnskap*, 114; see also even Samuel Huntington, *The Soldier and the State. The Theory and Politics of Civil-Military Relations* (Cambridge, MA and London, 1957),

199 (the American Military Academy, West Point 'produced more railroad presidents than generals').
38 See Slagstad, *Sporten*, 72-91 for the military frontiers as walking tourists and as name-givers of the most famous mountains. See also Peter Fjågesund and Ruth A. Symes, *The Northern Utopia. British Perceptions of Norway in the Nineteenth Century* (Amsterdam and New York, 2003) on the development of tourism in Norway during the nineteenth century.
39 Anderson, *Imagined Communities,* 163-85. The map has even been called the prime ideological apparatus for the education of citizens in the field of national consciousness during the nineteenth century, see John Rennie Short, *Representing the Republic. Mapping the United States 1600-1900* (London, 2001), 11 and passim.
40 Ibid., 15.
41 Berg, *Profesjon,* 16; Berg, 'Denmark, Norway and Sweden', passim.
42 Berg, *Profesjon,* 108-10, 92; Slagstad, *Sporten,* 22; Roald Berg, 'The 19th Century Norwegian-Swedish Border. "Imagined community" or "pluralist Security system"', *Journal of Northern Studies* 1 (2009), 91-103.
43 Sven Widmalm, *Mellan kartan och verkligheten. Geodesi och kartläggning 1695-1860* (Uppsala, 1990), 363f.; Berg, *Profesjon,* 108-110; Slagstad, *Sporten,* 22.
44 John Noble Wilford, *The Mapmakers,* revised edn (New York, 2000), 257f; Short, *Representing,* 100f.
45 Lars Ericson, *Svensk militärmakt. Strategi och operationer i svensk militärhistoria under 1500 år* (Stockholm, 2003), 155.
46 Rasmus Glenthøj, *En moderne nations fødsel. Norsk national identifikation hos embedsmænd og borgere 1807-1820* (Odense, 2008), 204.
47 William H. Goetzmann, *Exploration and Empire. The Explorer and the Scientist in the Winning of the West* (Austin, TX, 2000), 7; John Logan Allen, *Passage through the Garden: Lewis and Clark and the Image of the American Northwest* (Urbana, IL, 1975).
48 Berg, *Profesjon,* 122.
49 Huntington *The Soldier,* 30-9; Hans Hosar, 'Offiserane,' in Rune Slagstad and Jan Messel (eds), *Profesjonshistorier* (Oslo, 2014), 381.
50 Berg, *Profesjon,* 101f.
51 Ibid., 104-6.
52 Ibid., 114.
53 Ibid., 114f.
54 Jens Petter Nielsen, 'Novembertraktaten (1855-1907) – Norges første stormaktsgaranti,' in Roald Berg (ed.), *Selvstendig og beskyttet. Det stormaktsgaranterte Norge 1855-2008* (Bergen, 2008), 19-24; Bruno Naarden, *Socialist Europe and Revolutionary Russia. Perception and Prejudice* (Cambridge, 1992).
55 Karl Johan, *Karl Johans brev till Riksståthållaren Mörner 1816-1818,* Sofie Aubert Lindbæk (ed.). *Historiska Handlingar* 30:1 (Stockholm, 1935), 69.
56 Karl Johan, *Karl XIV Johans brev til Riksståthållaren J.A. Sandels 1818-1827.* Elise Adelsköld (ed.) *Historiska Handlingar* 35:2 (Stockholm, 1955), 39.
57 Richard J. Evans, *The Pursuit of Power. Europe 1815-2014* (New York, 2016), 178.
58 *Stortingsforhandlinger* (Parliamentary Records) 1836-5 (Okt.), 178-80.
59 Harald Høiback, '1814-1914: Forsvaret som nasjonsbygger,' in Håkan Edström and Palle Ydstebø (eds), *Militærstrategi på norsk – en innføring* (Oslo, 2011), 163.

18

The Construction of the Boundaries in Restoration Italy: A Comparative Perspective

Marco Meriggi

One of the factors which most characterized the daily experiences of Europeans during the Napoleonic era was surely the growth of government control, which the state systematically and relentlessly exerted over their lives.[1] The Napoleonic state was, on the one hand, a military state and on the other, a police state.[2] This meant that it did not fear competition from any alternative jurisdiction (for instance: the Church, feudal overlords and municipalities), whereas in the recent past conflicts with competing particularistic and privileged institutions had characterized the experience of government for nearly all *ancien régime* societies.

Since this new kind of state held the monopoly on public power it was natural for it to aspire to exercise its authority in the most extensive way possible. One of the tools by which this claim to supremacy was concretely put into practice consisted in the introduction of a civil registration system, which was based not on the place of birth (prior to this parishes, by dispensing baptismal certificates, monitored and vouched for the identity, not to mention good morals, of the souls entrusted to their care) but rather, on the place of residence for each individual.[3]

Thanks to these new administrative practices, an individual identity recognition system was introduced into each of the three jurisdictions into which Napoleonic Italy was divided (that is the kingdom of Italy in the north; the kingdom of Naples in the south; and finally the Piedmontese, Ligurian, Tuscan and Roman *départements réunis*, which were directly ruled from Paris). According to this system, in principle every adult male was required to carry a personal identity document issued by the state, which provided information about his physical characteristics (i.e. height, facial features, hair, distinguishing marks and so on), in order to render himself easily recognizable to the authorities.[4]

To move outside of his district (that is beyond the 'face-to-face society' in which he could be recognized directly by other fellow local residents), every individual had to obtain a 'pass' or a security card, that is an official document which allowed him to move from one of the state's districts to another. A case in point can be found in the diary, kept during these years, by Luigi Mantovani, a Milanese chronicler. Carrying identity papers was not a mere formality; the Napoleonic authorities took this system extremely seriously. On 5 February 1808, shortly after the regulations relating to identity papers came into force, the police decided to carry out spot-checks, during Carnival, to audit how many people were carrying their papers. These pre-Lenten days coincided with large public festivities and *soirées* held in Milan, the capital of the kingdom of Italy. Over four hundred people were arrested as the police surprised them without their 'security cards' that authorized them to transit from one district to another.[5]

Most of these unfortunates, who came to Milan to attend these festivities, were provincials who had not yet, evidently, become familiar with the new system. In the following years the possession of a security card became the norm for anyone wishing to move within the territory of the state, whereas, for those who intended to go beyond the boundaries of the state, the authorities introduced and imposed the duty on travellers to obtain a passport. In the absence of this document the authorities could refuse access to travellers intending to cross the border.

The process one had to follow to get the various cards which allowed freedom of movement was quite complex. It also involved costs, which especially for the lower and middle strata of the population were far from negligible. Apart from these issues, there was an underlying reason that rendered these innovations particularly unwelcome. Previously, both internal mobility within the territory of the state and travel abroad were on the whole devoid of binding rules.

Passports for foreign countries had already been in existence for centuries, but they were generally reserved for people of rank, for those travelling for pleasure or on the grand tour, and for merchants who used them in order to get support, or protection, from their consular authorities abroad.[6] Ordinary people, on the move for work, often travelled without any official document. At most they carried in their pocket a simple baptismal certificate, issued by the parish priest of their place of birth. It is difficult to assess how deep the influence exerted by these new measures was on the relationship between citizens and state authorities. One can say that, together with the introduction of compulsory military service and the attack on the power and influence of the Church, the 'bureaucratic revolution' unleashed by this new state documentation and identification system can be regarded as a source of strong dissatisfaction which ordinary people bore against the Napoleonic regimes. This was especially the case in the last years of the Empire just before the fall of Bonaparte.[7]

In fact, freedom of movement was an essential prerequisite, not only for those who practised a trade, but also for the many people who lived permanently in search of seasonal occupations and temporary work. Moving not only became more expensive, due to stamp duties and other charges connected with the issuing of identity documents (which were valid for one year, after which they had to renewed yet again for more fees), but also uncomfortable, becoming materially slower and more complex. The decision to go on a journey became a psychological burden given that there were so many formalities attached to a process that once had been taken for granted.

Moreover, the introduction of this system highlighted a deep change in the way in which authorities treated their subjects. An anonymous journalist, with pro-Bourbon leanings, in a gazette published in Messina, in June 1808 (at that time under British control), mused about how times were changing. He waxed lyrical about the 'beautiful' golden age, which sadly these new laws and administrative practices were effacing on the continental side of the kingdom of Naples (where a Napoleonic government was in charge). It is worth quoting him directly:

> The legitimate monarchs of Naples and Sicily had never needed such cards to acknowledge their subjects. Educated to reign, they always used noble and virtuous means to win the hearts, love and charity [of their people]. Gratitude and duty formed the sweet ties which bound together the throne and the people, making it a single whole. These [practices] combined the interests of both, and produced that mutual confidence, which results in public peace. Now, however, distrust and suspicion arrive in Naples [highlighting] the threshold where the tyranny begins.[8]

Perhaps ironically, at the end of the Napoleonic period, this 'tyranny' was confirmed rather than reversed. In the age of Restoration, the states of the Italian peninsula which had fallen under Bonaparte's yoke did not abolish (for the most part) the legislation relating to individual identification and personal mobility that had been introduced prior to 1814.[9] Despite the official promises on the rebuilding of the old regime, the so-called age of 'mutual confidence' between rulers and ruled was over. During the years of French occupation the state controlled and monopolized all institutional machinery and thus maintained a position of absolute dominance over society. Unlike what happened in other European countries – previously subject to Napoleonic rule – in the Italian states the subjects of each country continued to depend directly on the central state authorities. In some states – it is true – the system of military conscription was abolished, as it had caused so much resentment during the Napoleonic period. This was the case, for example, within the Papal States.

Yet for the most part, the detailed control and surveillance procedures of the adult male population, which under Napoleon had accompanied the introduction of military service, continued to be developed by state authorities. Such procedures were grounded on the close relationship between the identification of individuals through documents and the corresponding restriction of the freedom of movement. This topic is very well documented by extensive research in the archives of the kingdom of Lombardy-Venetia, the Grand Duchy of Tuscany and the kingdom of Two Sicilies.[10] In each of these states internal mobility was subject to many controls and restrictions. This caused, on the one hand, the construction of a large and close net of internal borders, and on the other the strengthening of those supervisory bodies responsible for ensuring their effectiveness.

Internal borders came into existence that divided not only one administrative province from another but also subdivided each province into networks of districts and municipalities. Take the case of the kingdom of Lombardy-Venetia, the heart of Habsburg Italy, which was examined exhaustively and studied meticulously by Andrea Geselle more than fifteen years ago.[11] Though it was a single state, subjected to one viceroy, the kingdom itself was divided into two administrative regions, each with a distinct regional government: that is, Lombardy and Venetia. Both the Emperor's Lombard subjects and his Venetian ones suffered limitations on their freedom of movement within the territory of this state. Such restrictions impacted the Venetians far worse than they did the Lombards. They needed, as had already been the case in the Napoleonic era, an identity card to move from one district to another, which essentially acted as a passport that allowed them to cross the River Mincio which acted as the 'natural' boundary between their region and Lombardy. For the Lombards, things were a bit better. A special pass was all that was needed to enter the Veneto. Within Lombardy itself, it was no longer mandatory when moving between one district and another, as had happened during the Napoleonic era. The kingdom of the Two Sicilies was the Restoration state in the Italian peninsula that remained most faithful to the Napoleonic administrative legacy. This was especially so, in terms of those territorial control arrangements adopted by the kingdom's public authorities in relation to the internal mobility of its subjects. Identity cards (that were equivalent to the Lombard-Venetian security cards) had to be shown to authorities whenever a person crossed the line between a district and a neighbouring one. Such checks could take place within a short distance of a dozen kilometres, or sometimes even less.

Moreover, in the decades following 1815, this system, which was initially limited to the continental part of the Kingdom and to the adult male population, was also extended to Sicily and to the female population. Similarly, in Tuscany, the rules regulating movement were – in continuity with Napoleonic tendencies – particularly rigorous. They concerned – so stated the laws – 'foreigners'. Such were considered not only the inhabitants of other states, but also Tuscan subjects who happened to find themselves outside the boundaries of their residential community. To move from one place to another, then, a traveller had to be in possession of documents authorizing their travel. These could be granted or refused by the authorities depending on the profile and background of the applicant. If they were considered a danger to public order their request for papers could be rejected outright. Ignoring this outcome carried the risk that a clandestine traveller could be intercepted by the very same police officer who had refused his request. Equally if chance and luck were kind to him he could be spared this unwelcome encounter. It was almost impossible, by contrast, for anyone without documents to enter walled cities. At the gates were stationed not only police officers, but also customs officials who exerted rigorous surveillance of those entering and exiting. They also collected tolls and customs duties on goods brought into the city. This was the so-called 'duty on consumption', which represented a very important element of the indirect tax system.[12] Here we come to another fundamental issue. It was not only ordinary folk, but also traders and smugglers (who often worked at the behest of the former), who had to deal with and find accommodation with the state's impressive apparatus for controlling the movement of goods and people.

Walled cities, subject to joint supervision by the police agents and customs officials, were many, spread all over the territory of every state in Restoration Italy. More rigorous measures and controls on access were reserved for capital cities. Such stringent regulations sough to protect and maintain public order especially in those places, and buildings, which were considered the political 'heart' of the state itself. Even if a 'foreigner' – understood in the broad sense discussed earlier – had managed to enter undetected through the city gates, without documents, it would still have been very difficult for him to settle, or remain unnoticed, in the city.

Let us dwell again on the case of Tuscany, whose characteristics were similar to those of the kingdom of Lombardy-Venetia and the kingdom of the Two Sicilies. Here 'special registers were provided by the courts, every three months, to innkeepers and all those involved in the hospitality industry. These tribunals then proceed to carry out detailed inspections of these records.'[13] Each innkeeper was obliged to verify – or face criminal prosecution – that his customers had a certificate granting free circulation within the city. These were granted by the municipal police officers to every foreigner on his entrance into the city. Simultaneously these authorities provisionally withdrew the traveller's original pass. Subsequently, and within twenty-four hours, the innkeepers would have to present the traveller's arrival declaration (and, later, departure declaration), 'if in Florence to the police inspector's office, and if in the province to the respective chanceries and courts'.[14]

Similar systems were in use in Lombardy-Venetia, in the kingdom of the Two Sicilies, and even in the Papal States, as the tale of Fabrizio del Dongo's entrance and stay in Bologna narrated so suggestively by Stendhal in *La Chartreuse de Parme* epitomizes.[15] Potentially, the subject on the move was continually subject to direct or indirect supervision by the state. Governments, at this time, regarded human mobility as a danger, capable of jeopardizing the static order and hierarchies that were imposed on society; movement essentially posed a permanent challenge to peace. In addition to the internal borders, which fragmented the internal territory and space within a state into a myriad of separate administrative units, there were, of course, the external frontiers, which coincided with the lines at which the sovereignty of each state ceased to be exerted.

In *La Chartreuse de Parme*, Stendhal offers some very effective illustrations of the problems related to crossing state borders at this time. He presents the hero of his story, Fabrizio del Dongo, firstly on the run from the Duchy of Parma, then from the kingdom of Lombardy-Venetia and finally from the Papal States. In order to escape arrest, in one single day he is obliged to cross the border no fewer than three times. Furthermore, to evade and thwart the surveillance of border officials, he resorts both to false documents and to the help of boatmen who, for a fee, transport him clandestinely from one bank of the River Po to the other. Then, at the decisive moment, when the situation seems to go wrong for him, a stroke of good fortune allows him to escape unscathed into the neighbouring state.[16]

How the borders of the Restoration states of the Italian peninsula were defined and delineated was a complex matter. In general – or rather when it was materially feasible – the key points of reference were offered by the summits of the mountain ranges, and by the course of rivers, canals and streams. The geographic sciences of the time tended to label such features as 'natural frontiers'. But all too often it was difficult to identify these precisely. Unsurprisingly this gave rise to disagreements and disputes which sometimes lasted until the national unification of the peninsula.

The story of Italian borders pre-unification had been, even before the Napoleonic period, very problematic. Around the middle of the eighteenth century each state had built up border agencies, which had the task of monitoring travellers entering and exiting their frontiers. They also had to ensure that communities living close to the frontier would not seek – as had often been the case – to claim portions of territory, which according to the rival neighbouring state were instead part of their own territorial jurisdiction. When it came to drawing formal boundary lines controversy and conflict were almost permanent.[17] Such tensions were hardly isolated to Italy alone and border disputes erupted in many other places across Europe at that time. The border region of the Pyrenees between France and Spain has been the subject of a famous study by Peter Sahlins.[18] During the second half of the eighteenth century, frequent talks were held between diplomats from various states in order to stipulate treaties which would hopefully settle and fix a shared interpretation of where boundary lines between states actually lay. When the Napoleonic era exploded onto the international scene, such negotiations were very far from concluded. Eventually, in the Final Act of the Congress of Vienna, it was decided to restore the borders between the various states of the peninsula as they had been before the arrival of Bonaparte in Italy. The language of continuity which characterized this decree actually concealed vast changes in the territorial configuration of Italy post-1814 (great changes resulted from the erasure of previously independent states, such as the republics of Genoa and Venice). Such diplomatic ambiguity was a simple repetition of the same uncertainty which had characterized the late eighteenth century.[19]

Almost everywhere negotiations on this issue, once resumed, lasted decades in many cases. In some instances, they were only concluded in the 1850s, well beyond the Restoration. Having said this, in the decades prior to 1848 key problems had emerged, which this chapter will try now to explain briefly. It will do so by referring, on the one hand, to the negotiations between the kingdom of the Two Sicilies and the Papal States; and on the other, with reference to those between Austria's domains (Lombardy-Venetia), Parma, Modena and the Papal States, with particular attention given to how the border areas along the River Po were delimited.[20]

As much in one case as in the other, what emerged during the negotiations was the growing importance of a 'Raison d'État', which was basically antithetical to the sensibilities of local communities living on the border. In order to provide legitimacy to their jurisdictional claims, frontier communities often referred to old customs and traditions. The problem was that every community in conflict, of course, believed that their own customs and traditions were valid, while those of neighbouring communities were fraudulent. During the eighteenth century, diplomats charged with conducting negotiations on border controversies often listened to the voices of local communities. During the Restoration decades, on the contrary, the local community's perspective received less and less attention from the negotiators. They preferred to follow the guidelines prescribed by documents and reports received from technical experts like geographers, engineers and surveyors. These professionals were despatched from the capital to the marches of the state. Their task was not so much to identify the existing, traditional boundary, but rather to delineate a modern, scientific boundary which was to be built from scratch. On this basis, diplomats tried to negotiate an agreement with their counterparts, even if it could imply surrendering portions of actual state territory, in exchange for the simultaneous acquisition of portions of the neighbouring state territory.

The new boundary was dictated by reason of state and not by conflicting local traditions and customs. It was constructed on the most suitable location to ensure not just military defence but also to exercise control over the movements of human beings and goods. Science and technical expertise, not tradition, became the preferred tools deployed to preserve order and peace. Thus – gradually and laboriously – capillaries of borders spread throughout the peninsula reinforced by concomitant plans to control human mobility by the state. This modus operandi was basically shared by all the governments of the time. Symbols of this system were the large number of border stations and checkpoints at which people on the move were obliged to show those documents necessary for their expatriation and for the circulation of goods destined for foreign trade.

Who then travelled at this time? First of all, ordinary people, often suffering from precarious economic plight, and for this reason they were motivated to go abroad to find their means of subsistence. There were also young people not at all eager to perform military service, and many vagabonds used to living in perpetual motion. Large numbers of merchants and, from the 1820s onwards, political dissidents who opposed the existing authoritarian regimes, and were forced to emigrate to escape arrest and persecution. These were, in broad strokes, the categories most touched by the new frontiers, and who were particularly subject to the attention and scrutiny of the state's surveillance institutions. To carry out their work successfully, these agents of the state relied on the verification of personal identity documents, which the Napoleonic regimes had introduced, and the Italian Restoration states subsequently confirmed. Indeed, they extended them to women following the revolutions of 1848.

This obsession for individual and documentary identification during the Restoration had as its primary goal as much the defence of public order (which had to be protected from threats both from social outcasts and political opponents) as the growth of tax revenues for the state. If one wants to gauge the effectiveness of this system, one can say that it was probably effective in general, especially in relation to controlling the movements of the ordinary people. Indeed, one of the prices of maintaining peace post-1814 was the rigorous limitation of the freedom of movement which previous generations had enjoyed. Of course, the system worked, at least in part, in controlling the spread of political opposition. Much less successful were the results when it came to regulating the movement of goods and of those who accompanied them to the other side of the border. Smuggling thrived, and there was no way of stopping it; so much so, that the population of Italy came to consider and condone it as a quasi-legal practice.

Even before the push towards political liberalism began, a popular, almost spontaneous drive towards laissez-faire economics and free trade practices emerged which deeply embarrassed and upset the Restoration states' claims to control their markets. The relationship between the state and its subjects had been deeply affected, as we have seen, by the general introduction of systems of personal identification and the strict regulation of state boundaries, which were essentially two sides of the same coin. In the 1850s it became apparent that the well-being of state finances paradoxically had more to gain from the liberalization of trade than from protectionist customs legislation, especially given the Restoration states' inability to thwart endemic smuggling. In the history of borders and of free movement thus was opened a new 'liberal' phase, which sadly falls outside the remit of this chapter.

Notes

1. Marco Meriggi, 'La cittadinanza di carta', *Storica*, VI/16 (2000), 107–20.
2. Livio Antonielli, 'Le istituzioni dell'età napoleonica', in M. Meriggi and L. Tedoldi (eds), *Storia delle istituzioni politiche. Dall'antico regime all'era globale* (Rome, 2014), 81–102. On this issue see also Howard G. Brown, *Ending the French Revolution: Violence, Justice and Repression from the Terror to Napoleon* (Charlottesville, 2000), as well as the essay review by Peter Hicks, 'The Napoleonic "police" or "security state" in context', *Napoleonica. La Revue*, 1/4 (2009), 2–10.
3. Olivier Faron, *La ville des destins croisés. Recherches sur la société milanaise du XIXe siècle* (Rome, 1997).
4. For the Kingdom of Italy: Andrea Geselle, 'Bewegung und ihre Kontrolle in Lombardo-Venetien', in W. Heindl and E. Saurer (eds), *Grenze und Staat. Passwesen, Staatsbürgerschat, Heimatsrecht und Fremdengesetzgebung in der österreichischen Monarchie 1750–1867* (Vienna, 2000), 347–515. For the Kingdom of Naples: Laura Di Fiore, *Alla frontiera. Confini e documenti di identità nel Mezzogiorno continentale preunitario* (Soveria Mannelli, 2013). On the general features of the Napoleonic personal identification system: Gerard Noiriel, 'Surveiller les déplacements ou identifier les personnes? Contributions à l'histoire du passeport en France de la Ire à la IIIe République', in Idem, *État, nation et immigration. Vers une histoire du pouvoir* (Paris, 2001), 309–29; Vincent Denis, *Une histoire de l'identité. France, 1715–1815* (Champ Vallon, 2008). See also: John Torpey, *The Invention of the Passport. Surveillance, Citizenship and the State* (Cambridge, 2000), 21–51.
5. Luigi Mantovani, *Diario politico ecclesiastico*, vol. 3 (Rome, 1991), 300.
6. Valentin Groebner, *Who are You? Identification, Deception, and Surveillance in Early Modern Europe* (New York, 2007).
7. Michael Broers, *Europe under Napoleon 1799–1815* (London, 1996).
8. Quoted in Patrizia De Salvo, *Sicilia inglesa. Una metáfora del constitucionalismo mediterráneo* (Madrid, 2016), 33.
9. Marco Meriggi, 'Sui confini nell'Italia preunitaria', in S. Salvatici (ed.), *Confini. Costruzioni, attraversamenti, rappresentazioni* (Soveria Mannelli, 2005), 37–53.
10. Geselle, *Bewegung und ihre Kontrolle*; Antonio Chiavistelli, *Dallo Stato alla nazione. Costituzione e sfera pubblica in Toscana dal 1814 al 1849* (Rome, 2006); Di Fiore, *Alla frontiera*.
11. Geselle, *Bewegung und ihre Kontrolle*. On the Lombardo-Veneto Kingdom in general, see: Marco Meriggi, *Il Regno Lombardo Veneto* (Turin, 1987) and David Laven, *Venice and Venetia under the Habsburgs 1815–1835* (Oxford, 2002).
12. Edith Saurer, *Strasse, Schmuggel, Lottospiel. Materielle Kultur und Staat in Niederösterreich, Böhmen und Lombardo-Venetien im frühen 19. Jahrhundert* (Göttingen, 1989).
13. Chiavistelli, *Dallo Stato alla nazione*, 80.
14. Ibid., 81.
15. Stendhal (Henry Beyle), *La Chartreuse de Parme*, chapter XII.
16. Ibid., chapter XI.
17. Marco Meriggi, *Racconti di confine. Nel Mezzogiorno del Settecento* (Bologna, 2016).
18. Peter Sahlins, *Boundaries. The Making of France and Spain in the Pyrenees* (Berkeley and Los Angeles, 1989). For the French sea borders see Renaud Morieux, *The Channel: England, France and the Construction of a Maritime Border in the Eighteenth Century* (Cambridge, 2016).

19 *Atto finale del Congresso di Vienna del 9 giugno 1815 ed altri trattati che vi si riferiscono* (Milan, 1859), 59–62.
20 Antonio Cantalupi, *Appendice al manuale delle leggi, regolamenti, discipline intorno alle strade, alle acque e alle fabbriche* (Milan, 1855), 148–61.

19

When Size Mattered: The Threshold Principle and the Existential Fear of Being too Small

Rasmus Glenthøj

Introduction

Nationalism is in general understood as an ideology that strives for the creation or the maintenance of nation-states and is often linked to aggressive and chauvinistic notions. In this chapter, I will argue that although this definition of nationalism may capture the essence of many instances of modern-day nationalism it does not capture much of nineteenth-century nationalism, as many national movements of the era sought at most limited autonomy or tied their nationalist aspirations to pan-nationalist or federalist projects. This suggests that Eric Hobsbawm may have been right in claiming that liberal nationalism between 1830 and 1870 was characterized by a 'threshold principle', a principle which affirmed that only states of a certain seize could survive.

This may in turn explain why many nationalist movements prior to 1870 were defined by unification nationalism and pan-nationalism. Even though there are all too many examples of nationalist chauvinism, I will argue that the movements of national unification and macro-nationalism that flourished in the wake of the Napoleonic wars to a larger extent were motivated by existential fear and fears of foreign oppression. To support these points, this chapter will use Pan-Scandinavism in Denmark as a case study.

Pan-Scandinavism

Pan-Scandinavism derived from the idea that the historical, cultural, linguistic and religious commonality between the Scandinavian countries warranted integration or union. As such Pan-Scandinavism transcended Danish, Norwegian and Swedish national identities and nationalism. Some wished merely for closer cultural, literary and scientific cooperation: this may be termed 'cultural Pan-Scandinavism'. Others wished for a fully fledged political union or a Scandinavian nation-state: this may be termed political Pan-Scandinavism. At the heart of Scandinavism lay the notion that, after centuries of war, rivalry and hatreds, the nineteenth century signalled an era of Scandinavian fraternity.

Political Pan-Scandinavism in Denmark, Norway and Sweden spanned from the end of the Napoleonic wars through the German Wars of Unification. It played a role in First Schleswig War (1848–51) and a vital role in the Second Schleswig War (1864), also known as the First War of German Unification. Scandinavists had envisioned that this war would serve the same unificatory purpose as military strife had in the Italian case and would have in the German instance. However, the movement ultimately failed as the Swedish government chose not to ratify a Danish-Swedish military alliance, which hindered Charles XV's plans for a federation and his efforts to draw Sweden and Norway into the war. Because of its failure, political Pan-Scandinavism has been dismissed by the clear majority of Scandinavian historians as a project doomed to fail as the Scandinavian nations-states of today are perceived as the only logical outcome of nineteenth-century Scandinavian history and nationalism. This traditionalist and theological approach blocks a more open understanding of (pan)nationalist movements in the period.

Defining nationalism in the nineteenth century

Few ideologies had a greater impact on the European continent during the long nineteenth century than nationalism. Most students of nationalism see it as a modern-day invention that arose from the turmoil of the French Revolution and spread across Europe during the Revolutionary and Napoleonic wars. But what did this ideology entail and can it be defined? There is no clear answer as the concept of nationalism is ambiguous and the field of nationalism studies is divided. However, within the dominant modernist school, the majority rely on some version of Elie Kedourie's definition of nationalism. That is:

> Nationalism is a doctrine invented in Europe at the beginning of the nineteenth century.... Briefly, the doctrine holds that humanity is naturally divided into nations, that nations are known by certain characteristics which can be ascertained, and that the only legitimate type of government is national self-government.[1]

Ernst Gellner adopted this definition in a shorthand version that holds that '[n]ationalism is primarily a political principle, which holds that the political and the national unit should be congruent'. This definition was later embraced by Eric Hobsbawm amongst others.[2]

To Kedourie this nationalist principle introduced a new style of politics that overrode existing treaties, dissolved allegiances and legitimized all acts in its name. 'By its very nature', he states, 'this new style ran to extremes.'[3] These lines of thought are not only mirrored in the writings of Gellner, Hobsbawm and other scholars of nationalism,[4] but also reflect a general post-1945 perception of nationalism as an aggressive and chauvinistic notion.

An alternative approach to nineteenth-century nationalism

This is not without reason. There are all too many examples of aggressive nationalism within world history, not to mention present-day populism, and there are plenty of examples of the nationalist principle put into political motion. However, when dealing with nationalism in *vormärz* Europe most cases were far from clear cut. Historians and students of nationalism tend to forget that the goal of nationalist movements, at this time, was not necessarily a nation-state. On the contrary, many nationalists were satisfied with a more limited degree of independence within a multinational empire or a federation.[5]

Accordingly, it may be more appropriate to see nationalism as an ideology or movement that strove to attain or maintain autonomy and unity, that is to achieve as much independence as possible.[6] Ideally, this may have involved the creation of nation-states, but it was not necessarily always the case. Even if pan-nationalism is left out of the picture, it was far from clear *who* or *what* belonged to the 'nations' of mid-nineteenth-century Europe. Some ardent German nationalists, for example, claimed that the Danes and Dutch in truth were Germans even if they did not realize it. Moreover, the borders between nations were blurry at best. Hungarian, Polish and Danish nationalists wanted their 'historic' borders, French nationalists wanted their 'natural' borders, while German professors in Frankfurt debated where Germany was to be found.

As stressed by Benedict Anderson, nationalism does not only entail feelings of hate and aggression, but also inspires love and self-sacrifice.[7] Even though visions of national grandeur and chauvinism certainly did play into nineteenth-century nationalist thought, national aspirations were just as much driven by existential fears and fears of foreign domination. This link between nationalism and existential fear should be seen in the light of external threats, wars and defeats that had a mobilizing effect and affected ideas of national identity.[8]

This is evident in German and Italian unification nationalisms, as nationalists in both cases argued that it was the absence of a united nation-state that time and again had allowed foreign invasions and subjugations. This was articulated in a prize-winning essay on the future government of Italy in 1796:

> For countless centuries our soil has been the theatre over which foreigners have disputed their claims. . . . it is therefore best to provide her [i.e. Italy] with the sort of government capable of opposing the maximum of resistance to invasion. That government is beyond question a unitary republic: *vis unita fortior*.[9]

In the case of the smaller nations, there was a Darwinist logic to national thought that can be expressed as 'expand or perish'; expansion meaning either unification with similar nationalities or national aggrandizement. In this respect, what appeared to be wars of national expansion could be driven by defensive considerations. This was evident in the nationalisms of Eastern Europe and Scandinavia that often tied into the macro-nationalisms of Pan-Slavist and the Pan-Scandinavian movements.

The threshold principle

But how are we to explain unification nationalisms and the macro-nationalism that emerged following the Napoleonic wars? This chapter claims that we need to look at the so-called 'threshold principle'. The threshold principle may be understood as an immanent heuristic tool within the liberal nationalist ideology of the age. The idea of the principle was advanced by Eric Hobsbawm.[10]

Even though Hobsbawm adhered to the equation of nationalism with the creation or the maintenance of nation-states, he recognized that the nationalist principle in the classical liberal era was only applied in and to some nations as it was curtailed by a threshold principle. Many liberals only supported the creation of nation-states if they were part of the progressive advancement of world history. Accordingly, the principle of nationality was only to be applied to nationalities that not only wanted independence, but were also feasible as nation-states. The latter entailed a certain size as only larger nations were culturally, economically, politically and militarily viable. Without the necessary resources, nations would not be able to evolve as nations nor survive as states. Liberals belonging to larger nationalities, in particular, saw human history as an evolution towards large national polities with sophisticated national cultures. To many British or French liberals, states such as Belgium or Portugal were too small to make sense, to say nothing of even smaller nationalities.[11]

The economic argument was most strikingly brought home by the German economists, most notably Friedrich List. He stressed that a national economy had to be of a sufficient size to be sustainable. To liberal Europeans progress meant growth, growth meant evolution and evolution meant expansion and ever larger units.[12] For List a state without a large population, an extensive territory and the necessary resources could only 'possess a crippled literature, crippled institutions for promoting art and science' and would 'never bring to complete perfection within its territory the various branches of production'.[13] To many intellectuals, the size of the nation indicated human progress and was to some extent seen as a precondition for national statehood. Small peoples whose cultural standards did not measure up to those of the great nations had to accept a subordinate role. This point was bluntly put by John Stuart Mill:

> Nobody can suppose that it is not more beneficial to a Breton, or a Basque of French Navarre, to be brought into the current of the ideas and feelings of a highly civilised and cultivated people – to be a member of the French nationality, admitted on equal terms to all the privileges of French citizenship, sharing the advantages of French protection, and the dignity of French power – than to sulk on his own rocks, the half-savage relic of past times, revolving in his own little mental orbit, without participation or interest in the general movement of the world.[14]

The boundaries of the state and government need not wholly coincide with those of a single nation. A given state or federation could encompass several nationalities per se, but they needed to be similar in their outward features to enhance the 'blending of their attributes and peculiarities in a common union', to quote Mill.[15]

Even the apostle of radical, democratic nationalism, Giuseppe Mazzini, believed in a hierarchy of nations dominated by larger and 'historic' ones such as the Italians, Germans, Poles and Hungarians. As 'people without histories' were of less importance, the Italian nationalist argued that Europe ideally should be comprised of 12 nation-states or federations of certain sizes, with similar cultural and linguistic features and with certain historical pedigrees such as Scandinavia, Germany and the Netherlands, Spain and Portugal, Greece and Bulgaria as well as Hungary and Rumania. The only 'true' nation-state in Mazzini's Europe was perhaps, not surprisingly, Italy.[16]

The period did see secessionist nationalisms such as in Greece, Belgium, Ireland, Serbia, Sicily and to a certain extent Hungary. However, these cases were not necessarily clear cut. Serb nationalism tied into Pan-Slavism (cf. Yugoslavia), Sicilian nationalism into Italian nationalism, and the success of Belgian nationalism and the break-up of the United Kingdom of the Netherlands was not a forgone conclusion. Moreover, liberal nationalists in regions such as Lombardy, the Rhineland, Bohemia and Moravia generally aspired less to individual nation-statehood than to fulfil their national aspirations as parts of a greater nation-state. Thus, the threshold principle may be seen as one of the main sources of unification nationalism or macro-nationalism.[17]

Unification and pan-nationalism

Unification nationalism and macro-nationalism were closely related movements to such a degree that some scholars believe the latter to be an 'aspect' of, or a certain type of, the former.[18] Indeed, the unification of Italy served as a model not only to German nationalists, but also to Pan-Scandinavists. Sweden was seen as the Piedmont of Scandinavia, Charles XV was referred to as the Victor Emmanuel of the North and politicians were hailed either by themselves or by others as 'our Cavour'.[19] But how should we understand these movements? Louis L. Snyder has defined pan-nationalism as a:

> [P]olitical-cultural movements seeking to enhance and promote the solidarity of peoples bound together by common or kindred language, cultural similarities, the same historical traditions, and/or geographical proximity.[20]

This definition is open to cases of both cultural pan-nationalism and political pan-nationalism, the former often being the stepping-stone of the latter, as is the case with nationalism at large. The major difference between pan-nationalism and unification nationalism is that the second only strives to unify one nation, while the first seeks to unite related nations. The supranational element in pan-nationalism has been seen by some students of nationalism as the reason why it has often failed as a political movement.[21] The unifications of Germany and Italy, on the other hand, have been seen as inevitable in national and traditionalist historiography, with Borussian tradition as the prime example.[22]

Three things need to be considered when comparing unification and pan-nationalisms. Firstly, the threshold principle underscored both types of movements.

Secondly, the transition between the two movements was fluid and the goals of unification nationalism were not necessarily any clearer than those of pan-nationalism, as a comparison of German unification nationalism to Pan-Scandinavism shows. The latter wanted to unite the Kingdoms of Denmark, Norway and Sweden, but Danish Scandinavists wanted the national ambivalent duchy of Schleswig to become part of Denmark while Swedish Scandinavists wanted a re-conquest of Finland, which had been lost to Russia in 1809. Equally, the problems facing German nationalism were considerable. There was the question of whether to create a *Grossdeutschland* or a *Kleindeutschland*, which in both cases would result in a state with significant national minorities.[23] Furthermore, German nationalism from the outset often slipped into a Pan-German nationalism that entailed a 'nation'-state which included parts of – or all of – Denmark, France, Italy, Bohemia, the Baltic States, Belgium, Luxembourg and the Netherlands. The Netherlands may itself serve as case in point as Dutch nationalists disagreed on the future of their state and their nationality. Should, for example, the Dutch unite with the Flemish or perhaps become part of state-speaking *Plattdeutsche* spanning from Dunkirk to Königsberg?[24]

Thirdly, the goals of unification nationalism were not necessarily easier to attain than those of pan-nationalism. As noted by John Breuilly, the severe limitations of Italian and German nationalisms prior to unification have been obscured by the success of unification. Many liberals saw it as a positive thing if smaller nationalities or nation-states accepted their integration into larger nation-states or federations. These ideas were not only found amongst men from larger nations, such as Mill, List and Mazzini, but also amongst Danish, Swedish and Norwegian liberals. We need to keep in mind that complex national and political identities were a common feature of the age. A Scotsman could be both Scottish and British at the same time, while a Bohemian could perceive himself as being a Czech in a cultural sense, a citizen of the Habsburg Empire in a political sense and loyal to the *Kaiser*.[25]

Even some secessionist nationalists aspired to create new nation-states in which they would unite with other people of similar cultural and linguistic features. The Illyrian movement tried from the 1830s and onwards to unite Serbs, Croats, Bosnians and Montenegrins into a South Slav nation-state, Yugoslavia, while Polish nationalists dreamed of a reunited Poland-Lithuania. The Pan-Slavist wished for greater national autonomy under the rule of either the Habsburgs or the Romanovs. Even though the goals of the Pan-Slavic movement were never attained it did result in the creation of Czechoslovakia and Yugoslavia.[26]

Prior to 1848, sentiments of nationality and the threshold principle were primarily advocated amongst liberals and radicals in opposition. However, these ideas were not alien to the governments of Great Britain, France and Piedmont: especially not *after* 'the Spring Time of Peoples'. In the eyes of James Hudson, British minister to Piedmont, the merging of smaller states with greater ones would benefit international politics as a strong Piedmont in the north would make sure that '[t]hat eternal source of discord, the "Italian question", would gradually dry up'.[27] Moreover, the threshold principle tied into Napoleon III's *politique des nationalités*. Despite its name this policy was not a policy of a Europe of nation-states. European states ought to be 'agglomerates' of peoples of the same race united under one ruler. Napoleon III's plans involved the creation of a Slavic principality consisting of Serbia, Montenegro, Hercegovina and parts of Bosnia, a Hungarian-Slavic Danube confederation, a greater Greek kingdom, an Iberian Union and a Scandinavian Union. These ideas may seem far-fetched, but both the Latin Monetary Union and the unification of Italy were partly a result of the Emperor's *politique des nationalités*.[28]

For Hobsbawm, the threshold principle was very much a theory, which few scholars have pursued let alone explored empirically. The threshold principle can help to better understand the unification movements of Germany and Italy as well as the macro-nationalism of Eastern, Central and Northern Europe. As for how to explain the emergence of the threshold principle itself, we should look at the recent historical events in Europe.

Experiences and lessons of the Napoleonic wars

The politics of nineteenth-century Europe were partly shaped by the experiences of wars and the lessons drawn from them. This is especially true of the Revolutionary and Napoleonic wars. The Congress of Vienna, the Holy Alliance and the European Concert were all responses to the great upheaval. Within this post-Napoleonic system, the great powers tried to find a European equilibrium to avoid or contain conflicts. This great power system was far from perfect, but compared to its recent past it was fairly successful. The security that this great power system partially provided may explain why less attention may have been given to another important legacy of the wars: a political sense of insecurity within smaller states and nations. Millions of Europeans had experienced that states with a long history could disappear overnight.

In the name of modernity the French Emperor had reorganized the continent time and again in a rationalization process.[29] Small political units such as city states, bishoprics, duchies and petty kingdoms did not make sense to the modern mind, as multinational and dynastic empires later in the century did not make sense to national liberals. Some states, as allies of Napoleon, had profited from the experiences; others were his creations and many adopted the legal and administrative reforms of the French along with a more modern conception of politics. However, the states of Germany and Italy had once more been either dominated or occupied by France and become the theatres of war for the great powers.

A couple of interwoven lessons could be drawn from these experiences. Firstly, small states had a limited sovereignty which could easily be undermined. This made fear of foreign domination a common theme in much of Europe in the following decades. Secondly, size *did* matter as small states had been swallowed by larger states. Hence, to survive one either had to be large or become large. In short, the wars had created an existential fear within many small European states and nations. These concerns were reinforced by ideas within the philosophy of history and economics which bound economic development and the progress of civilization with growth and expansion.

The German *Zollverein* can be seen as an economic response to the Napoleonic experiences, whereas the German Confederation with its parliament and army was a political and military response. The first was built on ideas of rationalization and economic nationalism and a step towards the creation of the infrastructure of a modern territorial state. The second was hampered by interstate rivalry in the realm of foreign policy, while its opposition to liberal reforms alienated German liberals and radicals alike.[30]

In Germany, as in other cases, the existential fear and historical experiences spilled into the new ideas and ideologies of the age: nationalism, romanticism, political and economic liberalism and popular sovereignty. Together they made up a part of the foundation for a threshold principle within liberal nationalism, which in turn underpinned unification nationalism and pan-nationalism alike. Hence, one of the main political lessons of the Napoleonic wars was that small states and nations had to unify if they were to avoid paying the price for their size or for territorial fragmentation; that is, foreign domination or extermination. The threshold principle should in this manner be seen as a product of modernization in general and the Napoleonic experiences in particular. Political Pan-Scandinavism may serve as a case in point as Scandinavist adherence to the threshold principle was, perhaps above all, born out of fear and trauma in the shape of a perceived quest for future national survival. This is most evident in the Danish instance.

Danish traumas and fear of Germany

The Napoleonic wars nearly brought about the dissolution of the Danish state. Their result was nothing short of a catastrophe for the Danish monarchy. It lost its navy, most of its merchant marine, it went bankrupt and was forced to cede Norway to Sweden, thereby losing more than 80 per cent of its territory and 40 per cent of its population. Moreover, 'the loss of Norway' changed the make-up of the Danish composite state. Prior to 1814, 75 per cent of the population had been Scandinavian and 25 per cent German. Now the numbers were 60/40.[31]

Moreover, the state's sovereignty was partly undermined not only by the Vienna System, but also by its ties to the German Confederation through the German duchies of Holstein and Lauenburg. The latter gave the confederation a say not only in matters relating to the duchies, but increasingly also in constitutional issues connected to the entire Danish state. To make things even worse it became clear that the Oldenburg dynasty would die out. As the line of succession was disputed in the German territories of the state, a change of dynasty made the future very uncertain.[32]

These fears for survival were enhanced not only by its loss of political, military and economic power, but also by the threat of being caught up in the German unification process. These worries should be seen in the perspective of Pan-German nationalism, Prussian policies and the budding conflict between Danish and German nationalism in Schleswig. The duchy of Schleswig was Danish, the majority spoke Danish, had a regional identity and their loyalty was towards the dynasty. However, Schleswig was historically, administratively and commercially tied to Holstein, the elites in the duchies were intertwined and their language and culture was German. Constitutional concerns, liberalism, regionalism, nationalism and the question of the succession evolved into a regionalist movement that demanded the unification of the duchies into a state only tied to Denmark by a loose personal union (i.e. only having the prince and defence in common).

These demands fuelled the existential fears of many Danes, especially as the population of Middle-Schleswig increasingly switched its language from Danish to German. Danish nationalists dreaded not only that Schleswig would be lost, but that German language, culture and nationality would expand into Denmark proper, spelling the end of the nation. Such concerns, however, worked both ways as a Danish cultural offensive into Schleswig fuelled the fears of Holsteiners and German-minded Schleswigers. These fears turned the regionalist movement towards German nationalism. Thus, the Schleswig-Holstein question became the litmus test of German unification nationalism.

The existential fear in Denmark was also fed by Pan-German assertions. The brothers Grimm, for example, suggested that the population of Jutland was German and saw its Danish national identity as a false consciousness, while the economist Friedrich List stressed that a unification of Germany could not be complete without Denmark becoming economically, politically and nationally German. A German state would need Denmark's coastline, maritime commerce, naval power and colonies. For List, this process was unavoidable, as Denmark was too small to survive on its own and unproblematic as Danes were Germans even if they didn't realize it.

Similar ideas in the German press can be traced back to Prussian government circles. It was advocated in the German press that Denmark should become a part of the *Zollverein* and the German *Bund* as the 'admiral state' of Germany. These articles were followed by a diplomatic advance. The reasoning behind these initiatives was that Prussia as an expanding state needed colonies, hence it needed Denmark with its sailors, harbours and navy. However, with the First Schleswig War Prussian policies changed towards a partition of either Schleswig or the entire Danish state. The latter possibility was suggested several times in Stockholm. These proposals made some Danes draw parallels between their situation and the fate of Poland in the eighteenth century.[33]

Strategies of survival

Danish politicians feared for the existence of the nation, but they disagreed on how to respond. The conservatives wanted to preserve the Danish *Gesamtstaat*. Further cessions would spell the end of an independent state. Hence, these politicians feared Danish nationalism, German nationalism, regionalism in the duchies and Pan-Scandinavism all alike. Danish nationalists wanted to excrete Holstein from the state as they feared that the German duchy would drag either Schleswig or all of Denmark into the unification of Germany. Schleswig was deemed vital as they believed Denmark would become too small to survive without it. Hence, Schleswig should be incorporated into Denmark proper to create a nation-state. The Pan-Scandinavists also feared the unification of Germany and their policies towards the duchies were the same. However, they believed that the Danish state had already become too small due to the Napoleonic wars. A united Scandinavia was the only salvation for the Danish nation. While there was strong disagreement between the advocates of the *Gesamtstaat* and the nation-state, there was a smooth transition between nationalism and Pan-Scandinavism. As the conflict between Denmark and the German Confederation escalated, Danish liberals believed that Denmark only had the choice between two polices: a 'German' policy and a 'Scandinavian' policy; and the clear majority of national liberals chose the latter.[34]

Nationalism and pan-nationalism

On their own the Scandinavian states felt exposed to the expansion of their neighbours, most evidently in the Danish case. In the eyes of the Pan-Scandinavists a Scandinavian federation offered Denmark, Norway and Sweden the possibility of becoming politically relevant, economically viable, more independent and less exposed to external threats as a union would have a sufficient population, a sizeable army and a strong navy. As stated by the prominent Pan-Scandinavist, Orla Lehmann, unification would ensure that the 'North' regained its power and its significance within world history.[35]

Some nationalists in Scandinavia, especially in Norway, saw Pan-Scandinavism as a threat to national identity. However, to Pan-Scandinavists, especially in Denmark, a united Scandinavia was the only way to secure the survival of their national identities as the interrelated national cultures of Denmark, Norway and Sweden would strengthen one another. Some went further and believed the three nationalities were one and the same. In the Danish case nationalism and pan-nationalism were two sides of the same coin in the same manner as mid-nineteenth-century Czech nationalism can hardly be separated from Pan-Slavism. Therefore, the widespread scholarly definition of nationalism as an ideology that aimed to create or maintain nation-states is problematic when dealing with the nineteenth century. Moreover, it must be concluded that existential fear was just as much a driving force within nationalist thought as chauvinism. In short, the threshold principle is vital in understanding nationalism in the wake of the Napoleonic wars.

Notes

1 Elie Kedourie, *Nationalism*, 3rd edn (London, 1986), 9.
2 Ernest Gellner, *Nations and Nationalism* (Oxford, 2002 [1983]), 1; Eric J. Hobsbawm, *Nations and Nationalism since 1780*, 2nd edn (Cambridge, 2002), 9.
3 Kedourie, *Nationalism*, 18.
4 Cf. Hobsbawm, *Nations*, 9; Dieter Langewiesche, 'Was heist "Erfindung der Nation"?', in Mathias Beer (ed.), *Auf dem Weg zum ethnisch reinen Nationalstaat? Europa in Geschichte und Gegenwart* (Tübingen, 2004), 19–40.
5 Monika Baár, *Historians and Nationalism* (Oxford, 2010), 9.
6 Smith, *Nationalism*, 9; Breuilly, *Nationalism*, 2.
7 Anderson, *Imagined*, 141–2.
8 Antony D. Smith, *The Ethnic Origins of Nations* (Oxford, 1999 [1986]), 7.

9 Denis Mack Smith (ed.), *The Making of Italy 1796-1870* (New York, 1968), 13, 15. As for Germany see Sabine Freitag, 'National Union or Cosmopolitan?', in Axel Körner (ed.), *1848: A European Revolution?* (Houndmills, 2000), 108.
10 Hobsbawm, *Nations*, 33, 42.
11 Ibid., 24, 30-3, 41; John Stuart Mill, 'Nationality', in Stuart J. Woolf (ed.), *Nationalism in Europe, 1815 to Present* (London, 1996), 43-4.
12 Gustav Cohn, *Grundlegung der Nationaloekonomie*, vol. 1 (Stuttgart, 1885), 447-9; Hobsbawm, *Nations*, 31, 35, 38.
13 Friedrich List, *National System of Political Economy* (Philadelphia, PA 1856), 262ff; Hobsbawm, *Nations*, 29-30.
14 Mill, 'Nationality', 44.
15 Ibid., 44.
16 Hobsbawm, *Nations*, 31-2, 37-8; Smith, *The Making*, 11; Stefano Recchia and Nadia Urbinati (eds), *A Cosmopolitanism of Nations. Giuseppe Mazzini's Writings on Democracy, Nation Building, and International Relations* (Princeton, NJ, 2009), 141-2, 236.
17 Cf. Dominuque Kirchner Reil, *Nationalists Who Feared the Nation* (Stanford, 2012); Hans Kohn, *Pan-Slavism*, 2nd edn, revised (New York, 1960); Hobsbawm, *Nations*, 33; Joep Leerssen, *National Thought in Europe* (Amsterdam, 2006), 154ff.
18 Breuilly, *Nationalism*, 255; Leerssen, *National Thought*, 154.
19 Rasmus Glenthøj, *1864: Sønner af de slagne* (Copenhagen, 2014), 266-7.
20 Louis L. Snyder, *Macro-Nationalisms* (London, 1984), 5.
21 Ibid., 6, 247-54.
22 For a revisionist perspective on Italy, see David Gilmour, *The Pursuit of Italy* (London, 2011).
23 Cf. Mark Hewitson, *Nationalism in Germany, 1848-1866* (Houndmills, 2010).
24 Leerssen, *National*, 18.
25 Linda Colley, *Britons. Forging the Nation 1707-1837* (New Haven, CT, 1992), 117ff; Rasmus Glenthøj, *Skilsmissen* (Odense, 2012), 177-88; Laurence Cole, 'Differentiation or Indifference?', Maarten van Ginderachter and Marnix Beyen (eds), *Nationhood from Below* (Houndmills, 2012), 100.
26 Cf. Kirchner Reil, *Nationalists Who Feared the Nation*; Kohn, *Pan-Slavism*; Hobsbawm, *Nations*, 33; Leerssen, *National*, 154 ff.
27 Smith, *The Making*, 193.
28 Roger Price, *The French Second Empire* (Cambridge, 2001), 43; William Echard, *Napoleon III and the Concert of Europe* (Baton Rouge, LA, 1983), 1-8, 163, 209, 295; Denis Mack Smith, *Cavour* (London, 1985), 140-2; Harry Hearder, *Cavour* (London, 1994), 100; Marc Flandreau, 'The economics and politics of monetary unions: A reassessment of the Latin Monetary Union, 1865-71', *Financial History Review*, 7(1), 2000.
29 Breuilly, *Nationalism*, 99.
30 Breuilly, *Nationalism*, 100-1.
31 Glenthøj, *1864*, 24ff.
32 Orla Lehmann, *Det gamle Mellemværende mellem Dansk og Tysk* (Copenhagen, 1868), 20-1. Cf. Glenthøj, *1864*, 20-3.
33 Aage Friis, *Skandinavismens kulmination* (Copenhagen, 1936).
34 Cf. Glenthøj, *1864*, chapter 4.
35 Povl Bagge and Povl Engelstoft (eds), *Danske politiske breve fra 1830erne og 1840erne* (Copenhagen, 1945), 332, 341.

Part Six

Re-Imagining Restoration

20

Was Moderate Representative Government Possible in Spain (1814–32)?[1]

Gonzalo Butrón Prida

Spain's transition to Liberalism

The debate on the Restoration in Spain has traditionally focused on the violent opposition between reaction and revolution, while the prospect of a moderate, representative government has attracted less attention from historians. The fact that the political transition to Liberalism was undertaken in exceptional circumstances has led to an underestimation of the forces of moderation in Spain, since the climate of political polarization tended to encourage division into two opposing and irreconcilable camps. Firstly, by 1808 Napoleon's invasion had initiated a long and multifaceted war, which must be examined at local, national and international levels.[2] During the war of 1808–13, in the absence of the king, the *Cortes* (Spanish parliament) was convened and the Liberal Constitution of 1812 (soon overthrown by Ferdinand VII on his return to Spain in 1814) was enacted. Furthermore, in the post-war years, military and social unrest, together with national bankruptcy and the colonial crisis, laid the foundations for the success in 1820 of a *pronunciamiento*[3] leading to the reinstatement of the Constitution of 1812 and the opening of a period of political confrontation that became especially critical in the last two years of the so-called Liberal Triennium (1820–3).

Moderation, inspired by old *afrancesados*, those who had followed King Joseph Bonaparte, and the more moderate elements among the liberals – and, to a lesser degree, among supporters of royal absolutism – lost relevance and visibility in these circumstances and the attempts of moderate politicians to install a more inclusive representative order in Spain failed. From 1814 onwards, they were inspired by the liberal political systems of France, Britain and the Netherlands. The French and British models were especially influential. They were well known thanks to the experience of Spaniards in exile. According to the moderates, those models, together with policies of forgiveness and forgetting about the political past would have enlarged the social basis of a new political order by attracting the king and privileged members of the old regime to constitutionalism. More than this, these policies would have given Spain the means to enter the ranks of liberal European states.

Spain's first Restoration (1814)

Ferdinand VII returned from France at the beginning of 1814 in a context of political uncertainty, given that the end of the Napoleonic menace had reopened political confrontation in Spain, which had been relatively dormant during the war. The return of the king led to the clash of two concepts of sovereignty. On the one hand was the sovereignty of the nation, presented by the liberals as legitimated by popular resistance to France; on the other was monarchical sovereignty, claimed by Ferdinand, whose supporters alleged that the *Cortes* convened in Cadiz lacked a constitutional mandate and was, therefore, devoid of power to change the political status quo of 1808. However, the return to 1808 was also controversial, since Ferdinand had not come to the throne through normal succession, but by backing an uprising against his father.

In a matter of months, the latent conflict between the king and the *Cortes* was resolved in favour of Ferdinand, due mainly to the huge popularity he had acquired during the war, when official propaganda presented him as 'the Desired One', an innocent victim of Bonaparte's ambitions. Once released, Ferdinand VII did not publicly manifest his plans for the character of his restoration and played skilfully for time. He intentionally delayed his entry into Spain, and on his return to Madrid, he refused to acknowledge any authority other than his own.[4]

The liberal government was weakened by the king's silence, the lack of popular demonstrations of support for it and its diplomatic isolation. In fact, the liberals found it much harder to exert their authority in Madrid in 1814 than in Cadiz during the French siege, when conditions had been more advantageous to Liberalism and neither the parliament nor the government had to concern itself with the king's opinions. Given that the king's consent was now essential to the fate of constitutional government, the liberals tried to force Ferdinand to swear allegiance to the Constitution. However, neither the *Cortes*, nor the provincial authorities, nor political propaganda was strong enough to raise sufficient support to force the king to accept the Constitution.

This political impasse briefly allowed moderates to enter the political debate. In early 1814, they focused their attention mainly on France and the Netherlands, whose political solutions to the post-Napoleonic era were influential for them. Articles were published in several journals in favour of the supposed policy of reconciliation based on forgiveness and forgetting which were guiding the restoration in Paris and The Hague.[5]

However, the carefully prepared coup by Ferdinand in May 1814, studied by Emilio La Parra,[6] ended moderate hopes. Ferdinand refused to accept not only the Constitution of 1812, but any limits on the exercise of his royal power. Ferdinand even waived convening the old *Cortes*, as had been proposed by both the famous 'Manifesto of the Persians' signed by absolutist deputies before the dissolution of the *Cortes*, and the royal decree signed by the king in Valencia on 4 May 1814. The announcement of the convening of 'legitimate *Cortes*' raised the hopes of some moderates, like Alejandro Oliván, who likened Ferdinand's proposal to Louis XVIII's Declaration of Saint-Ouen.[7] Instead, the return to the ancien regime, before 1808, was complete.

The reforms of the *Cortes* were annulled; the Constitution of 1812 was abolished; the liberal leaders were either imprisoned or fled into foreign exile. Ferdinand was, for the first time, effectively at the head of the government of Spain and he exercised his powers in a more absolutist manner than his predecessors. As Pedro Rújula recently pointed out, Ferdinand opted for a counter-revolutionary restoration inspired by intransigency,[8] which eroded the expectations of reformists and prevented them from cooperating with the monarchy in the difficult circumstances of 1814, when Spain needed to recover from political, social and economic disruption both at home and in its American empire. Ten years later, Lord Castlereagh, in a parliamentary debate about Spain's 1820 revolution, blamed Ferdinand and his reactionary policy for having betrayed his kingdom:

> The Spaniards had formerly been in possession of a free constitution, and by their exertions during the late war had again shown themselves worthy to enjoy it. They had obtained one by their blood and treasure, and Ferdinand had just promised to maintain it; and then, after destroying it, he held out hopes to the nation that he would give them another. This he had failed to do.[9]

The difficult defence of moderation under Ferdinand's early rule (1814–20)

Although politics in Spain entered a process of radicalization from 1814 onwards, there were some clandestine discussions among liberals about reform, outside the political mainstream. Certain texts attest to continued support for moderate representative government among some prominent political opponents of absolutism.

Moderation formed part of Díaz Porlier's manifesto published in Corunna (September 1815), in the context of one of the first liberal *pronunciamientos* against Ferdinand's absolutist rule. The document reveals that the possibility of amending the Constitution of 1812 along moderate lines was already being contemplated as early as 1815. In particular, Díaz Porlier – an old war hero – advocated a settlement modelled on the constitutional monarchies of Europe. However, he also acknowledged that the foundation of any change should emanate from the people, not from the king:

> Our object – like that of all Spaniards – is a Monarchy under fair and prudent laws, and constituted in such a way that ensures the prerogatives of the Throne and the rights of the Nation. We request the convening of *Cortes* chosen by the people, capable to make in the Constitution proclaimed by the Extraordinary *Cortes*, the changes demanded by our situation, that experience has taught us and that are demanded by the Constitutions of the moderate monarchies of Europe.[10]

Three years later, in 1818, Flórez Estrada, a former liberal deputy in the *Cortes*, exiled in England since 1814, published his *In Defence of the Cortes*, a document demanding that Ferdinand accept the 1812 Constitution after its revision along less radical lines, including the renunciation of the principle of popular sovereignty and the incorporation of un upper house of parliament appointed by the monarch.[11]

The documents associated with the El Palmar conspiracy – discovered and dismantled in 1819 – confirmed the existence of a detailed moderate alternative to Ferdinand's system of government. The conspiracy was organized by troops stationed in the province of Cadiz, destined to set sail for the Americas to fight the insurgency there. Unlike most previous conspiracies, its aim was not to reinstate the Constitution of 1812. Among its documents, studied by Claude Morange, was the *Constitutional Act of the Spaniards of Both Hemispheres*, drafted by a group of liberals and former *afrancesados* led by Juan de Olavarría, who proposed the creation of a new political order based on post-revolutionary liberal ideas.[12] Their Constitutional Act proposed establishing a bicameral system with a 'perpetual chamber' that would provide a moderating body which was clearly influenced by the ideas of the French liberals Benjamin Constant and Destutt de Tracy.[13]

The defence of moderation during the Liberal Triennium (1820–3)

In 1820 Ferdinand VII accepted the Constitution of 1812 after the triumph of a *pronunciamiento* led by Rafael del Riego, a radical officer, in the Cadiz garrison. Absolutists were relegated to minor roles in the new political circumstances, and adoption of the 1812 Constitution, now regarded as a symbol of liberty, met with little criticism in liberal ranks. However, both domestic and international circumstances gradually eroded this initial enthusiasm for the reforms of 1812. Political practice soon revealed the impossibility of reaching an understanding between the king and the *Cortes*. It was the first time that the Constitution of 1812 was in force while Ferdinand was present in Spain, and it was genuinely difficult to reconcile the interests of a king steeped in the values of the old regime with a constitution centred on the *Cortes*. Moreover, the impact of the Spanish revolution on Naples, Portugal and Piedmont in the late summer of 1820 made Spain a source of concern for the great powers, who were genuinely concerned about the survival of the Restoration settlement, and to prevent the spread of revolution throughout Europe.

The desire for stability led some among the anti-absolutist ranks to consider reforming the 1812 Constitution along more moderate lines. They hoped this would broaden support for it both within Spain, and with the great powers. Former *afrancesados* – beneficiaries of the amnesty decreed in 1820 and the restoration of the freedom of the press – publicly defended this course of reform, whereas less radical liberals preferred a more cautious approach.

The former *afrancesados* Gomez Hermosilla, Alberto Lista and Sebastian Miñano published a number of pamphlets and articles, mainly in the weekly journal *El Censor*. They sought to broaden support for constitutionalism by winning over the king and the more moderates absolutists, and so escape the predictable hostility of reactionaries in both Spain and the rest of Europe. Their proposals included the incorporation of an upper house into the Constitution, either through the creation of a new chamber, or through the conversion of the Council of State, which was appointed by the king, into an upper house.[14] They also proposed the reinforcement of the king's political position, the abandonment of the concept of popular sovereignty, and the imposition of property requirements for political participation. They continued to advocate conciliation, rather than confrontation, until radicals came to power in July 1822 after the failure of a counter-revolutionary conspiracy by the royal guard.[15]

In contrast, moderate liberals were more guarded in their defence of a revision of the Constitution. Although they controlled the government until mid-1822, they preferred secrecy to prevent radicals from discovering their plans, because, from the outset of the revolution in 1820, radical clubs and journals had openly proclaimed their refusal to accept any change in a constitution they considered perfect.

Apart from their preference for secrecy, the moderate liberals' revisionism largely conformed to that of the former *afrancesados*: Both groups supported a constitutional amendment that would bring the system in liberal Spain closer to those of Britain and France, which entailed a more balanced relationship between king and parliament.

This form of revisionism was supported by a group of influential politicians who were known as *los importantes*.[16] Many among them looked to the French Charter, regarded as a concise text which outlined the key framework of a modern political system, and could provide stability for Spain, because its abstract nature made it adaptable to different national political circumstances.[17]

Prominent moderates, as Count Toreno and Martínez de la Rosa, played a vital role in formulating these proposals. The latter, secretary of state from February to August 1822, is credited with having designed a political system that sought to reconcile order and freedom through a secret plan known at that the time as the *Plan of the Chambers*. Although unpublished, the plan was the object of several contemporary commentaries and critiques.

Radicals opposed these proposals in both parliament and political journals.[18] A pamphlet, *French Charter with Spanish Notes*, by Ruiz del Cerro in 1822, provides a good example of radical opposition to moderate proposals. While more general criticisms revolved around the idea that a constitutional amendment would divide and weaken the liberals, Ruiz del Cerro warned specifically about the personal and political interests of moderates. He accused them of caring only about business and obtaining high public offices. However, he also blamed them for trying to betray the social contract between the Spanish people and the state, embodied in the 1812 Constitution, by adopting the French Charter of 1814.[19] Ruiz del Cerro then made a severely critical analysis of the Charter, refuting the two main points of the moderate proposals. First, he argued that reinforcing royal power would betray the principle of national sovereignty; it would give one man 'complete authority', reducing the rest of the population to 'slavery'.[20] Second, he criticized the creation of an upper chamber as a return to 'old times when everything was arbitrary and power was abused'. He was particularly scathing on the appointment of peers to the upper house by the king, as this would convert the second chamber into 'an auxiliary army of the throne', an image reiterated in his conclusion:

> If we saw an upper house in Spain, we can rest assured that, from the day it is established, it would go to war with Liberalism and it would not stop until absolute rule in all its purity was restored.[21]

At the beginning of October 1823, a few days after the surrender of Cadiz, Salvador Manzanares, a former government minister, confided that the creation of a second chamber was unfeasible; the ignorance of the Spanish nobility made them 'incapable of forming a distinct legislative body'.[22]

Many liberal leaders also referred to the *Plan of the Chambers* later, mainly in publications in exile, and through autobiographical writings, published after the fall of liberal Spain in 1823. In London, *El Español Constitucional* and *Ocios de españoles emigrados* attributed the plan to Martínez de la Rosa and Toreno.[23] In his memoirs, Espoz y Mina (a former guerrilla leader) referred to Ferdinand's involvement in the plan; in particular, he recalled having been asked, during the summer of 1822, to support a project to impose a 'national representation divided into two chambers' on Spain. Mina described the plan as very advanced and as having already won Ferdinand's support.[24] The king's involvement was also indicated by the radical Benigno Morales, who thought that Ferdinand pretended to agree with the plan not out of conviction, but through pragmatism, in order to gain time until he could reclaim his absolute power.[25] Ultimately, the king's refusal to accept limits on his power frustrated any constitutional reform. Henry Wellesley, then the British Ambassador in Madrid, had already warned Castlereagh of Ferdinand's attitude, in February 1821, when he realized that the king was only prepared to accept the restoration of his own sovereign power and, at most, the convening of a traditional *Cortes*. This led Wellesley to express his disappointment about Ferdinand's 'very erroneous notion, both of his own situation and of the modifications of the Constitution to which the people might be willing to submit'.[26]

According to Fernando Fernández de Córdova, a young moderate, the plan was floated in 1822. Initially, Ferdinand was to commission Martínez de la Rosa to draft a conservative and authoritarian constitution, which would be imposed by a coup; only later would the government convene the *Cortes* to sanction the new constitution. However, Ferdinand rejected this and it was abandoned. Despite these difficulties, a fresh attempt was made in July 1822, led by Fernando's elder brother, Luis Fernández de Córdova, who again advocated the establishment of a moderate regime capable of reconciling 'the authority and the prestige of the monarchy with public freedoms'. It failed due mainly to the lack of any practical or ideological agreement among its supporters,[27] and because the government of Martínez de la Rosa did not rely on French support for constitutional reform.[28]

Although members of most political groups refer to the existence of these plans, the historian Clara Álvarez has only recently found a written version of them, the manuscript titled *Royal 'Fuero' of Spain*.[29] Dated 18 May 1823, the manuscript is not signed, but Álvarez attributes its authorship to Martínez de la Rosa.[30] Significantly, the text is dated a few days before French troops seized Madrid,[31] where Martínez de la Rosa had remained after having decided not to follow the *Cortes* and the king in their escape to Seville.[32] It is possible that Martínez de la Rosa raced against the clock in order to submit it to the French. Above all, the real significance of this document is that an alternative to the Constitution of 1812 was at last drawn up.

Clearly inspired by moderate models which the radicals had recently denounced, the *Royal Fuero* respected the requirements of both moderate discourse, advocating a limited monarchy for Spain, and official French declarations aimed at preventing a military intervention in Spain similar to those carried out in 1821 by Austria against the liberal regimes established in Naples and Piedmont. Louis XVIII's speech at the opening session of the French chambers in January 1823 was clear about this. It justified the envisioned changes by the moderates to the existing Spanish Constitution 'because [that constitution] did not emanate from the Crown'. A declaration made by France the following March stipulated the three constitutional changes required to avert war: the suppression of the principle of national (that is, popular) sovereignty; strengthening royal power; and the acceptance of a second chamber.[33]

The *Royal Fuero* proposed the restoration of the king to the central political position he had lacked under the Constitution of 1812. The text also accepted the creation of a second chamber, and set out a concrete plan for a bicameral system. The upper house, the *Estamento Real,* was reserved mainly for the nobility (fifty seats) and clergy (ten), but it was also to include twenty-five important individuals distinguished by their civil and military services, all appointed by the king. The lower house – or *Estamento de los Procuradores* – with about 200 seats, would be elected on a limited franchise.

In general, there is a clear parallel between the *Royal Fuero* and the French Charter. Their differences arose from the powerful influence of historical precedents among prominent Spanish liberals, who supported the restoration of an earlier Spanish constitutional tradition. Parallel to this conservative tradition of political representation stood the radical influence of the Constitution of 1812, itself. Another crucial difference between the French model and Spanish circumstances was that Louis XVIII voluntarily granted the constitutional charter to his subjects. The Spanish project retained the Council of State as the king's advisory board, it limited the number of seats in the upper chamber (which was unlimited in the French Charter) and the public character of parliamentary sessions, which were secret in the case of French peers and optionally secret in the case of the French Chamber of Deputies.

It remains unknown if the *Fuero* was forwarded to the French at the gates of Madrid. Nevertheless, it was clearly drafted to satisfy foreign pressure to reform the Constitution, in that it not only corrected most of the 'defects' in the Spanish Constitution officially noted by France as a pretext for war. It also considered British recommendations made during negotiations with the Spanish government to prevent the outbreak of war with France: Lord Fitzroy Somerset was sent to Spain in January 1823 to support and advise Sir William A'Court, Britain's ambassador in Madrid, to negotiate a moderate settlement with Spain. Wellington had specifically instructed Somerset to promote an increase in royal power to put Ferdinand VII more at ease with the constitutional system. It was expected that reform of this kind would not only promote tranquillity within Spain, but deter France from invading.[34] According to Evaristo San Miguel – Spain's secretary of state from August 1822 to March 1823 – the British suggested a shift from popular to royal sovereignty, the modification of the Council of State (which in their plan would henceforth be appointed by the king and thus serve as a kind of non-elected upper chamber), the addition of property requirements for election to the representative chamber, and the declaration that the time for making reforms in the Constitution had arrived despite the time limit established by its article 375.[35]

While the *Royal Fuero* remained unpublished, other proposals were published in Madrid. In *On amending the Constitution*, Alejandro Oliván advocated a bicameral system of shared sovereignty between king and parliament, and a restricted electorate;[36] simultaneously, an anonymous constitutional project sought to revive the traditional, pre-1808 *Cortes* by combining some authoritarian principles drawn from the Napoleonic Constitution of Bayonne, of 1808, along with other, more liberal principles, taken from the Constitution of 1812.[37]

Despite these final attempts to reach a settlement, the moderates' hopes for Ferdinand in 1823 were wholly unfounded. The easy advance of the French army, which took Madrid in May and initiated the siege of Cadiz in June, allowed France to tighten the conditions for an agreement, to the point of making the reformers' projects unrealizable. Not even Britain's efforts to push Spain into negotiations during that summer were successful, because of the Spanish government's intransigence. In April, San Miguel made clear the rebel government's determination to prevent any modification to the Constitution: 'Neither the Spanish Government, nor the Cortes, can enter upon negotiations or conventions whilst foreign troops occupy the territory of Spain.'[38] The proposals made by the Duke of Angoulême to the Liberals besieged in Cadiz confirm the renunciation of France's ambitions for a moderate settlement, which by then was reduced only to an amnesty for the rebels, and the convening of a traditional *Cortes*,[39] a proposition very close to those made in 1814, as a prelude to the first absolutist restoration of Ferdinand VII.

Increasingly besieged and abandoned, Spain's liberal government finally collapsed at the end of September 1823, unable either to find any international support against France, or to initiate a reform process which would prepare the way for a moderate regime. Ferdinand was finally 'liberated' by the French army, and any hopes for the establishment of a limited monarchy soon vanished. It was not until his death in 1833 that a moderate regime could be created in Spain, that of the *Estatuto Real*, a charter largely inspired by the *Royal Fuero*, but also influenced by the French Charter and by the guidance of George Viliers, the new British Ambassador in Madrid.

Notes

1 This work was carried out thanks to a research stay at the University of Oxford with the support of the 'Salvador de Madariaga' Programme, Government of Spain.
2 Gonzalo Butrón and José Saldaña, 'La historiografía reciente de la Guerra de la Independencia', *Mélanges de la Casa de Velázquez* 38 (1) (2008), 243–70; Jean-Philippe Luis, 'Balance historiográfico del bicentenario de la Guerra de la Independencia: las aportaciones científicas', *Ayer* 75 (2009), 303–25; Pedro Rújula, 'A vueltas con la Guerra de la Independencia. Una visión historiográfica del Bicentenario', *Hispania* LXX/235 (2010), 461–92.
3 The conditions of repression and violence imposed in 1814 reduced the channels of opposition to a clandestine one, hence the series of conspiracies that united civilians and military circles in their struggle against absolutism. See Irene Castells, 'El liberalismo insurreccional español (1815–1833)', in X. R. Barreiro (ed.), *O liberalismo nos seus contextos: un estado da cuestión* (Santiago de Compostela, 2008), 71–88.

4   Emilio La Parra, 'La Restauración de Fernando VII', *Historia Constitucional* 15 (2014), 205-22.
5   For instance, *El Conciso*, one of the most important journals at that time, published several articles on this matter: 'Nueva Constitución política de Holanda' (9 March 1814), 'Sobre la resolución del Stadhouder mandando hacer una Constitución política para Holanda' (20 April 1814), 'Las tres nuevas Constituciones' (1 May 1814) and 'Reflexiones' (2 May 1814).
6   Emilio La Parra, 'Napoleón y el golpe de Estado de 1814 en España', in X. Huetz de Lemps and J. -P. Luis, *Sortir du Labyrinthe. Études d'Histoire Contemporaine de l'Espagne* (Madrid, 2012), 171-91.
7   Alejandro Oliván, *Ensayo imparcial sobre el gobierno del rey D. Fernando VII* (Madrid, 1824), 61, available at: http://www.saavedrafajardo.org/FichaLibro.aspx?libroTitulo= EnsayoimparcialsobreelgobiernodeFernandoVII&id=1734787 (accessed 27 March 2017).
8   Pedro Rújula, 'El mito contrarrevolucionario de la "Restauración"', *Pasado y Memoria* 13 (2014), 79-94.
9   *Hansard* HC Deb 21 February 1821, vol. 4, cols 873-4.
10 *Manifiesto que dirige a la nación española la Junta Provincial del Reino de Galicia, de la que es presidente el mariscal de campo don Juan Díaz Porlier, comandante general interino del Reino* (Corunna, 1815).
11 Álvaro Flórez Estrada, *Representación hecha a S. M. C. el Señor Don Fernando VII* (London, 1818).
12 Claude Morange, *Una conspiración fallida y una Constitución nonnata (1819)* (Madrid, 2006).
13 Ignacio Fernández Sarasola, 'Conspiraciones constitucionales en España (1819-1834)', *Historia Constitucional* 10 (2009), 489-91.
14 Ignacio Fernández Sarasola, 'Las primeras teorías sobre el Senado en España', *Teoría y Realidad Constitucional* 17 (2006), 190.
15 Juan López Tabar, 'Por una alternativa moderada. Los afrancesados ante la Constitución de 1812', *Cuadernos Dieciochistas* 12 (2011), 79-100 and 'La moderación como divisa. En torno al ideario político de los afrancesados', in Rújula and J. Canal (eds), *Guerra de ideas. Política y cultura en la España de la Guerra de la Independencia* (Madrid, 2013), 135-55.
16 Joaquín Varela Suanzes-Carpegna, 'La monarquía imposible: la Constitución de Cádiz durante el Trienio', *Anuario de Historia del Derecho Español* LXVI (1996), 683.
17 Jean-Baptiste Busaal, 'Constitution et "gouvernement des modernes" dans l´Espagne du Trienio liberal (1820-1823)', in J. -P. Luis (ed.), *La Guerre d'Independance espagnole et le libéralisme au XIXe siècle* (Madrid, 2011), 122.
18 Clara Álvarez Alonso, 'Las bases constitucionales del moderantismo español: el Fuero Real de España', in I. Fernández Sarasola (ed.), *Constituciones en la sombra. Proyectos constitucionales españoles (1809-1823)* (Oviedo, 2014), 465-70.
19 Manuel Ruiz del Cerro, *La Carta francesa con notas españolas* (Madrid, 1822), 3.
20 Ibid., 7-8.
21 Ibid., quotations from 11, 23 and 39 respectively.
22 Thomas Steele, *Notes on the War in Spain* (London, 1824), 186.
23 Joaquín Varela Suanzes-Carpegna, 'La prensa liberal española en Londres y París ante la Constitución de Cádiz, 1824-1830', *Cuadernos de Ilustración y Romanticismo* 22 (2016), 331. Toreno, exiled in France in 1814, returned to Paris in 1822, where he was influenced by post-revolutionary liberals.

24 Álvarez Alonso, 'Las bases constitucionales', 457.
25 Iris M. Zavala, 'La prensa exaltada en el trienio constitucional: "El Zurriago"', *Bulletin Hispanique* 69/3-4 (1967), 383-4.
26 Mark Jarrett, *The Congress of Vienna and its Legacy: War and Great Power Diplomacy after Napoleon* (London, 2013), 311.
27 Fernando Fernández de Córdova, *Mis memorias íntimas* (Madrid, 1886), vol. I, 41-3.
28 Marqués de Miraflores, *Apuntes histórico-críticos para escribir la historia de la revolución de España, desde el año 1820 hasta 1823* (London, 1834), vol. I, 155.
29 The term 'Fuero' referred intentionally to the Middle Ages, when the different Spanish kingdoms had their own compilations of laws.
30 Álvarez Alonso, 'Las bases constitucionales', 453-99.
31 French troops entered Spain in April 1823 and in May they reached Madrid. The liberals only resisted in some coastal areas, like Barcelona, Corunna, Alicante or Cadiz, where the government and the *Cortes* sought refuge, forcing the king to follow them. See Emilio La Parra, *Los Cien Mil Hijos de San Luis* (Madrid, 2007) and Emmanuel Larroche, *L'expédition d'Espagne. 1823: de la guerre selon la Charte* (Rennes, 2013).
32 Pérez de la Blanca, *Martínez de la Rosa*, 215-16.
33 The consequences of the speech were debated mainly in the lower chamber. Louis XVIII's exact words were 'Let Ferdinand be free to give to his people the institutions they cannot hold but from him', and Canning was fearful that this would imply 'that the free institutions of the Spanish people can only be legitimately held from the spontaneous gift of the sovereign, first restored to his absolute power, and then divesting himself of that power as he may think proper to part with' (*Hansard* HC Deb 14 April 1823, vol. 8 cols. 872-96). The *Déclaration du gouvernement français sur l'expédition d'Espagne* (Paris, 14 March 1823) in Archive du Ministère des Affaires Étrangères, Correspondance Politique, Espagne, t. 721, fo. 135-7.
34 Wellington to Somerset (undated), attached to Canning to A'Court, United Kingdom National Archives, Public Record Office, Foreign Office, 6 January 1823, FO 72/268, fo. 5-12v.
35 'Note' (Seville, 24 April 1823), in *British Foreign State Papers 1822-1823* (London, 1850), 977-9. The article 375 stated that no alteration, addition or reform might be proposed until after eight years have elapsed from the implementation of the Constitution in all its parts.
36 Gómez Ochoa, Fidel, 'El liberalismo conservador español del siglo XIX: la forja de una identidad política, 1810-1840', *Historia y Política* 17 (2007), 48.
37 *Anónimo que tiene por objeto establecer el orden de sucesión en la Corona de España y establecer bajo una forma nueva las antiguas Cortes por medio de Procuradores y una Diputación Permanente*, in Fernández Sarasola, *Constituciones en la sombra*, 573-84.
38 *Memorial of the Minister for Foreign Affairs of Spain to the Cortes, 24 April 1823* (Seville, 24 April 1823), in *British Foreign State Papers*, pp. 968-77.
39 Archive du Ministère des Affaires Étrangères, Correspondance Politique, Espagne, t. 723, f. 126. The Duke of Angoulême to Ferdinand VII (Siege of Cádiz, 17 August 1823).

21

The Poles and their next 'Saviour': Alexander I and the Kingdom of Poland

Jarosław Czubaty

The role played by the so-called 'Polish question' in the process of the creation or, perhaps more accurately, the reconstruction of the political order in Europe after the collapse of the Napoleonic empire, is best approached with direct reference to the years preceding the Congress of Vienna.

The Kingdom of Poland ceased to exist in 1795. Its territory was divided among Austria, Prussia and Russia. A few years later, the dynamic changes in European balance of power created by Napoleon's victories gave Poles hope for the restitution of their own state under the protection of the French Emperor. The creation of the Duchy of Warsaw under the Treaty of Tilsit (1807) was perceived as a first step towards this goal. The second was the enlargement of its territory after the war with Austria in 1809. The next – in the opinion of many Poles – was the outbreak of war with Russia and proclamation of the restoration of the Kingdom of Poland by the *sejm* (parliament) of the Duchy (28 June 1812). Napoleon's defeat and his abdication (on 6 April 1814) seemed to mark the end of these plans. From 1813, the territory of the Duchy of Warsaw remained under Russian occupation, while the remnants of the Polish army fighting alongside Napoleon stayed in France until 1814. A new partition of Polish lands between Russia, Prussia and Austria now seemed inevitable.[1]

However, a new, more promising political project emerged from the initiatives of the Russian tsar Alexander I, who was supported by a group of Polish statesmen – initially few but growing with time – led by Prince Adam Jerzy Czartoryski, the tsar's friend and former head of Russia's diplomatic service (1804-6).[2] The Russian ruler, in assuming the role of protector of Polish national aspirations, returned to his old plan (previously considered by him in 1805, 1807 and 1810–11) to realize his *idée favorite*, the creation of a Kingdom of Poland under his personal rule, thus enlarging the Russian sphere of influence in Europe, and simultaneously gaining him prestige as the liberator of nations, a new 'saviour of the Poles', to take the place of Napoleon. He realized these hopes at the Congress of Vienna, although not without making necessary concessions to other European powers. The price for agreement in Polish matters was the cession of two departments of the Duchy of Warsaw (Poznań and Bydgoszcz) to the Prussians in exchange for renouncing their demand for the whole of Saxony.[3]

The Kingdom of Poland proclaimed in 20 June 1815 was smaller than the Duchy of Warsaw (by approximately 30,000 square kilometres). Nonetheless, its constitution seemed to guarantee the national rights of Poles, civil liberties and some forms of parliamentary control over the government. The constitution was granted by the tsar but prepared by a circle of prominent Polish notables, headed by Czartoryski, together with a few Russian advisers of Alexander I.[4]

The Kingdom's administrative and legal systems differed somewhat from the essentially Napoleonic patterns of the Duchy of Warsaw. The new organization of the administration appealed to the Polish tradition of collegiality. The system of one-man management of ministers or prefects which was in force in the Duchy of Warsaw was replaced by one based on collective bodies – government and district commissions (*komisje wojewódzkie*). Equally close to Polish tradition were the prerogatives of the parliament (*sejm*). The competences of the *sejm* of the Kingdom were wider in comparison to its equivalent under the Duchy. The parliament of this Napoleonic protectorate was supposed to be a kind of efficient machine for voting on projects submitted by ministers of the ruler. The right to debate was limited to the small number of deputies designated to work in committees assessing government projects. The *sejm* had no possibility of holding ministers to political account too.[5] The constitution of the Kingdom of Poland adapted the Napoleonic principle of superiority of the executive power over the legislature but the parliament had the right to debate on the government's bills, to accept or reject the government's reports concerning the state of the country, to submit questions to the ministers or to hold them to parliamentary account. Such prerogatives gave hope that the deputies could become the real representatives of public opinion. It also seemed that parliamentary opposition – if not against the king himself, then at least against his ministers – would become a natural element of the political system of the Kingdom. In contrast to Napoleon's constitution of the Duchy of Warsaw, the Constitutional Law of 1815 listed a number of civic rights such as freedom of religion, free press, inviolability of property and prohibition of imprisonment without trial.[6]

Napoleon was to disappear from Polish historical consciousness as – according to Alexander I's proclamation to Poles – the Duchy represented a 'wrong way'[7] to independence. Nevertheless, a great part of his heritage was considered useful. There were some elements of continuity in the administrative and legal spheres. Similar to the Napoleonic constitution, which granted by Alexander I concentrated full executive power in the hands of the king, strengthening his position through his influence on the judiciary and entrusting legislative initiative to him, not the *sejm*. The wide powers of the executive, alien to Polish political tradition until 1807, were also taken from the Napoleonic organization of the Duchy. The organization of the judiciary also remained unchanged. Moreover, there was no attempt to overthrow the principle of equality before the law. Political rights depended on wealth or education – the change in this sphere was the deprivation of the right to vote at assemblies previously held by officers or persons considered meritorious for services to the state, such as former distinguished soldiers who were not officers. According to Polish legal historians the political system of the Kingdom of Poland was more liberal but less democratic than that of the Duchy of Warsaw. The guarantees of the civic rights were clearly declared in the constitution while in the Napoleonic period some of them (like the freedom of the press) were not mentioned and the others resulted only from the Napoleonic Code. In the sphere of political rights in the Kingdom, the number of voters in parliamentary and local elections was reduced by property requirements higher than those in place under the Duchy of Warsaw. Another conservative principle – less democratic in nature than under the Duchy – limited the right to hold some posts in the administration to the class of noble landowners. In spite of formal equality in face of the law the nobility was also freed from corporal punishments.[8] Nevertheless it is worth emphasizing that the act of 1815 still gave the right to vote to almost 100,000 of the Kingdom's inhabitants – a number greater than in France under the *Charte constitutionnelle* of Louis XVIII.[9]

The final form of Alexander's constitution was the result of an attempt to reconcile the modern conception of the state outlined in Napoleon's constitution for the Duchy of Warsaw with Polish political tradition, Alexander I's fascination with liberal principles and his wish to maintain the dominant role of ruler in the state.[10] In practice, the new solutions outweighed Polish tradition. This satisfied all of Napoleon's former adherents among Poles who sought the strong state as a tool to modernize the country. More conservative circles of dignitaries and deputies were focused on the committee (*Komitet Cywilny Reformy*) set up by Czartoryski to prepare a draft for changes in the administrative and legal systems. The debates of its members showed considerable criticism of Napoleonic principles of government, particularly of the *Code Napoléon* as a civil law alien to Polish tradition, and of the enormous (from the pre-partition era perspective) growth of a powerful administration. This is evident in the emotional tone one member of the committee took against the Duchy's bureaucracy:

> Who ... squandered public revenues collected by the sweat of one's brow, usurped them and misappropriated them shamelessly? Always officials.... Who impudently denied an account of the citizens' contributions so generously dispensed? Officials, wicked officials, this villainous tribe of our common mother![11]

Although the Code was maintained as the civil law of the Kingdom and the number of bureaucrats was not reduced, the opponents of the Napoleonic model of state could still be satisfied by some solutions which referred back to practices and institutions derived from the 'national' past. These included the guarantee of citizens' liberties, like the principle dating back to the fifteenth century of *neminem captivari permittemus nisi iure victum* ('we will not allow anyone to be imprisoned without a court judgement'), relatively free parliamentary debates and the reserving of higher posts in the administration and judiciary exclusively for large landowners.

Shortly after the announcement of the decisions of the Congress of Vienna, the mood of Poles in the Kingdom, and many of their compatriots under Austrian, Prussian and Russian rule, was far from enthusiastic, as vast areas of old Poland remained outside the frontiers of the new state. Most of them agreed, however, that the results of negotiations among the European powers concerning the future of Poles – the most loyal of Napoleon's allies – could have gone much worse for them. The state was smaller, but the name of Poland appeared on the maps again. The Kingdom was connected with Russia only by the person of Alexander, who was simultaneously the king of Poland

and tsar of Russia, and by a common foreign policy. The Kingdom's own constitution, parliament, army, administration and legal system seemed to guarantee a sort of independence, no less than under the Duchy of Warsaw. The character of the ruling elite of the Kingdom appointed by Alexander I was also cause for hope. Composed of almost the same people who had ruled the Duchy, it was based on that group of aristocrats who had supported the reform during the so-called Great Diet (1788–92).[12] Alexander's personal decisions of this kind seemed to indicate his intention to rule the Kingdom in cooperation with men of public standing and authority, although many commentators were incensed by his choice of governor for the Kingdom: General Józef Zajączek. This choice of a former staunch supporter of Napoleon, instead of Czartoryski, the most independent and powerful of the Polish leadership, seemed to indicate that Alexander sought a mere executor of his orders, rather than genuine political partners.[13]

The attitudes of Poles were influenced by the new position the country found itself in, but also by their own expectations. The Final Act of the Congress of Vienna left the tsar the possibility to enlarge the territory of the Kingdom from lands of the pre-partition kingdom of Poland which remained under direct Russian rule (Lithuania, Volhynia, Podolia and part of Ukraine).[14] This possibility was gently hinted at in Alexander I's proclamation to Poles. The new ruler realized the Poles' disappointment at the smallness of their new state and explained the decision of the Congress concerning the territory of the Kingdom as an essential consequence of having to compromise with the demands of the remaining powers: 'A fatherland had to be retained for you that could not become a cause of envy, or an object of anxiety to its neighbours, or a reason for a European war.' Nevertheless, at the same time he stated:

> Let this memorable epoch which is changing your fate fulfill forever your wishes, your hopes and your feelings! May you prove you are worthy of benefits of your new existence and worthy of further improvement of your fate by your zeal for the glory of Our state and by unshaken faith in Our intentions![15]

Clear promises to incorporate parts of pre-partition Poland still under Russian rule after 1814 into the Kingdom of Poland frequently appeared in Alexander's conferences with his trusted adviser, Czartoryski, which helped influence public opinion. Most Polish observers realized that such a plan would meet angry opposition from Russian generals and politicians, and understood the need for caution. In such situations, gestures and symbols were of special importance. Alexander's decision to organize a separate corps of the Russian army was carried out in the territory of pre-partition Poland, uniformed in Polish style and subordinated directly to the tsar's brother Grand Duke Constantine, who was commander-in-chief of the Polish army. This act was widely recognized as the first step towards the unification of the Kingdom with other Polish provinces of the empire.[16]

Public opinion in 1815 was divided over the results of the Vienna negotiations on the 'Polish case', but it is difficult to assess precisely the influence of the different parties and coteries among the Poles. The most ardent of Napoleon's adherents kept quiet, although Czartoryski and his collaborators were afraid of their continuing influence on townsmen, poorer nobles and the lower ranks of the army. Some of them decided to demonstrate their objections to the new order: General Stanisław Małachowski, a prisoner of war in Russia, after returning home, placed a banner in the gate of his palace with the inscription: 'It is not over yet'. Many others resigned from service to avoid serving under the Grand Duke Constantine, who was known for his brutality and impetuosity.[17] Nor was there a lack of sceptics disappointed in the Congress's decision over Poland. The most eminent among them was Tadeusz Kościuszko. The former head of the Polish insurrection of 1794 initially supported Alexander's ambitions to reach the Polish throne, but he ultimately rejected any engagement with the politics of the Kingdom, writing to Czartoryski:

> Let us give thanks and eternal gratitude to the emperor for resurrecting the name of Poland ... but the name by itself does not constitute a nation, only the size of territory and [number of] citizens. ... In the current situation ... Russians would treat us as their subordinates because so small a handful of population would never defend itself against the intrigue, predominance and violence of Russians.[18]

The prevailing opinion was probably that of the realists. Notwithstanding the imperfections in the Congress settlement, and the risk resulting from the dangerous relationship with Russia, they nevertheless saw many benefits in the new situation. The existence of even a small Polish state created favourable conditions for the development of a national culture, education and institutions, allowing the new Kingdom to become a centre of gravity for the unification of all provinces of former Poland in the future. Two opinions emerged as typical of this group. A former Napoleonic enthusiast, General Antoni Sułkowski, wrote to his wife: 'This new Poland under the sceptre of noble Alexander will be small and poor, but it will be Poland, it will have this holy name ... it will be a centre of ideas and activities.' At the same time the former republican, Andrzej Horodyski, stated that admittedly, although the Kingdom was a kind of 'political purgatory', its creation gave Poles the chance to improve their administrative skills and 'political virtues', and one day to 'attain glory and the good opinion of strangers'.[19]

The legal and political system of the new state amazed many observers, who wondered how Alexander I, as the Orthodox, despotic ruler of Russia, could govern Catholic Poland as its constitutional king. The first years of the Kingdom seemed to justify more optimistic expectations. Their apogee came in 1818, when Alexander came to Warsaw to take part in the first session of parliament. He was welcomed by an anthem with chorus calling: 'we carry our supplication to Your altars/ Save our King, oh Lord'. His opening speech emphasized his respect for the Polish nation and his concern for its common happiness. He stated that constitutional experiences, collected in the reality of the Kingdom, would be useful for the framing of a constitution for Russia. The king appealed to Poles for patience and perseverance, referring almost directly to the plan of incorporating the Polish provinces in Russia into the Kingdom of Poland: the future would show if 'being faithful to my intentions I would further expand this, which I had already done for you'.[20] The parliament, although criticizing some administrative practices, accepted the government's report on the state of the country and almost all the bills prepared by ministers. Closing the session Alexander stated: 'You justified my expectations.... Oh Poles, I am going to realize my intentions. You are familiar with them.'[21]

Behind these scenes of liberal idyll, there were hidden tensions. Public opinion was shocked by Constantine's excesses as commander of the army. His brutal attitude towards subordinates caused several suicides by officers who felt that their honour had been offended.[22] The activity of the secret police intensified over time, as did the number of cases of unconstitutional arrest of individuals accused of insulting the authorities or disobedience. In 1819 a decree introducing censorship was issued.[23] All this was perceived as a result of interference in matters of state by the mentally disturbed brother of the tsar. More pessimistic yet was the opinion of Czartoryski. In November 1817 he explained to Alexander the necessity of acting in accordance with the constitution and of returning Constantine to Russia. The course of the conversation convinced the prince that Alexander's intention was gradually to extinguish the real independence of the Kingdom. As he wrote in his secret diary, Alexander wanted to:

> ... observe some forms which could ensure him the applause of the newspapers, to destroy the national character and courage, to separate the army from the country creating from it an instrument to act even against the country; to play at smelling incenses burning here and abroad to his alleged liberality; to have a constitution like a bauble using it in a way which would not limit his despotism.

Searching for motives of such a change in the currents of politics, Czartoryski found in Alexander 'fear of [his] brother, fear of Russians, fear of Poles, the desire to appease all, the desire to be considered as a liberal and great man ... adding some rightness, gentleness and the desire to do good ....'[24]

The course of events in the next few years proved that the pessimistic vision of the tsar's former friend was not unfounded. Already in August 1817, the minister of state of the Kingdom, Ignacy Sobolewsk, explained to the governor Zajączek the political *credo* of the ruler: 'His Majesty acknowledges these provisions [constitution of the Kingdom] in force for the nation, but not for himself. He will respect them as long as, in his wisdom, he considers them appropriate for the good of the nation.'[25]

The change of political course in the Kingdom was accompanied by a conservative turn in Alexander's European policies. Administrative abuses, and then cases of violating civil rights, provoked firm opposition from liberal deputies during the parliamentary session of 1820. Two government bills were rejected. About ninety petitions concerning violations of the constitution by the government were accepted by the parliament. 'You have delayed the progress of the restoration of your fatherland', said Alexander in his final speech to the *sejm*. The next parliamentary session was only convoked five years later. Its freedom of debate was reduced by many new restrictions.[26] The limited possibility of legal opposition led to conspiracies, especially among students and young officers devoted to liberal principles and the idea of national sovereignty. Growing political tensions led to the outbreak of the so-called November Uprising in 1830 and the deposition of the Romanov dynasty by the parliament of the Kingdom. After the crushing of the uprising in 1831, the constitution of the Kingdom was abolished.[27]

It would be difficult to consider the case of the Kingdom of Poland as a part of a modernizing *ancien régime*. Its territorial shape was the price paid for peace in Europe, but its creation was a kind of political experiment going beyond the idea of restoration. The political system of the Kingdom referred mainly to the Duchy of Warsaw. Its territory and ruling dynasty had no references to the past. The motives that led Alexander I to create this liberal constitutional monarchy remain something of a riddle to historians. The combined influence of personal and political motives is a viable possibility. The Kingdom could be simultaneously a kind of political dream entertained by a despotic ruler, and an experiment preceding reforms in Russia.[28] Its collapse was caused by the essential difference in political mentality between Alexander and the Polish political elite. Perhaps Czartoryski was right writing in his memoirs: "The emperor liked some forms of liberty such as one likes performances. ... he would gladly agree that all were free only if all voluntarily followed his will".[29] During the nineteenth century, hopes for the restoration of Poland under Alexander I's protection almost disappeared from Polish historical memory, although the anthem written for him became one of the most popular patriotic songs.[30] However, a fundamental change occurred in the chorus: 'Return to us our free Fatherland, oh Lord'.

Notes

1 Jarosław Czubaty, *The Duchy of Warsaw 1807–1815. A Napoleonic Outpost in Central Europe* (London, 2016), 13–36, 63–77, 169–89.
2 Jerzy Skowronek, *Adam Jerzy Czartoryski* (Warsaw, 1994), 177–98.
3 The Final Act of the Congress of Vienna, art. 1; Władysław Zajewski, 'Kongres wiedeński i Święte Przymierze', in Władysław Zajewski (ed.), *Europa i świat w epoce restauracji, romantyzmu i rewolucji* (Warsaw, 1991), 47–9.
4 Skowronek, *Adam Jerzy Czartoryski*, 211–12.
5 Czubaty, *The Duchy of Warsaw*, 41–2.
6 Zbigniew Stankiewicz, 'Królestwo Polskie 1815–1863', in Juliusz Bardach and Monika Senkowska-Gluck (eds), *Historia państwa i prawa Polski*, vol. 3 (Warsaw, 1981), 287–90, 295–7, 317–30.
7 Alexander I proclamation in: *Gazeta Warszawska*, 20 June 1815, 49, 887.
8 Marian Kallas, *Historia ustroju Polski* (Warsaw, 2006), 212.
9 Andrzej Ajnenkiel, *Polskie konstytucje* (Warsaw, 1983), 147.
10 Hubert Izdebski, 'Ustawa konstytucyjna Królestwa Polskiego z 1815 r.', in Marian Kallas (ed.), *Konstytucje Polski. Studia monograficzne z dziejów polskiego konstytucjonalizmu*, vol. 1 (Warsaw, 1990), 203.
11 Maciej Mycielski, *Rząd Królestwa Polskiego wobec sejmików i zgromadzeń gminnych 1815–1830* (Warsaw, 2010), 36.
12 Czubaty, *The Duchy of Warsaw*, 25, 47. See also: Richard Butterwick, *Poland's Last King and English Culture. Stanisław August Poniatowski 1732–1798* (Oxford: Clarendon Press, 1998), 275, 280–1, 289–303.
13 Skowronek, *Adam Jerzy Czartoryski*, 213–14.
14 The Final Act of the Congress of Vienna, article 1: 'His Imperial Majesty reserves to himself to give to this State, enjoying a distinct Administration, the interior improvement which he shall judge proper.'

15 *Gazeta Warszawska*, 20 June 1815, no. 50, 888.
16 Maciej Trąbski, *Armia wielkiego księcia Konstantego* (Oświęcim, 2013), 45.
17 Czubaty, *Wodzowie i politycy. Generalicja polska 1806-1815* (Warsaw, 1993), 217–18; Leon Drewnicki, *Za moich czasów* (Warsaw, 1971), 62.
18 Czubaty, 'A Republican in a Changing World: The Political Position and Attitudes of Tadeusz Kościuszko, 1798–1817', *The Polish Review*, vol. 59, no. 3, 2014, 77.
19 Antoni Paweł Sułkowski, *Listy do żony z wojen napoleońskich* (Warsaw, 1987), 35–36; Skowronek, *Adam Jerzy Czartoryski*, 205.
20 Alexander I speech in: *Gazeta Warszawska*, 28 March 1818, supplement to no. 25, 637–41.
21 Andrzej Ajnenkiel, *Historia sejmu polskiego* (Warsaw, 1989), 45–6.
22 Wacław Tokarz, *Armia Królestwa Polskiego 1815-1830* (Piotrków, 1917), 103–4.
23 Anna Barańska, 'Polityka polska Aleksandra I', in Wiktoria Śliwowska (ed.), *Wolnomularstwo Narodowe. Walerian Łukasiński* (Warsaw, 2014), 59.
24 Małgorzata Karpińska (ed.), *Dziennik ks. Adama Jerzego Czartoryskiego 1813–1817* (Warsaw, 2016), 415–16.
25 Barańska, 'Polityka polska Aleksandra I', 56.
26 Barańska, 'Polityka polska Aleksandra I', 60–2.
27 Władysław Zajewski, 'Powstanie listopadowe', in Stefan Kieniewicz, Andrzej Zahorski and Władysław Zajewski, *Trzy powstania narodowe* (Warsaw, 2006), 173–8, 193–4, 271–2.
28 Discussion concerning this matter referred in Barańska, 'Polityka polska Aleksandra I', 70–2.
29 Adam Jerzy Czartoryski, *Pamiętniki i memoriały polityczne 1776–1809* [ed. Jerzy Skowronek] (Warsaw, 1986), 381.
30 Stefan Kieniewicz, *Powstanie styczniowe* (Warsaw, 1983), 85.

22

Peace through Legislation: Law Codes and Social Control in Restoration Italy

Marco Bellabarba

In his book *Law and Revolution*, Harold J. Berman points out that 'the concept of a "body" of law that consciously develops in time, that "grows" over generations and centuries' is typical of the Western tradition. He states that it is assumed 'that legal change does not occur at random but proceeds by conscious reinterpretation of the past to meet present and future needs'. Furthermore, Berman argues that 'the law evolves, is ongoing, it has a history, it tells a story. Yet the evolution of law in the West began with a Great Revolution and has been interrupted periodically in the past five centuries by a series of [them]. Every nation of the West traces its law back to such [events]. The interaction of long-term evolution and periodic Great Revolutions is an essential part of history.'[1] If by 'Revolution' Berman means a fundamental change in the political and social system of a society – a rapid, violent and lasting change that also fundamentally alters the people themselves (their attitudes, character and belief system) – then there can be no doubt that the eighteenth- and nineteenth-century *Sattelzeit* (saddle period) experienced such a revolution.

It is well known that during this time all great Western European countries went through a phase of intense legal-code writing. These texts tell a story of their own, we might say. From a number of accounts, we know the story told by these texts rested on the belief – typical of eighteenth-century culture – that society could be reformed through the power of law. Yet eighteenth-century culture now faced the traumatic 'reframing'[2] of political structures brought on by the Revolution and by Napoleonic rule. Indeed, a transitional period started after 1815–16, very complex at the outset both from a political-ideological point of view and in practical terms.[3] The sovereigns of Restoration Italy were confronted with a set of problems that were modern, not ancient. The first task at hand was building a more centralized and effective government structure, particularly police forces able to rein in crime and vagrancy that jeopardized the security of cities and rural areas in regional states.[4]

In addition to strengthening government institutions, the second order of business, which the Italian ruling classes possibly felt to be even more pressing, was to stop the dissolution of social solidarity – the bonds between individuals, families and social bodies, now dangerously weak. One of the most obvious legacies of the Napoleonic era had been the creation of 'a society that was infinitely vast and complicated', more modern than that of the *ancien régime*, but also comprised a 'multitude of different situations',[5] a myriad of social strata and population segments that no longer rested in a state of equilibrium. This increase in social complexity resulted in broadening the application of legislative instruments believed to be necessary to ensure an orderly society.

To examine the process of (civil and criminal) codification as a means 'to rebuild the social edifice from the beginning' ... once the modern State has been founded and become effective',[6] as Damiano Casale suggests, is first and foremost to reflect on territorial and legal spaces. In Revolutionary and Napoleonic France, the *Code civil* was an ideal tool to rearrange the land and cancel the particularism of provinces, through a new system of national departments. For all its differences, the Austrian civil code (*Allgemeines Bürgerliches Gesetzbuch* or ABGB) introduced in the new Italian provinces pursued very much the same goal – to bring on the end to the *ancien régime's* pluralism, to its mixture of legal and administrative powers, and to the privileges enjoyed by individual classes. Published in 1811, as a code for only the German provinces 'for the whole German hereditary lands', it was later automatically extended to all lands annexed to the Empire after the Congress of Vienna. At least on paper, it left no space for local rights or for privileges granted to single provinces.

In effect, Habsburg authorities moved to introduce the civil code, as well as the 1803 criminal code, as quickly as possible. Starting in January 1815, a series of imperial *Patenten* ordered their immediate implementation. As pointed out by Pieter Judson, between 1815 and 1848, 'the Austrian regime preferred to spend its limited resources on achieving administrative centralization in its newly acquired provinces, rather than target resources to raise economic or cultural standards there. More precisely, when it did consider investing in infrastructure or education or in the local economy, the State always sought to create centralized Empire-wide institutions first, which added decades onto the time it took to establish new institutions.'[7]

Still, in spite of policymakers' intentions, the Austrian codes set forth in the early 1800s had to come to terms with the Empire's enormous heterogeneity. They accomplished this not by giving space to the particularisms of any given region or class. Indeed, such interests played no part in early nineteenth-century codes, which yielded to a principle of legal uniformity (*Rechtseinsheit*) reminiscent of the one that had inspired the French code. Rather, the Empire's vastness and diversity was confronted with difficulties on another important plane, namely that of relationships that existed between norms, individuals and social groups (families, but also associations, for instance). Each code possessed, one might say, a sense of society's stratification.[8] In other words, it offered a representation of individuals and of their placement within social hierarchies. This accounts for the usefulness of addressing – from a historical perspective – the relation between written norms and the image the latter provide of society, in order to examine how legal texts might contribute to the construction of social models and assess their 'performative' potential.

The fear emerged, among men in power and intellectuals of the time, that, following the decline of traditional institutions and the trauma of revolution, a society too fractured to sustain itself[9] might become increasingly prone to conflict.[10] The 'political instability and social unrest that were the hallmarks of Italy in the half-century that preceded Unification'[11] required prompt answers. In the field of law, it was this sense of weakness that put questions that many had thought solved, through the publication of the codes, back on the agenda. There were three key questions that confronted law makers at this time. First, what relationship was to exist between individuals – deemed the sole protagonists of civil rights – and social groups (families, associations, communities, churches and so forth)? Secondly, how was their place within the political sphere to be defined? Finally, what limits might be placed on the actions of individuals in relation to the system of power?

Piedmont's case is instructive here. During the crisis that took place in the late eighteenth century, the breaking up of traditional loyalty towards the ruling house had mostly presented itself as an affirmation of autonomy on the part of cities and peripheral communities.[12] This conflicting relationship between Turin's court and peripheral communities forcefully re-emerged after 1814, when Savoy was returned to Piedmont, and became the central element of all attempts at legal reform launched after 1819, by a commission led by Prospero Balbo. Not by chance did the issues touched upon have to do with the reform of criminal proceedings. The commission's most conservative members – among whom, notably, Joseph De Maistre – refused to acknowledge that the crisis of the justice system required a change in the laws, that is, in the royal constitutions (*Regie costituzioni*).[13] Other members in Balbo's commission called for the introduction of a procedure akin to the one in place under Napoleon, to reduce the influence of elites governing local communities.[14]

Overall, the proposed reforms aimed to strengthen the authority of judges, people endowed with the gift 'of knowing men, and the ability to access the darkest depths of their hearts,' magistrates whom the people were 'accustomed to venerating' and whom the sovereign could trust wholeheartedly. It was during these years of reform (interrupted by the 1821 revolution) that, slowly, 'the option of favouring codified law increasingly [tended] to appear merely as preferable for a certain, more modern legislative policy, over another, more traditional one aimed at conserving the so-called common law system.'[15] In the early 1830s, in his well-known report, 'On the progress of European legislation after the resurgence of civilization and science,'[16] Federico Sclopis endeavoured to prove that the road to 'civilizing' a people rested on the level of perfection reached by its legislation, the last stage of which appeared to him to be codification.

The code was thus viewed as a sign of 'civilization'. As noted by Sclopis in another passage, in the Kingdom of Sardinia 'public order [was] threatened by the widespread perception of an arbitrary administration of justice, which lacked certainty and uniformity'. The only remedy to this state of affairs was codification.[17] Therefore, concrete measures strengthening the authority of the restored monarchy were poured into this new container – the modern code system – primarily in an effort to ensure public safety.

This interweaving of old and new may be found, even more, in the Austrian civil code. The ABGB was presented to the Italian public as being more conservative than the French code, and indeed in many regards it was. The jurist Franz Zeiller, its de facto author, underlined that his code had not been 'born of the revolution,'[18] and that consequently – unlike the *Code civil* – it took citizens' different nationalities into account. Between 1816 and 1817, some commissions proposed developing a version of the codes specific to the Italian provinces.[19] In 1816, the jurist Carl Joseph Pratobevera published an initial summary on the reception of Habsburg laws in Italy in the magazine *Materialien für Gesetzkunde und Rechtspflege*. While acknowledging that the new subjects were somewhat familiar with them (these laws were an eighteenth-century legacy for Lombard provinces), Pratobevera did not fail to note that Italian provinces possessed a 'moral' sensitivity and political constitution unlike those found in the rest of the Empire. The government had to take the specificities of Lombard-Venetian provinces into account, for instance by introducing state functionaries such as pretors and district commissioners. These were supposed to replace the judges who serviced the feudal signorie still present in the Habsburg hereditary lands. As a matter of fact, Pratobevera feared all this merely served the purpose of rebuilding the traditional bonds of respect and obedience that bound peasants to their landowners.[20] His concerns were shared by other members of the *Umsetzung-Kommissionen* (one of which was active in Milan, and the other in Venice) charged with the task of studying the application of Habsburg codes in provinces where Italian was spoken.

A long report prepared between 1816 and 1817 by Giuseppe (Joseph) von Sardagna, a noble from South Tyrol,[21] in his capacity as president of the commissions, illustrates this perspective very well. The starting point is the ideological distance from the Napoleonic codes: a paternal, non-despotic sovereign like Francis I could not afford to impose his laws in the top-down way Napoleon had. Secondly, because of its degree of civilization, the Italian people would not have accepted an act of force by the government.

Sardagna quickly turned to more practical matters, and it is no surprise that his report to the emperor addressed the criminal code first. He believed the 1803 *Strafgesetzbuch* needed to be corrected – that is, made more repressive – to suit the behaviour of Italian populations. A code conceived for 'German races', among whom loyalty, religious piety and sincerity were shared virtues, clearly could not be applied to 'Latin races', devoid of such virtues. Indeed, the lack of these collective virtues affected civil laws as well, as exemplified by instances of forged wills, false witness depositions and border disputes, which the ABGB regulated too imprecisely.[22] The government's measures were thus motivated by a detrimental lack of 'morality' in the Italian temperament. This trait appeared to Sardagna to be almost more threatening than political disloyalty, for it had the potential to break society's foundations from within, turning citizens into 'irrational and dangerous individuals' – that is, individuals destined to make up what nineteenth-century critics were now beginning to call 'dangerous classes'.[23]

In 1815, the *Kreishauptmann* (district captain) of Rovereto, in Italian Tyrol, pleaded with the town *podestà* (mayor) to know which course of action he intended to pursue 'to improve morality, arouse fear in the perpetrators of crimes, and ensure, if possible, [the inhabitants'] safety and [their] properties'.[24] Spurred more or less by the same concerns, in 1828, Milan's Chamber of Commerce denounced before the city's governor the risks posed by the unruly behaviour of city workers: 'It is essential to put an end once and for all to the insubordination of the labourers; clear regulations must be laid down for all apprentices and for the training they must undergo; their exorbitant demands must be checked; they must be forced by means of fines to respect their obligations.' As a result, Milan's merchants further pressed for 'comprehensive legislation to discipline workers and workplaces, the need for which has frequently been voiced'.[25]

To face these demands, Austrian codes distanced themselves from the doctrines of eighteenth-century natural law and from the Napoleonic *Code*, too compromised by revolutionary ideologies. At the same time, however, they could not entirely yield to the temptation of reinstating a society based on class differences, as had occurred in Prussian codification, for example. The feeling of living in a period of great changes was pervasive in the Austrian society of the *Vormärz*; particularly in more conservative circles, this manifested itself in nostalgia toward a traditional world, in which the boundaries between privileged classes (aristocracy, urban bourgeoisie) and working classes were still clear.[26] Some scholars have spoken of a 'neuständische Kodifikation'(codification that continued to recognize social distinctions based on an individual's membership of a privileged estate)[27] with regard to Habsburg civil and criminal codes, to indicate their conservative characteristics. Yet this revival of an estate-based structure should be viewed not as a return to the past, but rather as an attempt to steer a very complex social and political transition from the top down, in an orderly fashion.

The illusion of achieving equality through abstract and general norms therefore clashed against the representation of society as being made up of very diverse individuals, families, social groups, mind-sets and behaviours. In other words, the Austrian legislation had to strive to create a new society, in the wake of what an important functionary of the Habsburg administration in Italy, Carl von Czoernig,[28] called the 'the catastrophe of 1814'. For Czoernig, it had not been a political upheaval (the collapse of institutions) as much as a social and cultural disaster, which had broken 'the ethical bonds which linked the prince and the people' creating a society based on selfishness and material interests.[29] All of the above made it necessary for the codes to strive to lay the foundations for a new social order, which 'should not proceed from assumptions of methodological individualism, but from the community in its appearance as a single, historical subject'.[30]

Family was one social aggregate the Italian and Austrian legislators of the Restoration focused on with great resolve. In this case too, the law makers had to distance themselves, at least at first, from the model of the *Code civil*, which had introduced meaningful changes with regard to paternal authority and the mechanisms of hereditary succession. The prevailing opinion was that it had been the French code's fault if marriage had been turned into a mere legal transaction, stripped of its sacramentality and rendered dissoluble through divorce. According to Giuseppe Sardagna's report, these norms had exacerbated Italians' proclivity for restlessness and individualism, favouring the continuous patrimonial disputes that had resulted in the 'ruin of many families'.[31] Even though divorce provisions were 'already a dead-letter'[32] in those years, many Italian commentators believed one of the Austrian code's more positive aspects was the reaffirmation of the religious nature of marriage. The mere possibility of divorce – lawyer Giovanni Maria Negri of Vicenza,[33] one of the staunchest supporters of the Austrian laws, wrote in 1815 – had shaken traditional Italian religiosity, bringing about 'scandals, turmoil, inconveniences and division' within common people's already precarious morality.[34]

The ABGB, those laws promulgated on their return by the Restored Savoy dynasty, and later Charles Albert's civil code, all placed the marriage contract front and centre on their agenda.[35] From a legal point of view, the attention paid to family and to its duration resulted in the dowry system being reinstated, and in the end of the institution of divorce and of equal inheritance among all children, as prescribed by the *Code civil*. But most importantly, the ruler's first concern was to restore the idea of family based on *patria potestas* (the power of a father, or *paternal* authority), perceived as an 'irreplaceable element of tradition and social order'.[36] It was partly a French legacy, for the *Code civil* had expressly sanctioned the bride's inferiority to her husband, effectively viewed as the only 'representative of the conjugal society' before the law and the State.[37] In part it was the result of the notion – expressed in the projects for the 1837 Savoy civil code – that the *paterfamilias*, viewed as the only source for family authority, was a reflection of that 'political paternalism' of sorts that belonged to the sovereign. In the words of a commission of jurists that was working on the code in 1831, the father, in his capacity as 'the sole source of family authority ... sets forth a living image of that sort of political paternalism with which the sovereign must be vested'. The principle of unity that family was based on thus served as the deepest guarantee for monarchy's own principle of unity.[38]

To educate subjects to feel respect for their king, they must be accustomed to submit to the absolute power of their natural 'father' since childhood. For the same reason, paternal authority was made to be long-lasting: in Habsburg territories, children were subordinated to their father until they were aged twenty-four (the legal age was twenty-one in the *Code civil*). Under the Albertine Code, women's legal subordination lasted even longer, until they were thirty or forty. Thereafter, they continued to owe their father, or grandfather, deference and respect even if they were married and had children.[39] Therefore, creating a sort of parallel between biological blood ties and the political bonds and allegiances that early nineteenth-century governments sought to create. Obviously, this entailed the careful supervision of family as an institution. The latter thus fell within the jurisdiction of criminal courts or the police, which were charged with the vast task of controlling private and public morality.

The insertion into the Habsburg criminal code, published in 1803, of concepts of 'public morality' and 'public scandal' redefined a series of behaviours as 'obscene' and offensive to 'public opinion' which now became entangled in the nets of the courts and the police. These expressions did not refer to a generic 'bourgeois public opinion' made up of newspapers, parties and political associations, but rather to the more restricted views of local elites, neighbours and family members.[40] Even according to Franz von Zeiller, the first objective of political authority was to be 'the promotion of public morality, and the removal of any obstacle [to its accomplishment]'.[41] In fact, it was no coincidence that, before the civil code even entered into force, the Austrian governors hurried to introduce norms pertaining to marriage law in the Kingdom of Lombardy-Venetia. Pratobevera claimed that the marriage law, in these years, was undoubtedly 'the most important' of the rights brought by the Austrians, and the only one that managed to keep the distinctive value of marriage 'as a counterweight' preventing its devaluation to a mere private contract, as had been the case in Napoleonic laws.[42]

Right from the start, safeguarding public morality was among the chief concerns of the Savoyard government as well. During a ministerial conference in 1817, the latter unanimously passed a resolution whereby it was 'necessary for the police to penetrate the secrets of subjects' domestic lives'.[43] In particular, it was deemed necessary to encroach on the private lives of members of elites in small towns in provincial areas, who, with their conduct, were expected to set an example for lower classes in terms of morality. So pervasive an intrusion into people's private lives – in the event of concubinage, adultery, illegitimacy or even conjugal violence – would have been unimaginable in the Napoleonic era. Conversely, public interest not so much in family itself as in family values now allowed broad discretionary powers over private life – even to the benefit of wives against their husbands, and of children against their fathers, as was often seen in courts of law at the time.[44]

Once again, upon coming in touch with everyday life – issues of public order, tensions between centre and periphery, and the procedures used by the police and the tribunals called upon to end such conflicts – the individualism underlying the codes fragmented, replaced by a more communitarian dimension. By the late 1700s, in much of Europe, criminal legislation had equipped itself with the necessary instruments to protect the 'quiet life' of their communities. Those laws mirrored the crisis of a society in which the ancient relations of patronage and friendship that had local noble classes and their lineages as their linchpin had stopped working. The *ancien régime*'s judges had always pursued the goal of resolving family conflicts through arbitrary punishments, extrajudicial compromises or friendly agreements between parties; but now that the foundations of that order had forever vanished, the old remedies of 'informal justice' no longer sufficed. For this reason, the supervision of private and family life had become a vital task. As law professor Theodor Hamer of the University of Innsbruck wrote in 1807, in the face of 'disordered families',[45] laws and court practices had to penetrate into the most intimate spheres of domestic life. It was by such means that the elites of the Restoration intended to rebuild the public sphere that had lost its old points of reference when it came to 'customs and habits, gender and family relations, religion and economics [which] were all political questions'.[46]

Notes

1   Harold J. Berman, *Law and Revolution*, vol. 2, *The Impact of the Protestant Reformation on the Western Legal Tradition* (Cambridge, MA, 2003), 3.
2   See Jeremy Adelman, 'An Age of Imperial Revolutions', *The American Historical Review* cxiii/2 (2008), 319–40. In analysing the transition from the eighteenth to the nineteenth century as it occurred in Iberian colonies, the author effectively portrays the features of the age of 'imperial revolutions', which resulted in a traumatic 'reframing' of those colonies' political structures.
3   Michael Broers, 'Cambiamenti ideologici e frontiere nazionali tra Stato napoleonico e restaurazione sabauda nella zona subalpina, 1814–1821', in L. Antonielli and S. Levati (eds), *Controllare il territorio. Norme, corpi e conflitti tra medioevo e prima guerra mondiale* (Soveria Mannelli, 2013), 509–19, here 509. As observed by M. Meriggi, in D. Laven and L. Riall (eds), *Napoleon's Legacy: Problems of Government in Restoration*

Europe (Oxford and New York, 2000), 49–64, 57: 'None of the series of institutions that had been overthrown during the Revolutionary and Napoleonic era was reborn after 1815: the feudal rights and estates, special citizen statutes, fiscal and judicial immunities that had been abolished during the *decennio* were not reintroduced.'

4 John A. Davis, *Conflict and Control. Law and Order in Nineteenth-Century Italy* (Basingstoke and London, 1988), 105: 'Following precedents set during the period of French administration, the policing of the pre-Unification Italian cities was also directed mainly towards maintaining and widening the separation between, on the one hand, the "fixed" or permanent population and, on the other, the more floating and marginal elements.' On border control policies in this period, see Marco Meriggi, *Racconti di confine. Nel Mezzogiorno del Settecento* (Bologna, 2016).

5 These forceful expressions are François Guizot's; they are quoted in Sandro Chignola, *Il tempo rovesciato. La Restaurazione e il governo della democrazia* (Bologna, 2011), 87 and 109.

6 Damiano Casale, 'The Many Faces of the Codification of Law in Modern Continental Europe', in D. Casale, Grossi and H. Hofmann (eds), *A Treatise of Legal Philosophy and General Jurisprudence*, vol 9, *A History of the Philosophy of Law in the Civil Law World, 1600–1900* (Dordrecht, Heidelberg, London and New York), 135–83, here 148.

7 Pieter M. Judson, *The Habsburg Empire. A New History* (Cambridge, MA, 2016), 128.

8 Pio Caroni, *Saggi sulla storia delle codificazioni* (Milan, 1998).

9 Pierre Legendre, *Trésor historique de l'État en France: l'administration classique* (Paris, 1992), 412.

10 Pierre Rosanvallon, *L'État en France de 1789 à nos jours* (Paris, 1990), 108 and 111.

11 Davis, *Conflict and Control*, 119.

12 Michael Broers, 'Revolution as Vendetta. Patriotism in Piedmont 1794–1821', *The Historical Journal* xxxiii/3 (1990), 573–597 and xxxiv/4, 787–809.

13 Isidoro Soffietti, 'Sulla storia dei principi dell'oralità, del contraddittorio e della pubblicità nel procedimento penale. Il periodo della restaurazione nel Regno di Sardegna', *Rivista di storia del diritto italiano*, xliiii–xlv, (1971–72, 125–241, 193 here.

14 Ibid., 161.

15 Gian Savino Pene Vidari, 'Problemi e prospettive della codificazione', in *Ombre e luci della Restaurazione. Trasformazioni e continuità istituzionali nei territori del Regno di Sardegna*, Proceedings from the conference held in Turin, 21–24 October 1991 (Rome, 1997), 174–218, here 191.

16 Federico Sclopis, *De' progressi delle legislazioni europee dopo il risorgimento della civiltà e delle scienze* (Turin, 1835), passim.

17 Ibid., 211–212.

18 Wilhelm Brauneder, 'Das österreichische ABGB: Eine neuständische Kodifikation', in G. Klingenberg, J. M. Rainer and H. Stiegler (eds), *Vestigia iuris romani. Festschrift für Gunter Wesener zum 60. Geburtstag* (Graz, 1992), 67–80; here 80.

19 Antonio Trampus, 'Le traduzioni italiane dell'ABGB: orientamenti istituzionali e politiche del diritto', in Caroni and R. Ferrante (eds), *La codificazione del diritto fra il Danubio e l'Adriatico. Per i duecento anni dall'entrata in vigore dell'ABGB (1812–2012)* (Turin, 2015) 79–85.

20 Carl Joseph von Pratobevera, 'Nachrichten über die neueste Gesetzgebung und Rechtspflege in den österreichischen Staaten', *Materialien für Gesetzkunde und Rechtspflege in den österreichischen Staaten*, ii (1816), 292–353, here 340.

21 The *Pro Memoria über die Einführung des österreichischen Zivil-und Criminal-Gesetzbuches in Italien*, referenced and used, among others, by Maria Rosa Di Simone, *Percorsi del diritto tra Austria e Italia (secoli XVII–XX)* (Milano, 2006), 163–7, is now transcribed in its entirety in Daniele Mattiangeli, *Die Anwendung des ABGB in Italien im 19. Jahrhundert und seine historischen Aspekte* (Frankfurt am Main, Berlin, Bern, Bruxelles, New York, Oxford and Vienna, 2012), 118–129. The *Pro-Memoria*, preserved in the Haus-Hof-und Staatsarchiv Wien, *Staatskanzlei*, Provinzen, Lombardo-Venetien, K. 33 (alt. 40), is anonymous, but attributed by Mattiangeli to one 'Herzog' Giovanni Battista Sardagna, whereas Di Simone believes its author was Giuseppe (not Giovanni Battista) Sardagna. The latter attribution is the more likely one, based on some internal notes in the manuscripts, the many references to Sardagna's doings, and the brief biography dedicated to him in Arthur G. Haas, *Metternich, Reorganization and Nationality 1813–1818. A Story of Foresight and Frustration in the Rebuilding of the Austrian Empire* (Wiesbaden, 1963), 190 in particular.
22 Mattiangeli, *Die Anwendung des ABGB*, 120.
23 Louis Chevalier, *Classes laborieuses et classes dangereuses à Paris pendant la première moitié du XIXe siecle* (Paris, 1958).
24 Biblioteca civica G. Tartarotti, Rovereto, *Archivio storico del comune*, Polizia, 1815, folder 33, n. 605.
25 Davis, *Conflict and Control*, 106.
26 Edith Saurer, *Strasse, Schmuggel Lottospiel. Materielle Kultur und Staat in Niederösterreich, Böhmen und Lombardo-Venetien im frühen 19. Jahrhundert* (Göttingen, 1989), 222–3.
27 This interpretation is proposed by Brauneder, *Das österreichische ABGB*.
28 On Czoernig's character and on his role in the Lombard-Venetian administration, first and foremost, see Marco Meriggi, *Amministrazione e classi sociali nel Lombardo-Veneto (1814–1848)* (Bologna, 1983).
29 Haus-Hof-und Staatsarchiv Wien, *Kabinettsarchiv*, Kaiser Franz Akten, K. 33 (alt 226): c. 375v, § 8: 'Über die Ursachen der Revolution in Italien August 1833. . . . Einfluß der Regierung auf Beförderung der Revolution- I. Durch die Gesetzgebung'. This paragraph lists the circumstances in which the administration of justice was not renewed: 'hier und dort befanden sich nach der Catastrophe des Jahres 1814 alle gesellschaftlichen Verhältnisse in einer Art von Auflösung, die moralischen Bande, welche Fürst und Volk verknüpften, waren zerschnitten, dem gröbsten Egoismus welchem durchaus nur materielle Interessen anerkannt, herrschet überall, die ewige Grundlage alles menschlichen Wirkens, die Religion, befand sich in fürchterlichen Verfalle.'
30 Inge Kroppenberg and Nikolaus Linder, 'Coding the Nation. Codification History from a (Post-)Global Perspective, in T. Duwe (ed.), *Entanglements in Legal History: Conceptual Approaches* (Frankfurt am Main, 2014), 67–99, here 148.
31 Mattiangeli, *Die Anwendung des ABGB*, 125.
32 Davis, *Conflict and Control*, 123.
33 On him, see Chiara Maria Valsecchi, 'L'avvocatura veneta tra diritto comune e codici: il caso del vicentino Giovanni Maria Negri', in A. Padoa Schioppa (ed.), *Avvocati e avvocatura nell'Italia dell'Ottocento* (Bologna, 2009), 521–624.
34 Giovanni Maria Negri, *Dei difetti del codice civile italico che porta il titolo di Codice Napoleone e dei pregi del codice civile austriaco* (Vicenza, 1815), 14.
35 Barbara Dölemeyer, 'Frau und Familie im Privatrechtdes 19. Jahrhundert', in U. Gerhard (ed.), *Frauen in der Geschichte des Rechts: von der Frühen Neuzeit bis zur Gegenwart* (Munich, 1997), 633–58, here 639.

36 Marco Cavina, *Il padre spodestato. L'autorità paterna dall'antichità a oggi* (Rome-Bari, 2007), 207.
37 Maria Sole Testuzza, 'Matrimonio e codici. L'ambiguo statuto della corporeità', *Quaderni fiorentini per la storia del pensiero giuridico moderno*, xlii (2013), 281-321, here 301.
38 Cavina, *Il padre spodestato*, 204.
39 Manlio Bellomo, *La condizione giuridica della donna in Italia* (Rome, 1996), 180.
40 Edith Saurer, 'La secolarizzazione dei peccati', in *Donne sante sante donne. Esperienza religiosa e storia di genere* (Turin, 1996), 255-84.
41 Franz von Zeiller, 'Dissertazioni e commenti sulla Giurisprudenza e Scienza politico-legale austriaca', Section I, *Giurisprudenza pratica*, xxi (1833), Part II, 68.
42 Pratobevera, *Nachrichten über die neueste Gesetzgebung*, 302; on 287-90 of the text, Pratobevera published Francis I's ordinance issued on 20 April 1815 on the introduction of laws pertaining to marriage. On this topic, see also Di Simone, *Percorsi del diritto*.
43 Broers, *Sexual Politics and Political Ideology*, 622.
44 Ibid., as well as the articles cited in Cavina, *Il padre spodestato*.
45 'In das Innere des häuslichen Lebens', see, Theodor Hamer, Civil- und Criminal-Justiz-Behörden in Tirol, *Sammler für Geschichte und Statistik von Tirol*, i/3 (1807), 195-289.
46 Bee Wilson, 'Counter-revolutionary thought', in G. Stedman Jones and G. Claeys (eds), *The Cambridge History of Nineteenth-century Political Thought* (Cambridge, 2011), 9-38, here 22.

Conclusion

Conclusion

23

Metternich-Kissinger: Interpreting the Restoration

Luigi Mascilli Migliorini

On 18 July 1814, prince Metternich returned from Paris and made his formal entry into Vienna. The crowds that greeted him triumphantly recognized him as the true victor of a struggle that had engulfed Europe for over two decades. He was the saviour of a state that had several times, in these past twenty years, been faced with the threat of extinction. He was the defender of a monarchy, the most ancient on the continent, that had sat apprehensively on the brink of a precipice throughout this time. The Emperor had even been forced to agree to marry his daughter to his most relentless enemy, the Corsican ogre, who had a singular and almost unpronounceable name: Napoleon.

That evening, at the theatre, he was welcomed by the notes of Beethoven's *Prometheus* overture: a tribute – or so said the newspapers – to a man who remained stalwart both in his principles and policies, when everything around him seemed to be on the verge of shipwreck and everybody wavered unsteadily, visibly shaken by fear. On that same 18 July, the common enemy that had been defeated by such iron determination, thus succeeding where so often cannons and bayonets had failed, now frolicked in the countryside of a tiny island on the Tuscan archipelago. Here, he organized with imperial resolve the lives of the miniature community of subjects entrusted to his care. These islanders reacted with that disenchantment and patience which was, and is, so much a part of life on any Mediterranean island. Nobody on that day could have imagined that the music of Beethoven would once again be needed to celebrate the glory of the man who, after Waterloo and a new exile and a new island (this time a remote one in the middle of the South Atlantic) would appear to the new generation of Romantic Europe as the true, suffering and heroic Prometheus of their age.[1]

Equally nobody, that day, could have imagined that the great Congress in Vienna, desired with such vigour by Metternich, would become the origin and basis of a century – though filled with alternating cycles of wars and revolutions – that could be defined as the age of European equilibrium. When Henry Kissinger wrote of the world born of restoration, in his now old, but celebrated book *A World Restored*, he had no doubts. The Congress of Vienna assured a hundred years of peace for Europe, unsteady but long-lasting, because for Kissinger it was bereft of those naïve and risky aspirations to universal peace that so quickly had corroded the edifice that had been built in 1918 at Versailles.[2] There is a phrase by Metternich – written probably after 1848 and, thus, by a man who was weighed down by the burden of defeat and the realization that his political season was closed – to which Kissinger is very attached. 'Only a shallow historicism – one reads – would maintain that successful policies are always possible.'[3] For the Habsburg chancellor, as for the American secretary of state for that matter, it was not, therefore, from its isolated diplomatic and territorial outcomes that one should judge the Congress of Vienna. Rather, it should be understood more holistically, with a complete appreciation of its logic and meaning, visible through the politico-diplomatic edifice that was constructed during these months. Individual territorial outcomes – it shall be emphasized later in this chapter – were characterized by a constitutive fragility tied to the dynamics of the many diplomatic adjustments and decisions made at Vienna. These were linked, it could be said, to a re-balancing of balance, that is to a continuous reassessment of relative power that in any system of balance of power is by its very nature in constant flux. The other side of the system of equilibrium created at Vienna is to be found in its static dimension, so to speak, which forms a sort of perimeter that constrains the forces in play, and forms a benchmark to which one can return, after the necessary adjustments have been made between competing powers, and despite such alterations, in terms of detail, the system and its guiding principle remain intact.

Vienna was born from a cold evaluation of the forces in play and from a need to give these forces, so as to avoid their being in conflict, a point of equilibrium capable of impeding any temptation towards hegemony, a temptation that had possessed, and at the same time had destroyed, a great protagonist of history like Napoleon. This was a Europe that was, therefore, multipolar and rich in political actors, and furnished with a well-heeled synthetic form of governance vested in the five great powers – France, Great Britain, Prussia, Russia and Austria – to whom fell the responsibility to calibrate and adjust the scales of the international system each time shifts of power made adjustments in weights and measures necessary. It was also thanks to this arrangement that the Congress of Vienna would never become a victor's peace (like Versailles was from the outset and remained throughout). Equilibrium cannot be constructed on the annihilation of the enemy, but rather is assembled on the stable restructuring of those principles and practices that give rise to a healthy system of international relations.[4]

Vienna finds its most natural comparison with the, by then distant, peace of Westphalia, much more so than with the subsequent peace of Versailles, to which it is so often wrongly juxtaposed. This earlier peace was the object of a number of reflections on the part of Metternich in the years following the Congress and is epitomized – with the force of a thunderbolt – in a singular pamphlet, written by an anonymous Italian, which found its way onto the crowded desk of the chancellor:

> Give back everything to everybody – one reads – re-establish ancient dynasties and principalities, return the world to the state in which it was half a century ago; is this really the principle and aim of the great alliance? It is impossible, without creating dangerous upheavals, to reverse the changes unleashed in the past fifty years within the policies of states, nature of government, the habits of

individuals, and the thoughts and aims of enlightened monarchs. Rather will not the reorganisation of Europe, on the basis of the great equilibrium that was introduced, by the well-known treaty of Westphalia, not give rise to changed circumstances, by which new powers will emerge, and others will be enlarged?[5]

It appears immediately evident, thus, that the construction of a new principle, on which rested the European equilibrium, required that Metternich broaden both his thinking and his policies. Restoration cannot be seen, in any sense, as a return to that *ancien régime* – as he himself would observe years later – which in any case had collapsed even before the French Revolution had cut it down. Restoration is a uniquely delicate architectural process, indeed like a real restoration, it uses materials from the past, including ruins and debris, and then erects a solid, new and long-lasting building.[6]

This period marks a watershed in the history of the World. It was a time of transition. At this moment in time, the edifice of past was in ruins; and the new edifice was not yet standing. It remains in construction and our contemporaries are the workmen building it. From every corner, there arrive architects; but none of them will see their work ever finished, because a human life is too brief.[7]

Prince Metternich was over seventy when – in December 1844 – he wrote these lines that were to open the *avant-propos* of his eight-volume memoirs, which appeared thanks to, as is well known, the efforts of his son Richard. In 1880 simultaneous French and German editions were published, and they are both a linguistic and intensive tribute to the man born in the Rhineland; a man who, on the banks of this river, the Rhine, had always appreciated the need to bring together rather than distance its two banks (a tragic lesson that would eventually be learned in the twentieth century).[8]

The imagery he uses – that of buildings and architecture – is not unusual and frequently appears in his writing, especially (notes, family and private correspondence) where he tells of himself, and where his interior life becomes most manifest. Thus, we find such imagery at different times and in different circumstances: even later than the previous example, in 1852, when he returns from the exile imposed on him by the 1848 Revolution and when he reweaves, together with the new Emperor Franz-Josef, the threads of a political discourse that sought to rebuild an Austrian Empire swept by revolution.[9] Or earlier – in October 1822 – when on the contrary, he was at the zenith of his power and might in Europe. Indeed, exactly on this occasion – the Congress of Verona – which appeared like a triumph, does prince Metternich abandon himself to an unusual confession which he uses as a *topos* that will become habitual in his writings:

I arrived in the world either too early or too late – he writes – at this moment I do not feel good for anything. If I had been born earlier I would have savoured the joys afforded by that time; If I had come later I would have been useful in helping with rebuilding; today I pass my days trying to restore crumbling buildings.[10]

Just a short step away, on the opposite side, so to speak, of the barricades to those ruins on which sat a *jeunesse soucieuse* (anxious youth) described so well in the

Confessions d'un enfant du siècle, which was the manifesto of a disgruntled generation for which Alfred de Musset made himself the mouthpiece (staying with ruins, one could even take a step back, and recall the memorable reflections of Volney in his *Ruines ou méditation sur les révolutions des Empires* of 1797) and the situation becomes clearer.[11]

Recovered within its architectural etymon, or if one prefers its larger historico-artistic dimension, the Restoration assumes a comprehensibility on which only a few historiographical reflections, in its now 200-year history, have guided interpretation.[12] The burdensome, sometimes vain, attempt to reconstruct buildings from their debris, that is to say, buildings which – obviously – can be political, institutional, social, cultural, mental – has nothing to do with the idea that the Restoration is a simple mechanical operation of temporal readjustment, a winding backwards – if one likes – of the hands of the clock.

Among the sharpest political actors of the age, where one certainly finds prince Metternich, there was a realization that what they were surrounded by was a theatre of relics and wreckages. Reconstruction meant, therefore, to collect with patience, where possible, that which had survived, and try to return it to a form and function fit to give meaning to what would otherwise merely seem a desolate landscape. Such relics cannot be relegated simply to a distant past, to the *ancien régime*, inspired by Tocqueville's masterpiece, many will assert, with ever greater insistence, that they are also of the present. The collapse of the old world did not just affect the remote past, but also a more recent past, as a matter of fact, it had even touched a future once known with the appellation of Revolution. It would have been naïve after 1815 to design a clock that went backwards in time, so it would have been equally naïve (and recalled many traumas) to rewrite and fast forward time, forcing the calendar towards new, ephemeral rhythms, to rename the months and years that already belonged, as one should remember, to the baggage of an almost exotic age.

The materials to be used for the foundations of the post-Napoleonic edifice were very jumbled and spoke the language of two equally lost illusions. It was pointless to hope that from this confusion could be born a solid edifice, which could clearly return to an era, an ideology or a style. One needed to dig, to sort out the different accumulations and contaminations of time. It was as if this was a first experiment in the 'post-modern' that now – in this delicate and enchanting changeover, in this transition, as described by Metternich between 1815 and 1818, which we prefer to designate as the age of Romanticism – re-proposed the question 'what was modern?'

This was a difficult question and the Revolution had both reinforced its meaning and its contractions. If, indeed, the substantial victory of the 'Moderns' in the *Querelle* that had been waged towards the end of the seventeenth century had traversed the subsequent hundred years with a general sense of consensus, then the Revolution with its excesses had revealed all the harshness of that superiority with which the present had affirmed in its ultimate victory. The revolutionary rupture, with its scorched earth policy towards the past, burned every vessel, and its content, in port. This gave rise to a Terror, which many imputed to such temporal abstractions, in which the Revolution perhaps wished or rather had ended up situating itself. Even more so, the Revolution had sought to transfer 'the Modern' onto the terrain of politics with a force undoubtedly motivated by circumstances. This accelerated processes that up to that time had remained imprecise, often consciously and deliberately imprecise in a European culture – that of Enlightenment – that found it difficult to translate into a political language – especially the concept of sovereignty from below and consequently the notion of individual representation – that modernity that was imposing itself in the sphere of culture and customs.

It was unimaginable, however, after 1815, that all this had not happened. It was impossible to think, or plan, without taking into account that modernity had shown its face in the historical process and that, after withdrawing like a wave, had left on the beach all manner of relics and shipwrecks. Indeed, it was at this juncture that the restored monarchies reluctantly needed to make some room for limited but significant 'constitutionalizations' –for example the *chartes octroyées* – that provided legitimation and concrete practices. Equally, the process of Napoleonic legal codification imposed itself, even for them, as an indispensable reference point of a juridical culture whereby the relationship between individual and equal subjects before the law was defined. On the other hand – as was the case in the reflections of a man such as Benjamin Constant – the apparently democratic excesses of the Terror, and subsequent regimes, forced 'new men' who lived and survived through the revolutionary experience to rethink the question of how to represent popular sovereignty. They started a journey in this time of *instaurazione/restaurazione* (that is, inauguration-creation/restoration) towards a political culture of the Modern in which, not the French Revolution, but that singular hircocervus of modernity, the two English revolutions of the second half of the seventeenth century, became the key points of reference.[13]

From one side, as on the other, everybody was impelled toward rediscovery, towards the restoration of a tradition that could never be ... Some had believed – and this was completely Winckelmann's case – that tradition could be entirely founded on antiquity. In Europe, too much water has flowed, during the Revolution and Empire, under the bridge of the old seventeenth-century *Querelle des Modernes*. One needed to widen the horizons of the past, seek out new chronologies and new legitimations. Essentially, 'the century of history' had opened up; it was a spectacular collective dig into the past, in which all European culture participated, with goals and results that were to be extremely diverse. Yet it was held together by the common realization that a tradition was necessary, especially after the radical rupture represented by the French Revolution (and the Napoleonic adventure), but this tradition could not have the character, content and especially the same spaces as that which had preceded it.[14] Totally European in essence, this effort in recasting tradition, in fact, poured itself out onto frameworks that always more clearly would appear and define themselves as national spaces. To return, it is true, to the reconstruction of a shared Europe, but a Europe of Nations, in which the work of reconstruction had been placed at the service of the identification and legitimation of specific communitarian identities. Those familiar with the teachings of men like Giuseppe Mazzini, who are so difficult to define according to their political battles, so ponderous in their struggle to establish a tradition that would not inextricably link them to the French Revolution, will easily understand the sheer variety of opportunities and inspirations they draw from the Restoration and its lexicon.

The central concern, therefore, of the men of the European Restoration was to avoid that fragmentation, beginning with political fragmentation, which could be perceived in the many struggles to build a tradition, would end with compromising, not the possibility of a tradition, but rather causing its very subject matter to disappear; that is a mutated Europe, which this tradition, in its final analysis, sought to settle. From such concerns were born fundamental works of the historical culture of the nineteenth century, such as Francois Guizot's *History of European Civilization*. Such works were born of the conviction that painstaking, and at the same time strong, efforts would weave together those forgotten linkages scattered throughout national biographies. This scholarly effort mirrored the craft of the restorer. These men ventured into the hidden depths of events, examined specific communities of varying sizes and differentiated amongst themselves, before which national space opened itself before them. At end of their journey they beheld a complete fresco, a civilization, which was hardly less authoritative than those of the past, which were built on different spaces and sources of legitimacy.[15]

The Protestant Guizot, therefore, could indulge in a different type of Universalism, while for the Catholic world there was more an inclination towards a renunciation of Universalism. Indeed, the years of the Restoration offer Catholicism an extraordinary opportunity to rethink its relationship with political reality and history. In truth, this had been begun many years previously by a determined romantic, like Novalis, who in 1799 in his *Christianity and Europe* had produced the manifesto of a Europe that could survive the crisis and lesson of Revolution through an innovative reconsideration of its origin and religious tradition. It was on this road that the Catholicism of the Restoration drove forth with determination. Chateaubriand, Lamennais, de Maistre, Lacordaire are but a few of the names that can be cited so as to recall how much poorer we would be if the relationship between Restoration and Catholicism were merely reduced to the political resistances and rejections of the Church of Rome.

It almost seems, at times, that the 'new man' who the Revolution sought out in its battles, on the streets of Paris, Chateaubriand glimpsed in the forests of America that hosted him as an exile. An innocent and original being that through his relationship which nature cultivated a relationship with the divine. Religiosity during the age of Restoration is a complex story, to say the least: a history that was probed – at the height of the last World War – by a richly sophisticated and intellectual personality as was the Italian historian Adolfo Omodeo. His reflections, incipient, unfinished, but extremely lively appeared in instalments between May 1940 and July 1943 in the journal *Critica*. These articles were commissioned and edited by Benedetto Croce who was the first at this other time of ruins and reconstruction, of deserts and new horizons, to describe these reflections, in his *History of Europe*, not by accident dedicated to Thomas Mann, as the 'religion of freedom.'[16]

Translation by Dr Ambrogio A. Caiani

Notes

1   This, and what follows, is treated with much greater breadth in my *Metternich* (Rome, 2014).

2   H. Kissinger, *A World Restored* (Boston, 1957); the Italian edition was published as *Diplomazia della Restaurazione* (Milan, 1973).
3   Ibid., 322, English edn.
4   In the almost infinite number of comparisons drawn between Vienna and Versailles bequeathed to us by twentieth-century European historiography, it is worth dwelling on a passage from the Introduction of a biography of *Metternich* (1936) by the British historian Algernon Cecil, which was added to the 1946 edition, and on p. 12, it states: 'after this book was published for the first time, we had time to observe Europe freed from the dominion of priests and witnessed it instead dominated by an Austrian painter, by an Italian school teacher and by a Georgian kinti from Tbilisi. All of these personages are the non-hereditary, intellectual descendants of the Corsican adventurer and are sons of the people more so than even he could have claimed to be.'
5   This document, is preserved at the StaatsArchiv of Vienna in a series relative to the Congress of Vienna and further details can be found in my *Metternich*, op. cit., on p. 132.
6   For examples see a letter dated 6 October 1822, in *Mémoires documents et écrits divers laissés par le prince de Metternich chancelier de Cour et d'Etat*, publiés par son fils le prince R. de Metternich, classés et réunis par M. A. de Klinkowstroem (Paris, 1880), III, 369.
7   *Mémoires, documents et écrits fivers laissés par le prince de Metternich chancelier de Cour et d'Etat*, publiés par son fils le prince R. de Metternich, classés et réunis par M. A. de Klinkowstrom (Paris, 1880), I, 1.
8   The principal biography of prince Metternich, in which significant space is afforded to the Rhenish education of the future Habsburg chancellor, remains the monumental three-volume biography by the German historian Heinrich von Srbik, *Metternich der Staatsmann un der Mensch* (Munich, 1925). To this can be added the much more recent one by W. Siemann, *Metternich. Stratege und Visionar* (Munich, 2016), and to which can be included my own *Metternich* (Rome, 2014).
9   This can be found in a report addressed to Franz Joseph, who had requested it after the publication of the so-called 'patent of Saint Sylvester'. It bears the date of 2 January 1852 and can be read in Metternich, *Mémoires*, op. cit., VIII, 538–44.
10 Ibid., III, 369.
11 A. De Musset, *La confession d'un enfant du siècle*, texte établi et annoté par G. Barrier, préface de C. Roy (Paris, 1993); and C. F. Volney, *Les ruines ou méditation sur les révolutions des Empires* (Paris, 1797).
12 Please see, in the best traditions of Italian historiography, the works of Walter Maturi which are now collected amongst the volumes of *Storia e storiografia*, edited by L. S. Massimo and N. Tranfaglia, with an introductory volume by G. Galasso, *L'ambiente culturale napoletano e gli studi sull'età della Restaurazione*.
13 Among the many available options, one recommends the excellent read afforded by G. Sciara, *La solitudine della libertà. Benjamin Constant e i dibattiti politico-costituzionali della prima Restaurazione e dei cento giorni* (Soneria Mannelli, 2013).
14 See Benedetto Croce in the opening of his *Storia d'Europa nel secolo decimonono*; the latest edition is that by G. Galasso, published in Milan by Adelphi, 1991.
15 On Guizot, one recommends the biography of L. Theis, *François Guizot* and from the same perspective one could also profitably read his *Histoire de la Révolution d'Angleterre*, also edited by Theis, published in Paris by Laffont, 1997.
16 This obviously refers to Omodeo's two substantial studies on the period: one on *Cultura francese nell'età della Restaurazione* and the other on *Aspetti del cattolicesimo della Restaurazione*, subsequently published together as A. Omodeo, *Studi sull'età della Restaurazione*, prefazione di Alessandro Galante Garrone (Turin, 1970).

Index

Aachen, Congress of 43
Abbenhuis, Maartje x (*see also* chapter 1)
Abel, Jakob Friedrich 136
absolutism
   constitutions and 122
   enlightened 8
   of Ferdinand VII of Spain 10, 79, 190, 191, 261, 264
   House of Savoy and 174, 176
   neo-absolutism in Spain 109, 118n.2
   neo-absolutism in the Austrian Empire 155
   Sweden 202
A'Court, William 265
afrancesados, Spain 259, 261, 262, 263
Africa, settler colonialism 9
Aix-la-Chapelle, Congress of 1818 62
Alexander I of Russia 7, 29–30, 31–3, 34–5, 58, 60, 209, 269–75
Allied Administration 41
Allied Council of Ambassadors 39–47
Álvarez, Clara 264
American Civil War 4
Americas
   American empire of Spain 191–2
   independence movements 191
   post-imperial and colonial instability 4
amnesia 98–9, 103
ancien régimes
   administrators during 8
   diversity of 1
   fluidity of status in 10
   government and 235
   Louis XVIII of France and 109, 111
   ultra-royalists and 102
Anderson, Benedict 226, 247
Angoulême, Louis Antoine Duc d' 85, 101, 106n.36, 183, 184–9, 266
Anker, Peder 205–6, 208
Antonetti, Guy 213
Archangel 231

Ardazun, Juan 189
art
   Jean-Baptiste Isabey 67–74
   performances of paintings 69
Artois, comte d' 95
Asia, settler colonialism 9
Asinari di San Marzano, Carlo 83, 85
associations, revolutionary 81
Attellis, Orazio de 82, 84
Atthalin, General 218
Augustenborg dynasty 206
Austrian Empire (*see also* Habsburg monarchy)
   Austrian civil code (*Allgemeines Bürgerliches Gesetzbuch* or ABGB) 278, 279–80, 282
   as a composite monarchy after 1815 147–55
   Congress of Vienna and 148, 149–51
   constitutions and 151
   constitutions of Baden and Bavaria and 128
   Fifth Coalition War (1809) with France 152
   German confederation and 19
   the Habsburg monarchy and 148–9
   Hungary and 152
   internal structures of 148–9
   Napoleonic wars and 154
   neo-absolutism in 155
   Provincial Homage of 1816 150
   reform projects of 151–3
   Russia and 32
autocracy 109–11

Babeuf, Gracchus 80
Baden
   constitutions and 115, 121, 123, 124, 127, 128
   French *Charte constitutionnelle* and 7
Bagration, Catherine 69

Balbo, Prospero 279
Banda Oriental 45
banking houses, of the European great powers 43
Barante, Prosper de 92
Barbaro, Ermolao 57
Barbaroux, Count 176
Barton, Arnold 208–9
Basque country, Spain 192
Batavian Commonwealth 165
Bavaria
  ceding Tyrol and Vorarlberg 149
  constitutionalism 9–10
  constitutions and 115, 121, 123–4, 126, 128
  French *Charte constitutionnelle* and 7
  reform in 151, 154
  Vorarlberg and 150
  'War' of the Bavarian Succession 56–7
Bayly, Christopher 4, 35
Beach, Vincent 185
Beauharnais, Hortense de 45
Befreiungskriege 113
Belgium
  Belgian revolution of 1789 166, 167
  Belgian revolution of 1832 7
  Belgian uprising of 1830–1 62–3, 166, 167
  benefits of neutrality 24
  creation of a new state of 63
  German invasion of 20
  nationalism 249
  Netherlands and 1, 159
  neutralization of 20–1, 63
Bellabarba, Marco x (*see also* chapter 22)
Bentham, Jeremy 80
Berg, Roald x (*see also* chapter 17)
Berman, Harold J. 277
Bernadotte, Jean Baptiste 126, 201–10 (*see also* Charles XIV John of Sweden and Norway)
Berry, Duc de 185, 188
Bertier de Sauvigny, Guillaume de 2
Beugnot, comte 93–6
Bilbao, siege of 194
'The Birth of the Modern World' 4
Bisinger, Joseph Constantin 148
Black Sea 20, 30, 34
Bloch, Marc 6

Bodø Affair 207
Boigne, Mme de 214
Boilly, Louis-Léopold 71, 73
Bolaños, B. 195
Bolivar, Simon 84
Bonaparte, Joseph 259
Bonaparte, Louis-Napoleon 159, 165
Bonaparte, Napoleon
  deposition of 93
  Hundred Days 73, 96, 102, 103
  legacy of 188
  power of 58
  return of 60, 61
  Russia and 29
Bonapartist sympathizers, removal of 43–5
Bórbon, Carlos María Isidro de. *See* Don Carlos of Spain
Borch, Gerard ter 70, 76n.23
borders
  border disputes 240
  identity papers 235–9, 241
  Italy and 235–41
  new territorial boundaries 18
Bourbon monarchy (*see also* names of individual monarchs)
  exiling of political enemies 81
  martial image of 196
  restoration of 4, 91, 186
  restoration project of 109, 117
  searching for a *roi de guerre* 183
  Spain 79
Bowring, John 83, 84, 85
Breuilly, John 250
Briot, Pierre-Joseph 80–1, 82
Broers, Michael x, 2–3, 9, 122
Broglie, duc de 95
Brun, Johan Nordahl 225, 229
Bucharest, Treaty of (1812) 30
Bull, Hedley 17
Buonarroti, Philippe 80, 82, 86
bureaucracy(ies)
  inherited from the French Empire 8
  the Revolution and 101
Burke, Edmund 136
Butrón Prida, Gonzalo xi (*see also* chapter 20)

Cadiz Constitutions of 1812 6, 7, 113, 190, 259, 260, 261, 262, 265

Caiani, Ambrogio xi (*see also* Introduction)
Camp, Louis Marie de 206
Campbell Orr, Clarissa 219
Campo Formio, Peace of (1797) 150
Canal, Jordi 193
Carbonari 79, 80–1, 81–2, 83–4, 85, 86
Carlist Wars, first (1833–9) 6, 184
Carlists 194, 195
Carlowitz, Congress of (1699) 56
Carlsbad Decrees 124, 128
Caron, Jean Claude 3, 85
cartography, politicized 229
Casale, Damiano 278
Castlereagh, Lord (Robert Stewart) 31, 39, 40, 41, 46, 57, 59–61, 72, 261, 264
Catalonia, 'Sacred Battalion' 85
Catherine the Great of Russia 57
Catholic Church
    Charte constitutionnelle of 1814 and 100
    Great Britain 8, 100–1
    Netherlands 166
    the Restoration and 294
    Spain 189, 191
El Censor 262
censorship
    Allied Council of Ambassadors and 45
    July Monarchy and 219
    Poland 274
Central Administration (1814) 40
Chamber of Deputies, France 99–100
Chamber of Peers, France 99–100
Chambre Introuvable 42, 44
change
    education and 136
    Württemberg and 137
Charles-Albert of Sardinia 173, 174, 176–7, 282
Charles-Felix of Sardinia-Piedmont 171–2, 173, 174
Charles II of England 56
Charles IV of Spain 189
Charles IX of France 97
Charles X of France 97, 116, 184, 187–8, 215, 217, 220
Charles X of Sweden 56
Charles XII of Sweden 227
Charles XIII of Sweden 203

Charles XIV John of Sweden and Norway 125, 126, 128, 204–9, 225, 226, 231, 233n.27 (*see also* Bernadotte, Jean Baptiste)
Charles XV of Sweden 249
Charte constitutionnelle ('Constitutional Charter') of 1814 6, 7, 9, 91–104, 109–11, 114, 116, 187, 263
La Chartreuse de Parme 239
Chateaubriand, François-Réné de 103, 185, 294
Chaumont, Treaty of 60, 61
China
    first Opium War 1839-1841 24
    Qing dynasty 4, 24
Christian August (Charles August), Crown Prince of Sweden 203
Christian Frederik, Crown Prince of Denmark 127, 203, 225, 226 (*see also* Christian VIII of Denmark)
Christian VIII of Denmark 123, 124
Christiania 204, 205, 206, 225, 227, 228
Christiania Military Society 230
Christianity and Europe 294
Christie, Wilhelm F.K. 229
Church, power of 236 (*see also* Catholic Church; religion)
Cisalpine Republic 150
civic rights, Poland 270–1
Civil Code, Sardinia 177
civil engineering, Norway 229, 231
civil liberties 109
civil rights 114, 116, 274
civil servants
    Netherlands 167
    Württemberg 134, 136–7
civil society 8, 80
class, rise of the middle classes 23 (*see also* elites)
Clausel de Coussergues, Jean-Claude 94
Clausewitz, Carl von 18
Clemente Solaro, della Margarita 176
Code Napoléon 271
Cold War 59
collegiality, Polish tradition of 270
Collett, Jonas 208
Collins, Christian 229
Colombian independence 84
colonialism (*see also* imperialism)

the Americas and 4
internal colonizing projects 40
Napoleonic Empire and 9
New World 23
post-colonial understandings of the Restoration 9
settler colonialism 9
Commentaries on the grievances of the nobility of Poitou to the estates general of 1789 102
communities, imagined 226
composite monarchy 7, 10, 147–55
Comuneros 84, 85
Concert of Europe 5, 9, 25, 54, 57, 64 (*see also* Congress system)
Conference des Ministres Alliés. See Allied Council of Ambassadors
Confessions d'un enfant du siècle 292
Congress of Verona. See Verona, Congress of
Congress of Vienna. See Vienna, Congress of
Congress system 17–25, 35, 62 (*see also* Concert of Europe)
Conny, Félix de 104
conservatism
  conservative Empires of eastern Europe 6
  constitutional conservatism, Norway 205
  constitutions and 122, 205
  France 8
  ultra-conservativism, of Don Carlos 190, 191
conspiracies
  Carbonari 81–2, 85
  against the Holy Alliance 79–86
  Jacobin 44
  Poland 274
Constant, Benjamin 99, 100, 101, 293
Constantine, Grand Duke 272, 273, 274
constituent power 7
Constitutional Act of the Spaniards of Both Hemispheres 262
constitutional conservatism, Norway 205
constitutional monarchism 6, 109–18, 122, 127
constitutionalism
  Bavaria 9–10

  European 112–18
  foreign policy incentives for 124
  French revolutionary 113, 114
  Norway 9–10, 112
  parliamentary constitutionalism 112, 114, 115
  parliamentary-corporatist constitutionalism 112
  parliamentary-monarchical 112
  Scandinavia and South Germany 9–10, 128–9
  sovereignty, division of power and equal rights and 122
constitutions
  absolutism and 122
  Austrian Empire 128, 151
  Baden 115, 121, 123, 124, 127, 128
  Bavaria 115, 121, 123–4, 126, 128
  Cadiz Constitution of 1812 6, 7, 113, 190, 259, 260, 261, 262, 265
  Charte constitutionnelle ('Constitutional Charter') of 1814 6, 7, 9, 91–109, 109–11, 114, 116, 187, 263
  constitution of 1791, France 101
  constitution of United Netherland 1814 113, 159–67
  democracy and 122
  Denmark 121, 122, 123, 127
  following the model of 'constitutional monarchism' 112
  foreign policy concerns and 123–5, 128–9
  French revolutionary and Napoleonic constitutions 113
  Germany and 114–15, 121, 123
  Jacobin constitution of 1793 6–7
  Norway 6, 7, 113, 121, 124–6, 204, 205, 210, 225
  Piedmontese Constitution (*Statuto Albertino*) 173, 178
  Poland 6, 7, 113, 270, 274
  Scandinavia 121
  Sweden 113, 121, 126, 127, 204
  Württemberg 115, 121, 123, 124, 126–7, 133, 134, 138–9
Copenhagen 202
Corcelle, Claude de 81
Córdoba, Fernando Fernández de 195

El Correo Español 195
Correspondance politique et administrative 102
corruption 206–7
cosmopolitanism 79–82, 86
Cotta, Johann Friedrich 138
Cracow, neutralization of 19–20
Crimean War 24, 25, 35
Critica 294
Croce, Benedetto 294
Cuba 191
culture(s)
  cultural identity 1
  cultural imperialism 9
  cultural Norwegianization 228–30
  cultural Pan-Scandinavism 245
  eighteenth-century 277
  Nordic political culture 201–10
  political 6, 201–10, 293
  revolutionary visual culture 73
  salon culture 74, 80, 81, 206
  of subaltern peoples 8–9
Czartoryski, Adam Jerzy 269, 270, 271, 272, 274, 275
Czechoslovakia 250, 254
Czoernig, Carl von 281
Czubaty, Jarosław xi (*see also* chapter 21)

Dambray, Charles-Henri 94, 95
David, Jacques-Louis 72–3
de la Rosa, Martínez 263, 264
De Maistre, Joseph 279
de Olavarría, Juan 262
Deak, John 147–8
debts, of France 43, 100
Decazes, Elie 99, 100
del Cerro, Ruiz 263
del Riego, Rafael 262
Delaroche, Paul 188–9
demilitarization, of France 42–3
democracy
  Charte constitutionnelle ('Constitutional Charter') of 1814 and 111
  constitutions and 122
  the democratic principle 116
  monarchical-constitutional systems and 118, 122
Denmark

  civil war 1848–51 128
  constitutions and 121, 122, 123, 127
  the Danish Restoration 4
  First Schleswig War (1848–51) 245, 253
  Germany and 252, 253
  Holstein and 123, 128, 252, 253
  liberalization of 202
  multi-ethnic empire of 227
  nationalism 253, 254
  Norway and 124, 125, 202–3, 207, 225, 227, 252
  Oldenburg dynasty 252
  Pan-Scandinavianism 245–6, 250
  public sphere in 128
  Schleswig and 128, 252, 253
  Second Schleswig War (1864), (First War of German Unification) 245
  struggles between monarch and parliament 116
  traumas of 252–3
dependency, inter-imperial 46
Descazes, Élie 44
desire, management of 69
despotism, enlightened 136
di Villamarina, Emanuele Pes 176
diplomacy
  concert diplomacy 20
  the Congress of Vienna and 1, 5, 19
  diplomatic developments of 1813–15 57
  effective European system of 34
  inter-state 5
  international relations and 54, 55–64
  Jean-Baptiste Isabey and 67–74
  neutrality and 18, 25
  promoting cooperation 57
  Russian 29, 32
Diplomatic Theory of International Relations 53
Directory of 1795–9 80
discourse, public constitutional 113, 114–15
domination, fear of foreign 251
Don Carlos of Spain (Carlos de Borbón) 183, 184, 189–96
Don Carlos y su acompañamiento 194
Don Carlos, Zumalakarregi y el Estado Mayor 194
Droz, Jacques 2

Duyn van Maasdam, Frans Adam van der 161

Eckert, Georg xi (*see also* chapter 10)
economic capital, nobility and 175
economics, laissez-faire 241
Economist 23
economy(ies)
    Belgium 24
    economic role of Switzerland 19
    eighteenth-century slave plantation 4
    globalization of 23
    Great Britain 23–4
    open economic systems/free-trade liberalism 18, 23
    size of and sustainability 248–9
Edinburgh Review 133, 135, 140
education
    change and 136
    educational policies 7
Egyptian crises, 1830s and 1840s 20
elites
    composite 10
    in the duchies of Germany/Denmark 252–3
    Italy 279, 283
    liberal 79
    Netherlands 166
    Norway 203, 204–5, 207, 208, 209, 225, 226, 227, 228, 231–2
    old-new 8
    Piedmontese and Savoyard 172–4, 177–8
    Poland 272
    political 2
    of post-revolutionary European society 68
    service elites 8
    Sweden 126
    Württemberg 127, 135, 136, 138
Elizabeth of Russia 209
Elliott, John 7, 147
Elout, Cornelis Theodorus 163
émigrés
    Adélaïde d'Orléans and 215
    returning to France 101–2
England. *See* Great Britain
L'Enjambée Impériale 188
Enlightenment 36n.5, 293

Enskilda Byrån 206
Erbvergleich of 1770 136
eroticism, representation of the Congress of Vienna and 71, 74
El Español Constitucional 264
Essay on the French Restoration 99
Estates-General, Netherlands 162–3
Estrada, Flórez 261
Etzioni, Amitai 226
Eugen, Karl 136
Europe
    civil society/public sphere 8
    conservative Empires of eastern Europe 6
    constitutionalism 112–18
    the end of 'restoration Europe' 24–5
    great powers 55, 57–8
    international and interconnected nature of 3
    Post-Napoleonic 2
    the re-ordering of 9
    social order, Western Europe 113
    Southern Europe, representative governments in 6
    stability of 17–18
    subaltern 9
    western Europe, liberal constitutional monarchies of 6
Evans, Richard 231
exiles, as international conspirators 81 (*see also émigrés*)

Fabvier, Colonel 83, 85
Faget de Baure, Jacques-Joseph 96
Falsen, Christian Magnus 126
family, Italy and the 281–2
Faulcon, Felix 92
fear
    nationalism and 254
    security and 55
    of small states 251–3
    of social and moral disaggregation 5
Felbinger, Udo 68
Fenimore Cooper, James 80
Ferdinand VII of Spain
    absolutism of 10, 79, 190, 191, 261, 264
    Don Carlos and 189, 191–2, 193
    early rule of (1814–20) 261–2
    Louis XVI and 93

Plan of the Chambers and 264
    restoration of 186, 190, 194, 260–1
Fernández de Córdova, Fernando 264
Fernández de Córdova, Luis 264
Ferrand, comte 93, 94, 95
Ferreira, Silvestre Pinheiro 83
Fiévée, Joseph 102
Finland 202, 203
foreign policy
    constitutions and 123–5, 128–9
    neutrality as 21–2
    Russian 29
    war avoidance as 18
Forging a Multinational State 147–8
forgiveness 103
Forsting, Richard Meyer xi–xii (*see also* chapter 14)
Fouché, Joseph 44, 101
Four Sergeants of La Rochelle 85
Fox, Charles James 133
France (*see also* Bourbon monarchy; Paris)
    Carbonarism 82, 83
    Chamber of Deputies and Chamber of Peers 99–100
    Chambre Introuvable 43, 44
    Charte constitutionnelle ('Constitutional Charter') of 1814 6, 7, 9, 91–104, 109–11, 114, 116, 187, 263
    conservatism in 8
    constitution of 1791 101
    constitutions; revolutionary and Napoleonic 113
    cultural imperialism of 9
    debts of 43, 100
    demilitarization of 42–3
    Directory of 1795–9 80
    émigrés returning to 101–2
    Fifth Coalition War (1809) with Austria 152
    'first Entente Cordiale' with Britain 217
    French Grand Orient Lodge 81
    French intervention in Spain 79–86
    French Requisition Committee 41
    French Revolution 292–3
    Hundred Days 73, 96, 102, 103
    inherited bureaucracies from the French Empire 8
    invasion of by Russia (1814) 231
    invasion of Spain 1823 6, 186, 264, 266, 268n.31
    Jacobin Republic of 1792–4 80
    July Monarchy 213–20
    July Ordinances of 1830 116, 215
    July Revolution of 1830 4, 86, 112, 185, 187–8, 215
    legacy of the French Empire 3
    liberalism 84
    massacres of Protestants 44
    military occupation of 1815-18 39–47, 49n.32
    monarchical succession and the role of the military 183–9, 196
    Orléanist régime 213–20
    persecutions of protestants in 44
    role of the military in restoration France 183–96
    Third Estate 98, 103
    ultra-royalism 8, 44, 102
    Villèle government (1822-1827) 8
franchise, introduction or extension of 116 (*see also* suffrage)
Francis I Emperor of Austria 33, 280
Francis II/I, Emperor of Austria 148–9, 150, 153
Franz-Josef I, Emperor of Austria 155, 291
Fredriksten fortress 227
free-trade liberalism 18, 23
free trade, political radicalism and 83
freedom of movement 236–41
freedom of speech, Norway 207, 208
freedom of the press 45, 128, 164, 207, 208, 270
Freemasonry 80, 81, 83, 84, 204
Freire, Colonel 83
French Charter with Spanish Notes 263
Frénilly, baron de 102
Friedrich I of Württemberg 133, 134, 135, 138, 139
Friedrich Wilhelm III of Prussia 44, 149
Frydenlund, Bård xii (*see also* chapter 15)
Fulda 164, 165

Garcia-Llera, José Luis Comellas 79
Gellner, Ernst 246
Gelykheid-Vryheid-Broederschap. 1795. Politiek Belang-Boek voor dit

Provisionele Tydperk. Gewigt tans, Gedenkwaardig hierna 163
gender
  Congress of Vienna and 71
  politics and 219-20
general alliance, Russia and the 29-35
Genlis, Mme de 214
Genta Ternavasio, Enrico xii (*see also* chapter 13)
Gentz, Friedrich 40, 61, 72
George IV of England 73
Germany (*see also* Baden; Bavaria; Württemberg)
  anti-French resentments 113, 114
  Carlsbad Decrees and 128
  Charte constitutionnelle ('Constitutional Charter') of 1814 and 114
  Congress of Vienna and 134
  constitutional monarchism 112-13
  constitutions and 114-15, 121, 123
  Denmark and 252-3
  First Schleswig War (1848-51) 245, 253
  the German confederation 7, 19, 251-2
  German Customs Union of 1833 (Zollverein) 23
  German Federal Act of 1815 115, 123
  invasion of Belgium and Luxembourg 20
  liberal German nationalism 125
  nationalism and 125, 247, 250, 252-3
  Second Schleswig War (1864), (First War of German Unification) 245
  South German constitutionalism 128
  South German states 125, 126, 128
  unification of 249, 250, 251, 252, 253
  Wars of Unification 245
Geselle, Andrea 237
gift giving, Charles XIV John of Sweden and Norway and 206
Glenthøj, Rasmus xii, 226 (*see also* chapter 19)
globalization, of economies 23
Gneisenau, Neidhardt von 41
Godefroy, Jean 73
Gothenburg 204
governance, vested in five great powers 290
government
  Napoleonic era 235

  in Norway and Sweden 205
  representative 6-7
  in Sardinia 171-8
Graaf, Beatrice de xiii (*see also* chapter 3)
Great Britain
  Adélaïde d'Orléans and 217
  Catholic Emancipation and the Great Reform Act of 1832 8
  Catholicism and 8, 100-1
  Corn Laws and Navigation Acts 23
  Denmark-Norway and 202
  economy of 23-4
  'first Entente Cordiale' with France 217
  first Opium War 1839-1841 24
  the Ionian isles and 45
  parliamentary constitutionalism 112, 114, 115
  primogeniture in 179n.7
  the rise of 23-4
  Russia and 32
  Tories/Conservative party 8
Great Diet (1788-92) 272
great power system 251
great powers, Europe 55, 57-8, 290
Greece
  establishment of an autonomous Greece 37n.22
  Greek crisis 36n.9
  Greek rebellions 30-1, 36n.8
  Ionian islands 20, 45
Grigorios V, murder of 31
Grimm brothers 253
Grotius, Hugo 110
Gruder, Vivian 220
Gruner, Justus von 41, 43-4, 45
Gueniffey, Patrice 202
Guilleminot, Armand Charles 85, 187
Guizot, Francois 92, 104, 218, 220, 294
Gustavus Adolfus IV of Sweden 203

Haan, Ido de xiii (*see also* chapter 12)
The Habsburg Empire: A New History 148
Habsburg monarchy (*see also* Austrian Empire)
  composite monarchy 10
  Congress of Vienna and 149-50
  constitutional structure of 148, 151
  Cracow and 20
  the functionality of 147

Holy Roman Empire and 149, 154
Hungary and 149, 151, 152, 153
internal structures of the 154
Lombardy returned to the Habsburgs 149, 151
taxation and 150
Tyrol returned to the Habsburgs 149, 150, 151, 154
Vorarlberg returned to the Habsburgs 149, 150
Württemberg and 134–5
Hague, The 160, 161
Hamer, Theodor 283
Hardenberg, Karl August von 39, 41, 60
Harkett, Daniel xiii (*see also* chapter 5)
Haussez, Baron d' 187
Haynes, Christine 43
Hegel, Georg Wilhelm Friedrich 135, 137, 139
Hegermann, Diderik 227
Heligoland 207
Hermosilla, Gomez 262
Herrschaft durch Verwaltung ('ruling by management') 40
Hinsley, F.H. 53
Histoire de la monarchie de juillet 213
historiography, French 4
history, international 5
History of Europe 294
History of European Civilization 294
Hobsbawm, Eric 245, 246, 248, 251
Hogendorp, Gijsbert Karel van 160–1, 162–3
Hohenlinden, Battle of 185
Holstein, Denmark and 123, 128, 252, 253
Holy Alliance (1815) 5–6, 29, 79–86
Holy Roman Empire 19, 149, 154
Holy See 149
homosociality, Congress of Vienna and 71
Horodyski, Andrzej 273
Hudson, James 250
Hugo, Victor 214
humanitarian interventionism, military invasion as 6
Humboldt, Friedrich Wilhelm von 41, 72
Hundred Days 73, 96, 102, 103
Hungary, the Habsburgs and 149, 151, 152, 153
Huntington, Samuel 230

identity(ies)
Belgian 21
cultural/civic 1
identity papers 235–9, 241
noble 173
Norwegian Officers Corps, 1814–45 225–32
'Norwegianness' and 'Swedification' 226, 228, 231–2
Pan-Scandinavianism and 254
social and political 10
Swiss 19
ideology, of revolution 54, 58
Illyrian movement 250
imagined communities 226
imperialism (*see also* colonialism)
the Americas and 4
cultural 9
industrial 23
the Restoration as a post-imperial time 9
In Defence of the Cortes 261
independence movements, Americas 191
industrial revolution, neutrality and the 22–4
innovation, the king of Württemberg and 133
instaurazione 10
international organizations 79–82
international relations 18, 53–4, 55–64
Ionian isles 20, 45
Isabel II of Spain 184, 189, 192, 193, 194
Isabey, Jean-Baptiste 67–74
Italy (*see also* Lombardy-Venetia; Piedmont; Venice and the Venetia)
Carbonarism 82
the construction of boundaries in 235–41
the family and 281–2
identity papers 235–9
law codes and social control in 277–83
marriage and divorce 281–2
Milan 236, 280–1
nationalism and 247, 250
paternalism 282
social control 277–83
Statuto Albertino (Piedmontese Constitution) 173, 178
subaltern 9

taxation 238
unification of 249, 251

Jacobins
   Jacobin conspiracies 44
   Jacobin constitution of 1793 6–7
   Jacobin Republic of 1792–4, France 80
   rehabilitation of 86
Jaucourt, comte de 97
John, Charles 229
Joseph II, Holy Roman Emperor 151
Judson, Pieter 148, 278
De jure naturae et gentium 110
juste milieu 8
Jutland 253

Kahan, Alan 127
Kantian philosophy 136
Karls-Schule 136, 137, 138
Kaunitz-Rietberg, Wenzel Anton von 58
Kedourie, Elie 246
Kiel, Treaty of (1814) 207, 208, 225
Kissinger, Henry 30, 289–90
Knesebeck, Karl Friedrich von dem 149
Koenigsberger, H.G. 147
Kopetz, Wenzel Gustav 148
Kościuszko, Tadeusz 273
Krakow, Free City of 5

La Garde-Chambonas, Auguste de 68, 69
La Parra, Emilio 260
Lafayette, General 80, 81, 83, 84–5, 86
Laffitte, General 83, 84, 85
laissez-faire economics 241
Lajer-Burcharth, Ewa 73
L'Ami des peuples 83
landständische Verfassung 113, 114, 115, 119n.16, 123
Langhorne, Richard xiii (*see also* chapter 4)
language policy, Netherlands 166
Latin Monetary Union 251
Lauenburg, Denmark and 252
Laven, David 3
Law and Revolution 277
law(s)
   budgetary law 1814, France 100
   Constitutional Law of 1815, Poland 270, 271
   Corn Laws and Navigation Acts, Britain 23
   criminal legislation 283
   evolution of 277
   July Ordinances of 1830, France 116, 215
   law codes and social control in Italy 277–83
   Napoleonic legal codification 5, 293
   neutrality law 22
   the political field and 116
Le Brun, Charles 69
League of Nations 54
Lee, Loyd 122
legitimacy, concepts of 116–17
Lehmann, Orla 254
Leipzig, Battle of 1, 59
Levine, Philippa 23
Liberal International 79, 85
liberalism
   France 84
   free-trade 18, 23
   international 80
   Liberal Triennium (1820–3), Spain 186, 189, 192, 259, 262–6
   Spain 84, 259, 260
   Württemberg 137
Ligne, Charles-Joseph de 69
Liguria 1
Limburg Stirum, Leopold van 160–1
List, Friedrich 137, 139, 248, 253
Lista, Alberto 262
literacy, Scandinavia 204
Lok, Matthijs 8
Lombardy-Venetia
   ancien régime statehood and 10
   establishment of 150
   freedom of movement 237–8
   Lombardy returned to to the Habsburgs 149, 151
   marriage law 282
London Protocol of 21 June 1814 161
London, Treaty of 1839 20
Loning, Adolf 195
López, Vicente 194
Louis IX of France 186
Louis Philippe I of France 213–20
Louis XI of France 97
Louis XIV of France 97

Louis XVI of France 81, 93, 101, 102, 103, 184
Louis XVII of France 98
Louis XVIII of France
   Charte constitutionnelle ('Constitutional Charter') of 1814 and 91–104, 109–11
   conspiracies and 44
   Duc d'Angoulême and 184, 188
   Duke of Wellington and 41–2
   liberals and 81, 82
   power of 100, 101
   restoration project of 109, 117
   rights of 99
   royal prerogative of 99
   royal sovereignty of 96, 97–8
   Spain and 82, 186, 187, 264, 265, 268n.33
Ludovika, Maria 69
Luis, Jean-Phlippe 3
Lutheranism 204
Luxembourg 20

Maanen, Cornelis Felix van 163
Małachowski, Stanisław 273
Malet, General 226
manifiesto de los persas 5
Manno, Antonio 174
Mantovani, Luigi 235
Manuel, Jacques-Antoine 85
Manzanares, Salvador 264
map making 229
Maria Amalia of Naples and Sicily 214, 215
María Luisa of Parma 189
Maria Theresa, Empress 71, 147–8, 151
Marie Antoinette, Queen consort of France 81, 103, 219–20
marriage, Italy 281–2
Mascilli Migliorini, Luigi xiii–xiv (*see also* chapter 23)
Masson, Victor Alexandre 94
Materialien für Gesetzkunde und Rechtspflege 280
Maturana, Don Vincente 190
Maximilian I Joseph of Bavaria (Max Joseph of Bavaria) 124
Mazzini, Giuseppe 249, 293
McNeil Kettering, Alison 70

media
   Adélaïde d'Orléans and 219–20
   campaign of Don Carlos 194–5
   Charles XIV John of Sweden and Norway and 206
   'mediatization' of Western society 117
   politics and the 117
   sexual slander 219–20
Mehrkens, Heidi xiv (*see also* chapter 14)
Meijer, Jonas Daniel 163–4
Mélanges historiques 185
Meriggi, Marco xiv, 2 (*see also* chapter 18)
Metternich, Clemens Wenzel 151–2
Metternich, Franz Georg von 134
Metternich, Klemens von
   the Allied Council and 41, 45
   Bavarian constitution and 124
   Congress of Vienna and 60–1, 62, 63, 71, 72, 289–91
   European police directory and 45, 46–7
   international conspiracy and 81
   Norweigan constitution and 126
   reconstruction and 292
   Russo-Ottoman war scare of 1821–2 and 31, 32, 33
   South German states and 128
   war of 1815 and 39
   Württemberg and 134
Mexico, independence of 84
Meydell, Jacob Gerhard 230–1
Miel, François 74
Milan 236, 280–1
military
   compulsory military service 236, 237
   professionalization of 230
   role of in restoration Spain and France 183–96
Military Committee, Allied Council of Ambassadors 41
Mill, John Stuart 248–9
Miller, Marion S. 79
Mina, Espoz y 264
Miñano, Sebastian 262
La Mode 218, 219
modernity 293
modernization
   the threshold principle and 252
   Württemberg 135, 136, 140
Mohl, Benjamin Ferdinand von 137

Mohl, Robert von 138
Moldavia, Greek uprising in 30–1
Molé, Louis-Mathieu 217, 218, 220
Molitor, General 160
monarchy
   composite 7, 10, 147–55
   constitutional monarchism 6, 109–18, 122, 127
   dual monarchy of Sweden and Norway 205
   limited monarchy 110
   monarchical legitimacy 117, 118
   monarchical power 111, 184
   monarchical sovereignty 109, 110, 124, 127
   monarchical succession in restoration Spain and France 183–96
   parliamentary representation and 6–7, 9
   restoration of 17
Le Moniteur 95
Monroe Doctrine 24
Montalivet, Camille de 216
Montesquiou, abbé de 93, 94, 96
Montet, Alexandrine du 68
Montgelas, Maximilian von 123, 154
Morales, Benigno 264
morality
   fear of moral and social disaggregation 5
   of Italians 280
   public 282–3
Morange, Claude 262
Moresnet, neutralization of 19, 20
Morgenbladet 206
mortgages, restructuring of in Sardinia 171
Motzfeldt, Peter 227
Moxo, Manuel 190
multi-polarity, management of 53–64
Münchengrätz convention 6
Münster, Treaty of 70
Munthe, Gerhard 229
Musset, Alfred de 292
Müssig, Ulrike 127

Naarden, Bruno 231
Nantes, edict of (1598) 98
Naples
   military invasion of 6
   Napoleonic era 237
   parliamentary-monarchical constitutionalism 112
   revolution of 1820 31, 126
   Troppau protocol and 36n.11
Napoleon III, *politique des nationalités* 250–1
Napoleonic Empire, colonialism and 9
The Napoleonic Empire in Italy 9
Napoleonic wars 154, 203, 251–2
'Napoleon's Legacy' 3
Nassau, constitutions and 123
nation-states 79–80, 248 (*see also* states)
nationalism
   Belgium 249
   cosmopolitanism, international organizations and 79–82
   Czech 254
   defined 246
   Denmark 253, 254
   fear and 254
   Germany 125, 247, 250, 252–3
   as an ideology 247
   Italy 247, 250
   liberal 125, 252
   Netherlands 250
   nineteenth-century 245–54
   pan-nationalism 249–51, 254
   Pan-Scandinavism and 254
   Piedmont 250
   secessionist nationalisms 249
   the threshold principle 248–9, 252, 254
   unification nationalism 249–51
nationality, principle of 248
Navarino, Battle of 37n.22
negotiations, representation of 70–4
Negri, Giovanni Maria 281
Nesselrode, Karl von 41
Netherlands
   Belgian revolution of 1789 166, 167
   Belgian revolution of 1832 7
   Belgian uprising of 1830–1 62–3, 166, 167
   Belgium and 1, 159
   constitution of United Netherland 1814 113, 159–67
   Estates-General 162–3

first constitution, the Staatsregeling
   1798 162
Kingdom of the Netherlands 19
language policy 166
monarchy of 159
nationalism and 250
neutrality and the 24
Patriot movement 159
religion and 166
restoration of the Orange dynasty 103
revolution of 1813 160–1
rights and 164
sovereignty 159, 162–3
United Kingdom of the Netherlands 7, 159–67
networks, cross-border/social 80
neutrality
   diplomacy and 18, 25
   the industrial revolution and 22–4
   neutralization of the Ionian islands 20
   the permanence of 21–2
   the rise of 24–5
   as a tool of territorial equilibrium 18–21
Nicholas I of Russia 209
Nielsen, Jens Petter 231
Nijmegen, Congress of (1676–9) 56
Nipperdey, Thomas 2
nobility (*see also* elites)
   as a concept 174
   primogeniture and 175–8
Normann-Ehrenfels, Philipp Christian Friedrich von 137
Norway
   ancien régime statehood and 10
   civil engineering 229, 231
   constitution of 1814 6, 7, 113, 121, 124–6, 204, 205, 210, 225
   constitutionalism 9–10, 112
   Convention of Moss/joint Act of Union (Riksakten) 205
   Denmark and 124, 125, 202–3, 207, 225, 227, 252
   freedom of speech/the press 207, 208
   national assembly of 205
   Norwegian Officers Corps, 1814–45 225–32
   Pan-Scandinavianism and 245–6
   parliament session of 1821 207–9
   parliamentary-monarchical constitutionalism 112
   popular sovereignty 7, 125
   Russia and 231
   sovereign and executive power in 127
   Sweden and 124–5, 203, 225, 229–30
   transferred from Denmark to Sweden 203
Norwegian Military Journal 230–1
Novalis 294

Oath of the Horatii 72
The Oath of the Tennis Court 72
occupation, of France 39–47, 49n.32
Ocios de españoles emigrados 264
Ohme, Johan Andreas Cornelius 227
Oldenburg dynasty, Denmark 252
Oliva, Congress of 56
Oliván, Alejandro 260, 266
Oliveira, João Francisco d' 83, 84
Omodeo, Adolfo 294
On amending the Constitution 266
On War 18
Orange dynasty, restoration of 103
organizations, international 79–82 (*see also* Freemasonry)
Orléanist régime, France 213–20
Orléans, Adélaïde d' 213–20
Orléans, Louis-Philippe-Joseph, duc d' 214
Osiander, Andreas 17
Ottoman empire
   composite monarchy 147
   Russia and 30–5, 37n.22
Ottosen, Morten Nordhagen xiv (*see also* chapter 9)
oubli/oubliance 98

Palmella, count de 46
Palmerston, Lord 63–4
pan-nationalism 249–51, 254
Pan-Scandinavianism 125, 245–6, 247, 249, 250, 252, 253–4
Pan-Slavist movement 247, 250, 254
Papal States 237, 239, 240
Paris
   capture of by Russia (1814) 231
   liberation of 42
   Paris salons 74, 81
   Revolution of 1830 4

Paris, Declaration of (1856) 25
Paris, first Treaty of 30, 70, 149
Paris, Peace of (1763) 55
Paris, second Treaty of 41, 61
parliamentarianism, monarchical-constitutional systems and 118
parliamentary constitutionalism, Great Britain 112, 114, 115
parliamentary-monarchical constitutionalism 112
parliamentary representation, monarchy and 6-7, 9
Pasquier, Étienne-Denis 99, 218
passports 42, 235-6
paternalism, Italy 282
Patriot movement, Netherlands 159
Pavels, Claus 225, 226, 229
Pax Britannica 24
peace
   maintenance of 55, 61
   peacekeeping troops, France 42
   process of peace making 34
   restoration of 58, 92
   sociability and 74
peasant revolt, in Wallachia 31
peasantry, Norway and Baden 127
Peninsular War (1808-14) 7, 183, 186, 189
Pepé, General 81, 83, 84
Pérez Galdos, Benito 195
performances, of paintings 69
Périer, Casimir 217-18
persecutions, of protestants in France 44
Philip V of Spain 194
Philippe-Egalité 214
Philippines 191
Piat, General 85
Piedmont
   crisis of the eighteenth century 279
   ennoblements in 173-4
   nationalism and 250
   Piedmontese Constitution (*Statuto Albertino*) 173, 178
Pirala, Antonio 191, 195
Pisa, Colonel 84
'Pitt-plan' (1805) 40
Pitt, William 58-9, 61, 161
Pius VII, Pope 149
Plan of the Chambers 263, 264
Plessis, Armand Émmanuel du 41

Poland
   Alexander I of Russia and 7, 269-75
   ancien régime statehood and 10
   civic rights 270-1
   Congress of Vienna and 269, 271, 272-3
   constitution of Congress Poland 1815 6, 7, 113, 270
   Constitutional Law of 1815 270, 271
   Duchy of Warsaw/Treaty of Tilsit (1807) 269
   Kingdom of Poland 269-70
   November Uprising (1830) 274
police
   European police directory 45, 46-7
   Metternich's 81
   secret 45, 274
   Verbündetenpolizei 41
policies, educational and welfare 7
politics
   cartography and 229
   concepts of legitimacy and 116-17
   female political power 213-20
   gender and 219-20
   international 53
   mass accessibility of 117, 118
   the media and 117
   neutrality and 22
   Pan-Scandinavianism 125, 245-6, 247, 249, 250, 252, 253-4
   political authority 282
   political culture 6, 201-10, 293
   political identities 10
   political pan-nationalism 249
   political power 110, 115, 116
   political radicalism and free trade 83
   post-Vienna 10
   radical in Spain 261
   Restoration 3, 121-2
   sexual slander and 219-20
   wars and 251
politique des nationalités 250
Pontecorvo 206
popular sovereignty
   constitutional monarchy and 127
   Netherlands 159, 162, 163
   Norway 7, 125
   Sweden 126
Porlier, Díaz 261

Portugal, invasion of the Rio Plata (1817) 45–6
post-colonial studies 8
power
   of the Church 236
   conflict between monarchical and parliamentary 116
   constituent 7
   divine 96–7
   female political 213–20
   great power system 251
   of Louis XVIII of France 100, 102
   maintaining the balance of 17, 18
   monarchical 111, 184
   multi-polar distribution of 53
   of Napoleon 58
   Napoleonic era 235
   Norway and Sweden 205
   political power 110, 115, 116
   power sharing in Sweden 126
   separation of 101, 125–8
   sovereign powers in Sweden and Denmark 127
   of tradition 135–6
Power and the Pursuit of Peace 53
Pozzo di Borgo, Carlo Andrea 41, 46
Pragmatic Sanction, Spain 192
Pratobevera, Carl Joseph 280
press
   Charles XIV John of Sweden and Norway and 206
   freedom of the 45, 128, 164, 207, 208, 270
   increasing importance of 117
   monarchs and 167
Pressburg, Peace of (1805) 149, 150
Price, Munro xiv (*see also* chapter 16)
'The Price of Peace, 1815–1848' 6
primogeniture
   in England 179n.7
   nobility and 175–8
Prince of Orange. See William I of the Netherlands
private life, supervision of 283
private/public sphere, women and 219–20
privateering, right to 25
propaganda, of ultra-royalists 79
Protestants, massacres of in France 44

Prussia
   constitutions of Baden and Bavaria and 128
   First Schleswig War (1848–51) 245, 253
   German confederation and 19
   Saxony and 1
   Second Schleswig War (1864) 245
   struggles between monarch and parliament 116
Prutsch, Markus J. xv, 7, 122 (*see also* chapter 8)
public sphere
   Denmark 128
   Europe 8
   Norway and Sweden 204, 206
   Scandinavian countries 128
Pufendorf, Samuel von 110

Qing dynasty 4, 24
quadruple alliance of 1834 6, 43
The Queens of Persia at the Feet of Alexander 69
Queenship in Britain, 1660–1837 219
Queenship in Europe, 1660–1815 219

Rainer, Archduke 151–2, 153
Raison d'État 240
Ranke, Leopold von 1, 99
reconciliation 92, 102–3
reforms, Napoleonic 171
regicides 81, 101, 103
Reichsdeputationshauptschluß 137
religion, Netherlands 166 (*see also* Catholic Church; Church)
reparations 41, 42, 43
republicans, Ligurian 1
résistance, policy of 217
resistance, Spanish 79
Restoration, post-colonial understandings of 9
restraint, principle of 22
Retrato del Infante Carlos María Isidro Bórbon 194
revolutionaries
   of the 1820s 7
   liberal 79
   professional 80

revolution(s)
　armed forces' potential as an instrument for 196
　French Revolution 292–3
　ideology of 54, 58
　international dimension of 80
　July Revolution of 1830, France 4, 86, 112, 185, 187–8, 215
　of the late 1840s 20, 21, 24
　revolutionary constitutionalism 113, 114
　revolutions of the 1820s 7, 79, 262
　royal revolution of Louis XVIII 93
Rey, Joseph 81
Riall, Lucy 3
Rials, Stéphane 96, 100
Richelieu, Armand Jean du Plessis de 44, 45, 101
Riego, General 84
Rien appris, rien oublié? 3
rights
　Charte constitutionnelle ('Constitutional Charter') of 1814 and 111
　civic rights, Poland 270–1
　civil rights 114, 116, 274
　of the King 99
　Netherlands 164
Riste, Olav 25
Rodil, general 193, 195
Roncal, Antonio Moral 190
Rosanvallon, Pierre 104
Rousseau, Jean-Jacques 57
Royal 'Fuero' of Spain 264, 265
Rújula, Pedro 261
Russia
　Austria, Great Britain and 32
　Black Sea and 30, 34
　Finland and 203
　foreign policy 29
　the general alliance and 29–35
　Napoleon's invasion of 1812/invasion of France by Russia 231
　Norway and 231
　Ottoman empire and 30–5, 37n.22
　Russo-Ottoman war scare of 1821–2 30–5
　Russophobia 231
　Scandinavia and 209
　Turkey and 56
Ryswick, Congress of (1697) 56

Sahlins, Peter 240
Saint-Ouen, declaration of 93, 98, 105n.9, 106n.24
Sainz, Francisco 194
salon culture 74, 80, 81, 206
Salzburg, Prince-Archbishopric of 149
Samlinger til det norske Folks Sprog og Historie 229
San Miguel, Evaristo 265, 266
Sandin, Per 209
Santa-Rosa, Comte de 81
Sant'Albano, marquis of 174
Santo-Lorenzo, Duke 84
Sardagna, Giuseppe (Joseph) von 280, 281
Sardinia
　Civil Code 177
　government in 171–8
　Kingdom of Sardinia-Piedmont 171
　law codes in 279
　Moti of 1821 171, 172
　restructuring of mortgages in 171
Sauquaire-Souligné, Martial 83, 84
Savigny, Friedrich von 5
Savoy, House of 171–2, 174, 176, 178, 282
　(*see also* Charles-Albert of Sardinia; Charles-Felix of Sardinia-Piedmont)
Savoy, returned to Piedmont 279
Saxony, Prussia and 1
Scandinavia
　before 1810 202–3
　constitutionalism 9–10, 128
　constitutions in 121
　literacy 204
　Pan-Scandinavianism 125, 245–6, 247, 249, 250, 252, 253–4
　public sphere in 128
　Russia and 209
　trade 202, 207
Schiller, Friedrich 136
Schimmelpenninck, Rutger Jan 165
Schleswig
　Denmark and 128, 252, 253
　First Schleswig War (1848–51) 245, 253
　Second Schleswig War (1864) 245

Schneider, Karin xv (*see also* chapter 11)
Schönbrunn, Peace of 152
Schroeder, Paul 5, 17, 53, 61
Schwarzenberg, Karl Philipp Prince of 44
Scio, Fernando and Felipe 189
Sclopis, Federico 279
seas, freedom of the 24, 25
Sébastiani, Horace 217, 218
secret societies, European 81–3 (*see also* Freemasonry)
security
    fears about 55
    inter-imperial security arrangements 39–47
Sémonville, Charles Louis Huguet de 94
Serbia, nationalism 249
Sérent, Armand Louis de 185
settler colonialism 9
sexual slander, women and 219–20
Sharp, Paul 53
Short, John 229
Sicily 172, 238, 249
Sixth Coalition 40, 41
smuggling 207, 241
Snyder, Louis L. 249
Sobolewsk, Ignacy 274
sociability, peace and 74
social achievements, of the Revolution 100
social and moral disaggregation, fear of 5
social capital, nobility and 175
social control, Italy 277–83
social mobility 174–5, 201
social networks 80
social order, Western Europe 113
social prestige, states and 8
social solidarity, Italy 277–8
social stratification 278
Society of Perfect Sublime Masters 82
society, Restoration 8
Solórzano Pereira, Juan de 147
Somerset, Fitzroy 265
South America, Portuguese invasion of the Rio Plata (1817) 45–6 (*see also* Americas)
Southern Europe, representative governments in 6
sovereignty
    division of power and 125–8
    monarchical 109, 110, 124, 127

Netherlands 159, 162–3
popular 7, 125, 126, 127, 159, 162, 163
Sardinia 173
small states and 251
Spain 190, 260, 262, 263, 265
Spain
    absolutism 190, 191, 261, 264
    afrancesados 259, 261, 262, 263
    American empire of 191–2
    Angoulême's Spanish campaign of 1823 186 (*see also* Angoulême, Louis Antoine Duc d')
    Basque country 192
    Bourbon Monarchy 79
    Cádiz Constitution of 1812 6, 7, 113, 190, 259, 260, 261, 262, 265
    Carlists 194, 195
    Catholic Church 189, 191
    civil war in 6
    composite monarchy 147
    Don Carlos. *See* Don Carlos of Spain (Carlos de Borbón)
    El Palmar conspiracy 262
    the *Estatuto Real* of 1834 7, 266
    Ferdinand VII and. *See* Ferdinand VII of Spain
    First Carlist War (1833–9) 6, 184
    first Restoration (1814) 260–1
    French intervention in 79–86
    French invasion of 1823 6, 186, 264, 266, 268n.31
    Liberal Triennium (1820–3) 186, 189, 192, 259, 262–6
    liberalism 84, 259, 260
    los importantes 263
    Louis XVIII of France and 82, 186, 187, 264, 265, 268n.33
    monarchical succession and the role of the military 183–4, 189–96
    neo-absolutism 109, 118n.2
    Peninsular War (1808–14) 7, 183, 186, 189
    Portuguese invasion of the Rio Plata (1817) 45–6
    Pragmatic Sanction 192
    resistance in 79
    revolution of 1820 262
    role of the military in restoration Spain 183–96

Royal 'Fuero' of Spain 264, 265
siege of Bilbao 194
sovereignty 190, 260, 262, 263, 265
transition to liberalism 259, 260
ultras 189
War of Independence. *See* Peninsular war
Speranskii, Mikhail M. 29
spies 44
Spivak, Gayatri Chakravorty 8–9
stability, European 17–18
Stadion, Johann Philipp 151
Staël, Mme de 101
Stassart, Goswin de 160
state(s)
  composite monarchy and 7
  Napoleonic 235
  nation-states 79–80, 248
  neutralization of. *See* neutrality
  new territorial boundaries 18 (*see also* borders)
  size of and nationalism 245–54
  small states and sovereignty 251
  society and 8
  surveillance 241
status quo, restoration of 59, 61
Statuto Albertino (Piedmontese Constitution) 173, 178
Stein, Lorenz von 40
Stendhal 239
Stewart, Robert 41
Stites, Richard 3
Stockholm 202, 203, 204, 205
Stockton, C.H. 25
Strangford, Lord 34
Stroganov, Grigorii A. 31
subaltern peoples 8–9
Sublime Porte 31, 32, 33, 34, 37n.21, 37n.22
Suez canal, neutralization of 20
suffrage 7, 127, 271
Sułkowski, Antoni 273
surveillance
  Charles XIV John of Sweden and Norway and 206
  Napoleonic era 237
  state 241
Sweden
  before 1810 202–3

absolutism 202
constitution of 1809 113, 126, 127, 204
constitutions in 121
Finland and 202, 203
Napoleonic wars and 203
Norway and 124–5, 203, 225, 229–30
Pan-Scandinavianism 245–6
parliamentary-corporatist constitutionalism 112
policy of 1812 203
popular sovereignty 126
Stockholm 202, 203, 204, 205
Swedish Age of Liberty (1719–72) 204
Swildens, Johan Hendrik 163
Switzerland
  Carbonarism 82
  neutralization of 19, 21

tableaux vivants 69–70
Talleyrand, Charles-Maurice de 41, 44, 60, 67, 70–1, 72, 92, 93, 95, 165, 217
Tardy, Jean-Noël xv (*see also* chapter 6)
Tatishchev, D.P. 30, 32–3, 34
taxation
  Habsburg monarchy and 150
  Italy 238
  Württemberg 134, 135
technocracy, Württemberg 134, 136–8, 139–40
La Tercerola 191
Teschen, Congress of 56–7
Teschen, Peace of (1779) 56
Thiers, Adolphe 215–16
Third Estate, France 98, 103
threshold principle, nationalism 248–9, 252, 254
Thureau-Dangin, Paul 213
Tidemand, Nicolai 230, 231
Tilsit, Treaty of (1807) 269
Toreno, Count 263, 264, 267n.23
trade
  free-trade liberalism 18, 23
  free trade practices 241
  freedom of movement and 236
  political radicalism and free trade 83
  Scandinavia 202, 207
tradition
  necessity of 293–4
  power of 135–6

The Transformation of European Politics, 1763–1848 53
Transpadanian Republic 150
Transylvania 151, 153
Trocadero, Battle of 186
Troppau protocol 31, 33, 36n.11
Tübingen, Treaty of (1514) 136
Tübingen, University of 138, 139
Turin 173, 185, 279
Turkey, Russia and 56
Tuscany, Grand Duchy of 237, 238–9
Two Sicilies, kingdom of 237, 238
Tyrol, returned to the Habsburgs 149, 150, 151, 154

Uhland, Ludwig 139
ultra-conservativism, of Don Carlos 190, 191
ultra-royalists
    France 8, 44, 102
    propaganda of 79
ultras, Spanish 189
Umsetzung-Kommissionen 280
unification nationalism 249–51
United Nations 54
United States
    American Civil War 4
    Constitution of 1787 113
    Monroe Doctrine 24
    neutrality and the 24
universalism 294
Utrecht, Treaty of (1713) 172

Vasa dynasty 206
Venice and the Venetia 149, 150–1 (*see also* Lombardy-Venetia)
Verbündetenpolizei 41
Verona, Congress of 5, 291
veterans, Napoleon's 187
Vick, Brian 5
Victor Amadeus II of Sardinia 172
Victor Emmanuel I of Sardinia 171, 172, 173, 174
Vienna, Congress of
    Austrian Empire and 148, 149–51
    borders and 240
    civic identities of Europeans and 1
    collapse of 6
    Congress system 17–25, 35, 62

diplomacy and 1, 5, 19
European equilibrium and 289–90
the Free City of Krakow and 5
the French Restoration and 109
gender and 71
Germany and 134
Habsburg monarchy and 149–50
international politics and 53
Jean-Baptiste Isabey and 67–74
Kingdom of Sardinia-Piedmont and 171
Metternich and 60–1, 62, 63, 71, 72, 289–91
monarchy and 7
opening of the 60–1
Poland and 269, 271, 272–3
politics and 10
territorial settlement and 61
Vienna, Leopoldstadt 68
Vienna settlement 62, 81, 82
Viliers, George 266
violence, imperialism and 23
visual culture, revolutionary 73
Vitrolles, baron de 92, 95, 105n.9
Vladimirescu, Tudor 31, 36n.8
Vorarlberg, returned to to the Habsburgs 149, 150
Vorderösterreich 135
Voyer d'Argenson, Marc-René de 80–1

Wallachia, peasant revolt in 31
Wallmark, Pehr Adam 206
Wangenheim, Karl August von 139
Waresquiel, Emmanuel de xv, 2 (*see also* chapter 7)
war(s)
    American Civil War 4
    civil war in Denmark 1848–51 128
    civil war in Spain 6
    Cold War 59
    Crimean War 24, 25, 35
    Fifth Coalition War (1809) 152
    First Carlist War (1833–9) 6, 184
    first Opium War (1839-1841) 24
    First Schleswig War (1848–51) 245, 253
    the limiting/avoidance of 17–18, 21–2
    Napoleonic wars 154, 203, 251–2
    Peninsular War (1808–14) 7, 183, 186, 189

politics and 251
between the Russian and Ottoman empires 30–5, 37n.22
Second Schleswig War (1864), (First War of German Unification) 245
War of Independence, Spain. *See* Peninsular war
'War' of the Bavarian Succession 56–7
wars of succession 5
World War I 20, 21
Warsaw, Duchy of 269
Wedel Jarlsberg, Ferdinand Carl Maria 227
Wedel Jarlsberg, Herman 205–6, 208, 227–8
Weibull, Jørgen 209, 210
Welcker, Theodor 128
Wellesley, Henry 264
'Wellington-Barrier' 42, 43
Wellington, Duke of 41–3, 44, 45, 46, 47, 72, 265
Wergeland, Henrik 226, 228, 232
western Europe, liberal constitutional monarchies of 6
Westphalia, peace of 290, 291
Wilhelm I of Württemberg 133, 138
William Frederick of the Netherlands. *See* William I of the Netherlands
William I of the Netherlands 45, 49n.39, 81, 159, 161, 164–7
Wilson, Robert 83, 85
Wirtschafter, Elise Kimerling xv–xvi (*see also* chapter 2)

women
  female political power 213–20
  private/public sphere and 219–20
  sexual slander and 219–20
A World Restored 289
World War I 20, 21
Wright, Frances (Fanny) 80, 84
Wulfsberg, Niels 206
Württemberg
  change and 137
  constitution of 1819 124, 126–7, 133, 134
  constitutions and 115, 121, 123, 134, 138–9
  education 136
  French *Charte constitutionnelle* and 7
  Karls-Schule 136, 137, 138
  modernization 135, 136, 140
  Neu-Württemberg 137
  royal opposition against the *Ancien Régime* 133–40
  taxation 134, 135
  technocracy 134, 136–8, 139–40

Ypsilantis, Alexandros 30–1
Yugoslavia 250

Zajączek, Józef 272, 274
Zéa, Don Francesco-Antonio 84
Zeiller, Franz 279, 282
Zumalacárregui, general 193, 194